Multimodal Processing and Interaction

Audio, Video, Text

MULTIMEDIA SYSTEMS AND APPLICATIONS SERIES

Consulting Editor

Borko Furht
Florida Atlantic University

Recently Published Titles:

THE VC-1 AND H.264 VIDEO COMPRESSION STANDARDS FOR BROADBAND VIDEO SERVICES by Jae-Beom Lee and Hari Kalva; ISBN: 978-0-387-71042-6

SIGNAL PROCESSING FOR IMAGE ENHANCEMENT AND MULTIMEDIA PROCESSING edited by E. Damiani, A. Dipanda, K. Yetongnon, L. Legrand, P. Schelkens, and R. Chbeir; ISBN: 978-0-387-72499-7

MACHINE LEARNING FOR MULTIMEDIA CONTENT ANALYSIS by Yihong Gong and Wei Xu; ISBN: 978-0-387-69938-7

DISTRIBUTED MULTIMEDIA RETRIEVAL STRATEGIES FOR LARGE SCALE NETWORKED SYSTEMS by Bharadwaj Veeravalli and Gerassimos Barlas; ISBN: 978-0-387-28873-4

MULTIMEDIA ENCRYPTION AND WATERMARKING by Borko Furht, Edin Muharemagic, Daniel Socek: ISBN: 0-387-24425-5

SIGNAL PROCESSING FOR TELECOMMUNICATIONS AND MULTIMEDIA edited by T.A Wysocki,. B. Honary, B.J. Wysocki; ISBN 0-387-22847-0

ADVANCED WIRED AND WIRELESS NETWORKS by T.A.Wysocki,, A. Dadej, B.J. Wysocki; ISBN 0-387-22781-4

CONTENT-BASED VIDEO RETRIEVAL: A Database Perspective by Milan Petkovic and Willem Jonker; ISBN: 1-4020-7617-7

MASTERING E-BUSINESS INFRASTRUCTURE edited by Veljko Milutinović, Frédéric Patricelli; ISBN: 1-4020-7413-1

SHAPE ANALYSIS AND RETRIEVAL OF MULTIMEDIA OBJECTS by Maytham H. Safar and Cyrus Shahabi; ISBN: 1-4020-7252-X

MULTIMEDIA MINING: A Highway to Intelligent Multimedia Documents edited by Chabane Djeraba; ISBN: 1-4020-7247-3

CONTENT-BASED IMAGE AND VIDEO RETRIEVAL by Oge Marques and Borko Furht; ISBN: 1-4020-7004-7

ELECTRONIC BUSINESS AND EDUCATION: Recent Advances in Internet Infrastructures edited by Wendy Chin, Frédéric Patricelli, Veljko Milutinović; ISBN: 0-7923-7508-4

INFRASTRUCTURE FOR ELECTRONIC BUSINESS ON THE INTERNET by Veljko Milutinović; ISBN: 0-7923-7384-7

DELIVERING MPEG-4 BASED AUDIO-VISUAL SERVICES by Hari Kalva; ISBN: 0-7923-7255-7

Multimodal Processing and Interaction

Audio, Video, Text

Edited by

Petros Maragos
National Technical University of Athens
Greece

Alexandros Potamianos
Technical University of Crete
Greece

Patrick Gros
INRIA, Rennes
France

Editors:
Petros Maragos
National Technical University of Athens
School of Electrical & Computer Eng.
Athens 15773, Greece
maragos@cs.ntua.gr

Alexandros Potamianos
Technical University of Crete
Dept. Electronic & Computer Eng.
University Campus-Akrotiri
731 00 Chania, Crete, Greece
potam@telecom.tuc.gr

Patrick Gros
INRIA Rennes
Campus de Beaulieu
35042 Rennes Cedex, France
Patrick.Gros@inria.fr

Series Editor:
Borko Furht
Florida Atlantic University
Department of Computer Science & Engineering
777 Glades Road
PO Box 3091
Boca Raton FL 33431
borko@cse.fau.edu

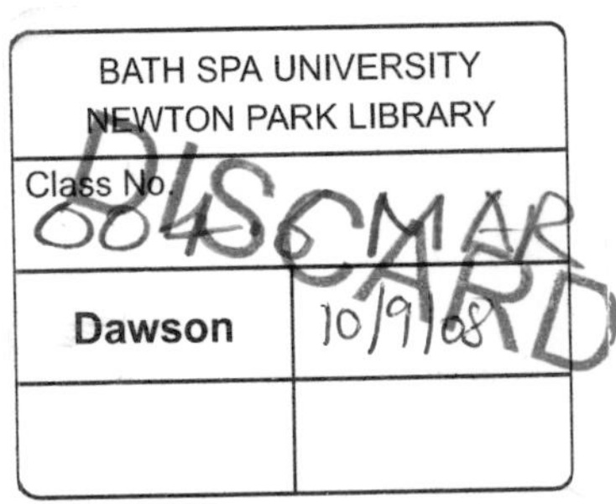

ISBN: 978-0-387-76315-6 e-ISBN: 978-0-387-76316-3
DOI: 10.1007/978-0-387-76316-3

Library of Congress Control Number: 2008926090

Printed on acid-free paper

9 8 7 6 5 4 3 2 1

springer.com

To our families and students

Preface

This is a book on multimedia information processing and multimedia systems. It grew out of a four-year collaboration among research groups participating in the European Network of Excellence on Multimedia Understanding through Semantics, Computation and Learning, abbreviated as "MUSCLE". It focuses on thematic areas that are scientifically and technologically important for multimodal processing and interaction. Specifically, it addresses the state-of-the-art research and new directions on the theory and applications of multimedia analysis, approaches that improve robustness and performance through cross-modal integration. It also focuses on interaction with multimedia content, with special emphasis on multimodal interfaces for accessing multimedia information.

This volume contains contributions by experts in the ubiquitous scientific and technological field of multimedia. The purpose of this book is twofold: (i) to present the *state-of-the-art* in the areas of multimedia processing and interaction from the theoretic, algorithmic and application viewpoints, and (ii) to present *in-depth* novel perspectives, analytic tools, algorithms, design practices and applications in selected areas of multimedia processing and interaction. Emphasis is given on multimodal information processing aspects of multimedia and cross-integration of multiple modalities. This book can be used either as an additional textbook for an advanced multimedia course or as a research aid for investigators in the area of multimedia processing and interaction.

The MUSCLE Network of Excellence is a microcosm of the multimedia world and contains members from the multimedia signal processing, computer systems, machine learning and human-computer interaction areas. However, MUSCLE by design is somewhat biased towards the media processing and machine learning communities. One of the main goals of the MUSCLE Network of Excellence is to integrate and synthesize the work of researchers with different media processing backgrounds and multimedia systems expertise. This is especially evident in the research area of multimodal processing and interaction of which this book is an outgrowth. Our goal in this book is to bring together the multimedia processing and multimedia systems communities, identify common problems and synergies, and propose solutions that significantly improve on the state-of-the-art. This book demonstrates these views and this synthesis. However, due to the vast area that this book covers, exposition will not be complete; not all multimedia research and application areas will be covered.

The authors would like to thank the members of the EU-IST INFSO.E2 unit, and especially Dr. Stefano Bertolo, for providing their support in this effort. We also would like to thank members of the MUSCLE Network of Excellence, especially, Dr. Eric Pauwels who served as the network coordinator during the formation of this book. Several people have provided additional editorial support for this book, notably, Nassos Katsamanis, George Papandreou, and Manolis Perakakis. In particular, we wish to thank Nassos Katsamanis and George Papandreou for setting up and maintaining an automated LaTeX collaboration system and for their editorial processing of the bibliography and other typesetting details of this book. Many thanks to Nancy Zlatintsi for designing the book cover figure. We also acknowledge help from many people from our research groups who have provided proofreading comments for chapters. Finally, we wish to thank Susan Lagerstrom-Fife and Sharon Palleschi at Springer for their support, valuable edits and the timely publication of this book.

Petros Maragos, Alexandros Potamianos, Patrick Gros

January 2008

Introduction

Ἄνδρα μοι ἔννεπε, Μοῦσα, πολύτροπον, ὃς μάλα πολλὰ
πλάγχθη, ἐπεὶ Τροίης ἱερὸν πτολίεθρον ἔπερσε·
πολλῶν δ' ἀνθρώπων ἴδεν ἄστεα καὶ νόον ἔγνω,
πολλὰ δ' ὅ γ' ἐν πόντῳ πάθεν ἄλγεα ὃν κατὰ θυμόν ...

"Tell me, O Muse, of the **multimodal**[1] man, who wandered full many ways after he had conquered the sacred castle of Troy. Many were the men whose cities he saw and whose mind he learned, and many the woes he suffered in his heart upon the sea ..." (Homer, *Odyssey*).

In multimedia analysis, most of the tools are devoted to a single modality, the other ones being treated as illustrations or complementary components. For example, web search engines and image retrieval systems barely mix textual and visual descriptions; video processing is usually done separately on sound and images. The main reason for this is that the different media concern different and sometimes very separate scientific fields. However, even without learning, performance of multimedia analysis and understanding systems (especially in terms of robustness) can be greatly enhanced by combining different modalities through interaction or integration. Thus, one of the goals of this book is to present algorithms and systems processing several different media present in multimedia and exploit their interaction. This requires a strong synergy between various scientific fields and many research methodologies. Examples of modalities to integrate include all possible combinations of: (i) vision and speech/audio; (ii) vision (or speech) and tactile; (iii) image/video (or speech/audio) and text; (iv) multiple-cue versions of vision and/or speech; (v) other semantic information or meta-data.

[1] The word "multimodal" is a free (but etymologically precise) translation of the greek adjective "$\pi o \lambda \upsilon \tau \rho o \pi o \nu$", which, for Homer's Odysseus or any man, means the "man of many ways" or the "man of many devices".

Multimedia information retrieval via an interactive human-computer interface is a complex task that requires feedback from the user and a complex negotiation between the user and the machine. The grand challenges are to research, design and build natural and efficient human-computer interfaces for performing multimedia information retrieval tasks that allow for negotiation (dialogue) between the user and the system. Three broad thematic areas in research on human-computer interfaces are multimodality, adaptivity and mobility.

The field of multimedia is truly interdisciplinary and so is this book. Two diverse research communities are the main drive behind multimedia technology and applications. One driver is the media processing community that produces algorithms for analyzing, encoding and recognizing patterns in multimedia streams. This community is in itself diverse and its members are identified by their specialization into speech processing, audio processing, image processing, video processing, and natural language processing. Some community members work on multiple media, e.g., speech and text, speech and audio, image and video, or more rarely, speech and video. The second driver behind multimedia technology and applications is the computer systems community that combines media processing algorithms with its own building blocks to create multimedia systems. Again a diverse number of research areas are involved in multimedia systems from this community, namely, agents and web technologies, ontologies and semantic web, databases, human-computer interaction. This community deals with a number of important problems, such as data and meta-data formalisms, semantic representation and inference, multimedia indexing and search, interface design. Last but not least, a community that significantly contributes to multimedia processing is the machine learning community that provides general purpose algorithms for modeling of the media, but also multimedia application control and interfaces to multimedia.

Fundamental Concepts

The field of multimedia processing gained momentum in the early 1990's when video processing experts began to realize the advantages of joint processing of the audio and visual streams. It is not surprising that the problem of modality combination or *fusion* remains central to the multimedia community to this day. Fusion, or the merging of various input or information streams, can be performed at the feature or model level, known as early and late fusion, respectively. Multimodal (or cross-modal[2]) fusion is important for many multimedia applications because of the big gains that can be achieved in performance due to the complementarity of the information available in the different modalities; consider the examples of audiovisual speech recognition, movie indexing, content-based image retrieval. Since multimodal interaction is the focus of

[2] In this book, the terms multimodal and cross-modal are often used interchangeably.

this book the problem of fusion will be encountered throughout, starting from the basic concepts introduced in Chapter 1. The combination of output (instead of input) media for the purposes of presentation is known as the *fission* problem and is introduced in Chapter 2.

A fundamental issue in multimedia processing is that, although each modality is different, the major interaction modalities, namely audio, video, text, have a *sequential nature.* The notion of *time* is fundamental in audio, music and video data; text is a sequence of words. In addition, images and video have the notion of *space.* Inadvertently multimedia data demonstrate relationships in both time and space. Thus, multimedia processing deals with extracting features and modeling multidimensional sequences of data. Another characteristic of multimedia data is *variability.* There are many ways to convey the same (semantic) message using low-level instances of multimedia data, e.g., there is an infinite number of speech signals that all signify the same phoneme /ah/. Given this variability, it is not surprising that the most popular modeling tools for multimedia data are statistical, and specifically, Markov chains and hidden Markov models; these models are computationally simple and can model dependencies in sequences of data. Another important concept is that multimedia data exhibit different (time) *scales.* For example in digital video data, the audio stream is sampled typically at 44.1 kHz, while the visual stream is sampled at 25 Hz; a difference of over three orders of magnitude.

Multimedia data convey mostly high-level semantic information, i.e., human perception has mechanisms that abstract the signal to corresponding patterns and semantic representations. Humans transform automatically audio signals to text, and then text to semantics. Similarly video information is processed into audiovisual semantics, such as, actor identity, dialogue, plot line. Turning multimedia signals into semantics is the ultimate goal of multimedia processing. However, most of the multimedia processing applications today, ranging from translation to movie summarization, extract features at the raw signal level and are often *agnostic to semantics.* Nevertheless, the notions of *saliency*, i.e., parts of the multimedia stream where information resides, *information content* and *multimedia semantics* remain important for multimedia processing.

We have left for last the important role that human *perception* and *cognition* plays in multimedia processing and multimedia systems in general. Multimedia information is obtained and processed in the human brain in a fixed, often "hard-coded" way. Multimedia processing by humans is surprisingly robust, yet has some limitations that can be useful. For example, auditory masking has been extensively exploited in music processing to improve audio coders. In addition, interfaces to multimedia content have to respect basic human-computer interaction principles that are based on cognitive considerations. For example the magical number 7 that relates to the short-term human memory, as discussed in Chapter 2. Also multimedia presentation and interfaces to multimedia content have to respect human processing abilities and not incur disproportionate *cognitive load.* Multimedia processing and interaction that combines cognitive and perceptual considerations is an active research area.

The Book at a Glance

There are four parts to this book. Part I serves as an introduction to the areas of multimedia processing and interaction. It contains a review of the state-of-the-art in multimedia signal processing and interfaces to multimedia content. The focus of the review chapters is on multimedia theory, algorithms and applications. Basic concepts such as perception, feature extraction, statistical modeling, pattern recognition and multimodal fusion are presented together with corresponding multimedia processing applications. The basic notions employed in multimedia system and interface design are presented in the second review, namely, usability, fusion and fission, multimodality, adaptivity.

Part II, III and IV contain original contributions by multimedia experts in the areas of multimedia processing, systems and interaction. Each contribution deals with a specific area of applications, e.g., sports videos, multimodal dialogue interfaces. Most chapters start with a brief review of the state-of-the-art for the specific application area and then present original research results and future research directions.

The focus of Part II of this book is on integrated multimedia analysis and recognition. It contains seven chapters that cover a broad area of multimedia processing applications. A common theme in all of these chapters is multimodal processing, especially the problem of fusion of different media streams, features and models. The thematic areas covered in this part of the book are: multimodal video analysis, audiovisual speech recognition with emphasis on audiovisual fusion, action recognition in multimedia streams, dialogue and action scene detection in movies, audiovisual salient event detection with application to multimedia summarization and skimming and, finally, the fusion of acoustic and linguistic information in speech recognition. Almost all of these chapters deal with the visual and audio modalities, while the last chapter also deals with text. Most of the chapters attack the problem of audiovisual fusion for different end-user applications; both early and late fusion methods are presented and evaluated.

Part III of the book contains three chapters on search and retrieval of multimedia content. There are two chapters on image retrieval and one more chapter on music information retrieval. All contributions use more that one source of information to retrieve multimedia content. For example in the first chapter, visual and text/semantics are used for image retrieval, while in the last chapter text and web link information is used for a similar task. For the problem of music information retrieval, audio and lyric information is used. Experts from both the multimedia processing and multimedia systems communities contribute to these chapters, demonstrating different angles of attack to the problem of information retrieval.

Finally, Part IV of this book consists of three chapters that present interfaces to multimedia content. The area of human-computer interfaces to multimedia content is large and very diverse. The three contributions included here have a high tutorial value and as included in order to familiarize the multimedia processing expert with some aspects of interface design. The topics covered are: multimodal dialogue interfaces, eye-tracking interfaces for image retrieval, and mobile interfaces. In the first chapter, the idiosyncratic nature of speech interfaces is pointed out and guidelines of how to combine the speech modality with traditional keyboard and mouse input are discussed. In the second chapter, eye-tracking technology is reviewed, and the advantages of the eye-gaze modality as a mechanism to provide relevance feedback in image retrieval applications are presented. The book concludes with an extensive review of mobile interfaces that focuses on the consumption of multimedia content on the go.

A Detailed Look at the Book

Next we give a short description for each of the chapters of this book. We focus on the original contributions that identify new research directions, i.e., Parts II, III and IV, rather than the introductory two chapters that review the state of the art in multimedia processing and interaction.

Integrated Multimedia Analysis and Recognition

In Chapter 3, *multimodal analysis of video* data is performed in order to extract high-level information, e.g., structure or genre, from raw video data. Video is by nature multimodal as both the visual and audio modalities encode semantic information. Therefore, modality fusion either at the feature or the model level is essential to achieve state-of-the-art performance. In this work, multimodal extensions of hidden Markov models (HMMs) are evaluated for video analysis and indexing, e.g., multi-stream HMMs, product HMMs. However, multimodal HMMs suffer from shortcomings, most notably the requirement for synchronization between modalities. The authors propose a segment model (SM) that achieves more efficient and versatile multimodal fusion by relaxing synchrony constraints between modalities. Extensive experimental results are supplied comparing HMMs and SMs for a sports video structuring application. The authors also present a new decoding algorithm for SMs that improves on the state-of-the-art. This chapter provides a good review of popular models used in multimodal video analysis along with experimental results for tennis video structuring. An important message here is how to select the model that best matches your data; the authors maximize performance by selecting a model that takes advantage of the hierarchical structure of tennis video data.

The problem of *multimodal fusion* is attacked once more in Chapter 4; this time the application area is *audiovisual speech recognition.* The approach proposed here, however, is pretty general and is based on the concept that for each of the modalities there is uncertainty (or estimation errors) during both feature extraction and modeling. Classification and learning rules are adjusted to compensate for the effects of feature measurement uncertainty. This approach is particularly fruitful in multimodal fusion scenarios, such as audiovisual speech recognition, where multiple streams of complementary time-evolving features are integrated. For such applications, the proposed framework leads to highly adaptive multimodal fusion rules which are widely applicable and easy to implement. The authors show that established multimodal fusion methods relying on stream weights fall under the proposed scheme under certain assumptions. The potential of the proposed fusion algorithm is demonstrated for audiovisual speech recognition using synchronous or asynchronous HMM models. This chapter contains more advanced research material and provides a new perspective into the problem of multimodal fusion.

In Chapter 5, a broad range of applications are presented related to the problem of *action recognition in multimedia streams*. Parsing multimedia streams with the end-goal of detecting and classifying actions implies modeling the dynamic nature of visual and audio features as they evolve in time. Hidden Markov Models are used to capture complex behavior and to model the non-stationarity inherent in the video signals. The subtleties in the application of HMMs to visual processing are often unclear, and the latter portion of this chapter sets out to expose some of these. Three applications are considered to motivate the discussion: actions in sports, observational psychology and illicit video content. Experimental results are also supplied for these applications. This chapter is good review of the state-of-the-art in action recognition of audiovisual content and also offers new insights into the use of statistical models for such applications.

In Chapter 6, the application area of *intelligent surveillance* using both audio and visual cues is reviewed and new methods and algorithms are proposed. Recently, intelligent video analysis systems have been developed for surveillance applications that are capable of extracting various semantic knowledge from video data, e.g., detecting humans and cars. Typically such video based analysis systems detect important events using only features extracted form the visual stream. However, most cameras used in video-surveillance are equipped with built-in microphones. The sound signal captured with these microphones can be analyzed and used to model audio events such as broken glass sounds, car crash sounds and screams. By doing joint analysis and modeling of audio and visual events, the performance and robustness of state-of-the-art surveillance systems can be improved. This chapter provides good insight into the problem of multimodal event detection in audiovisual data for surveillance applications.

In Chapter 7, the problem of *multimodal analysis and modeling of movies* is presented. Among the many applications of movie analysis, emphasis is given to dialogue and action scene detection. As online distribution and consumption of movies becomes increasingly popular, multimedia data management becomes a necessity, i.e., users should be able to organize, navigate, browse, search, and consume their multimedia content. Semantic content-based video indexing offers a promising solution for efficient digital movie management. Semantic video indexing aims at extracting, characterizing, and organizing video content by analyzing the visual, aural, and textual information sources of video. The current approaches for automatic movie analysis and annotation mostly focus on the visual information, while the aural information receives little or no attention. However, the integration of the aural information with the visual one can improve semantic movie content analysis as discussed here. This chapter offers a good review of algorithms used in movie analysis and indexing. Detailed evaluation results are given over a broad range of competing algorithms for the problem of scene detection and classification.

Audiovisual attention modeling and *salient event detection* is addressed in Chapter 8. Audiovisual saliency is relevant for a variety of video processing applications, e.g., *movie summarization* and skimming. Based on recent studies on perceptual and computer attention modeling, the authors extract attention curves using features around the spatiotemporal structure of video and sounds. Audio saliency is captured by modulation-domain signal modeling, while visual saliency is measured by means of spatiotemporal attention models that combine various features such as intensity, color and motion. Audio and visual saliency curves are fused, and events are detected on the resulting audiovisual saliency curve by computing local extrema and sharp transition points. The potential of intra-module fusion and audiovisual event detection is demonstrated in applications such as key-frame selection, video skimming and summarization and audio/visual segmentation. Although, both this and the previous chapter deal with multimodal processing of movies, the material here is complementary to Chapter 7. The analysis here is purely frame-based and low-level features, e.g., energy, motion, are used successfully to detect high-level semantic events. This chapter serves as a good introduction to the concept of multimodal saliency and its many applications in multimedia processing.

In Chapter 9, the problem of *combining acoustic and linguistic information for speech recognition* is reviewed. Although speech recognition is a unimodal problem, speech recognition models combine information collected through both audio and text corpora. Combining these two sources of information is usually done at the probability computation level. This chapter focuses on recent research work toward a better integration between automatic speech recognition (ASR) and natural language processing (NLP) for the analysis of spoken documents. The problem of combining audio and text is an important problem that is often overlooked in the framework of multimedia analysis and interaction.

Searching Multimedia Content

In Chapter 10, the problem of *image retrieval* using both visual and semantic information is presented. The authors use keyword annotations available from an image database to create a feature vector. The features are combined with low level visual features. Support vector machines are used to model relevance feedback in a query by visual example context. The proposed method is supported by extensive experimentation.

Music analysis and retrieval is investigated in Chapter 11. Both audio and text features extracted from a song's lyrics are used for music analysis and modeling. Although text might be easier to search and conveys information about the semantics of a song, it does not provide much information about sonic similarity. Thus, audio and text features are complementary and can improve the performance of music retrieval algorithms. The authors propose a visualization method, i.e., a music map, that uses both audio and lyric data, and self-organizing map clustering. The map can be used to automatically create play-lists or for *music retrieval*. The proposed algorithms are evaluated on an extensive audio collection.

In Chapter 12, a review of *content-based image retrieval* algorithms for the web is presented. The author first reviews the feature extraction process both for text and images, and then moves on to review image retrieval models. An additional source of information, popular within the web information retrieval community, is provided by link analysis. The author reviews a system that utilizes also web link information for the problem of content-based information retrieval. The chapter concludes with an investigation of the problem of relevance feedback and an extensive evaluation. This chapter gives a good overview of the state-of-the-art in multimodal content-based image retrieval.

Interfaces to Multimedia

In Chapter 13, the authors review design principles for building multimodal interfaces with emphasis on the speech modality. It is shown that some of the basic human-computer interaction principles are violated by speech interfaces, e.g., consistency, while other principles should be updated for *multimodal dialogue design*. Two important issues with multimodal systems design, is the selection of appropriate modalities in a given context and the exploitation of the *synergies* between the modalities in order to design a consistent and efficient interface. The authors introduce the concept of *mode synergy* that measures the added value from efficiently combining multiple input modalities. A mobile multimodal system that combines pen and speech input is used as a design case study. User behavior and system evaluation results on this prototype system demonstrate how users and multimodal systems can (and should) adapt to maximize mode synergy to create efficient, natural and intelligent multimodal interfaces. This chapter serves as a good introduction to spoken dialogue and multimodal interface design.

Eye-tracking interfaces for visual exploration are reviewed in Chapter 14. Eye-tracking technology offers a natural and immediate way of communicating human intentions to a computer. Eye movements reflect interests and may be analyzed to drive computer functionality in games, image and video search, and other visual tasks. Experiments show that target images can be identified more rapidly by eye tracking than by using a mouse interface. Further, results show that eye tracking technology provides an efficient interface for locating images in a large database. Finally, the authors speculate about how the technology may enter the mass market as costs decrease. This chapter is a good review of eye-tracking technologies and interfaces.

The final chapter of this book, Chapter 15, is a review of *mobile interfaces.* Mobile interfaces are becoming increasingly important as the capabilities of devices improve and users access multimedia data on the go. The authors review the state-of-the-art in mobile devices and mobile displays and then move on to review the main interaction modalities. Differences between desktop and mobile interfaces are outlined. Then a number of applications are reviewed, e.g., interfaces to audio content, content aware applications, augmented reality applications. Mobile interfaces pose unique challenges, but also present new opportunities as these challenges are overcome. This chapter offers good insight on what the future holds for mobile applications and interfaces.

Contents

Part I Review of the State-of-the-Art

1 Cross-Modal Integration for Performance Improving in Multimedia: A Review
Petros Maragos, Patrick Gros, Athanassios Katsamanis, George Papandreou 3

2 Human-Computer Interfaces to Multimedia Content: a Review
Alexandros Potamianos, Manolis Perakakis 49

Part II INTEGRATED MULTIMEDIA ANALYSIS AND RECOGNITION

3 Stochastic Models for Multimodal Video Analysis
Manolis Delakis, Guillaume Gravier, Patrick Gros 91

4 Adaptive Multimodal Fusion by Uncertainty Compensation with Application to Audio-Visual Speech Recognition
George Papandreou, Athanassios Katsamanis, Vassilis Pitsikalis, Petros Maragos 111

5 Action Recognition in Multimedia Streams
Rozenn Dahyot, François Pitié, Daire Lennon, Naomi Harte, Anil Kokaram 127

6 Surveillance Using Both Video and Audio
Yigithan Dedeoglu, B. Ugur Toreyin, Ugur Gudukbay, A. Enis Cetin 143

7 Movie Analysis with Emphasis to Dialogue and Action Scene Detection
Emmanouil Benetos, Spyridon Siatras, Constantine Kotropoulos, Nikos Nikolaidis, Ioannis Pitas 157

8 Audiovisual Attention Modeling and Salient Event Detection
Georgios Evangelopoulos, Konstantinos Rapantzikos, Petros Maragos, Yannis Avrithis, Alexandros Potamianos 179

9 Toward the Integration of Natural Language Processing and Automatic Speech Recognition: Using Morpho-Syntax and Pragmatics for Transcription
Stéphane Huet, Gwénolé Lecorvé, Guillaume Gravier, Pascale Sébillot . . 201

Part III SEARCHING MULTIMEDIA CONTENT

10 Interactive Image Retrieval Using a Hybrid Visual and Conceptual Content Representation
Marin Ferecatu, Nozha Boujemaa, Michel Crucianu 221

11 Multimodal Analysis of Text and Audio Features for Music Information Retrieval
Robert Neumayer, Andreas Rauber 241

12 Intelligent Search for Image Information on the Web through Text and Link Structure Analysis
Euripides G.M. Petrakis 259

Part IV INTERFACES TO MULTIMEDIA CONTENT

13 Design Principles for Multimodal Spoken Dialogue Systems
Alexandros Potamianos, Manolis Perakakis 279

14 Eye Tracking: A New Interface for Visual Exploration
Oyewole K. Oyekoya, Fred W. M. Stentiford 297

15 User Interaction for Mobile Devices
Sanni Siltanen, Charles Woodward, Seppo Valli, Petri Honkamaa, Andreas Rauber 311

References 331

Index 365

List of Contributors

Yannis Avrithis
National Technical University of Athens
School of Electrical & Computer Engineering
Athens 15773, Greece
rap@image.ntua.gr

Emmanouil Benetos
Aristotle Univ. of Thessaloniki
Department of Informatics
Thessaloniki, Box 451, Thessaloniki 541 24, Greece
empeneto@aiia.csd.auth.gr

Nozha Boujemaa
Institut National de Recherche en Informatique et Automatique
BP 105 Rocquencourt
78153 Le Chesnay cedex, France
Nozha.Boujemaa@inria.fr

A. Enis Cetin
Bilkent University
Department of Electrical and Electronics Engineering
06800, Ankara, Turkey
cetin@ee.bilkent.edu.tr

Michel Crucianu
Conservatoire National des Arts et Métiers
292 rue St Martin
75141 Paris cedex 03, France
Michel.Crucianu@cnam.fr

Rozenn Dahyot
Trinity College Dublin
School of Computer Science and Statistics
Dublin 2, Ireland
Rozenn.Dahyot@cs.tcd.ie

Yigithan Dedeoglu
Bilkent University
Department of Computer Engineering
06800, Ankara, Turkey
yigithan@cs.bilkent.edu.tr

Manolis Delakis
University of Rennes 1
Institut de Recherche en Informatique et Systèmes Aléatoires
Campus Universitaire de Beaulieu
35042 Rennes Cedex, France.
manolis.delakis@irisa.fr

Georgios Evangelopoulos
National Technical University of Athens
School of Electrical & Computer Engineering
Athens 15773, Greece
gevag@cs.ntua.gr

Marin Ferecatu
Institut National de Recherche en Informatique et Automatique
BP 105 Rocquencourt
78153 Le Chesnay cedex, France
Marin.Ferecatu@inria.fr

Guillaume Gravier
Centre National de la Recherche Scientifique
Institut de Recherche en Informatique et Systèmes Aléatoires
Campus Universitaire de Beaulieu
35042 Rennes Cedex, France.
guillaume.gravier@irisa.fr

Patrick Gros
Institut National de Recherche en Informatique et Automatique
Institut de Recherche en Informatique et Systèmes Aléatoires
Campus Universitaire de Beaulieu
35042 Rennes Cedex, France.
patrick.gros@irisa.fr

Ugur Gudukbay
Bilkent University
Department of Computer Engineering
06800, Ankara, Turkey
gudukbay@cs.bilkent.edu.tr

Naomi Harte
Trinity College Dublin
Department of Electronic and Electrical Engineering
Dublin 2, Ireland
nharte@tcd.ie

Petri Honkamaa
VTT Technical Research Center of Finland
P.O. Box 1000 (Vuorimiehentie 3, Espoo)
FI-02044 VTT, Finland
Petri.Honkamaa@vtt.fi

Stéphane Huet
University of Rennes 1
Institut de Recherche en Informatique et Systèmes Aléatoires
Campus Universitaire de Beaulieu
35042 Rennes Cedex, France.
stephane.huet@irisa.fr

Athanassios Katsamanis
National Technical University of Athens
School of Electrical & Computer Engineering
Athens 15773, Greece
nkatsam@cs.ntua.gr

Anil Kokaram
Trinity College Dublin
Department of Electronic and Electrical Engineering
Dublin 2, Ireland
anil.kokaram@tcd.ie

Constantine Kotropoulos
Aristotle Univ. of Thessaloniki
Department of Informatics
Thessaloniki, Box 451, Thessaloniki 541 24, Greece
costas@aiia.csd.auth.gr

Gwénolé Lecorvé
Institut National des Sciences Appliquées de Rennes
Institut de Recherche en Informatique et Systèmes Aléatoires
Campus Universitaire de Beaulieu
35042 Rennes Cedex, France.
Gwenole.Lecorve@irisa.fr

Daire Lennon
Trinity College Dublin
Department of Electronic and Electrical Engineering
Dublin 2, Ireland
lennondh@tcd.ie

Petros Maragos
National Technical University of Athens
School of Electrical & Computer Engineering
Athens 15773, Greece
maragos@cs.ntua.gr

Robert Neumayer
Vienna University of Technology
Institute of Software Technology and Interactive Systems
Vienna, Austria
neumayer@ifs.tuwien.ac.at

Nikos Nikolaidis
Aristotle Univ. of Thessaloniki
Department of Informatics
Thessaloniki, Box 451, Thessaloniki 541 24, Greece
nikolaid@aiia.csd.auth.gr

O.K. Oyekoya
University College London
Adastral Park Campus
Martlesham Heath, Ipswich, IP5 3RE, UK
o.oyekoya@adastral.ucl.ac.uk

George Papandreou
National Technical University of Athens
School of Electrical & Computer Engineering
Athens 15773, Greece
gpapan@cs.ntua.gr

Manolis Perakakis
Technical University of Crete
Dept. of Electrical and Computer Engineering,
Chania, Greece
perak@telecom.tuc.gr

Euripides G.M. Petrakis
Technical University of Crete
Dept. of Electrical and Computer Engineering,
Chania, Greece
petrakis@intelligence.tuc.gr

François Pitié
Trinity College Dublin
Department of Electronic and Electrical Engineering
Dublin 2, Ireland
fpitie@mee.tcd.ie

Vassilis Pitsikalis
National Technical University of Athens
School of Electrical & Computer Engineering
Athens 15773, Greece
vpitsik@cs.ntua.gr

Ioannis Pittas
Aristotle Univ. of Thessaloniki
Department of Informatics
Thessaloniki, Box 451, Thessaloniki 541 24, Greece
pitas@aiia.csd.auth.gr

Alexandros Potamianos
Technical University of Crete
Dept. of Electrical and Computer Engineering,
Chania, Greece
potam@telecom.tuc.gr

Kostas Rapantzikos
National Technical University of Athens
School of Electrical & Computer Engineering
Athens 15773, Greece
rap@image.ntua.gr

Andreas Rauber
Vienna University of Technology
Institute of Software Technology and Interactive Systems
Vienna, Austria
rauber@ifs.tuwien.ac.at

Pascale Sébillot
Institut National des Sciences Appliquées de Rennes
Institut de Recherche en Informatique et Systèmes Aléatoires
Campus Universitaire de Beaulieu
35042 Rennes Cedex, France.
pascale.sebillot@irisa.fr

Spyridon Siatras
Aristotle Univ. of Thessaloniki
Department of Informatics
Thessaloniki, Box 451, Thessaloniki 541 24, Greece
siatras@aiia.csd.auth.gr

Sanni Siltanen
VTT Technical Research Center of Finland
P.O. Box 1000 (Vuorimiehentie 3, Espoo)
FI-02044 VTT, Finland
Sanni.Siltanen@vtt.fi

F.W.M. Stentiford
University College London
Adastral Park Campus
Martlesham Heath, Ipswich, IP5 3RE, UK
f.stentiford@adastral.ucl.ac.uk

B. Ugur Toreyin
Bilkent University
Department of Electrical and Electronics Engineering
06800, Ankara, Turkey
ugur@ee.bilkent.edu.tr

Seppo Valli
VTT Technical Research Center of Finland
P.O. Box 1000 (Vuorimiehentie 3, Espoo)
FI-02044 VTT, Finland
Seppo.Valli@vtt.fi

Charles Woodward
VTT Technical Research Center of Finland
P.O. Box 1000 (Vuorimiehentie 3, Espoo)
FI-02044 VTT, Finland
Charles.Woodward@vtt.fi

Part I

Review of the State-of-the-Art

1

Cross-Modal Integration for Performance Improving in Multimedia: A Review

Petros Maragos[1], Patrick Gros[2], Athanassios Katsamanis[1], and George Papandreou[1]

[1] National Technical University of Athens, Greece
[2] Institut National de Recherche en Informatique et Automatique, France

Our surrounding world is abundant with multimodal stimuli which emit multisensory information in the form of analog signals. Humans perceive the natural world in a multimodal way: vision, hearing, touch. Nowadays, propelled by our digital technology, we are also witnessing a rapid explosion of digital multimedia data. Humans understand the multimodal world in a seemingly effortless manner, although there are vast information processing resources dedicated to the corresponding tasks by the brain. Computer techniques, despite recent advances, still significantly lag humans in understanding multimedia and performing high-level cognitive tasks. Some of these limitations are inborn, i.e., stem from the complexity of the data and their multimodality. Other shortcomings, though, are due to the inadequacy of most approaches used in multimedia analysis, which are essentially monomodal. Namely, they rely mainly on information from a single modality and on tools effective for this modality while they underutilize the information in other modalities and their cross-interaction. To some extent, this happens because most researchers and groups are still monomedia specialists. Another reason is that the problem of fusing the modalities has not still reached maturity, both from a mathematical modeling and a computational viewpoint. Consequently, a major scientific and technological challenge is to develop truly multimodal approaches that integrate several modalities toward improving the goals of multimedia understanding. In this chapter we review research on the theory and applications of several multimedia analysis approaches that improve robustness and performance through cross-modal integration.

1.1 Motivations and Problems

Digital technology provides us with multimedia data whose size and complexity keeps rapidly expanding. To analyze and understand them we must face major challenges which include the following:

P. Maragos et al. (eds.), *Multimodal Processing and Interaction*,
DOI: 10.1007/978-0-387-76316-3_1, © Springer Science+Business Media, LLC 2008

Data are Voluminous: Nowadays we are witnessing a rapid explosion of digital multimedia data. They are produced by a variety of sources including: video cameras, TV, digital photography (personal and professional albums, photo agencies), digital audio and other digital entertainment devices, digital audiovisual libraries, multimodal Web. As a numeric example, 24 hr of TV produces 430 Gb (raw, uncompressed) data, 2.160.000 still (frame) images.

Data are Dynamic: Dynamic websites, TV and other broadcast news quickly get obsolete.

Different Temporal Rates are of importance in the various media. For example, 25-30 image-frames/sec in video, 44.000 sound samples/sec in audio, 100 feature-frames/sec in speech, 4 syllables/sec in language processing.

Cross-Media asynchrony, since image and audio scene boundaries may be different. Examples include possible asynchrony between the voice heard and the face seen, or between a sports visual event (e.g., a goal in soccer) and the speaker's comment that comes later.

Monomedia specialization: Most researchers and groups are specialists in a single modality, e.g., speech processing and recognition, or image/video processing and computer vision, or natural language processing.

The rapid explosion of multimedia data creates an increasing difficulty in finding relevant information, which has spurred enormous efforts to develop tools for automatic detection, recognition, and semantic analysis of multimedia content. The overall goal is multimedia understanding, which requires to use content in a nontrivial way. For example, understanding goes beyond just displaying images or playing a music CD, for which we do not need to analyze the content of the data. In contrast, examples that require understanding include multimedia archiving, re-purposing, making websites from TV streams. This multimedia explosion also poses the need to develop efficient solutions for problems in several ambitious technology areas. Two such grand challenges[3] are: (i) Natural access and high-level interaction with multimedia databases, and (ii) Detecting, recognizing and interpreting objects, events, and human behavior in multimedia videos by processing combined audio-video-text data.

Thus, as mentioned in this book's Introduction, one of the grand goals in multimedia understanding is cross-media integration for improving performance in the various scientific and technological problems that arise in systems dealing with multiple modalities. And this is exactly the central topic of this review chapter. Among the features of this chapter, we include brief reviews of ideas and results from cross-modal integration in human perception, since the multimodal human brain is a great source of inspiration. Further, we survey several types of probabilistic approaches and models for multimodal fusion. Examples of modalities to integrate include combinations of:

- vision and speech/audio

[3] These challenges were also identified at `http://www.muscle-noe.org/`

- vision (or speech) and tactile
- image/video (or speech/audio) and text
- multiple-cue versions of vision and/or speech
- other semantic information or metadata.

Many previous research efforts in (human or machine) cross-modal integration deal with combining multiple cues, i.e., multiple streams of information from the same modality. A frequent example is vision, where multiple cues are often combined to increase the robustness in estimating properties of the visual world scene; e.g., stereo disparity is combined with texture to estimate depth. In general, if we wish to refine the definition of multimodality, we shall call **multicue** the *intramodal* integration of several cues within the same modality and **multimodal** the *intermodal* integration of several modalities. For example, to estimate the depth of object surfaces by combining stereo and texture is a multicue approach, whereas combining vision and haptics is a multimodal approach. However, for expressional simplicity, we may often use only the term 'multimodal' to refer to both intermodal and intramodal approaches.

The combinations of modalities (or cues) can be either of the cross-interaction type or of the cross-integration type. Interaction implies an information reaction-diffusion among modalities with feedback control of one modality by others. Integration involves exploiting heterogeneous information cumulatively from various modalities in a data feature fusion toward improved performance. A simpler way to see this differentiation is to consider strong- versus weak-coupling of modalities (discussed later in Section 1.3). Some broad areas of research problems in multimedia where integration of (strongly-coupled or weakly-coupled) modalities occurs include the following:

- **Features:** The extraction of critical features in each modality, e.g., audio, vision, text, is in a well-advanced state and is served by the fields of signal processing and pattern recognition. See Section 1.4 for a brief survey. However, when combining several modalities, it is quite challenging to integrate monomodal[4] features in a way that is robust (since individual stream reliabilities may vary dynamically), efficient in terms of size and synchrony, and optimum in terms of overall performance. Thus, some ongoing research challenges in this classic problem of multimedia include: (i) Selection, robust extraction, and dimensionality reduction of each modality's features, given the presence of other modalities and their corresponding features. (ii) Optimal fusion of the separate feature streams (from different modalities or cues). A typical example is the area of audio-visual speech recognition, where the audio feature extraction has advanced, but there is still ongoing research for robust extraction of low-dimensional visual speech features and optimal fusion of the audio and visual features.

[4] In this chapter, the term monomodal is used as equivalent to unimodal.

- **Models:** Most aspects of multimedia understanding involve problems in pattern recognition and machine learning. One can select appropriate methodologies and algorithms from the vast arena of these fields, including both static and dynamic classification models. However, in multimodal processing and integration, the big challenge is how to adapt or extend these models so that they can work with and decide optimally for multimodal data. For instance, an important issue is whether to fuse the data at an early, intermediate, or late stage of the integration procedure. Another challenge is to deal with the time-dependent nature of these data when the modalities are not synchronous. These issues are discussed in Section 1.5.
- **Applications:** The application areas of multimedia are numerous and keep growing. Examples that involve cross-modal integration include the following: (See also Section 1.7 for a brief survey of some applications.)
  - *Audiovisual Speech:* The two problems of automatically recognizing speech and inverting speech, i.e., recovering the geometry of the vocal tract, are ill-posed. Integrating the auditory information with visual information (e.g., video features around the speaker's mouth area) imposes additional constraints which may help regularizing the solution of these problems.
  - *Cross-Media Interaction Scenarios in Human Computer Interfaces (HCIs):* Human-computer interaction has started becoming a reality due to recent advances in speech recognition, natural language processing, object detection-tracking using vision and tactile sensors. However, building a natural and efficient HCI that combines all the required different modalities (e.g., speech, vision, graphics, text, tactile) toward improving the overall performance becomes a significant technical challenge in this case where the modalities can interact strongly. A review of this area is given in the book's Chapter 2.
  - *Multimodal Saliency:* Audiovisual Attention Modeling and Salient Event Detection is a significant research problem with applications in audiovisual event detection, bimodal emotion recognition, dialogue detection, and video summarization. A significant effort in this area is spent on multimodal feature extraction and fusion for attention modeling. (See Chapter 8.)
  - *Video Analysis and Integration of Asynchronous Time-Evolving Modalities:* Video processing is usually done separately on sound and on images. However, the solution of many video analysis tasks can be improved and become more robust by integrating these two modalities and possibly text. Major difficulties exist, however, because the various media are not temporally coherent and provide different kinds of data. Several chapters in this book deal with these problems.
  - *Combining Text and Vision or Text and Audio for Semantic Labeling:* The challenging research goal here is to use structural and textual information for semantic interpretation of image or audio data. Such

technologies will empower a full semantic analysis and classification of data for which currently almost everything beyond text is ignored.

The areas of human or machine cross-modal integration are both huge, and hence our coverage in this chapter will *not* be exhaustive. Instead, we sample key ideas and survey indicative applications. The rest of this chapter is organized as follows. In Section 1.2 we briefly summarize how various branches of psychology view perception, how certain aspects of perceptual inference can be modeled via Bayesian estimation and decision theory, and then we present examples of multicue or multimodal perception from psychophysics. In Section 1.3 we classify sensor data fusion schemes using a Bayesian formulation. The following four sections review the main problem areas in multimedia analysis and integration: feature extraction from the three main modalities (speech-audio, image-video, and text) in Section 1.4; stochastic models for cross-modal integration in Section 1.5; integrated multimedia content analysis beyond descriptors in Section 1.6; and a few sample applications areas in Section 1.7. Finally, we conclude in Section 1.8 by outlining promising future directions.

1.2 Multimodality in Human Perception

Humans need to extract multi-level information about the structures and their spatio-temporal or cognitive relationships in their world environment. This information processing could either be innate (inborn) and possibly learned via evolutionary processes or stimulated by sensory data. This chapter mainly focuses on the latter. The polarity between innate vs data-driven inference is conceptually similar to (or inspired by) Plato's rationalism versus Aristotle's empiricism.

Three stages in sensory information processing are sensation, perception and cognition. **Sensation** is signal formation caused by the sense organs (i.e., the sensors) when excited by the external world stimuli. **Perception** is the collection of processes by which we filter, select, organize, recognize, and understand the sensations. There is an overlap between sensation and perception, but as broadly stated in [185], "sensations are usually viewed as simple, basic experiences caused by simple stimuli, whereas perceptions are usually considered as more complicated experiences elicited by complex, often meaningful, stimuli". Even more complicated is **cognition** which refers to information analyzing mental processes such as comprehension, learning, memory, decision-making, planning. A causal hierarchy may be the following:

$$\text{Sensation} \longrightarrow \text{Perception} \longrightarrow \text{Cognition}$$

Since the dividing line is usually hard to draw between sensations and perceptions as well as between perception and cognition, henceforth, we shall loosely refer to *perception as the sensory-based inference about the world state*, i.e., the process through which the mapping from world stimuli to sensory signals is inverted. Herein, inference is meant broadly as the collection of the main tasks of sensory information processing, e.g., spatio-temporal detection of objects and events, estimation of their properties, localization, recognition, organization.

Human perception as a means of daily exploration and survival in nature has been of vital importance since the dawn of humanity. As a physical process or result of sensor operation, it has attracted the interest of great scientists in the physical sciences (acoustics, optics, neurobiology). As a main ingredient of human awareness and consciousness, its understanding has also occupied the minds of great philosophers, artists and psychologists. Approaches to study perception range from physiology and neurobiology through cognition-related psychology disciplines to philosophy disciplines centered around the mind-body problem. A practical blend of the first two viewpoints is presented by *psychophysics*, a subdiscipline of psychology, which explores the relationships between the external world's physical stimuli and their induced percepts in the human mind.

In the rest of this section we summarize how various branches of psychology view perception, how certain aspects of perceptual inference can be modeled via Bayesian estimation and decision theory, and then we present examples of multicue or multimodal perception from psychophysics. Obviously, since this is a huge area, here we only summarize some indicative cases that have proven useful in monomodal or multimodal information processing.

1.2.1 Psychology Approaches to Human Perception

For the aspects of sensory-based human perception that we will need in this review chapter on multimodal integration, most important are the disciplines of gestalt psychology and cognitive psychology. Before we summarize their main ideas, we outline a few of their origins from philosophy.

Much like the mind-body debate, ideas and approaches in psychology evolved from the poles of philosophy and physiology. The former relies primarily on reasoning and introspection, whereas the latter on empirical methods and observations. As in other sciences, the evolution of ideas in philosophy [453] often followed a *dialectic* path, where a new theory was proposed (a *thesis*), soon countered by an opposite theory (an *antithesis*), until a *synthesis* of the best ideas was formed. This synthesis formed a new thesis, to be followed by a new antithesis, and so on dialectically. A classic pair of thesis and antithesis is Plato's *rationalism* versus Aristotle's *empiricism*. In the former we are supposed to acquire most knowledge mainly via theoretical analysis (understanding and reasoning) independently of the senses, in the latter mainly via empirical evidence (experience and observations, especially sensory perception) independently of innate ideas. A similar contrasting controversy continued in modern philosophy between the rationalist Descartes, whose assertion "I think, therefore I am" cannot be doubted and views the mind as more certain than matter, versus the empiricist Locke, who emphasized experience and learning and believed that everything knowable (with the possible exception of logic and mathematics) is derived from perception. Kant synthesized both their views. Such a synthesis is used in most modern theories of knowledge, where elements from both rationalism and empiricism are encountered.

Along the route of empiricism, *behaviorism* in psychology developed as a discipline that focuses on observable behaviors as responses to the environment, without any consideration to internal processes or mind theories. According to behaviorism, all what humans do, both externally (actions) and internally (thoughts), are behaviors.

An avid rival to behaviorism, **Gestalt psychology** is a mind-brain theory for which the most important process is the formation of perceptual groups of observations that correspond to conceptual equivalence classes. An abstraction of the justification for preferring this grouping is the Latin adage *multum non multa*, which distinguishes two meanings of 'much': The former emphasizes how a deeper understanding can grow from analyzing and grouping of fewer items, whereas the latter is based on quantitative detailed analysis of many data. Thus, the gestalt theory is a global, holistic approach (as opposed to the local, atomistic observations of behaviorism). It is concerned with *molar* behavior instead of molecular behavior, the former being a coarse-granule grouping of behavior in external settings, whereas the latter is the fine-granule behavior taking place internally inside an organism initiated by environmental stimuli. The gestalt thesis that the whole is greater than the sum of its parts is particularly relevant for multimodal processing. It implies that grouping in the sense of fusing modalities creates a unifying percept that subsumes their simple concatenation.

Founded by Wertheimer, Köhler and Koffka [269, 270] during 20th century's first half, gestalt psychology distinguishes between the geographical environment versus the behavioral environment and emphasizes that perception occurs in the latter. However, the behavioral environment B by itself is not sufficient to account for all processes and needs to be complemented by the physiological processes P active during perception. B and P are psychophysically isomorphic. Wertheimer's principle of *psychophysical isomorphism* is to think of physiological processes not as molecular but as molar phenomena. Köhler [270] refined this principle and proposed the following in the cases of spatial and temporal order: "(i) Experienced order in space is always structurally identical with a functional order in the distribution of underlying brain processes. (ii) Experienced order in time is always structurally identical with a functional order in the sequence of correlated brain processes."

The main ideas in gestalt psychology have been inspired by or geared toward problems in visual perception. The perceptual grouping forms objects by starting from local data or features who satisfy or share several grouping principles and recursively builds larger visual objects, the Gestalts. The most important of these principles is the law of Prägnanz, according to which we perceive a collection of visual parts in the simplest way that can organize the partial elements into a stable and coherent form. Other gestalt principles include proximity, figure-ground, closure, continuity, similarity, and symmetry. Additional characteristics of the gestalt theory are that, it focuses on a parallel and continuous processing and favors self-organization.

An outgrowth of gestalt psychology and Piaget's stage theory for child cognitive development is the field of **Cognitive psychology**, which (according to Neisser who introduced the term in 1967) is "the study of how people learn, structure, store and use knowledge." A comprehensive introduction can be found in [508]. This school of psychology is concerned with how humans process information for general tasks such as perception, learning, memory, language, problem-solving. Unlike behaviorism, it accepts innate mental states, but it also uses scientific methods of experimentation and observation without resorting to introspection. Due to its emphasis on the mental processes associating stimuli and responses, it uses computational concepts, like input and output of mental processes, algorithms and knowledge representation. As such, it is closer to artificial intelligence, and the two fields have benefited from cross-fertilization. Actually, cognitive psychology has contributed to artificial intelligence the very useful concept and tool of semantic networks. For example, WordNet [157] is a semantic network used in natural language processing.

The most often used practical tools to test gestalt and cognitive theories of human perception stem from psychophysics and statistics. The psychophysical methods deal with determination of sensory thresholds, measurements of sensitivity, and signal detection theory. From statistics, the Bayesian framework has gained popularity and is briefly summarized next.

1.2.2 Bayesian Formulation of Perception

Bayesian statistics provides a general framework for modeling and solving problems in pattern recognition and machine learning [145, 66, 519] and in computer vision [189, 180, 323, 99]. Its success in vision has also propelled its use for modeling perception as Bayesian inference [267, 583]. Elements of the Bayesian framework for perception can be found in Helmholtz's belief that retinal images alone do not carry sufficient information and need to be supplemented with prior knowledge; hence, he viewed perception as unconscious inference [204]. Although the Bayesian approach to perception has been mainly developed for vision, we shall use herein the Bayesian formalism to model multimodal sensory information processing, where 'multimodal' may mean 'multi-sensory'. A unifying Bayesian approach to computer vision, speech and signal processing and their associated pattern analysis and recognition tasks is also offered by the 'Pattern Theory' field [189, 348].

For intuition and simplicity, we will often restrict to the two main senses, vision and hearing, and use the term 'audiovisual' instead of 'multimodal sensory' stimuli/data. Let S be a configuration (of the properties) of an auditory and/or visual scene of the external world (e.g., a vector of variables representing numeric or symbolic features-parameters) that represents the state of external audiovisual stimuli. Let D be the monomodal or multimodal data representing signals collected by auditory and/or visual sensors; at a higher level, D may also represent features extracted from the raw signals. If we view the sensory signal formation as a mapping $S \mapsto D$ from world state S to sensory data D, then perception is essentially the inverse problem of estimating the world audiovisual state from the sensory observations. If the variations of the audiovisual state are random in nature, or there is uncertainty in modeling the signal formation or there is observation noise, then we can use a probabilistic interpretation of the above problem. In this case, Bayes' formula offers us a convenient decomposition of the probabilities involved into prior (before observing the data) and posterior (after observing the data) terms:

$$P(S|D) = \frac{P(D|S)P(S)}{P(D)} \tag{1.1}$$

where $P(\cdot)$ denotes probability distributions (i.e., probability densities or probability masses according to the case). The **prior** distribution $P(S)$ expresses the *a priori* probability of how likely is the world state S before observing the data; it models prior knowledge about the random nature (e.g. regularities) of the scene structure and may include various a priori constraints. The conditional distribution $P(D|S)$ expresses the probability of observing D given the world state S; if it is viewed as function of S for fixed D, then it is called the **likelihood** function of S. It statistically models the overall causal generation process of signal data formation from the world state (audiovisual scene); thus, this probabilistic mapping $S \mapsto D$ is called a *generative model* in Bayesian networks. The likelihood embodies the reliability of the observed signal or feature data D which can vary due to possible model uncertainty and observation noise. The *marginal* distribution $P(D)$, usually called the **evidence**, expresses the probability of observing the data under all mutually exclusive state configurations; it can be computed by summing the product of the likelihood times the prior over all such S. Herein, we shall assume that the world state variables vary continuously and hence $P(D) = \int P(D|S)P(S)dS$. The distribution $P(D)$ encapsulates data regularities that arise from similarities among audiovisual scenes in nature. Finally, the **posterior** conditional distribution $P(S|D)$ expresses the *a posteriori* probability of the audiovisual scene S after observing the data D.

The posterior distribution is the main tool for Bayesian inference since it allows us to use the data as observations to update the estimate of S based on Bayes' formula. This updating, applied to perception, agrees with cognitive psychology's view that, as we move in the environment we sense the world and our sensations get mapped to percepts which are accompanied by degrees of belief; these percepts may change as we acquire new information. In addition to the posterior, to complete the inference process, we also need a *decision rule*. For example, one of the most well-known solutions for finding S is to select the *Maximum-A-Posteriori (MAP)* estimate:

$$\hat{S}_{MAP} = \underset{S}{\operatorname{argmax}}\, P(D|S)P(S) \tag{1.2}$$

The marginal $P(D)$ is viewed as a normalization factor and hence is ignored in this maximization. The MAP estimate is influenced both from prior knowledge and from the data observed. Thus, assuming a uniform prior reduces the above to the equally well-known *Maximum Likelihood (ML)* estimate

$$\hat{S}_{ML} = \underset{S}{\operatorname{argmax}}\, P(D|S) \tag{1.3}$$

A unifying way to view these and other solutions is through Bayesian **decision** theory. First, we specify a *loss* (negative utility) function $L(S, A)$ that associates a cost L to the *decision* that assigns a solution A to the true scene state S. The *risk* is the expected loss over all possible scenes:

$$\text{Risk}(A) = \int L(S, A)P(S|D)dS \tag{1.4}$$

Then, we find an optimum Bayesian decision, i.e., solution $\hat{S}$, by minimizing this risk:

$$\hat{S} = \underset{A}{\operatorname{argmin}}\, \text{Risk}(A) \tag{1.5}$$

If we set $L(S, A) = c - \delta(S - A)$ where δ is the Dirac function, which means that we penalize equally (by a cost c) all wrong decisions, then $\text{Risk}(A) = c - P(A|D)$ and risk minimization yields the MAP estimate as the optimum Bayesian decision. Other well-known choices for the loss function include the quadratic error and the absolute error; i.e., assuming scalar S, A, we can select $L(S, A) = |S - A|^b$ with $b = 1, 2$. For $b = 2$ the risk is the Mean Square Error (MSE) and the optimum solution becomes the *mean* of the posterior distribution (i.e., the conditional mean given the data), whereas for $b = 1$ the risk is the Mean Absolute Error (MAE) and the optimum solution is the *median* of the distribution.

Returning to the view of perception as the process of inverting the world-to-signal mapping, this is generally an ill-posed problem. Thus, we need constraints to make it *well-posed*, i.e., to have a unique solution and the solution to depend continuously on the data. This approach is partially inspired by Tikhonov's *regularization theory* [520], which, to make inverse problems well-posed, proposes that we introduce some *constraints* by forcing the solution to lie in a subspace of the solution space where the problem is well-defined. For multimodal sensory perception, constraints can be of the following three types [99]: (i) Physical constraints, which stem from physical laws governing the multimodal world and are universally valid; (ii) Natural constraints that depend on the specific tasks (e.g., the smoothness constraints used in computer vision); and (iii) Artificial constraints that are imposed at some higher cognitive level. Two important problems are to determine which constraints to use and how to embed them into the information processing algorithms.

An intuitive approach to incorporate constraints is the Bayesian formalism, where the plausibilities of different solutions are quantified by probabilities based on stochastic sensor models for the signal formation and prior expectations of the world state; the latter are influenced by previous measurements (as in active vision or ecological optics) and by the constraints we impose on the system. Then, as true solution we choose the one with the highest probability. As described in [267], in psychophysics, *ideal observers* are considered the theoretical observers who use Bayesian inference to make optimal interpretations. Usually 'optimality' is the MAP criterion since this allows an ideal observer to take into consideration both prior knowledge about the world's audiovisual structure as well as knowledge about the audiovisual signal formation by the sensors. In psychophysical tests, the ideal observer's optimum performance is a useful reference that is compared with the performance of a human observer.

Another convenient way to embed constraints for making the inversion of the world-signal mapping well-posed is via the *energy minimization* approach, which has become quite popular in computer vision and is closely related to regularization [215, 405, 180, 323, 349, 582]. Here the optimum audiovisual scene state $\hat{S}$ is found as the minimizer of the energy functional

$$E(S; D) = E_{data}(S; D) + E_{smooth}(S) \tag{1.6}$$

where the energy term E_{data} expresses a norm of the deviation of the scene S from the data D, whereas the term E_{smooth} measures the non-smoothness of S and hence imposes regularization constraints on the solution. The minimization of E is equivalent to maximizing the following Gibbs probability distribution for the posterior

$$P(S|D) = \frac{\exp[-E(S; D)]}{Z} \tag{1.7}$$

where Z is a normalization factor (the partition function). In this case, solutions that are consistent with the constraints correspond to lower energy states, which are chosen by the minimization process. We can see several correspondences between the energy and the Bayesian approach if we take logarithms on both sides of the Bayes formula (1.1): the data-fitting error energy E_{data} corresponds to the log likelihood $-P(D|S)$ and the regularization energy E_{smooth} is the log prior $-P(S)$. Obviously, the Bayesian formulation subsumes the energy minimization approach and offers a richer interpretation using statistical tools. For example, using the popular quadratic energy functions corresponds to assuming Gaussian distributions. Further, regularization problems that use multiple energy constraint terms correspond to a Bayesian prior that is the product of the individual priors assuming independent sources.

1.2.3 Examples of Multicue or Multimodal Perception Research

In this section we outline the main findings from a few selected works on multimodal perception. The particular papers were selected either because they have become classic in the field, like [334] that presents an archetypal example of (i) the brain combining sound and vision, or because they represent different viewpoints of research in multimodal perception that are directly related to this chapter's scope, like (ii) promoting individual visual cue features in weak fusion to facilitate their integration [284]; (iii) exploring the difference between intramodal versus intermodal fusion [210]; (iv) integrating audio and visual modalities to improve spatial localization [44, 143, 555]; (v) investigating the temporal segmentation of multimodal time-evolving scenes into perceptual events [585]; and (vi) using gestalt principles to group audio and visual modalities [342].

McGurk effect: Hearing Lips and Seeing Voices

McGurk and MacDonald's 1976 paper [334] is a classic on human sensory integration. The McGurk effect is elicited when a listener's perceptual report of a heard syllable is influenced by the sight of the speaker mouthing a different syllable, inducing the report of another syllable. This effect can be explained by assuming that the finally perceived syllable is the one mostly compatible with both conflicting stimuli. Specifically, by synchronously combining the original vocalizations and lip movements, dubbed videos of the type [ba-audio/ga-visual] and [ga-audio/ba-visual] were shown to subjects under audiovisual and audio-only conditions. The audiovisual presentations of speech caused two distinct types of responses: **'Fusion'** where the information from the two modalities is transformed into something new with an element not presented in either modality, and **'Combination'** where a composite is formed comprising relatively unmodified elements from each modality. To [ba-audio/ga-visual] presentations, almost all adults gave fused responses [da]. To its complement, [ga-audio/ba-visual], more than half gave combination responses like [gabga]. The effect is generalizable to other stop consonants.

To explain the [ba-audio/ga-visual] case, first note that /ba/ sounds somewhat similar to /da/. Further, there is some visual similarity between (the articulation of) the back consonant in /ga/ and the middle consonant in /da/, whereas there is no such similarity between /ga/ and the front consonant in /ba/. If we assume that, when presented with the two modalities, perceivers attempt to interpret an event by searching for something that has the most common features or best matches with both modalities, then the unifying percept is /da/. However, in a [ga-audio/ba-visual] presentation, the modalities share no common features and hence are in conflict. The listener cannot decide between the two modalities and oscillates between them, hearing various combinations [bagba, gabga, baga, gaba].

The main conclusions from [334] include: (1) Speech perception seems to also take into consideration the visual information. Audio-only theories of speech are inadequate to explain the above phenomena. (2) Audiovisual presentations of speech create fusion or combination of modalities. (3) One possible explanation of the two response types is that a human attempts to find common information in both modalities and achieve a unifying percept.

The above paper has inspired much work in exploring and reaffirming the bimodality of speech perception. An interesting issue is that of *complementarity*, stated in [328] as: "Not only audible and visible speech provide two independent sources of information, but each also provides strong information where the other is weak." For example, /bi/ and /pi/ are visually indistinguishable but can be distinguished acoustically based on features such as voice onset time. In contrast, /mi/ and /ni/ sound very similar but differ visually in the place of articulation. In both cases, audiovisual speech can aid detecting the differences.

Modeling Depth Cue Combination using Modified Weak Fusion

Landy et al. [284], taking the application of scene depth reconstruction from various visual cues as a showcase, examined in detail how the different cues can be combined to yield a fused final result. For scene depth reconstruction, the different cues examined are motion parallax (with known camera egomotion), stereo, kinetic depth effect, texture, and shading. These alternative cues are quite different in nature: first of all, motion parallax can provide absolute depth estimates, whereas the other cues provide stereo measurements up to some unknown parameters, for example up to the unknown viewing distance parameter. Inter-cue interaction can be employed then to resolve these parameters and make the measurements from different cues commensurate, in a process the authors call *cue promotion*. After cue promotion, all measurements are on the same scale and in common units. Then, promoted cues can be directly fused in a modified weak fusion scheme. (The simple weak fusion scheme of [99] does independent processing of each cue followed by a weighted averaging; see also Section 1.3.)

Beyond cue promotion, the authors introduce in their modified weak fusion scheme two further important enhancements relative to [99]: First, they underline the importance of *dynamic cue weighting*, in response to the spatial (presense or absense of certain cues in the scene) and temporal relative reliability of each cue. Second, they highlight the issue of *robustness* in combining the different cues, proposing that an explicit mechanism should be present for outlier detection and down-weighting. The three constituents, namely cue promotion, dynamic weighting, and robustness constitute the main aspects of what they term the **modified weak fusion** scheme. This scheme generalizes the weak fusion scheme of [99] in the sense that it allows limited interactions between the different cues (most notably for cue promotion), while at the same time being modular and clearly more easy to verify than arbitrary strong fusion schemes. The authors give a methodology to assess the validity of the proposed fusion mechanism, as well as sufficient physiological experimental results in defense of their scheme.

Intramodal versus Intermodal Fusion of Sensory Information

Hillis et al. [210] explored human perception's capabilities for multimodal fusion to improve estimation of object properties (such as shape surface perception) both in an *intramodal* (within-senses) scenario of integrating the two visual cues of stereopsis-disparity and texture as well as in an *intermodal* (between-senses) scenario of integrating the two senses of vision and haptics. As optimal cue integration, they used a simple weak fusion [99, 583] where (under the Gaussian noise assumption) the Maximum Likelihood Estimate (MLE) becomes a linear weighted averaging with cue weights being inversely proportional to the variance of each cue noise. By performing psychophysical experiments and comparing the three cases of having (i) only single-cue estimators, (ii) only fused estimators (MLE), and (iii) both single-cue and fused estimators, they concluded to the following: Fusing cues (and losing information about the individual estimates) is more likely in the intramodal (disparity-texture) case than in the visual-haptic case. In the intermodal case, there may be natural circumstances where it is not beneficial to combine the two modalities (e.g., when one touches one object while looking at another).

Integration of Visual and Auditory Information for Spatial Localization

There is ample evidence that the human brain integrates multiple sensory modalities to accomplish various inference tasks such as spatial localization. In general, this integration improves performance. However, it may also lead to illusionary perception phenomena such as the "ventriloquist effect", where the movement of a dummy's mouth alters the perceived location of the ventriloquist's voice and hence creates a *localization bias*. Such phenomena are caused when there exist appropriate spatial and temporal disparities between the visual and auditory modalities. Experimental evidence [59, 555] has shown that the cross-modal localization bias decreases with increasing spatial and/or temporal disparity in the two stimuli.

Driver [143] explored variations of the ventriloquist illusion in the presence of a single visual and two auditory stimuli (target and distractor messages). He found that, under certain spatial combinations of the stimuli, the ventriloquist effect can actually help to enhance selective listening. Specifically, the simultaneous presence of a human face visually mouthing the target message and a mislocated sound source generating target and distractor messages can create an apparent visual source of the target sounds. Thus, before attentional selection is completed, ventriloquism causes a cross-modal matching that spatially shifts the target sounds to a virtual instead of the actual location. This enhances the selective listening of the target message by focusing attention on the virtual source.

In several controlled experiments on integration of auditory and visual stimuli with spatio-temporal disparities, Wallace et al. [555] explored the relationship between two important aspects of multisensory integration, the perceptual unification of the two stimuli and the dependence of localization bias on their spatio-temporal disparities. They found that: (i) "regardless of their disparity, whenever the auditory and visual stimuli were perceived as unified, they were localized at or very near the light. In contrast, when the stimuli were perceived as not unified, auditory localization was often biased away from the visual stimulus"; (ii) "localization bias was a reliable, significant predictor of whether perceptual unity would be reported".

Battaglia et al. [44] compared two theories of how human observers fuse the visual and auditory modalities for spatial localization. One theory predicts a nonlinear integration where the modality whose signal is more reliable dominates over the other in a winner-take-all scheme. This model is known as *visual capture*, because human perception is usually dominated by vision over hearing. A typical example is watching a film in a movie theater where the visual information comes from the screen whereas the auditory information (loudspeakers' sound) originates from the sides, but human observers usually perceive the sound origin as coincident with the location of the visual stimulus. The other theory advocates for a linear integration of the two modalities through a weighted *visual-auditory average*, which corresponds to a weak fusion scheme [99, 583]. The authors conducted experiments where human subjects heard broadband noise from several locations and viewed noisy versions of a random-dot stereogram of a Gaussian bump. In the multimodal phase of the experiments, a difference in location was introduced between the visual and auditory stimuli. The results indicate that, in low-noise conditions, the observers' judgement was usually dominated by vision only. But at large noise levels, the observers' judgement shifted to an averaging of the two modalities. The authors also investigated a hybrid approach and proposed a Bayesian model that combines both the linear weighted averaging and a prior expressing an overall bias to vision.

Temporal Segmentation of Videos into Perceptual Events by Human Brain

Given the major role that the temporal structure has in human perception, Zacks et al. [585] addressed the two fundamental questions of whether and how the human perceptual system performs temporal segmentation into perceptual events. Their experimental method involved participants who watched short videos of daily activities while brain images were acquired with fMRI scanning. All participants watched each video in three corresponding modes:

naive passive viewing, intentional viewing seeking active segmentation into coarse time units and active segmentation into fine time units. The hierarchy between segmentation into coarse events and fine segmentation into subevents is conceptually similar to the spatial vision task of segmentation into objects and subparts. The main authors' conclusions are that there is significant and detectable neural activity in the human brain during both intentional and passive viewing, and this activity occurs around the perceptual event boundaries. Further, there is a hierarchical structure between the coarse and fine levels of segmentation, which are aligned. Finally, the segmented events are well correlated with environmentally meaningful parts of the video activity. Regarding this chapter's scope, we emphasize that, one open research direction in the above area is to investigate the separate roles of the individual audio and visual modalities as well as their integrated multimodality in the above temporal percept segmentation.

Audiovisual Gestalts

Nowadays, gestalt psychology principles have become an inspiration for several approaches in computer vision. In a relatively new direction, Desolneux, Moisan and Morel [133] detect visual gestalts based on a perceptual principle due to Helmholtz by finding statistically meaningful parts to be grouped through searching for geometrical structures that largely deviate from randomness. This work was extended by Monaci and Vandergheynst [342] to detecting audiovisual events. The authors' work in [342] is motivated by strong evidences from previous computational (e.g., in [209, 122, 494]) and psychophysical experiments (e.g., in [143, 555]) that the integration of audiovisual information by humans is strongly assisted by the temporal synchrony of events in the two modalities. It uses the Gestalt psychology principle of time proximity to relate audiovisual fusion with gestalt detection where the audiovisual gestalts are co-occurrences of auditory and visual events. To develop a computational algorithm the authors used the Helmholtz principle, introduced in image analysis by [133]. By combining sequences of energy features for the audio and displacement features for the visual stream, they derive synchronization indicator sequences from which they detect statistically meaningful audiovisual events. Their results re-confirm the significance of the temporal proximity between audio and visual events for integrating the two modalities. Computational studies with a similar goal (i.e., the importance of audiovisual synchrony) have also been done in [209, 122, 494, 43, 255, 462].

1.3 Bayesian Formulation of Fusion

As discussed in Section 1.2.2, inference about the world state is the process through which the world-to-signal mapping is inverted. Since this inverse problem is generally ill-posed, we need constraints to make it well-posed.

Sensor fusion is needed to: (a) Reduce the dependence of a sensor on possibly invalid a priori (natural or artificial) constraints. (b) Reduce the uncertainty in parameter estimation due to errors in the sensor modeling of the world-to-signal mapping. (c) Reduce uncertainty due to measurement noise contaminating the noise free data. The book [99] dealt mainly with (a). An approach to incorporate uncertainty estimation into the fusion problem is proposed in Chapter 4 of this book.

Let S be the world state to be estimated, e.g., a vector of numeric or symbolic features-parameters representing properties of an audiovisual scene of the external world. Let D be the multimodal data representing signals collected by auditory sensors, visual sensors and other information sources (e.g., text), or D may represent features extracted from the raw signals. We write $D = (D_1, D_2, D_3, ...)$ to separate the modalities. For simplicity, in this section we assume only two modalities, aural and visual, producing data sets D_A and D_V, respectively; hence, $D = (D_A, D_V)$.

Clark and Yuille [99] have proposed a classification of fusion cases in terms of weak and strong coupling, which we shall call simply 'weak fusion' and 'strong fusion'. Next we summarize the main ideas for both cases in the Bayesian framework.

Weak Fusion

A clear case of *weak fusion* [99] occurs if the aural and visual information processing modules are independent and have their own likelihoods $P_A(D_A|S)$, $P_V(D_V|S)$ and priors $P_A(S)$ and $P_V(S)$ and produce two separate posterior distributions

$$\text{audio}: \quad P_A(S|D_A) = \frac{P_A(D_A|S)P_A(S)}{P_A(D_A)} \tag{1.8}$$

$$\text{vision}: \quad P_V(S|D_V) = \frac{P_V(D_V|S)P_V(S)}{P_V(D_V)} \tag{1.9}$$

See Fig. 1.1, where for simplicity we denote the audio data D_A by A and the video data D_V by V. Each monomodal posterior could give its own MAP estimate of the world scene:

$$\hat{S}_i = \operatorname*{argmax}_S P_i(D_i|S)P_i(S), \quad i \in \{A, V\}, \tag{1.10}$$

Afterwards, for fusion, the two separate estimates can be combined somehow to give a combined audiovisual estimate:

$$\hat{S}_{AV} = \text{fusion}(\hat{S}_A, \hat{S}_V) \tag{1.11}$$

where the fusion function can be either linear (e.g., a weighted average) or nonlinear (e.g., a max or min combination).

Consider the above case of weak fusion and suppose we wish to find the joint maximum a posteriori (MAP) estimate from the combined prior

$$P_{AV}(S|D_A, D_V) = P_A(S|D_A)P_V(S|D_V) = \frac{P_A(D_A|S)P_V(D_V|S)P_A(S)P_V(S)}{P_A(D_A)P_V(D_V)} \tag{1.12}$$

If the two monomodal MAP estimates $\hat{S}_A$ and $\hat{S}_V$ are close, then Yuille and Bülthoff [583] have shown that the joint MAP estimate is a *weighted average* of the two single monomodal MAP estimates $\hat{S}_A$ and $\hat{S}_V$. Specifically, assuming that the two single MAP estimates are close, expanding in Taylor series the log posterior around the point $\hat{S}_A \approx \hat{S}_V$ and keeping up to second order terms yields

$$\begin{aligned} \log P_{AV}(S|D_A, D_V) \approx \; & \log P_A(\hat{S}_A|D_A) + \log P_V(\hat{S}_V|D_V) \\ & -[w_{\mathrm{a}}(S - \hat{S}_A)^2 + w_{\mathrm{v}}(S - \hat{S}_V)^2]/2 \end{aligned} \tag{1.13}$$

where $w_i = -(d^2 \log P_i(S|D_i)/dS^2)(\hat{S}_i)$, $i \in \{\mathrm{a}, \mathrm{v}\}$. Maximization of (1.13) yields the following MAP estimate for the audiovisual problem:

$$\hat{S}_{AV} = \frac{w_{\mathrm{a}}\hat{S}_A + w_{\mathrm{v}}\hat{S}_V}{w_{\mathrm{a}} + w_{\mathrm{v}}} \tag{1.14}$$

Since $w_{\mathrm{a}}, w_{\mathrm{v}} > 0$, the combined MAP estimate (after weak fusion) is approximately a linear convex combination of the monomodal estimates.

For Gaussian distributions, the second-order expression in (1.13) becomes exact and the assumption about $\hat{S}_A \approx \hat{S}_V$ is not needed. In this case the weights are inversely proportional to each modality's variance σ_i^2, $i \in \{\mathrm{a}, \mathrm{v}\}$. Since $1/\sigma_i^2$ measures the reliability of each modality, the weights in the above scheme are proportional to each modality's reliability.

A similar situation, i.e., the combined optimum estimate to be the weighted average of monomodal estimates, would occur again in a weak fusion scheme where we wish to obtain maximum likelihood (ML) estimates. In this case too, the combined likelihood factors into two terms

$$P_{AV}(D_A, D_V|S) = P_A(D_A|S)P_V(D_V|S) \tag{1.15}$$

Then, by working as in the MAP case, a second-order Taylor series expansion of the logarithm of (1.15) would yield as optimum multimodal estimate again a weighted average as in (1.14), but the $\hat{S}$ symbols would mean ML estimates and the weights w_i would result from the values of the second derivative of the monomodal likelihoods at their maxima (which should be close).

Strong Fusion

In the previous weak fusion scheme, the two modalities are processed independently, their monomodal optimal (with respect to the MAP or ML criterion) estimates are found, and then fusion occurs by combining the two single estimates into a multimodal estimate with a linear or nonlinear function.

In contrast, we have *strong fusion* [99] if we have a non-separable joint likelihood and a single prior; this gives as posterior

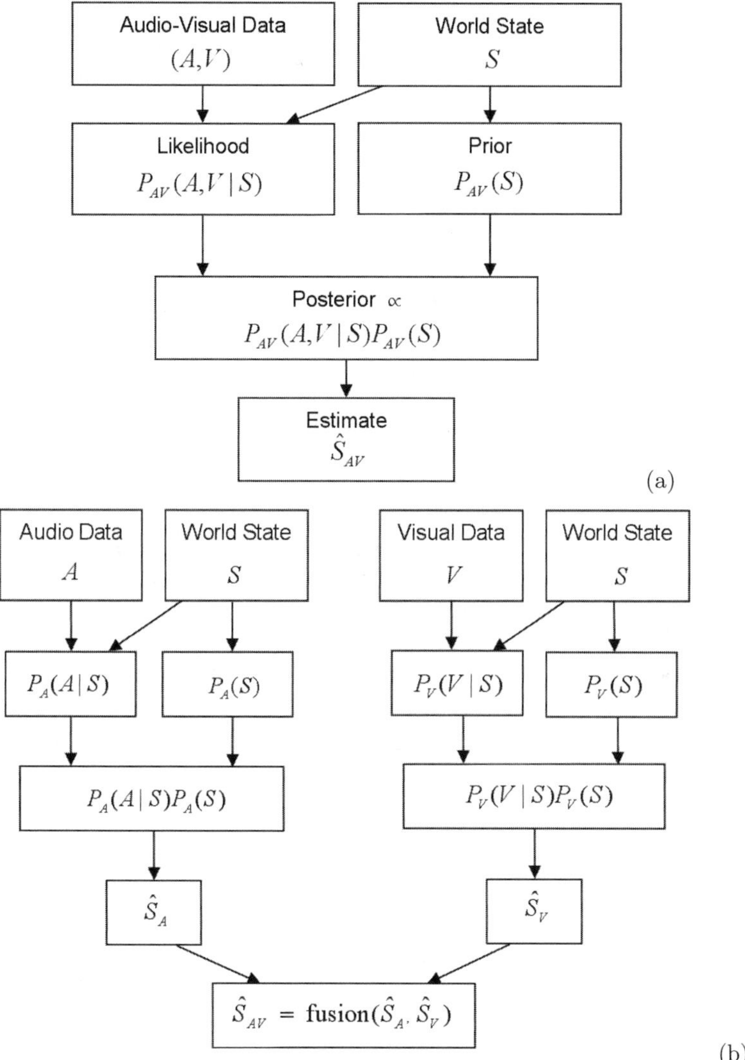

Fig. 1.1. Bayesian formulation of (a) Strong fusion and (b) Weak fusion schemes for two modalities, audio and vision.

$$P_{AV}(S|D_A, D_V) = \frac{P_{AV}(D_A, D_V|S)P_{AV}(S)}{P_{AV}(D_A, D_V)} \tag{1.16}$$

See Fig. 1.1 for diagrammatic illustration of strong fusion.

An *intermediate case* between weak and strong coupling is when the likelihood is separable and factors into two terms:

$$P_{AV}(S|D_A, D_V) = \frac{P_A(D_A|S)P_V(D_V|S)P_{AV}(S)}{P_{AV}(D_A, D_V)} \tag{1.17}$$

In this case, if the two modalities have the same prior, i.e., $P_{AV}(S) = P_A(S) = P_V(S)$, then we have a weak fusion scheme; otherwise we get a strong fusion.

Multi-stream Weights

In several cross-modal integration schemes used in multimedia applications, such as audiovisual speech recognition, the two modalities (or cues) are simply fused in the statistical models used for recognition by raising the respective monomodal likelihoods to various exponents, called *stream weights.* Without loss of generality, let us assume that we have two streams, say audio and video, with data or features D_A, D_V. The posterior probability of a property of an audiovisual scene S to be estimated given the multi-stream data $D = (D_A, D_V)$ is given by (1.16). If the two streams are statistically independent, the joint likelihood $P_{AV}(D|S)$ and marginal distributions $P_{AV}(D)$ become separable and we obtain (1.12). If needed, we can relax the independence assumption and assume only that the joint likelihood $P_{AV}(D|S)$ factors into the two corresponding monomodal likelihoods, in which case we obtain (1.17). The first case corresponds to simple weak fusion, whereas the second case is the aforementioned intermediate between weak and strong coupling. In both cases, raising each monomodal likelihood to a positive power, as usually done in multi-stream feature combination, creates a modified posterior-like function

$$B(S|D_A, D_V) = [P_A(D_A|S)]^{q_1} [P_V(D_V|S)]^{q_2} \frac{P(S)}{P(D)} \tag{1.18}$$

This may not even be a proper probability. Another artifact is the following: Since the rational numbers are dense in the set of reals, we can assume that the weights are rationals $q_i = n_i/n$, $i = 1, 2$, where n, n_1, n_2 are positive integers. If we ignore the common denominator n the integer stream weights correspond to replacing the product $P_A P_V$ of the marginal likelihoods with the power-weighted version $P_A^{n_1} P_V^{n_2}$. This corresponds to augmenting the multi-stream data (D_A, D_V) by replacing the ith stream with its n_i-fold repetition and treating the repetitions as independent. This repetition builds artificial correlations among subsets of the augmented data and may destroy any assumed independence of the separate streams. A better approach than power-raising the stream probabilities is proposed in this book's Chapter 4.

1.4 Monomodal Features

For multimodal integration, a proper representation of each single modality is very crucial. Multimedia description standards such as the MPEG-7 particularly emphasize the role of monomodal descriptors [319]. Two main types of elements that MPEG-7 uses to describe and manage audio-visual content are descriptors and descriptor schemes. The *Descriptors* convey information about low-level audio features (e.g. temporal and spectral envelopes, pitch, energy, and descriptors about musical timbre, spoken content and melody contour) or visual features (e.g. color, edges, shape, texture, motion), as well as attributes of audio-visual content (e.g. location, time, quality). The *Description Schemes* convey information about high-level features such as audio segments and events or visual regions and objects; they consist of a set descriptors and their relationship for a particular task or application, arranged in a tree structure. The domain of descriptor schemes categorizes them into three types: audio, visual, and multimedia. The latter combine content descriptions of audio, visual, and possibly text data. Overviews of the MPEG-7 audio, visual, and multimodal descriptors and descriptor schemes can be found respectively in [417], [488], [455].

Next we discuss some of the most popular techniques to extract features from the audio, visual, and text data for multimodal applications.

1.4.1 Audio Features

Information carried by the audio modality is certainly polymorphous and multi-level. Thus, choosing a proper audio representation is not always straightforward and depends on the specific application. For multimodal integration, the need to also compactly capture properties that are complementary to the other modalities poses additional requirements. This has led to the utilization of simpler and more focused audio feature extraction schemes in many multimodal scenarios. Alternatively, the audio frontend is adopted 'as-is' from the corresponding audio-only application, e.g., speaker identification.

From a different viewpoint, audio descriptions in the multimodal context, inspired from single modality approaches or not, can be either *generic* or *specific* [326]. Specific refers to high-level representations of audio content, as for example obtained by applying speech recognition or audio segmentation and classification; knowledge of the audio class, e.g., music, noise, speech, or of the words that have been uttered in the case when the audio contains speech, can be used in a successive multimodal analysis and fusion scheme as sketched in Section 1.5.1. Such representations can be very useful in multimedia applications and are usually devised via the employment of advanced pattern recognition techniques. The focus of the current discussion is however mainly on the generic, low-level audio features as they are extracted by a signal-processing front-end. These may be further categorized into spectral or temporal features or alternatively, according to [559], into short or long term audio representations.

Short-Term Features

Short-term features are normally extracted at a high rate and correspond to short audio segments, typically referred to as frames. They are advantageous in the sense that they allow the description of non-stationary audio signals whose properties vary quickly, e.g., speech. They cannot represent however long-term properties, as for example speech prosody. Probably the most widely used frame-level features are the short-term energy and variants as well as the zero-crossing rate [559, 575]. Their estimation is performed in the time-domain and when combined they can provide valuable information for speech/silence discrimination. Pitch, on the other hand, is extracted either by time or frequency analysis. It is the fundamental frequency of an audio waveform and it is very informative for speech and harmonic music. In speech, it mainly depends on the speaker's gender while in music it is influenced by the strongest note being played. In [333] the pitch is used, along with other features, for automatic meeting action analysis.

In applications such as audiovisual automatic speech recognition or audio-visual speaker identification, spectrum related representations are commonly preferred. This is justified by the relative success of the spectral feature sets in the corresponding audio-only based applications. Log-Mel filter-bank energies, Mel-frequency cepstral coefficients (MFCCs), linear prediction cepstral coefficients (LPCCs) [421], or perceptual linear prediction coefficients (PLP) are possible variants that have been successfully applied in various multimodal contexts [22, 147]. They practically provide a compact representation of smooth spectral information and their extraction is quite straightforward. For the most common ones, namely the MFCCs, the extraction process involves filtering the signal with a specially designed filterbank that comprises triangular or more elaborate filters properly localized in the frequency domain. The MFCCs are extracted as the first few Discrete Cosine Transform (DCT) coefficients of the log-energies of the signals at the filterbank output. Their efficacy is demonstrated in the context of audiovisual speech recognition in Chapter 4. Usually, to capture speech dynamics, these features are also accompanied by their first and second derivatives. These derivatives are approximated using information from neighboring frames as well and so they would be more appropriately characterized as long-term features.

Long-Term Features

Long-term feature estimation is based on longer audio segments, usually comprising multiple frames. In a sense, long-term features capture variations of the short-term ones and may be more closely related to audio semantic content. Many such features were originally applied for audio analysis in single-stream approaches and were or can be further customized for multimedia applications [591, 402]. Examples include various statistics of the short-time energy and the Zero Crossing Rate (ZCR), such as their average value or standard deviation. These indicate temporal changes of the corresponding quantities which in turn facilitate audio segmentation or classification in various classes, e.g., sports or news clips [559]; a sports clip would have a smoother ZCR contour than a news clip, since it is characterized by an almost constant noise background while clean speech during news exhibits a widely and quickly varying ZCR.

Long-term features based on *pitch statistics* can be equally useful. Only voiced speech and music have smooth pitch and thus pitch variations can help detecting voiced and music frames within an audio segment [559]. In a similar manner, spectral variations in time can help determining between speech and music; speech is expected to have much faster varying spectral characteristics. Indeed, temporal stability, i.e., a feature measuring these variations has been successfully applied in this direction at the first stage of a broadcast news multimedia indexing framework [375]. It is estimated as the variance of the generalized cross-correlation of the spectra of adjacent frames. At a different level, the *speaking rate*, i.e., how fast speech is uttered, can also be important; it may change a lot depending on speech pragmatics, namely the goal the specific speech utterance serves in communication. Being much different in a monologue or a presentation than during a conversation, the speaking rate has been exploited in [333] for multimodal meeting analysis.

1.4.2 Visual Features

The visual modality is an extremely rich source of information. Although high-level visual scene understanding of arbitrary scenes is beyond the reach of current technology, visual information processing plays a key role in various application areas, especially in domains where the image/video content is structured according to well-defined rules. In particular, visual information processing has proven beneficial in commercially-interesting domains involving sports video, broadcast news, and movies data, where it has been utilized in conjunction with audio and text for automatic content analysis, indexing, summarization, and re-purposing, among others.

A wide range of visual features has been proposed in the literature to address the requirements of different multimodal applications. We can categorize different visual information representations into two broad classes, low and mid-level generic visual features on the one hand, and high-level application-specific visual features on the other hand. We discuss next representative approaches from both categories.

Low and Mid-Level Visual Features

In the first category, low and mid-level visual features have been used to characterize basic image and video properties, such as color, texture, and motion. This class of features are broadly used as generic image descriptors, most notably for applications such as content-based image/video retrieval [222, 450, 559], see also Section 1.7.6, and variants of them have been included as descriptors in the visual part of the MPEG-7 standard [319, 488].

Among the generic visual features, *color* is perhaps the most widely used. Color is typically represented in one of standard color-spaces, such as the RGB or the perceptually better motivated HSV and $L^*u^*v^*$. The color content of an image or video frame is typically summarized in a low-dimensional color histogram signature, and color-based similarity metrics are defined in terms of these histograms. Since color is a per-pixel attribute, color representations can be computed very efficiently and are invariant to image scaling or view-point changes. However, color histograms can be significantly affected by illumination changes and, most importantly, completely discard geometric image information since they do not represent the spatial configuration of pixels. Color features are typically most appropriate either for applications in which their efficiency is crucial, such as real-time (audiovisual) face and hand tracking, or for scenarios in which a single color, such as grass' green in field games, dominates the scene and thus its detection safely identifies the video shot.

Another universal image attribute is its *texture*, roughly corresponding to a description of its periodic patterns, directional content, and structural/stochastic complexity. A popular way to describe texture is by the image response of a multi-scale, oriented transform, such as the Gabor or wavelet filterbanks. The textural content can then be characterized by the most dominant filterbank responses at each point, or by filterbank channel response moments across the whole image. Alternative textural representations, such as Markov-Random-Fields or co-occurrence matrices can also serve as powerful texture descriptors. Another successful recent advance in image texture modeling encompasses the mid-level vision class of distinctive image features popularized by the Scale-Invariant Feature Transform (SIFT) representation [308]. In the SIFT representation, a sparse set of salient scale-space image points is first selected, and then the image textural content around each salient point is described in a compact representation. This class of features has built-in scale invariance properties and has proven particularly effective for reliable image matching and higher-level object recognition.

The last large class of low and mid-level visual features represents *motion* in video, typically computed with block-matching or other optical flow techniques [42]. On the one hand, global scene motion can be used to recover camera attributes such translation, rotation, panning, and zooming, as well as detect scene changes. On the other hand, local object motion is often related to object saliency; motion features have thus been used widely as event detectors in surveillance and sports analysis applications. The down-side of motion-based features is that optical flow computation is a computationally demanding task.

We should note here that each of the low and mid-level visual feature classes described above is typically not adequate for describing by itself the semantic content of image and video. Thus, most applications typically utilize more than one visual cues in tandem (intramodal fusion), apart from combining them with audio or text information (intermodal fusion), or even allow the user participate in the processing loop, as in the relevance feedback approach of [452].

High-Level Visual Features

In certain domains high-level image and video understanding is indispensable and this is usually beyond the reach of the low and mid-level visual descriptors just described. Typical example applications are audiovisual speech/emotion recognition or face recognition, which all require high-level models for object analysis and recognition. We describe next representative models of object shape and appearance which are carefully tailored for the needs of high-level object understanding.

An important high-level visual attribute is the object's *shape*. Examples of generic shape representations are the region-based 'shape context' [52], which yields a histogram shape descriptor, and the classical contour-based Fourier shape descriptor which approximates a closed contour using the coefficients of a truncated Fourier series; variants thereof are included in the MPEG-7 standard [488]. A more powerful class of object-centric shape features are the parametric representations of [394] and [106]. Both these techniques capture shape deformation in a compact parametric shape model which is specifically tailored for a single class of objects. This object-specific shape model is derived either by a physics-based Finite Element Modeling (FEM) analysis in [394] or by a training procedure using a hand-annotated set as in the Active Shape Model (ASM) [106]. Given such a model, a target shape can then be described in terms of its first few eigen-modes or eigen-shapes, yielding a highly compact and specific representation. Such models have been used extensively in the past for applications such as tracking and feature extraction from human faces.

In parallel to shape, an important class of computer vision models is concerned with object *appearance* description. Popularized by the successful "eigen-face" model of [531], this class of models strives for accurate and compact representation of image appearance content. Such representations are typically learned from representative training images by means of principal component analysis or other unsupervised/supervised dimensionality reduction techniques. A significant recent advance in appearance models is the Active Appearance Model (AAM) [107] which combines the compact shape representation of the ASM and the PCA-based appearance modeling of eigenfaces in a new powerful blend, while at same time being amenable to efficient calculations. An application of the AAM model in audiovisual speech recognition is illustrated in the book's Chapter 4.

1.4.3 Text Features

The basics of text description

Text is a major medium carrying semantic information. In this section, we focus on the textual features that can be used to describe the content of a document for applications such as information retrieval for example. The basic paradigm consists in associating with each document a descriptor, called *index* in this domain, composed of a set of words called indexing terms. Such terms can be chosen from a predefined list (e.g., in a thesaurus) – in this case the correspondence between a document and this list is not trivial and is often done manually – or directly from the text itself. The latter is the usual way to proceed when large collections are to be processed automatically, i.e., in most search engines on the web.

To develop such a system implies first to choose the terms that should be extracted. The first stage in this process transforms the text in a sequence of words or tokens. If this is not too difficult in English, the absence of white spaces in Chinese for example can make this first step a rather difficult one. Next, the indexing terms are to be chosen among all the extracted tokens. They should be discriminant, and thus not appear in all documents, but they should not be too specific: they must appear in several texts and be informative [459]. The set of unordered words obtained by this process is called a bag-of-words.

Many systems associate a weight with each of the indexing terms, in order to designate which terms are more important or more meaningful. Three criteria are used: the importance of the term within the document, the importance of the term within the document collection, and the size of the document [456]. The first factor corresponds to a local weight and is usually based on the *term frequency* in the document. The second one is global and is often chosen as the *inverse document frequency* or one of its variants. The last factor tries to correct the effects of the size of the document.

Finally, a representation model defines the way the terms should be used or interpreted and how the query index should be compared to the collection indexes. Classical families of such models are the *set-theoretic* models like the Boolean model, where the documents are represented as sets of terms and where the comparisons are done using basic set-theoretic operations, the *algebraic* models like Salton's vector space model [458], where the documents are represented as vectors and the similarity is expressed as a scalar number, and *probabilistic* models [503] where the retrieval problem is seen as a probabilistic inference problem, making use of tools like Bayes' theorem.

Natural language processing for enhanced descriptions

The basic tools presented above fail to represent all the details and subtleties of natural languages, and natural language processing methods have been proposed in order to acquire linguistic information and to improve the performance of the description. These tools can work at various levels: at the morphological level, at the syntactic level or at the semantic level.

Morphology is concerned by the structure of the words, and explains the links between words like *transform*, *transforms*, and *transformation*. A basic idea, called lemmatization, is thus to replace all these words in the document index by the simplest one or the most basic one of the series: *goes* can be replaced by *go*, *bikes* by *bike*. According to experiments, such a technique allows to improve the precision and recall of an information retrieval system up to 20 %. A second technique pushes the idea further and replaces every word in the index by its stem, but the results are much dependent on the quality of the stemming algorithm used and on the language [31]: Swedish or Slovenian provide more convincing results than English.

The structure of the sentences and of the syntagms are the subject of syntax. Its use mainly consists in using syntagms as complex indexing terms. Although they present even more variations than simple terms, their use has been proven successful when they come in addition to the simple terms, directly in the same index [459] or in a separate index [278]. The gain in performance can reach 5 to 30 %.

At the semantic level, information about the meaning of words and relations between words can be taken into account. Possible relations are synonymy, hypernymy, or more complex relations like the one that links 'professor' with 'to teach' [100]. Such information can be used to expand the queries. Automatically extracted co-occurring words added to queries have been proved to improve the results [179], while the use of WordNet [157] leads to more deceiving results [549]. Another alternative is to use the semantic information in the index itself, by employing the meaning of the words as indexing criterion instead of viewing each word as a sequence of letters. Disambiguation is also an option [258]. In this case also, the use of WordNet does not clearly improve the results.

As a conclusion, if the basic ways to integrate linguistic information presented here have largely proven their relevance, really taking into account word meaning is still a challenge for which no universal technique is yet available. Tools developed for restricted domains (e.g., more restricted collections or specific languages) appear however very promising.

1.5 Models for Multimodal Data Integration

What tools can be used to analyze jointly the several media present in a document? Many authors tried to avoid developing ad-hoc methods for each new combination they encountered and relied on the classical techniques that were available in fields like data analysis, machine learning or signal processing. As a matter of fact, multimedia is yet another application domain for pattern recognition techniques.

Let us first categorize the tasks to be solved in four elementary problems. *Segmentation* aims at delimiting events. These events can be shots, scenes or sequences in an audiovisual stream. *Event detection* consists in finding predefined events in a document, such as advertisement, dialogues, and goals in soccer matches. *Structuring* is close to a complete segmentation of a document. Its goal is to provide the complete structure of a document, structure that can include some hierarchy (e.g., shots are gathered in scenes), or some classification (e.g., the various segments may be labeled). Finally, *classification* aims at providing labels to document parts. Of course, one major application of classification consists in associating more semantic labels to documents, but this leads to a very wide variety of problems, e.g., determining the language of a document, what is its genre, and what sport is shown.

These four categories have close links and many algorithms both segment and structure, or detect events and classify at the same time. It should be noticed that the first three tasks, as far as multimedia documents are concerned, deal most of the time with temporal documents and have to take this temporal dimension into account. On the other hand, the classification often arrives after other description steps and can be stated as a static problem. As written above, many temporal or dynamic algorithms also achieve classification tasks.

Several categorizations can be made of the various techniques. Section 1.5.1 introduces the distinction between early, intermediate, and late fusion. In [501], the authors present other typologies and separate statistical methods, ranging from rule-based techniques, or simultaneous methods where all the media are considered at the same time to methods where the media are processed one after the other. In Section 1.5.2 we describe appropriate representations, as well as classification tools for static modeling of multimodal data, while in Section 1.5.3 we describe tools suited for dynamic time-evolving modalities, including the Hidden Markov Model and its variants, as well as more general Dynamic Bayesian Networks.

1.5.1 Levels of Integration: Early, Intermediate, and Late Fusion Approaches

Integration of features extracted from diverse sources is not a trivial task. The two main problems encountered in this process are the following:

- A *decision* problem: what should be the final decision when the various media or sources of information provide contradictory data? Although the decision problem is common to all systems based on information fusion, it gets more difficult in the case of multimodal data because the different modalities are affected dissimilarly by environmental noise, and thus their relative reliability is time-varying.
- A *synchronization* problem, which is specific to multimodal integration of time-evolving data. Synchronization issues arise for two reasons. First, the natural representation granularity for heterogeneous modalities is different. For example, the elementary unit of video signal is the image frame,

typically sampled at 20-30 Hz, while audio features for speech recognition are usually extracted at 100 Hz, and the elements of text (words) are generated at roughly a 1 Hz rate. Second, the boundaries induced by a certain semantic event to different modalities are only loosely aligned. For example, applause (acoustic evidence) and score label update (textual evidence) typically lag scoring in sports, while visual evidence is concurrent to it.

One can generally classify the various approaches to multimodal integration into three main categories [205], depending on the stage that the involved streams are fused, namely early, intermediate and late integration techniques. In the early integration paradigm, corresponding to the strong fusion model of Section 1.3, we first concatenate all modality descriptors into a single multimodal feature vector; afterwards, processing proceeds by using conventional monomodal techniques. Late integration techniques, following the weak fusion model of Section 1.3, largely handle each modality independently using separate models; the corresponding partial results are subsequently combined to yield the final decision. While both early and late integration approaches build on established monomodal modules and are thus easily applicable, they cannot fully account for the loose synchronization and the fine interaction between the different modalities. Intermediate integration methods try to address this shortcoming by employing novel techniques specifically devised to handle multimodal data and properly account for multimodal interaction.

Early Integration

For early integration, it suffices to concatenate all monomodal features into a single aggregate multimodal descriptor, possibly compacted by a dimensionality reduction process. Since early integration corresponds to the strong fusion model of Section 1.3, it is theoretically the most powerful scheme for multimodal fusion. In practice, however, early integration schemes can only be effective if all individual modalities are synchronized. Moreover, early integration lacks flexibility due to its non-modular nature, and the whole system needs to be re-built in case the conditions affecting even a single constituent modality change. For example, in the case of audiovisual speech recognition based on early integration models, it is necessary to retrain all models for each acoustic noise condition.

Late Integration

In this approach, each modality is classified independently. Integration is done at the decision level and is usually based on heuristic rules. For example, audio and video streams are segmented and classified by two separate Hidden Markov Models. Dialogues are identified as segments where audio signal is mainly speech while visual information is an alternation of two views. The detection of such particular scenes is done by fusion of the decisions.

A particular instance of late integration techniques is based on the successive analysis approach. The principle of this scheme, as illustrated in video analysis applications, is the following: The audio or textual signal is employed in a first stage to detect interesting segments. Image analysis (tracking, spatial segmentation, edge/line/face detection) is then used in the regions previously detected to identify a particular event, or more simply to identify the video segment boundaries. In this first case, audio, or text, are used to restrict the temporal window where video analysis will be used. An implicit assumption of such a method is that interesting segment detection is faster with these modalities (applauds in the sound track or keywords in the textual stream). This constitutes the first stage of a prediction verification method, whose second stage is a verification and localization step done on the audio or on the visual stream. The use order of the various media may be inverted: in a first stage, visual features are used to detect interesting events. In a second stage, the state of excitement of the speaker or the public is measured to filter the most interesting shots. This process is no more a prediction/verification process, but the audio signal is used to order the visual segments by level of importance.

Intermediate Integration

Intermediate integration techniques lie in-between early and late integration methods and are specifically geared towards modeling multimodal time-evolving data. They achieve a good compromise between modularity and close intermodal interaction. Specifically, they are modular enough in the sense that varying environmental conditions affecting individual streams can be handled by treating each stream separately. Moreover, they allow modeling the loose synchronization of heterogeneous streams while preserving their natural correlation over time. This class of techniques has proved its potential in various application areas, such as audiovisual speech recognition presented in Chapter 4. Various intermediate integration architectures for handling time-evolving modalities are discussed in Section 1.5.3.

1.5.2 Static Models for Multimodal Data

We first consider static models for processing multimodal information. These are designed for data that are static themselves, but can also often handle satisfactorily dynamic data on a frame-by-frame basis.

Modeling Interrelated Multimodal Events

Multimodal data stemming from a common cause often have strong interdependencies. In the case of two sets of continuous vector variables, $\mathbf{x}$ and $\mathbf{y}$, canonical correlation analysis (CCA) provides a natural representation for analyzing their co-variability [322]. Similarly to the better-known principal component analysis (PCA), CCA reduces the dimensionality of the datasets, and thus produces more compact and parsimonious representations of them. However, unlike PCA, it is specifically designed so that the preserved subspaces of $\mathbf{x}$ and $\mathbf{y}$ are maximally correlated. Therefore CCA is especially suited for studying the interrelations between $\mathbf{x}$ and $\mathbf{y}$. In the case that $\mathbf{x}$ and $\mathbf{y}$ are Gaussian, one can prove that the subspaces yielded by CCA are also optimal in the sense that they maximally retain the mutual information between $\mathbf{x}$ and $\mathbf{y}$ [464]. Canonical correlation analysis is also related to linear discriminant analysis (LDA): similarly to LDA, CCA performs dimensionality reduction to $\mathbf{x}$ discriminatively; however the target variable $\mathbf{y}$ in CCA is continuous, whereas in LDA is discrete.

More specifically, in CCA we seek directions, $\mathbf{a}$ (in the $\mathbf{x}$ space) and $\mathbf{b}$ (in the $\mathbf{y}$ space), so that the projections of the data on the corresponding directions are maximally correlated, i.e. one maximizes with respect to $\mathbf{a}$ and $\mathbf{b}$ the correlation coefficient between the projected data $\mathbf{a}^T\mathbf{x}$ and $\mathbf{b}^T\mathbf{y}$

$$\rho(\mathbf{a},\mathbf{b}) = \frac{\mathbf{a}^T R_{xy}\mathbf{b}}{\sqrt{\mathbf{a}^T R_{xx}\mathbf{a}}\sqrt{\mathbf{b}^T R_{yy}\mathbf{b}}}. \tag{1.19}$$

Having found the first such pair of *canonical correlation directions* $(\mathbf{a}_1,\mathbf{b}_1)$, along with the corresponding *canonical correlation coefficient* ρ_1, one continues iteratively to find another pair $(\mathbf{a}_2,\mathbf{b}_2)$ of vectors to maximize $\rho(\mathbf{a},\mathbf{b})$, subject to $\mathbf{a}_1^T R_{xx}\mathbf{a}_2 = 0$ and $\mathbf{b}_1^T R_{yy}\mathbf{b}_2 = 0$; the analysis continues iteratively and one obtains up to $k = \text{rank}(R_{xy})$ direction pairs $(\mathbf{a}_i,\mathbf{b}_i)$ and CCA coefficients ρ_i, with $1 \geq \rho_1 \geq \ldots \geq \rho_k \geq 0$, which, in decreasing importance, capture the directions of co-variability of $\mathbf{x}$ and $\mathbf{y}$. For further information on CCA and algorithms for performing it, one is directed to [322].

Canonical correlation analysis and related ideas have proven fruitful in several multimodal fusion tasks. By searching in videos for the image areas that are maximally correlated with the audio one can spot audiovisual salient events. Applications include speaker localization and tracking, as well as video-assisted audio source separation (cocktail party effect) [209, 122, 255]. By maximizing the canonical correlation over a small shift window, one can also time-align asynchronous data streams, as demonstrated in [462]. Moreover, CCA is closely related to the optimal Wiener filter for linear regression [464]; this connection has been employed by [247] in recovering speech articulation from audiovisual data.

Classification of Static Multimodal Data

In the matter of classification with multimedia data, many techniques coming from classic pattern recognition can be used. Before discussing these techniques, several specificities should be outlined.

The algorithms can be employed at several levels. Their input can be descriptors or the output of monomodal classifiers [262]. Of course, the way the various media are mixed is important. The descriptors can be simply concatenated. When the various descriptors are of the same nature, the resulting vector can be reduced through a PCA or discriminant linear analysis. Concatenating descriptors of different nature like words with numeric descriptors is problematic since they correspond to very different kinds of distributions and metrics.

Simple Bayesian classifiers are a first class of possible classifiers for multimedia data. Support vector machines (SVMs) [540] are heavily used for at least three reasons. They are quite efficient in dealing with high dimensional data, they can manage non-linear separation boundaries, and, last but not least, free implementations are available which are quite simple to use[5].

Neural networks of different kinds, like multilayer perceptrons, are also classical tools in the domain. Convolutional networks have been used for face detection and proven to be well-suited tools for dealing directly with the signal [178]. Even if their use is more efficient in some cases, they remain difficult to apply, because of the complexity of the algorithms that are associated with them for training and because no widely available implementation exists (for the convolutional networks in particular).

Finally, Bayesian networks appear to be very flexible tools. Such networks allow to model any graph of dependency between random variables. The variables are simply represented as nodes in a graph where edges represent some dependence between two variables. One of the major advantages of Bayesian networks comes from the possibility to learn the structure of the network directly from data, e.g., using the K2 algorithm [104]. Of course, if many variables are to be taken into account and no hint is given to the algorithm, this requires lots of training data and the complexity becomes very high. This is a major difference with Markov models where the structure has to be *a priori* defined.

1.5.3 Models for Dynamic Data: Integration of Asynchronous Time-Evolving Modalities

In the case of dynamic data, two additional difficulties appear: The various data streams can have different rates and can also lack precise synchronization. As an example, movies can have 24, 25 or 30 images per second when sound frames have a rate of 16 kHz or 48 kHz and speech corresponds to four syllables per second. It is also clear that TV and radio commentators usually describe events that have already passed, for example, in live sport programs. Even if the interval between the event and its comments is rather small for human perception, it will be translated in terms of dozens of image frames and hundreds of sound frames. Choosing what part of each stream should be considered at a given instant is thus quite a complex problem. The two basic formalisms used in the domain are Markov models and Bayesian networks, the former being a particular case of the latter.

[5] A list is provided on the Wikipedia webpage on SVMs.

The Principle of Markov Models

Markov models are composed of a graph of states linked by oriented edges. Each edge represents a possible transition between two states or the possibility to stay at the same state for several periods of time. Time being assumed to be discrete, at each instant, the process makes a transition from its actual state to another one and emits an observation. Such a system is parameterized by several sets of probabilities. A first set provides the probability distribution of the initial state from where the process starts at $t = 0$. The second set provides the state transition probabilities. The last set provides the probability distributions of the observations emitted at each state.

Many variants of the basic model have been developed [413, 556]. The probabilities are usually constant over time, but one could use varying probabilities. The basic Markov hypothesis states that the observation emitted and the transition only depends on the current state: Past is reduced to the current situation. But here also, a variant is possible where the past could be reduced to the knowledge of a given number of past instants. That is for example what happens when using n-gram models.

A Markov model is said to be hidden when the sequence of states is unknown. This is the case for example when a sequence of observations is known, and the issue is then to determine the most probable sequence of states $s = (s_1, s_2, \ldots, s_T)$ which could emit this sequence of known observations $(o_1, o_2, \ldots, o_T)$. Mathematically, the problem is thus to find the optimal sequence of states s^* such that:

$$s^* = \arg\max_{s_{1:T}} (\log P(o_{1:T}|s_{1:T}) + \log P(s_{1:T}))$$

The Viterbi algorithm [169] is used to solve this problem and provides a global optimum.

It should be noticed that the structure of the hidden Markov model should be defined *a priori*. The parameters can either be predefined or estimated by the Baum-Welch algorithm from example data.

The Principles of Bayesian Networks

As mentioned earlier, the Bayesian networks allow a set of random variables and their dependencies to be represented by an oriented acyclic graph. Each node corresponds to an observed or hidden variable and the edges represent the dependencies. An edge between a node A and a node B indicates that the variable represented by B depends upon the variable represented by A. Of course, the absence of any edge between two nodes means these nodes are independent, or conditionally independent if they share a common parent.

The parameters of such a network are the conditional distributions of each node. These distributions provide the probabilities of each variable conditionally on its parent variables. The global joint probability of all variables can be computed:

$$P_\theta(x) = \prod_i P_{\theta_i}(x_i|\mathcal{A}_i)$$

where $\mathcal{A}_i$ is the set of parents of node i in the graph. The parameters θ_i correspond to the parameters of the conditional distribution at node i. The factorized form of this joint probability is the starting point of the algorithms that allow to learn the structure [104] and the parameters of such networks [260, 236].

Such Bayesian networks are called dynamic Bayesian networks when they represent a random process. Such a denomination is quite improper in fact, but it is largely accepted by the community. Dynamic networks are in fact static, but they present a pattern repeated over time. On the other hand, the parameters are time independent. As a consequence, the same training algorithms can be used, but learning the structure of such a network becomes intractable in most situations.

Hidden Markov Models for Multimedia Processing

When several streams of observations are to be taken into account, Hidden Markov Models (HMMs) can be adapted. If the streams are synchronized and share the same rate, a first solution is to fuse the descriptors at each instant in order to create larger multimodal descriptors. Such a method is restricted to the fusion of descriptors of the same nature. Mixing words with numeric descriptors makes it difficult to define a metric between descriptors. Furthermore, the constraint on the rate often implies to align one of the streams on the other one (e.g., to reduce the audio information to one descriptor per visual shot) (see Fig. 1.2).

There are many Markov model variants for processing multimodal data; a unified presentation of the most popular architectures can be found in [362]. *Multistream* HMMs were introduced to process several streams, using one HMM per stream and by adding synchronization points [77, 208, 147] (see Fig 1.3). Between two such synchronizations, the two streams are assumed to be independent and are modeled by their own HMM. In this case the observations of the various streams are supposed to be independent (conditionally to the hidden process). At each synchronization point, the scores corresponding to each stream have to be combined.

Two extreme cases of multistream HMMs are the synchronous and the asynchronous models. In the former, the two Markov models have a shared state sequence, and can be considered as synchronized at every instant. In the latter, there is no synchronization (except at the beginning and at the end of the process) and the model is equivalent to a synchronous model in the product state space. As a consequence, such a model is often called a *product* model. More specifically, let us consider a pair of bimodal sequences $\mathbf{y}^{(1)}$ and $\mathbf{y}^{(2)}$, each consisting of T (discrete or continuous) observation samples $\mathbf{y}^{(i)} = (y_1^{(i)}, y_2^{(i)}, \ldots, y_T^{(i)})$. Then, in the synchronous multistream HMM model the

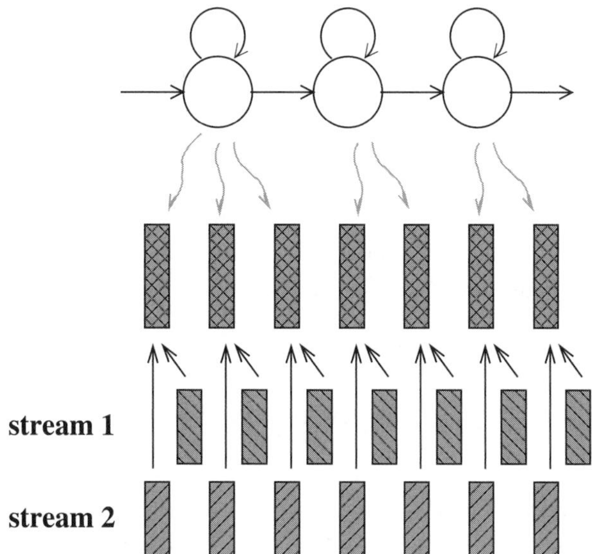

Fig. 1.2. Descriptor fusion with hidden Markov models. Grey arrows correspond to conditional probabilities and provide an exemple of alignment between states and observations. (Credits: G. Gravier)

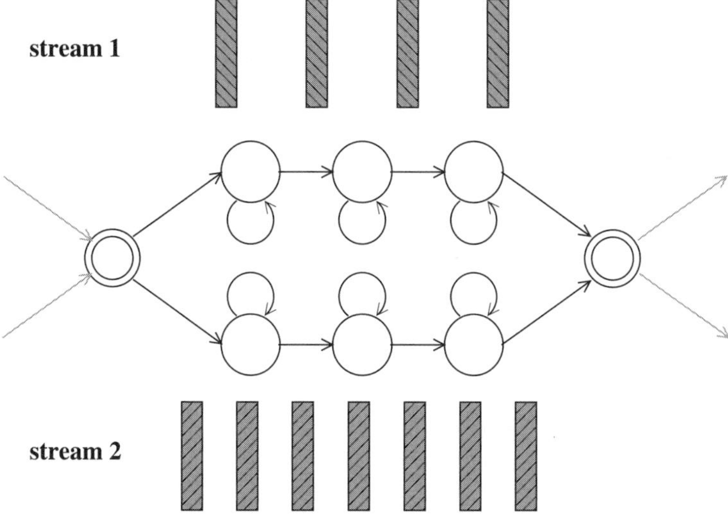

Fig. 1.3. Multistream hidden Markov model. The states represented by a double circle correspond to synchronization points. (Credits: G. Gravier)

data are explained by a common hidden state sequence $\mathbf{x} = (x_1, x_2, \ldots, x_T)$, with x_t taking values in the single label set $\mathcal{L}$, yielding the overall probability

$$p(\mathbf{y}^{(1)}, \mathbf{y}^{(2)} | \mathbf{x}) = p(x_0) \prod_{t=1}^{T} p(x_t | x_{t-1}) p(y_t^{(1)} | x_t) p(y_t^{(2)} | x_t). \tag{1.20}$$

In the case of the asynchronous multistream HMM model, however, each modality has its own dedicated hidden state sequence $\mathbf{x}^{(i)} = (x_1^{(i)}, x_2^{(i)}, \ldots, x_T^{(i)})$, with $x_t^{(i)}$ taking values in the possibly separate label sets $\mathcal{L}^{(i)}$, yielding

$$p(\mathbf{y}^{(1)}, \mathbf{y}^{(2)} | \mathbf{x}^{(1)}, \mathbf{x}^{(2)}) = p(x_0^{(1)}, x_0^{(2)}) \cdot \prod_{t=1}^{T} p(x_t^{(1)}, x_t^{(2)} | x_{t-1}^{(1)}, x_{t-1}^{(2)}) p(y_t^{(1)}, y_t^{(2)} | x_t^{(1)}, x_t^{(2)}). \tag{1.21}$$

The resulting product HMM allows for state asynchrony, since at each time instance one can be at any combination of unimodal states.

The Bayesian network framework allows to represent easily other variants by introducing new possibilities of dependency between the states of the model. For example, Fig. 1.4 represents a *coupled* multistream model with a coupling between the chains associated to each stream. The associated observation sequence probability is

$$p(\mathbf{y}^{(1)}, \mathbf{y}^{(2)} | \mathbf{x}^{(1)}, \mathbf{x}^{(2)}) = p(x_0^{(1)}) p(x_0^{(2)}) \cdot \prod_{t=1}^{T} p(x_t^{(1)} | x_{t-1}^{(1)}, x_{t-1}^{(2)}) p(x_t^{(2)} | x_{t-1}^{(1)}, x_{t-1}^{(2)}) p(y_t^{(1)} | x_t^{(1)}) p(y_t^{(2)} | x_t^{(2)}). \tag{1.22}$$

Figure 1.5 represents yet another popular alternative, the *factorial* model. In this model, at a given instant, all hidden states depend upon all observations, yielding

$$p(\mathbf{y}^{(1)}, \mathbf{y}^{(2)} | \mathbf{x}^{(1)}, \mathbf{x}^{(2)}) = p(x_0^{(1)}) p(x_0^{(2)}) \cdot \prod_{t=1}^{T} p(x_t^{(1)} | x_{t-1}^{(1)}) p(x_t^{(2)} | x_{t-1}^{(2)}) p(y_t^{(1)} | x_t^{(1)}, x_t^{(2)}) p(y_t^{(2)} | x_t^{(1)}, x_t^{(2)}). \tag{1.23}$$

The relative merits of both multistream HMM variants, as well as the coupled and factorial HMM models, are examined by [362] in the context of audiovisual speech recognition.

Segment Models

In all the models presented so far, both Markov models and Bayesian networks associate a hidden variable to each observation. As a consequence, modeling a

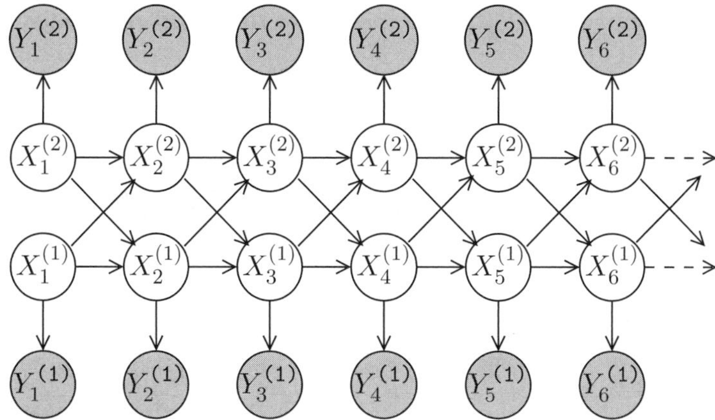

Fig. 1.4. Graphic representation of the coupled Markov model for two streams. States in grey correspond to observed states (the corresponding observations are not represented). (Credits: G. Gravier).

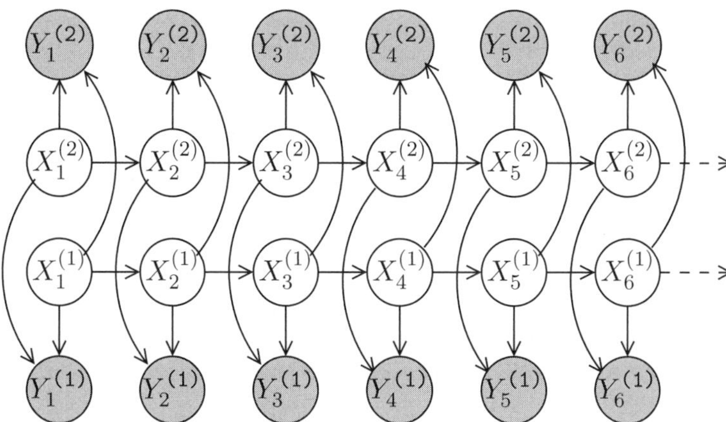

Fig. 1.5. Graphic representation of the factorial Markov model (Credits: G. Gravier).

process that should stay for some time in a given state implies an exponential distribution for this duration. This is not always realistic.

Segment models [136, 379] are a variant of Markov models in which every state can be associated to several observations. Their number is modeled by an explicit duration model, which can be parametric or not. The use of such a model is for example, explained in the book's Chapter 3.

1.6 Integrated Multimedia Content Analysis (Beyond Descriptors)

Although descriptor computation has attracted most of the attention of the video processing community, other aspects have also to be taken into account in order to derive complete systems. Several of these aspects are presented in this section, including metadata and the normalization problem, indexing techniques, and performance evaluation.

1.6.1 Metadata and Norms

The increasing number of digital photo and video collections raised the problem of describing them in a uniform way to allow an easier querying of these collections. One difficulty comes from the number of different communities that are concerned and have different habits and standards to describe their documents: documentalists used to manage libraries, the video community that developed the MPEG standards and wanted to enlarge their scope to include metadata through the MPEG-7 standard, the Web community which was confronted to the increasing number of images and videos and is working on the semantic web standards like RDF and OWL, some users like the American government defined their own system (the Dublin Core [125]). All these communities have their own standardization bodies like ITU for the telecommunication domain, ISO, IEC, the W3C, and this leads to a certain cacophony.

Another problem comes from the nature of the digital documents to be annotated. While books are material objects that do not change once published, even if a "book" may have several versions with differences between them, digital documents usually do not exist in a directly readable form but in compressed formats. They can be read through several software packages that provide different results which depend upon many factors like the screen used and the network bandwidth. Furthermore many versions of an original document can exist with various formats and resolutions. As a consequence, the concept of document has become quite fuzzy.

As far as digital videos are concerned, *metadata* can be separated into several categories. Some metadata describe the container of the document (e.g., name file, URL, compression format), some describe the physical aspects of the document when viewed (e.g., resolution, grey levels or color), others describe the content at various level: at low level with color histograms, at medium level with regions and spatial relations, at high level with faces / speakers and events. Another class of metadata is devoted to describing external elements: author, actors, how created, when broadcasted. Finally, some metadata describe the content from a human point of view, i.e., the story or the event. Such an annotation is not automatic because it requires some understanding of the document which is still impossible to achieve automatically with the current techniques.

The metadata normalization effort has led to different kinds of *norms*. First, some very general ones like the Dublin Core [125] which can be used for any digital document in fact. Although there are many variants, they all share a common basis and simplicity. Second, some attempts have been made to build a complete norm and led to MPEG-7 [319]. Such a norm suffers from several drawbacks: too general on the one hand, but not extensible on the other hand, not modular, based on a language that is not completely object-oriented and thus does not support inheritance although these properties were parts of the requirements [346]. MPEG-7 is a source of inspiration for many usages, but will probably not be used as such in practice.

Another norm very similar to MPEG-7 is nevertheless successful. TV-Anytime was developed at the same time but for a more focussed objective (the description of programs in TV streams) and, although based on the same concepts, was adopted and is used by many companies.

It is now accepted that conceiving a universal metadata norm is impossible and most standards plan to integrate and synchronize metadata with documents, but without specifying how these metadata should be written. This is, for example, the case of the MPEG-21 norm [345] or MXF [566].

1.6.2 Indexing Algorithms

Because in most libraries documents are described by words (authors, titles) and these words are sorted by alphabetic order, most persons fail to see the difference between a descriptor and an index which is a way to organize the metadata in order to retrieve easily the documents. As a matter of fact, the descriptors are used as indexes, and the alphabetic order is not seen as an external way to arrange them.

With images or sounds, the situation is different. Many descriptors are high dimensional numeric vectors subject to noise. Many of them cannot be compared directly, but through a distance or dissimilarity function and small differences may be considered as not significant. On the other hand, sorting such vectors in lexicographic order does not help to find the most similar vectors, whatever distance and search algorithm (ε-range or k-nearest neighbors searches) are used. Traditional database indexes of the B-tree family also fail to handle correctly such vectors for which all dimensions should be taken into account [26] at the same time.

A basic algorithm to solve this problem is the sequential and exhaustive search where all vectors are compared to the query vector. Such a simple algorithm has the major advantage to be absolutely linear in complexity. Many attempts have been made to improve this algorithm. A simple idea is to group the vectors in cells, and to be able to select the cells that should be read based on geometric properties.

Based on this idea, two main categories of algorithms have been proposed. Based on the seminal R-tree [192], some techniques called R+-tree [471], R*-tree [48], X-tree [56], SS-tree [564] and SR-tree [48] try to build the cells with respect to the data distribution. All these cells are organized in a tree structure. On the other hand, other algorithms based on the KD-tree [55], like the K-D-B-Tree [438], the LSD-Tree or the LSD^h-Tree [206], build the cells by cutting the vector space in hyperrectangular regions. These regions are also organized in a tree. All these techniques appear to have a time complexity that grows exponentially with the size of the vector space, and none can be used in practice as soon as the space has more than 10 or 15 dimensions. This is one of the effects of the *dimensionality curse.*

New techniques are appearing that solve this problem. First, they implement an approximate search: Although finding close vectors to a query vector is not so long and difficult, proving that they are the nearest is time consuming. It was thus proposed to avoid this second stage. The tree structures have been abandoned in favor of linear structures (projection on random lines or on space filling curve, hash tables). Finally, distance computations can be replaced by rank aggregation techniques, following ideas developed in the OMEDRANK algorithm [154]. Grouping all these ideas into a single algorithm led to the PvS algorithm [289] which has a complexity close to constant in time and can be used in practice with billions of descriptors.

1.6.3 Performance Evaluation

Performance evaluation is a twofold concept. Firstly, it consists in assessing the quantitative and objective properties of a system, in a way that allows comparison with competing systems. Secondly, its goal is to verify to which extent a system fulfills the users' needs. These two kinds of evaluation give rise to very different techniques and methods.

Quantitative evaluation is now organized along a well established and recognized protocol through competitive campaigns. A set of experts firstly establish a test corpus and a learning corpus. For the first one, the experts establish a reference, i.e., they manually provide what is considered as a perfect result to which the systems will be compared. The second one is provided to the participants in order to develop, tune and test their systems. Secondly, a metric is chosen in order to compare the reference to the results that will be provided by each system. Finally, each participant runs their system on the test corpus and the results are compared to the reference using the chosen metrics. A workshop is often organized where all results are published and discussed. Many such campaigns are annual such that participants can improve their system and that new tasks can be addressed.

For example, the National Institute for Standards and Technology in the US organizes lots of such campaigns on various topics like information retrieval (TREC campaigns), machine translation, speech recognition, language recognition, speaker recognition, and video analysis.

This existing protocol nevertheless does not suppress the difficulties. A large community has to agree on one common task to be solved when lots of systems can solve slightly different problems. A metric should be agreed on.

Gathering the data and establishing the reference can be extremely difficult and expensive, because most multimedia data are copyrighted and because the manual annotation process for the reference is an extremely long and boring process (imagine you have to annotate every pixel of a long video!)

User evaluation is a completely different problem. Since it should involve users in real conditions, it can be achieved only on complete systems with interfaces and thus requires more development most of the time. Furthermore, the actions and reactions should be recorded and analyzed without perturbing its use of the system. Finally, questionnaires and spoken debriefings can complete the analysis.

Here also, the difficulties are numerous. Most computer scientists are not trained to manage such evaluations. Establishing any result often takes a lot of time and needs to involve many users to reduce any bias due the order of the data presented to each of the users and to the order of the tasks proposed to the user. Eventually, quantitative results can be obtained on only few simple questions, although the oral debriefing can bring more qualitative pieces of information.

1.7 Application Areas

Next we describe some indicative application areas in which multimodal integration techniques have proven particularly beneficial.

1.7.1 Audio-Visual Automatic Speech Recognition

Commercial *Automatic Speech Recognition* (ASR) systems are monomodal, i.e., only use features extracted from the audio signal to perform recognition. Although audio-only speech recognition is a mature technology [421], current monomodal ASR systems can work reliably only under rather constrained conditions, where restrictive assumptions regarding the amount of noise, the size of vocabulary, and the speaker's accents can be made. These shortcomings have seriously undermined the role of ASR as a pervasive *Human-Computer Interaction* (HCI) technology [382] and have delayed the adoption of speech recognition systems in new and demanding domains.

The important complementary role that visual information plays in human speech perception, as elucidated by the McGurk effect discussed in Section 1.2.3, has provided strong motivation for the speech recognition community to do research in exploiting visual information for speech recognition, thus enhancing ASR systems with speechreading capabilities [510, 413]. The key role of the visual modality is apparent in situations where the audio signal is either unavailable or severely degraded, as is the case of very noisy environments, where seeing the speaker's face is indispensable in recognizing what has been spoken. Research in this relatively new area has shown that multimodal ASR systems can perform better than their audio-only or visual-only counterparts. The first such results where reported back in the early 80's by Petajan [398]. The potential of significant performance improvement of audiovisual ASR systems, combined with the fact that image capturing devices are getting cheaper, has increased the commercial interest in them.

The design of robust audiovisual ASR systems, which perform better than their audio-only analogues in all scenarios, poses new research challenges, most importantly:

- *Selection and robust extraction of visual speech features.* From the extremely high data rate of the raw video stream, one has to choose a small number of salient features which have good discriminatory power for speech recognition and can be extracted automatically, robustly and with low computational cost.
- *Optimal fusion of the audio and visual features.* Inference should be based on the heterogeneous pool of audio and visual features in a way that ensures that the combined audiovisual system outperforms its audio-only counterpart in practically all scenarios. This is definitely non-trivial, given that the audio and visual streams are only loosely synchronized, and the relative quality of audio and visual features can vary dramatically during a typical session.

These issues are discussed in detail in [413] and also in the book's Chapter 4.

1.7.2 Sports Video Analysis, Indexing and Retrieval

Sport videos, as well as news reports, have motivated lots of research work due to their large number of viewers and possible applications [274]. The main challenge is to structure such videos in order to retrieve their structure or the main events they contain in order to navigate more easily, to index them or to derive new services from these videos.

Two categories of sport were especially studied: score oriented sports like tennis or volley-ball, which are organized depending on the score, and time oriented sports like soccer or rugby which are mainly organized in time periods with a variable number of events in each period. For the former case, the main goal is to recover the structure of the game and to evaluate the interest of each action [131]. For the latter case, the goal is to detect the interesting events [149].

Another usual problem is to separate the parts of video where the game is going on from all other instants like commercials, views on the public, and breaks. Sport video analysis thus combines some processing tools at various levels. Detecting the playing area is often the first step, but many other indices can be used according to the concerned sport: detecting players, detecting lines or areas on the playing area, detecting text, extracting the ball and tracking it. The sound track can be of great help, especially for event detection: applauds, pitch variation, keywords are usual cues. All these detectors are to be assembled in a global system. Stochastic models like HMMs or Bayesian networks are a typical choice to fuse all the partial results in a global frame which allows recovering the structure of the video [257].

1.7.3 TV Structuring

TV structuring considers long and continuous TV streams of several days, weeks, or even months. In this case, the main goal is to compute an exact program guide, i.e., to segment the stream in smaller units and to characterize them by their start and end times and their title. These units are usually categorized into programs (e.g., weather forecast, news programs, movies) and non-programs (commercials, trailers, self-promotion of the TV channels, and sponsoring) TV structuring have mainly applications in the professional world for people working on TV archives, statistics or monitoring.

Two main methods have been proposed in the literature. A top-down approach [407] uses the regularity of program grids over years, and learns their structure from annotated data. The predicted grid is then compared to the stream to refine the detection of program separation. Such a method requires huge annotated data and was developed for TV archivers.

On the other hand, a bottom-up approach [359] tries to infer the stream structure directly from the stream itself. Most programs share no common information or structure that could be used to detect them. The segmentation thus starts by detecting the non-programs that have the common property to be heavily repeated in the stream. This can be achieved using a reference database or by directly comparing the stream with itself. Once the repetition are discovered and organized, the programs appear as the remaining segments. Their annotation can be done by comparing the stream with an Electronic Program Guide or the EIT tables associated with digital TV.

1.7.4 Multimedia Indexing of Broadcast News

Multimedia indexing of TV broadcast news programs is a very active application domain for the technologies of multimedia processing. There is significant interest in the potential of exploiting the vast amount of information carried over the TV networks on a daily basis. Exploitation in this context can be interpreted as the ability to efficiently organize, retrieve and reuse certain parts of the broadcasted information. This still poses various technological and scientific challenges and certainly effective multimodal integration of the involved audio, speech, text and video streams is one of the most important [87, 500, 375].

To classify broadcast news videos into various categories, in [87] they fuse low-level visual features such as color-histogram with audio class labels and high-level visual properties such as the number of faces appearing in the image. Classification is achieved via decision trees and the incorporation of multiple modalities is shown to play a key role in the achieved performance improvement. A similar conclusion is drawn from the evaluation results for the multimedia indexing system presented in [375]. Initial story boundaries are localized using audio, visual and speech information and these are then fused in a weighted voting scheme to provide the final news story segmentation. A more elaborate fusion scheme, which unfolds at the semantic level, is proposed in [500]. Essentially, the concepts conveyed by the involved modalities, video and speech, are constrained to have certain relations between them. The 'Semantic Pathfinder', as the corresponding system is termed, exhibits quite promising properties in broadcast news indexing experiments.

1.7.5 Biometrics, Person Recognition

Automatic person recognition or identification processes have nowadays become indispensable in various transactions which involve human-machine interaction. Commonly, as for example at bank ATMs (Automated Teller Machines) or in transactions performed online, identification processes require issuing a certain token such as a card or just its number and then a password or a PIN (Personal Identification Number). To achieve increased security and naturalness, the utilization of physiological and behavioral characteristics such as the person's fingerprints, iris, voice, face or signature for identification, i.e., biometric recognition, is considered to be a much more promising alternative. However, fingerprint, iris and signature recognition, though quite reliable, involves high-cost sensors in many cases and is regarded as obtrusive. On the other hand, audio-only (voice) recognizers are cheap and quite user-friendly but vulnerable to microphone and acoustic environment changes. Similarly, visual-only (face) recognizers can be quite sensitive to lighting conditions and appearance changes. Integrated exploitation of two or more biometric modalities, appears to give the solution that satisfies requirements in each case [445, 22, 444, 499, 233, 356]. Audiovisual person recognizers for example significantly outperform the single-audio or visual recognizers in terms of reliability while at the same time feature low cost and non-obtrusiveness [22].

1.7.6 Image Retrieval and Photo-Libraries

The management and use of photo libraries has motivated a very large literature that is impossible to fully reference here. Several technologies have to be assembled in order to build a complete system. The choice of the components of the system depends upon the context of use of the system: Is the photo collection to be managed homogeneous or heterogeneous? Is the user a specialist or not? How the queries will be formulated?

Images cannot be compared or matched to the query directly in most applications. They have to be described or annotated first and comparison or matching will be performed on that description or annotation. This can be done using low level descriptors based on the image signal itself (color, texture or shape descriptors) [74] or using only part of this signal (interest point, region descriptors) [308], using higher level processing tools (face detection, object recognition) [178], or keywords and text (coming from the image itself, associated to the image on a same web page or given by a human annotator). In association with these descriptors, a function must be defined in order to compare the image description with the query.

Another important question is the management of very large collections. When the descriptors are numeric, they are often represented as high dimensional vectors. Searching such vectors is a complex problem that is not solved by the use of database management systems [26].

Another key aspect is the user interface: this interface should allow the user to formulate its query and to see the results provided by the system. The user usually queries the system by presenting an image to the system (query by example) or by using words. Of course, the image descriptors used should be adapted to the queries; the matching between words and numeric descriptors remains a difficult challenge. Finally, the way the results are usually presented is a list of ordered images, although many works have also tried to develop other presentations.

1.7.7 Automated Meeting Analysis

Automated meeting analysis has lately come into the focus of interest in many diverse research fields, such as speech and speaker recognition, natural language processing and computer vision. The goal is to achieve systematic meeting indexing and structuring that would facilitate meeting information retrieval and browsing and would significantly favor remote meetings. In this direction, though speech is the predominant information carrying modality in this context, it has become clear that a meeting is essentially a sequence of multimodal human-human interaction processes and should be treated as such. Exploitation of video can help speaker and role identification in the meeting while the text of notes kept during the meeting may allow easier topic recognition and meeting segmentation. Proper consolidation of these modalities, i.e., video and text, in the analysis framework can lead to significant gains [333, 134, 73].

1.8 Conclusions and Future Directions

In this chapter we have surveyed some key ideas and results from research on cross-modal integration in multimedia analysis. We sampled problems from three major areas of research in multimedia: multimodal feature extraction, stochastic models for integrating dynamic multimodal data, and applications that benefit from cross-modal integration. In addition, we emphasized fusion of modalities or cues in various ways: explaining its weak- and strong-coupling versions with a Bayesian formulation, classifying it at various levels of integration in conjunction with the stochastic classification models, and seeing it at work in various applications. As a useful supplement, we also reviewed a few ideas and results from human perception and its Bayesian formulation.

Some interesting future directions include the following:

Optimal Fusion: What is the best way to fuse multiple cues or modalities for various tasks and noise environments? Which should be the optimality criteria?

Fusing numeric and symbolic information: Multimodal approaches are now common for audio and video, for still images and text (or at least keywords). Mixing text or transcribed speech with video and audio is still a challenge, since it brings together numeric information coming from sound or images with symbolic information.

Investigate how the cross-modal integration algorithms *scale* and perform on large multimedia databases.

Cross-modal integration for performance improving in two *grand challenges:* (i) Natural access and high-level interaction with multimedia databases, and (ii) Detecting, recognizing and interpreting objects, events, and human behavior in multimedia videos by processing combined audio-video-text data.

Anthropocentric system: The interaction with the system and taking the human user into account are still open issues. And they are very important, since in most multimedia applications it is humans who will ultimately evaluate and use the system. Many aspects of human-computer interfaces are reviewed in this book's Chapter 2.

Looking back at this chapter's journey, we attempted to take a few glimpses at a huge and fascinating field, that of multimedia understanding through cross-modal integration. We are still feeling that it is a very complex dynamic area. The understanding of each of the major sensor modalities, i.e., speech or vision, has not been "conquered" yet by science and technology, neither perceptually nor computationally. Imagine now their fusion! Nevertheless we must be brave and dare to keep researching this remarkable mapping from the combined audiovisual world to our multimodal percepts and inversely.

2

Human-Computer Interfaces to Multimedia Content: a Review

Alexandros Potamianos and Manolis Perakakis

Technical University of Crete

In the past few decades, there has been an explosive growth of multimedia content available both online and offline, in the personal collections of users. The majority of online content [522] is authored by individuals that are part-time content creators and is very diverse in style, often lacking semantic annotation and user quality ratings, e.g., blogs, home videos, personal images. In addition, multimedia content created by professionals often also lacks semantic and rating information, e.g., podcasts, mp3 music files, TV video clips. As a result, the user is faced with a tremendous amount of raw multimedia data that lacks annotation and cannot be possibly consumed within a lifetime, if accessed sequentially. It is not surprising that *designing interfaces for creating, searching, retrieving* and -most importantly- *consuming multimedia content* is quickly emerging as a top priority in both research and commercial product development.

Interface design is interdisciplinary by nature and requires both scientific expertise and creativity. Modality experts, multimedia experts, device experts, human factors experts, software designers, cognitive psychologists and graphic artists have to collaborate to create a successful interface. Creative thinking is needed in order to select the appropriate design among the numerous interface implementations possible for a specific task. An important interface design choice is the selection and mixing of input and output *modalities*, i.e., channels of communication, between the user and the system. In addition to traditional human-computer interaction (HCI) modalities, such as keyboard and mouse for input, and text and graphics for output, numerous "novel" modalities are available to today's interface designer, e.g., *speech*, *gestures*, *haptics*. New devices are becoming increasingly mainstream that can support *multi-touch* input, *augmented reality* displays, *force feedback* gloves, *virtual keyboards* and *eye-tracking*. The improved device capabilities and available interaction modalities have increased the freedom of choice for the designer, but also the complexity and challenges of interface design.

The purpose of this chapter is to familiarize the reader with fundamental concepts, review the state-of-the-art in multimedia interfaces and identify the

P. Maragos et al. (eds.), *Multimodal Processing and Interaction*,
DOI: 10.1007/978-0-387-76316-3_2,

most promising open research problems. The list of subjects covered is by no means exhaustive and is meant as an introduction to the more advanced topics covered in contributed research chapters. First, a short overview of human computer interaction is given, followed by a review of the various interaction modalities. Input and output modalities covered include graphical user interfaces (GUI), speech, gestures, eye-tracking, augmented reality, and haptics. Most interfaces are *multimodal*, i.e., employ more than one input or output interaction modalities. Multimodal interfaces pose interesting challenges related to the combination or *fusion* of input modalities, and the combination or *fission* of output media streams and are reviewed in Section 2.3. As interfaces to multimedia are becoming increasingly complex, personalization or adaptation of the interface to the user's needs and preferences is becoming a necessity. *Adaptive interfaces* use information from user profiles, user ratings or past user interaction patterns to update their behavior and to better serve the user or group of users, as discussed in Section 2.4. *Mobile interfaces* are becoming increasingly important as multimedia data is more and more stored and consumed from mobile devices. Mobile interfaces have to cope with small device size, limited processing power, and communication bandwidth, but also can take advantage of sensor input to improve *context awareness*, e.g., global position information, accelerometers, ambient light sensors. These issues are reviewed in Section 2.5. Example applications of interfaces to multimedia content are presented in Section 2.6. We conclude with a review of architectures, tools, and standards available for the design of multimedia interfaces.

2.1 Human Computer Interaction Basics

Human Computer Interaction (HCI) is the study of interaction between users and computer systems. HCI is a multi-disciplinary subject, combining topics such as: *psychology and cognitive science* that studies user's perceptual, cognitive, and problem solving skills, *ergonomics* (i.e., the study of the physical capabilities of the user), *design*, as well as *computer science, and engineering*. HCI is concerned among others with theories of interaction, development of new interfaces and interaction techniques, e.g. for mobile computing, methodologies for designing interfaces, implementation of software toolkits, design of hardware devices, and techniques for evaluating and comparing interfaces.

As the number, diversity, and complexity of interactive applications increases users need to continuously learn, adapt, and cope with new interfaces. As stated in [3]: "a long term goal of HCI is to design systems that minimize the barrier between the human's cognitive model of what they want to accomplish and the computer's understanding of the user's task." The call for interfaces that will be easier to learn and use is popularized by pioneers such as Dertouzos [132], and Shneiderman [484].

2.1.1 Theories of Interaction

The study of human beings in the context of HCI draws mainly from *cognitive psychology* that studies the capabilities and limitations of humans, how they perceive the world around them, how they store or process information and solve problems. Input-output channels (vision, hearing, touch, movement), human memory (sensory, short-term/working, and long-term memory), and processing capabilities (reasoning, problem solving, skill acquisition) should all be considered when designing computer systems with *usability* in mind. For more details refer to [139, 565, 460, 483].

Usability concerns the design of a system with the user's psychology and physiology in mind. The end-result should be a system that is easy to learn, efficient to use and promotes user satisfaction (refer also to Section 2.1.2). Based on cognitive psychology, ergonomics, and empirical results, *descriptive* or *predictive* models of human computer interaction have been devised to help designers analyze interaction and build efficient interfaces.

A fundamental empirical result concerns the limited capacity of working memory. Human memory consists of sensory buffers, short-term or working memory, and long-term memory. Short-term memory can be accessed rapidly but it also has a limited capacity. Miller in his classic article "The Magical Number Seven Plus or Minus Two" [340] found that human working memory can hold 7 ± 2 chunks of information. This finding has direct implications in the design of interactive systems; a complex interface may overload the short-term memory, resulting in poor and inefficient user interaction.

Another well-known result concerns information processing in choice reaction tasks. Reaction time increases logarithmically as the number of alternatives increases (Hick-Hyman law), while movement time to a target (ignoring initial reaction time) increases logarithmically with distance to target and inverse logarithmically with target's width (Fitts' law). These rules apply, for example, to the design of menu hierarchies. Another result concerning multimodal interaction is the "visual dominance" effect [506, 504], which states that "if percepts of varying modalities are of the same relative intensity, then information gathered via vision tends to have greater influence on perception, as compared to other modalities". The visual dominance effect applies, for example, to multimodal interface design and audiovisual speech recognition.

An early example of a descriptive/predictive model is the *Human Model Processor* [84], which is a simplified model of human processing when interacting with computer systems. The model comprises of three subsystems, namely: the *perceptual system* handling sensory stimulus from the outside world, the *motor system* that controls actions and the *cognitive system* that provides the necessary processing to connect the two [139]. "It is a synthesis of the literature of cognitive psychology of that time and sketches the framework around which a cognitive architecture could be implemented" according to [82]. It is also the basis of contemporary cognitive architectures that are used in HCI, such as EPIC (Executive Process Interactive Control), and ACT-R/PM

(Adaptive Control of Thought-Rational/Perceptual Motor) [82]. The *Goals, Operators, Methods and Selection* (GOMS) rules model analyzes routine human computer interactions and is used to make quantitative predictions about execution time for a particular task. The interested reader may refer to [84] for more details.

2.1.2 User Interface Design

The design of interactive systems follows the iterative process of the software life cycle, e.g., an iterative waterfall model, consisting of stages such as requirements specification, architectural design, implementation, and testing. For interactive systems, however, requirements specification is much harder to accurately define in advance. In order to achieve a highly usable system, designers continuously enhance the interface based on the feedback that evaluators provide on early prototypes. Various studies have shown that for interactive systems a large part of the development resources (up to 50% of total) are spent on the user interface. The design of interactive systems is not only highly demanding in terms of development efforts; it should also support usability to a high level in order to be successful.

When designing interactive systems, the notion of *usability* is central to the design process. ISO 9241 standard (Ergonomics of Human System Interaction) defines *usability* in terms of three attributes: the "*effectiveness*, *efficiency* and *satisfaction* with which users achieve specified goals using the system". According to this definition, effectiveness is the accuracy and completeness in achieving the user specified goals using the system. Efficiency relates to the resources expended in relation to the accuracy and completeness of goals achieved. Satisfaction is a measure of the user's comfort and acceptability towards the system. It is common to use objective metrics such as "task completion" and "time to completion" to measure the effectiveness and efficiency of a system, respectively, while satisfaction is measured using subjective metrics, e.g., evaluation questionnaires.

To make the development of interactive systems easier and ensure high levels of usability, a designer should create the interface with usability principles in mind. Since usability principles are essential but rather abstract properties, designers usually try to follow specific design rules such as user interface (UI) guidelines and standards. Applying design methodologies that promote usability such as "usability engineering" [139], using appropriate software toolkits and applying efficient designs such as the Model-View-Controller (MVC) architectural principle, are essential to successful design of interactive systems. The rest of this section focuses on usability principles, design rules, and the MVC paradigm.

Usability Principles

In [139], the authors list attributes that support usability under three different categories:

- Learnability: the ease with which new users can begin effective interaction and achieve best performance.
- Flexibility: the multiplicity of ways the user and the system exchange information.
- Robustness: the level of support provided to the user in the process of achieving his goals.

Learnability encompasses attributes such as *predictability*, i.e., determining the effect of future actions based on past interaction history, *familiarity*, i.e., the extend to which a user's knowledge or experience with other interactive systems can be applied when interacting with a new system, and *consistency*. Consistency, i.e., the likeness in behavior arising from similar situations, is the most important principle in user interface design, because users rely on interface consistency to carry out specific tasks. For example [175], to support internal consistency, the same conventions and rules for all aspects of an interface screen (GUI or web pages) should be followed, such as the organization, presentation, usage and location of screen components.

Related to flexibility is *customizability*, which refers to modifiability of the interface by the user (adaptable interfaces) or the system itself (adaptive interfaces); refer to Section 2.4 for more information on adaptive interfaces. Related to robustness are *observability* and *transparency* that allow the user to monitor the internal state of the system, and *recoverability* that allows the user to easily recover from errors, for example through "redo" and "undo" actions.

Design Rules: Guidelines and Standards

Design rules restrict the space of design options and prevent the designer from pursuing options that would likely result in less usable systems [139]. Design rules are often supported by psychological, cognitive or ergonomic theory, areas that the designer (typically a software engineer) might not be familiar with. Following design rules such as guidelines, style guides (e.g., look and feel for GUIs) and standards throughout the design process, is essential for the usability of the interactive system. An extensive list of guidelines for a broad range of topics such as data entry, screen design, graphics/icon design and proper use of GUI components exist in literature, e.g., [175]. An example of standards is ISO 9241, a multi-part standard covering many aspects of interaction such as menu and form-filling dialogues.

The MVC Design Paradigm

A computer system used to access multimedia information, or any HCI system for that matter, consists of three major parts: (i) the *model* or *application semantics*, (ii) the *view* or *interface implementation* and (iii) the *control* or *application logic*. The term model-view-controller has been extensively used in the HCI literature. The separation of these three key components both architecturally and in the system design process is known as the MVC paradigm [177]. The MVC paradigm goes beyond the traditional GUI community and extends also to state-of-the-art multimodal systems, see for example the latest W3C recommendations in [11]. Consider for example a spoken dialogue system: the term "model" could refer to the modules that perform speech understanding, i.e., turning speech into concepts, the term "control" could refer to the application manager that determines the next state of the interaction and the term "view" could refer to the implementation of the communication goals via the spoken dialogue interface.

2.1.3 Evaluation

An important step during the development of an interactive system is the evaluation of the interface design and implementation [139]. Although in practice evaluation takes place as the last step of the development process, ideally it should be integrated as soon as possible in order to provide feedback during the design life cycle, i.e., evaluation should be integrated in the *iterative design process*. Evaluation helps to ensure that the system functionality fulfills the intended requirements of the various tasks supported. It also allows the system designer to measure the effectiveness of the system in supporting the tasks, by measuring user performance. Finally, evaluation helps ensure that certain usability principles and guidelines have been followed, while common usability problems have been avoided, resulting in high levels of user satisfaction.

A variety of evaluation methods exist to test the design and the implementation of an interactive system. Methods that focus on the design can be used before implementation takes place to identify and eliminate possible interface related problems early in the design cycle. In *heuristic evaluation* [366, 368], usability criteria called *heuristics*, which are based on usability principles and guidelines, are used to identify usability problems, debug and effectively alter the design.

Actual testing of the interfaces with users (user-centered evaluation) includes a number of methods such as *experimental evaluation* and *query methods*, which use objective performance metrics and user satisfaction *subjective metrics* , respectively. With experimental evaluation, performance of different design options can be computed in order to decide the best alternative, e.g., "is interface A better than interface B"? Objective metrics such as speed, number of errors, task completion, are computed for the various system configurations and are statistically analyzed to determine the best system, for examples refer to [327, 351]. Alternatively, query methods can be used to elicit direct user feedback using either interviews or questionnaires. Query methods are simpler to carry out and analyze, and can provide useful information if well designed. Note, however, that the elicited information is subjective and may be less accurate than for objective evaluation methods.

We conclude with the notion of *participatory design* where users are not only involved in the evaluation phase of the system, but are also included as active participants during the design phase.

2.2 Interaction Modalities

Although GUIs have been the dominant user interface technology for the past two decades, today's computing platforms (ranging from mobile devices to large wall displays) call for new, more natural and efficient ways of interaction. Recently, there has been much interest in investigating alternative input/output interaction modalities that go beyond the traditional keyboard and mouse input, and text and graphics output. Such modalities may include speech, eye-tracking and haptics. In addition, various input/output devices [481, 83], such as glove mounted devices [586] and sensors ranging from accelerometers to GPS (global positioning system), open the door to new interfaces and applications.

In this section, various interaction modalities are reviewed such as speech, gestures, eye-gaze, augmented reality and haptics. First, graphical user interfaces are briefly reviewed. Speech is considered the most natural form of communication and although there are several limitations in speech recognition technology much progress in both system architectures and applications have been achieved in recent years. Visual based modalities, such as gestures and eye-gaze, are also quickly emerging as important complementary input modalities, especially given the recent progress in gesture recognition and eye-tracking technologies. Augmented reality environments offer visualization capabilities that are very rich and merge the physical with the virtual world. The review concludes with haptic interfaces that incorporate touch and/or force-feedback.

2.2.1 Graphical User Interfaces

Following the command-line and text-based interfaces, graphical user interfaces emerged and eventually dominated the past two decades. The Xerox Alto and Star (1981) [39] was one of the first personal workstations having significant local processing power and memory, networking capabilities, a high resolution bit-mapped display, a keyboard and a mouse. The user interface incorporated windows, menus, scrollbars, mouse control, and selection mechanisms (*WIMP* interface - windows, icons, menus and pointers) and views of abstract structures all presented in a consistent manner. These systems introduced several innovative concepts found in todays personal computers: the *desktop metaphor*, *direct manipulation* and WYSIWYG (what you see is what you get), where a user sees and manipulates on screen a representation of a document that looks identical to the eventual printed one. By offering a rich set of graphical elements (widgets) upon which users perform actions (direct manipulation), GUIs are easier to learn and operate compared to their command-line counterparts.

GUIs are the dominant interface technology in part due to the high bandwidth they provide on the output side. In general, information can be better organized and presented to the user using graphical output compared to other modalities. Thus GUIs today are used not only in desktop computers but also in a variety of other platforms such as intelligent information kiosks, portable and mobile devices and automated teller machines (ATMs). On the input side, GUIs use for selection, pointer devices such as mouse on desktop computers or pen devices on portable systems with touch-screens. Some touch-screens support touch or *multi-touch sensing*, allowing input through one or more fingers which is considered more natural than using a pen. A recent example is the Apple iPhone[1] that supports various gestures, e.g., the user can zoom in/out by spreading the two fingers closer together or farther apart. For text input, desktop computers use keyboard, while portable and mobile devices use methods such as miniaturized physical keyboards, keypads, virtual keyboards, or various handwriting recognition methods such as graffiti input.

Some recent advances in GUI interfaces include 3D interfaces and Zooming User Interfaces (ZUI). With the advent of powerful graphic processing power, 3D desktop environments have emerged as a replacement to their 2D counterparts. Other notable efforts include the Croquet project[2], a free software platform and a network operating system for developing and delivering deeply collaborative multi-user on-line applications. ZUIs extend GUIs by laying out information elements on a infinite virtual surface instead of windows. The user can pan across the surface and zoom into areas of interest. Examples of ZUI applications are mapping applications such as Google earth/maps and desktop-like environments such as the Sugar ZUI found in One Laptop Per Child initiative[3]. ZUIs are especially promising for mobile applications where screen real estate is limited.

2.2.2 Speech Modality

Speech is the most natural form of communication among humans, but it has several limitations when used in HCI. Although speech recognition technology has been studied actively during the past decades and highly sophisticated recognizers have been constructed, machines are far from matching human speech recognition performance, especially in adverse recording conditions. A second hurdle is the complexity of spontaneous human speech communication because it may contain a lot of ungrammatical elements such as hesitations, false starts and repairs. Finally, another issue is that people are used to talking differently to computers than to other people and often alter their speaking styles when talking to machines.

---

[1] http://www.apple.com/iphone/

[2] http://en.wikipedia.org/wiki/Croquet_project/

[3] http://wiki.laptop.org/go/HIG/

Spoken Dialogue Component Technology

Spoken Dialogue Systems (SDS) form the majority of speech applications. The main components of an SDS are: speech recognition, natural language understanding, dialogue manager, response generation and speech synthesis. Next a brief review of these technologies is presented. For more details refer to [98, 421, 217, 579, 541, 335].

Automatic speech recognition (ASR), is the process of transforming a spoken utterance into words. The audio signal is digitized and is transformed into a series of acoustic vectors $Y = y_1, y_2, \ldots, y_t$ (*feature extraction*) at a fixed rate [579]. To determine the most probable word sequence $\widehat{W}$ given the observed signal Y the following Bayesian formulation is used:

$$\widehat{W} = \arg\max_{w} P(W|Y) = \arg\max_{w} P(W)P(Y|W) \tag{2.1}$$

where $P(W)$ is the a priori probability of observing W, determined by the *language model*, and $P(Y|W)$ is the probability of observing the sequence Y given a word sequence W, determined by the *acoustic model*. For acoustic modeling, each phone (or sequence of phones) is usually modeled by a *Hidden Markov Model* (HMM). An HMM can be though as a random generator of acoustic vectors which consists of a sequence of states connected by probabilistic transitions. The language model provides a mechanism of estimating the probability of a word w_k in a utterance given the preceding words $w_1 \ldots w_{k-1}$. This is usually achieved by using N-grams, which assume that w_k depends only on the preceding N-1 words. Due to data sparseness problem, models with N equal to two (bigrams) or three (trigrams) are used in practice.

The output of the speech recognizer is analyzed by the Natural Language Understanding (NLU) component to derive meaning representations that will be used by the Dialogue Manager (DM). This involves syntactic and semantic analysis to elicit attribute-value pairs in a symbolic representation. A grammar that consists of hand crafted rules is sometimes used to produce a complete parsing of grammatically correct sentences. Techniques such as *robust semantic parsing* are often used instead, where only the essential items of meaning are extracted from the text.

The dialogue manager is responsible for the communication flow with the user. At each turn, the DM determines if sufficient information has been elicited in order to complete the user's request, e.g., information seeking. The DM is often implemented as a finite state machine (FSM) with conditions residing on the arcs and system actions residing on the nodes of the FSM. Various techniques are used for resolving errors and ambiguity in user input, such as implicit or explicit verification/confirmation.

Response generation deals with the construction of the message that will be sent to the user. Although complex natural language generation methods can be used, usually simpler methods such as template filling (insertion of retrieved data into predefined slots in a template) are the norm. The message is then send to the text-to-speech synthesis (TTS) component, which first analyzes the text message (text to phoneme conversion) and then generates the speech signal (phoneme-to-speech conversion).

Speech as an Input/Output Modality

Speech and GUI interfaces has been extensively studied and compared in the literature, e.g., [191, 283]. With GUIs everything the user wants to do at any given time must be presented at the screen, while speech interfaces lack visual information and require users to memorize all meaningful information. In addition, the sequential nature of speech loads the short-term memory and takes up the linguistic channel, which makes speech interfaces unsuitable for some tasks.

As an output channel, speech is too slow because of its sequential nature, while GUIs convey information in parallel thus making them suitable for presenting a large amount of information. Speech output may be more appropriate for grabbing attention and offering an alternative feedback mechanism to the user, rather than conveying a large amount of information [283].

Spoken interaction may be faster when users immediately say what they want to achieve without going through menu hierarchies. Spoken messages may also be more expressive and convey richer information compared to GUI actions, such as the selection of similar objects among a large number of them. However the freedom and efficiency that speech gives to user, makes speech harder for the computer to handle. It is also hard for users to know the limitations of what they can say and how to explore the set of possible tasks they can perform [283].

Finally, users interacting with speech interfaces do not have the same feeling of control usually offered by GUI interfaces. This is because speech input may be *inconsistent* due to recognition errors, i.e., the recognition result may be different for the same sentence spoken twice. Handling speech errors efficiently is a key issue for successful speech applications. Well designed spoken dialogue systems or the use of extra modalities in multimodal systems can alleviate these problems and allow for efficient and natural speech interaction.

How Speech Recognizer Features Affect Speech Applications

The capabilities and features of a speech recognition system can affect the design and interaction of a speech application [532]. Vocabulary size and recognition grammars characterize the interaction possibly better than other properties. For example, it is possible to construct a speech-only e-mail application with a dozen of words, but for building an information retrieval system at least a few hundred word vocabulary is needed. The possibility to change or dynamically construct vocabularies and grammars also affects interaction; e.g., allow the system to be context-sensitive and use user profiles with personalized recognition grammars.

Communication style can vary from speaker-dependent, discrete, read speech to speaker-independent, continuous, spontaneous speech. Speaker-dependent or adaptive models are suitable for some applications, e.g., dictation, while speaker-independent models are the norm. Although with current recognizers there is no need to speak in a discrete manner, it usually helps if words are pronounced clearly and properly. Most SDSs have to deal with various degrees of spontaneity in speech input, which is still a challenge for state-of-the-art speech recognition systems. Finally, capabilities like barge-in that can be used to interrupt the system output can influence the design and allow the system to generate longer and more informative responses.

Usage conditions can vary from clean to hostile environments, and low (public mobile phone usage) to high quality channels (close-talking microphones). Even with state-of-the-art recognizers, performance can dramatically suffer if usage conditions do not match recognizer training ones. This is usually compensated by using different acoustic models for each condition.

Speech Applications

Early speech applications included telephone-based interactive voice response (IVR) systems that used speech output and telephone keys for interaction. Such applications were designed to replace human operators. In the past decade, numerous spoken dialogue systems have been designed and deployed that fully automate simple interactive tasks usually performed over the telephone. Example applications that have dominated the field are information services (timetables, weather forecasting, e-banking), e-mail applications, ticketing and voice portals. Today's systems are fairly sophisticated and include state-of-the art recognizers, natural language understanding and response generation components, but still integration and interface design are the important factors for building successful applications [335, 532]. Recently, systems with more advanced natural language and spoken dialogue capabilities have been deployed for customer service applications, e.g., for telephony, cable TV[4], software retailers. Such systems automate complex interactions with complicated call-flows, but often run into miscommunication or other problems. When the system detects such problems a human operator is used as a bail-out.

Desktop applications such as dictation systems and command and control applications have also been deployed. Dictation systems[5] are popular for special user groups. Command and control applications usually control existing graphical applications, without using (or in conjunction with) mouse/keyboard, which can be very useful for mobile devices such as personal digital assistants (PDAs). Other spoken dialogue applications include automotive applications, e.g., navigational aids, gaming, and human-robot interaction.

[4] http://www.speechcycle.com/

[5] http://www.nuance.com/naturallyspeaking/

2.2.3 Visual Based Modalities

Gestures

Gesture based interfaces augment traditional graphical user interfaces, which are based on direct manipulation, by incorporating 2D and 3D gestures like manual gestures, head and body movements. Although people may occasionally use gestures as the only means of communication, e.g., to indicate disagreement by a head or hand gesture, in most cases gestures occur along with other modalities such as speech, as demonstrated in Bolt's "Put-That-There" prototype [69]. Apart from *deictic gestures*, *iconic gestures* that refer to objects or actions by describing them visually using familiar representations and *symbolic gestures*, e.g., thumbs-up, are also exploited in typical gesture interfaces. Gestures may be used to specify attributes, e.g., location, size, category of actions, or commands, e.g., creation, confirmation, selection.

Devices to capture 2D gestures include touch sensitive displays, digitizing tablets and light pens. Recognition of 2D gestures is either *template-based*, in which case gesture recognizers compare input patterns with prototypical templates to choose the best matched one, or *feature-based* where features extracted from the stream of input coordinates are first processed and then classified to a gesture class. 3D gestures such as hand and head or body movements can be incorporated either in active or passive mode. In *active mode*, dedicated devices are used, such as position trackers and sensing data gloves. In *passive mode*, user input is unobtrusively monitored using one or more cameras and computer vision algorithms are used to segment and classify the image data. In passive mode, no intrusive devices are necessary but recognition is much less accurate compared to the active approach. For a review of gesture-based interfaces refer to [54].

Eye-Tracking

Eye-tracking technology is mainly used as a way of revealing user's intention and attention. Thus it can be used as a replacement for the mouse in various applications such as visual search tasks. Recent technological advancements in the field have resulted in video based eye-tracking systems (apart from head mounted based ones) that unobtrusively monitor the user. These systems use infrared light to illuminate the eyes and an optical sensor such as a CCD (Charge Coupled Device) device to capture a reflection of the user's eyes in order to measure eye motion. Eye movements consist of abrupt fast movements called *saccades* followed by short stops called *fixations*, during which the eye acquires content. During fixations the eye-tracking system can identify what a user is looking at, and for how long. The data acquired (series of fixations and saccades) in the form of a *scanpath* or a gaze plot can then be used to analyze user gaze behavior.

Eye movement can be used in real-time interactive applications as a pointer to replace the mouse, which is especially useful for disabled people. When using eye-tracking to control an interface the problem of accidentally activating objects by looking at them (the "Midas Touch Problem" [230]) has to be addressed. By avoiding the extra muscular movement effort required in mouse usage, eye gaze may yield faster and more "natural" interaction. This has been confirmed in various studies (refer to Chapter 14) in which authors compared eye gaze with mouse performance in a image target identification task.

Eye-tracking has also found application in web usability studies because it allows to analyze user behavior between the clicks. Analysis of gaze data can identify the portions of a web page that attracted user attention. In [367], it was found that users read web pages in an F-shaped pattern; that is users focus on the left side of the body of a web page and fixate less on the right side.

Virtual and Augmented Reality

Head mounted displays (HMD) are devices worn on the head that include one or two miniaturized displays. HMDs are usually used in virtual or augmented reality environments. According to [34], virtual reality is defined as "a computer generated, interactive, three-dimensional environment in which a person is immersed". With the use of HMDs in virtual environments, the real world is replaced with a simulated world by accurately sensing how the user is moving in order to update the rendering on the HMD.

An augmented reality system generates a composite view where computer generated graphics are augmented in real world scene to provide additional information (contextual data). This is done with HMDs that support see-through functionality, by projecting the computer generated graphics through a partially reflective mirror. Various augmented reality applications that enhance the user's perception and performance are described in [539]. Augmented reality applications have been developed for the medical, e.g., superimposing MRI scans for surgeons, entertainment, manufacturing and maintenance/repair (access repair manuals and images of the equipment) sectors among others.

2.2.4 Tactile/Haptic Modalities

As noted in [226], haptics are difficult to synthesize compared to visual or auditory sensations. Unlike vision where the sensory input is gathered by specialized organs (eyes), the sensation of force can occur at any part of the human body and is therefore inseparable from actual physical contact. According to [479], the computer sensing of touch and force is especially important for building a proper feel of realism in virtual reality environments, adding an extra sense to previously visual-only solutions. The key idea is that by exerting force or touch on virtual objects the user will be able to manipulate the virtual environment in a "natural" manner. High-end wired gloves used in virtual reality systems can act as output devices by providing haptic feedback, e.g., the Rutgers force-feedback tactile glove [324] provides the user additional information about grasped objects (semantic association). Other common applications of haptic feedback is found in games (force feedback joysticks), telerobotics and teleoperators (exploration devices controlled from a remote location), and medicine (medical training simulation).

2.3 Multimodal Interfaces

Multimodal systems (or multimodal input/multimedia output systems) employ two or more input modalities and presentation media to interact with the user. Examples of input modalities include keyboard, pointing devices (mouse, pen), speech, eye-gaze, gestures, haptics. Examples of presentation media include text, audio, images, video, animation. Multimodal interfaces pose two fundamental challenges namely: the combination of multiple input modalities, known as *the fusion problem*, and the combination of multiple presentation media, known as *the fission problem*. "Optimal" solutions to the fusion and fission problems can significantly improve performance of multimodal systems over their corresponding unimodal constituents, both in terms of *efficiency* and *user satisfaction*. The improvement in performance of a multimodal interface over the "sum" of its unimodal parts is often referred to as *multimodal synergy*.

The most common multimodal interface is that of the personal computer that combines, since the 80's, keyboard entry with a pointing device (usually mouse). Although the two input modalities can typically be used only sequentially, the fundamental concepts of fusion, fission and synergy are still very relevant. Extensive experimentation (as well as cognitive considerations) have determined the rules and guidelines for the design of graphical user interfaces (GUIs). These guidelines are related to the fusion and fission problems. For example, guidelines about when and how to use "text entry" vs "pull down menus" are related to the keyboard and mouse fusion problem, while recommendations on the combination on text and graphics are related to the fission problem.

Recent bibliography on multimodal interfaces and systems focuses on novel interaction modalities, such as speech, gestures, eye-gaze or haptics. New modalities introduce new opportunities and challenges, e.g., speech interfaces are more natural but are prone to recognition errors. According to Oviatt [382], multimodal interfaces should be a paradigm shift away from conventional WIMP interfaces towards more flexible, efficient and powerfully expressive means of human computer interaction. Investigating new interaction modalities and concurrent multimodal interaction are active research directions in the field. Next the basic concepts of multimodal interaction, fusion, fission and design are presented.

2.3.1 Multimodal Interaction

In [12], multimodal interaction is categorized into: (i) *sequential* when at a specific point in the interaction only one input modality in active, e.g., keyboard and mouse on a typical desktop interface, (ii) *simultaneous* or *concurrent* when "simultaneous" input is received from multiple modalities but can be treated separately by the fusion module, e.g., eye-gaze combined with keyboard input, and (iii) *composite* (or synergistic [369]) when "simultaneous" input from multiple modalities has to be processed as a compound entity by the fusion module, e.g., the synchronized speech and gestural input "Put that [gesture pointing] there [gesture pointing]" from Bolt's famous demo [69].

Sequential multimodality is by far the most common in human-computer interaction. With the advent of "novel" modalities, such as eye-gaze and speech input, it is becoming increasingly common to have simultaneous input from different modalities. Composite multimodal interaction is especially relevant for a range of applications such as map navigation, course plotting etc. Although the basic principles of fusion are the same for all three interaction modes, the fusion module becomes more complex when allowing for simultaneous and (more so for) composite input.

According to [12], multimodal interfaces can alternatively be categorized into *supplementary* or *complementary* depending of whether all input and output tasks can be carried out by every modality or not. Supplementary interface design is the rule, because it results in a consistent user interface and improves usability. However, for modalities with limited interaction scope, e.g., eye-gaze or gestures, or for interaction tasks where one modality is clearly superior (in terms of efficiency) a complementary approach might be taken. Finally, *symmetric multimodality* [554] refers to interface design that has the same modalities available for both input and output.

2.3.2 Fusion Techniques and Data Integration

Multimodal systems require fusion in each of the three layers of the MVC paradigm, namely at the data (semantic fusion), at the view (interface fusion) and at the control level. It is customary in the literature for the term fusion to refer to *data fusion* or *semantic fusion*. However, *interface fusion* or *modality fusion*, i.e., the problem of fusing (or blending) the modalities at the interface level, is an equally important problem for interface design. Fusion at the control level is usually tackled by designing a multimodal application manager that manages all modalities. In fact, if the MVC paradigm is followed the application logic should be modality-independent and little integration is needed. Next we focus on the problems of data fusion and interface fusion.

Data fusion is usually categorized as *early fusion*, or *late fusion* [151]. The most common example of early fusion, also known as *feature-level fusion*, is the combination of the audio and video feature streams in audiovisual speech recognition. As discussed in [382], multimodal systems based on late fusion integrate common meaning representations derived from different modalities into a combined final interpretation. This requires a common meaning representation framework for all available modalities and a well-defined operation for integrating the partial meanings. Late fusion is more common in multimodal systems.

Depending on the multimodal interaction style (sequential, simultaneous or composite), the internal data representation, and the point of integration in the semantic chain, different fusion algorithms can be implemented. For sequential or simultaneous multimodal interaction the semantic information acquired from each modality can be processed more or less independently and thus late integration is the rule. The semantics extracted from each input stream are combined, often using a probabilistic framework, to resolve ambiguous or conflicting input. For composite multimodal interaction, integration typically occurs earlier in the process because input from various modalities has to be processed jointly. One popular approach is to design multimodal semantic grammars. For example, to handle composite speech and pen input a three-tape finite-state machine was proposed in [238].

According to [532, 369] one can consider fusion earlier or later in the semantic chain, i.e., at the *lexical, syntactic* or *semantic* levels. Lexical fusion is used when primitives, e.g., words, are mapped to application events. Syntactic fusion synchronizes different modalities and forms a complete representation. Semantic fusion represents functional aspects of the interface by defining how interaction tasks are represented using different modalities. Most advanced multimodal systems perform syntactic or semantic fusion.

Fusion also depends on the internal data representation. Application data can be represented in structures such as *frames* [341], *feature structures* [249] or *typed feature structures* [85]. Frames represent objects and relations as consisting of nested sets of attribute/value pairs, while feature structures go further to use shared variables to indicate common substructures. Typed feature structures are pervasive in natural language processing, and their primary operation is unification, which determines the consistency of two representational structures and, if consistent, combines them. As the data structures used become more complex and interdependent, the complexity of the fusion algorithm also increases. Various integration techniques have been devised: *frame-based integration* techniques use a strategy of recursively matching and merging attribute/value data structures (e.g., [478]) while *unification-based integration* techniques use *logic-based* methods for integrating the *partial meaning fragments*. Unification-based architectures have been applied to multimodal system design [239, 237]. Some important unification-based integration techniques include feature-structure and symbolic unification. *Feature-structure unification* is considered well suited to multimodal integration, because unification can combine complementary or redundant input from both modes, but it rules out contradictory input. *Symbolic unification* when combined with statistical processing techniques results in *hybrid symbolic/statistical* architectures that achieve very robust results.

Recently, with the advent of the semantic web, there has been much interest in using semantic mark-up languages such as DAML+OIL[6] to represent application semantics and perform discourse modeling. Such mark-up languages can be combined with reasoners that can perform automatic inference and consistency checking; refer to [554] for an example of a multimodal dialogue systems that uses these tools.

Example: QuickSet Fusion Mechanism

As an example of how fusion and semantic unification of two recognition based modalities is achieved in multimodal systems, the QuickSet multimodal system is described next [101, 380]. QuickSet supports both speech and pen (gesture) input. For pen input each stroke is timestamped and an internal data structure holding the x,y coordinates is sent to the gesture recognition component. The recognizer produces a N-best list of possible interpretations, each associated with a probability. These signal-level interpretations are then sent to the natural language agent to create a gestural parse N-best list before being integrated with the parallel speech interpretation. Like gesture processing, the speech recognizer generates an N-best list of interpretations, each associated with a probability estimate. These signal-level interpretations then are filtered by the natural language parser, which forms a spoken language N-best list.

To interpret a whole multimodal command, the time-stamps for speech and gestural input are compared by the integrator. Based on synchronization patterns typical of speech and pen input, an integration rule is applied to these time-stamped signals. The integrator will combine speech and pen signals and attempt to process their multimodal meaning when either a temporal overlap between signals exist or a speech signal begins within four seconds of the end of gesture (sequential signals). If synchronization rules permit joint processing, semantic unification will take place. The common meaning representation for speech and pen input, represented as typed feature structures are combined into a single complete semantic interpretation if compatible. Each item in the N-best list for both speech and pen input is processed by the unification parser to produce the feature structure representations which are combined during multimodal integration to produce full representations. The combined interpretations that do not unify are left out while the remaining ones are assigned probability estimates (by combining the unimodal scores) to build the final multimodal N-best list.

[6] http://www.daml.org/

2.3.3 Multimodal Interface Fusion and Fission

Interface designers can force or imply to the user what modality (or combination of modalities) should be used at each point of the interaction. For example, in GUI design, "radio buttons" and "combo boxes" imply mouse (or pen) input, while text fields imply keyboard input. This is also true for "novel" interaction modalities, e.g., for speech and pen interfaces a "click-to-talk" interaction mode biases the user towards the pen modality (refer also to Chapter 13). Designing interfaces that guide the user towards using the "optimal" input modality mix is the problem of *multimodal interface fusion* or fusion at the interface level. Few guidelines exist for selecting the "optimal" mix of modalities [58, 63]; these guidelines are mostly based on efficiency considerations. Overall, multimodal interface designers should respect all available input modalities, offer the user the flexibility to select (or override the default) input modality, and blend modalities having cognitive, efficiency and user satisfaction considerations in mind. The end goal is to create a truly multimodal experience, a user interface that maximizes *synergies* among the input modalities, by improving efficiency and robustness (error-correction capabilities).

The problem of *multimodal fission* is symmetric to that of fusion. Fission is the process of communicating an internal representation of the system to the user, via the co-ordinated action of multiple output modalities and output media. Selecting the appropriate output media, their relative importance for each communication act, and, most importantly, co-ordinating the presentation in time and space are some of the important issues in fission [532, 408]. Fission has not attracted as much research interest as fusion, and often ad hoc solutions are adopted for the fission problem. According to [532], most of the work in this area has been done by the multimedia research community, e.g., in the area of automated multimedia systems [27]. Such systems often focus more on how to render the information for different media and devices, rather than investigating the "optimal" blending of media or the selection of appropriate output modalities.

According to [408], fission algorithms should respect the MVC paradigm and separate communication acts from the interface implementation of these acts. In addition, there should always be output presentation for internal system representations (system states) and vice versa. This later principle is referred to as "*no presentation without representation*" [553]. Co-ordination and synchronization of the various output modalities is also an important problem. For example, for *embodied conversational agents* (also known as talking-heads) [86, 191] system output is presented via both audio and video streams that have to be synchronized to achieve a realistic effect (lip-syncing). Overall, selecting the appropriate mix of media to visualize system information and communicate with the user is an important open research problem that requires contributions from researchers, technologists and artists.

2.3.4 Multimodal Interaction Patterns and Usage

An important issue when implementing multimodal systems is the choice of interaction style (simultaneous vs. sequential), but also the internal implementation of input and output events in a synchronous or asynchronous manner. According to [12], synchronization of input events can occur instantaneously at the *event* level, at the *field* (concept) level or at the *form* (groups of concept) level. User behavior can serve as a guide for the selection of interaction style and synchronization granularity. In [383], the authors found that users adopt either a simultaneous or a sequential integration pattern during speech and pen multimodal input (70% simultaneous and 30% sequential). Their findings also show that user's dominant integration pattern is predictable early and remains consistent (89-97%) over time.

As discussed also in [102], multimodal interfaces may have many advantages: error prevention, robust user interface, easy error correction or recovery from errors, increased communication bandwidth, flexibility and alternative communication methods. Disambiguation of error-prone modalities is the main motivation for using multiple modalities in many systems. Multimodal interfaces offer improved robustness to errors due to both user behavior and system support [380]. During the evaluation of the QuickSet system, it was found that users tend to use simplified language (briefer utterances, fewer referring expressions) when interacting multi-modally than when interacting using a unimodal spoken dialogue interface. It is also reported that users tend to use the less error-prone modality in a certain context (error avoidance) and switch modes after system errors, thus facilitating error recovery. As far as system support is concerned, temporal, semantic and other constraints can be exploited to rule out candidates. This *mutual disambiguation* and *synergistic error correction* features make multimodal interfaces more robust compared to unimodal ones.

It should be noted, however, that multiple modalities alone do not bring these benefits to the interface: currently there is too much hype in multimodal systems, and the use of multiple modalities may be ineffective or even disadvantageous in some cases [381]. Following good system and interface design principles is essential for building successful multimodal applications.

2.3.5 Multimodal Applications

Numerous multimodal systems have been reported in the literature, a large number of which are cited in [382]. In [54], multimodal applications are categorized according to application domain, input/output modalities and fusion type. ¿From the historical perspective, multimodality offers promising opportunities, as presented in Bolt's "Put-That-There" system [69]. Bolt's system combined pointing and speech input as a natural way to communicate; gaze direction tracking was added in a later prototype and used for disambiguation. Other early systems used speech input along with keyboard and mouse in an effort to support better complex visual manipulation. Technology advances in late 1980s allowed speech to become an alternative to keyboard, leading to map and tourist information systems such as CUBRICON [360] and Georal [492]. For a more detailed analysis of multimodal spoken dialogue systems refer to Chapter 13.

Bimodal systems that combine speech and pen-input, or speech and lip-movements emerged in 1990s leading to work on integration and synchronization issues and the development of new architectures to support them. Speech and pen-input (2D or 3D gestures) involving hundreds of different interpretations beyond pointing have advanced rapidly both in research, e.g., Quickset [101], and commercial systems. Speech and lip movement systems exploit the detailed classification of human lip movements (visemes) and offer speech recognition robustness in noisy environments. Lip movement is also used in coordination with text-to-speech output in animated character systems (*talking heads* or *speaking agents*). Examples of such systems include include the Rea system [86], KTH's August, Adapt and Pixie systems [191]. These systems use audiovisual speech synthesis and anthropomorphic figures to convey facial expressions and head or body movements. Systems with animated interactive characters have also been constructed [27, 7]. These systems mainly focus on multimedia presentation techniques and agent technologies. Information kiosks (*intelligent kiosks*), such as SmartKom, use speech and haptics to provide an interface for users in public places, e.g., museums. Animated characters may have a strong motivational impact, since they are considered as being more lively and engaging for many users [347].

As noted in [382], systems combining three or more modalities such as biometric identification and verification systems [234], which use both physiological (retina, fingerprints, face or facial thermograms) and behavioral (voice, handwriting) modalities have also been developed. There is also increased interest in *passive input modes* [382], which refer to naturally occurring user behaviors that are unobtrusively monitored by a computer, e.g., eye gaze or facial expressions. *Ambient intelligence* and blending of active and passive modes is a promising direction to this end.

2.4 Adaptive Interfaces and User Modeling

As applications are becoming increasingly complex both in terms of functionality and interface design, it is also becoming increasingly hard to build applications and interfaces that satisfy the needs of all users. For example, users have different capabilities and preferences when multiple modalities are made available to them. New applications and interaction modes make user diversity even more apparent. As a result the need for *adaptation*, i.e., modification of the data model, application control and/or application interface to the specific user characteristics, needs, capabilities and preferences, is becoming increasingly apparent. Adaptation has been used for a large variety of tasks and applications, often successfully, improving the interaction efficiency and the user experience. However, despite the promise that adaptive interfaces hold, designing interfaces that are adaptive and also appear consistent to the user is a challenging task. In addition, adaptive interfaces are complex and the consequences of adaptivity on the user experience is sometimes unpredictable. As a result, system designers often opt for *adaptable interfaces*, i.e., interfaces that can be modified/adapted explicitly by the user, or limit the functionality of the adaptive algorithms.

2.4.1 A High Level View of User Adaptive Systems

The literature on adaptive interfaces is rich and very diverse, as researchers with different research backgrounds attack the problem. A number of definitions for adaptive systems can be found in the literature [446]. The definition of a user adaptive system given in [235] follows: "An interactive system that adapts its behavior to individual users on the basis of processes of user model acquisition and application that involve some form of learning, inference, or decision making." Thus, in a user adaptive system, the system gathers information about certain aspects of user interaction (*user model acquisition*) and performs learning and/or inference based on that information in order to create or update a *user model*. The system then applies the user model in order to determine how to adapt its behavior to the user (*user model application*). Although much of the adaptation literature focuses on user adaptation, there are also other aspects of adaptation, e.g., adaptation (or updating) of the system model or adaptation of the user interface that are equally important (refer to Section 2.4.3).

User model adaptation algorithms can be categorized based on the ways in which information about users is acquired. As discussed in [235], information about users can be acquired either as *explicit* input to the system or in a *implicit* way. In the first case, the system requests information relevant to the adaptation that may be difficult to elicit otherwise, e.g., location, user's age, topics of interest. In the second case, the system collects relevant naturally occurring actions or past interaction information and exploits it in the adaptation process. Examples include user location information extracted using GPS-capable mobile devices, or emotion detection, such as anger or attention. Often a pattern recognition system is used to extract this information leading to *unsupervised adaptation* algorithms, e.g., emotion recognition.

Another way to categorize adaptation is based on the learning, inference and decision making algorithms used, i.e., model acquisition and application. According to [235], these adaptation algorithms can be categorized into classification algorithms that employ no general knowledge about users and goals, and decision theoretic methods, e.g., Bayesian networks. Classification methods range from simple ones, such as naive Bayes, to more complex ones, such as advanced probabilistic classifiers, decision trees, and neural networks. For example, the SwiftFile system [470] classifies incoming email messages to user folders and uses text classification methods from the information retrieval field for archiving. Decision-theoretic systems explicitly define models of interaction, using tools such as Bayesian Belief Networks (BBNs). The models incorporate variables, for which the system has only an uncertain belief to begin with, and are connected in a probabilistic network in which the relationships among them can be interpreted as causal effects. As the system acquires new information, beliefs about network nodes are updated. For example, in the Lumiere project [216], the authors use a BBN to decide whether a user may need assistance based on user's expertise and task complexity. Other approaches include the use of stereotypes and plan recognition. A stereotype is a class of categories that a user may belong to. The system employs rules to assign users to classes and takes actions based on this classification. Plan based approaches consider user actions as steps towards achieving a certain goal; such techniques are employed in dialogue and help/tutoring systems.

User Adaptable Systems

There is a clear distinction between user adaptive and user adaptable systems. User adaptive systems implicitly adapt their user model to user preferences. An *adaptable* system, on the other hand, allows the user to explicitly tailor the interface to his preferences. A number of systems are adaptable but not adaptive. The main advantage of adaptable interfaces is that the user is in control and unwanted side-effects of adaptation can be avoided. The main drawback is that the user might not know how to effectively tune the system to his preferences. Next we focus on user adaptive multimedia systems.

2.4.2 A Probabilistic Framework for Adaptive Multimedia Systems

Multimedia retrieval and recommender systems search for the most relevant multimedia content based on information extracted by one (or more) queries from the user. Examples include web search engines that retrieve documents, images, music or video, and recommender systems for music, books and movies. Adaptive multimedia systems use implicit information extracted from past user behavior or explicit information provided by the user, such as user ratings, to improve retrieval performance. In essence, adaptive multimedia systems adapt their retrieval or content ranking model using information that is specific to a user or a group of users.

To better understand the adaptation process it is useful to pose the multimedia content retrieval and recommendation problem in a probabilistic Bayesian framework as follows:

$$\hat{d} = \arg\max_d p(d|\hat{q}, u) = \arg\max_d p(d, u|\hat{q}) \tag{2.2}$$

where d is the multimedia content available, $\hat{d}$ is the retrieved (or recommended) content, u is the user identity, and $\hat{q}$ is the user query. Note that

$\hat{q}$ signifies the internal system representation of the user request r. In many cases, the mapping from r to $\hat{q}$ is not deterministic due to using error-prone interfaces or due to inherent ambiguity in input semantics, e.g., for speech or natural language input respectively. In such cases, the problem of semantic interpretation of user input can be also expressed in a Bayesian framework as follows[7]

$$\hat{q} = \arg\max_q p(q|r, u) = \arg\max_q p(q, u|r) \qquad (2.3)$$

where q are the possible interpretations of the user input and r is the user input, e.g., features extracted from the speech signal for a spoken dialogue interface.

Most multimedia systems ignore the user term u in the probability maximization formulas shown above. In essence, for user adaptation systems the user u term is not dropped and the joint probability is maximized in Eqs. (2.2), (2.3). User adaptation can be applied either to the problem of user input interpretation (refer to Eq. (2.3)) or to the problem of multimedia retrieval (refer to Eq. (2.2)) or to both. Adaptation of the user input model is very much input modality dependent, for examples refer to the literature on acoustic model adaptation for speech input [454] or language model adaptation for natural language input [50]. We focus next on the problem of user model adaptation for multimedia content retrieval, i.e., on Eq. (2.2).

Most information retrieval systems ignore the u term and maximize $p(d|\hat{q})$, while user adaptive systems attempt to compute the joint distributions $p(d, u)$ instead. However, the joint distribution of "documents" d and users u is hard to compute due to the very large number of multimedia documents and the sparse information available about user preferences or ratings of these documents. A variety of smoothing techniques have been devised to estimate the joint probability $p(d, u)$ and overcome the information sparseness on the (d, u) manifold. These smoothing techniques are rather elaborate because it is hard to define a distance metric between multimedia documents (or between users for that matter). As a result smoothing techniques well-known for metric spaces cannot be easily applied for multimedia content retrieval, e.g., spline interpolation. Instead document and user similarity is used to classify documents and users into groups, and the joint probability distribution is typically computed for groups of documents and users.

There are two main groups of algorithms for user model adaptation of multimedia systems. One group of algorithms that is employed mostly by multimedia content retrieval systems uses user "document" ratings to compute the joint distribution $p(d, u)$ by smoothing along the d "dimension"; *relevance feedback* belongs in this group of algorithms. The second group of algorithms, employed mostly by multimedia content recommender systems,

[7] Note that one should actually preform a joint probability maximization over both d and q. However, in practice, most systems solve the query and content maximization problems separately as shown here.

uses user "document" ratings to compute the joint distribution by smoothing along the u "dimension"; *collaborative filtering* belongs in this group of algorithms. Examples of these algorithms are discussed next. It is important to keep in mind though that (independent of whether a probabilistic model is employed by the multimedia system or not): (i) *user model adaptation for multimedia systems involves the estimation of joint functionals of documents and users*, and (ii) *due to the sparseness of available user-specific data, a variety of smoothing techniques are employed to estimate these functionals.*

2.4.3 Adaptation Examples in the Context of the MVC Paradigm

An alternative view of adaptivity is through the model-view-controller (MVC) paradigm. Although adaptivity may cut through all the components of the MVC model, usually the adaptation algorithm may concern only one of the three components of the system architecture. As discussed next, adaptivity may focus on the interface (view) level of the application, the data (model) or the application control (controller). Most of the discussion up to this point has been on user model adaptation. Next we present examples of the two major applications of user adaptation, namely relevance feedback and collaborative filtering, but also present adaptation examples at the interface and controller level.

Adaptation at the Interface Level

An example of interface adaptation is the Smart Menus feature introduced in Windows 2000. The idea is to hide infrequently used menu items, so the user can faster access one of the most frequent used ones. For hidden menu items, the user has to fully extend the menu in order to view and select them. Clearly, there is a trade-off between accessing frequent items faster and "missing" infrequent menu items. The effect might be frustrating or confusing to some users; the list of items in each menu changes over time, which is highly inconsistent. For users that prefer to have the full list of menu items showing at all times this feature can be disabled.

Since many applications have become too complex and feature rich, *help systems* are needed that can guide users to effectively use the application. Adaptive help systems can potentially detect when the user needs advice, introduce concepts or features relevant to the given situation or even directly propose a solution to a given problem. An example of an adaptive help system is the Office Assistant agent, a derivation of Lumiere research prototype [216]. Lumiere uses decision theoretic methods (Bayesian networks) to decide if help should be given spontaneously. This is done if the computed likelihood that a user needs help, exceeds a given threshold. In the Office Assistant, the decision theoretic methods have been replaced by a relative simple rule-based mechanism. For an example system that adapts the default interaction mode of a multimodal spoken dialogue interface refer to Chapter 13.

Adaptation at the Model Level : Collaborative Filtering

Another example of adaptation is collaborative filtering for recommender systems, where the system tries to predict the user's interests based on the interests of groups of users, e.g., for recommendation of books, music, movies. The main idea is that, users sharing similar interests would give similar ratings for a given item. Such systems initially require the user to rate a small number of items in order to classify the user to a class of users with similar interests. Thus the rating of items is only indirectly used in order to propose similar items to the user. As discussed above collaborative filtering, in essence, smooths the joint functional of "documents" and users by grouping users together. Note that the interaction paradigm of recommender systems differs from that of information retrieval systems or web browsing discussed next.

Adaptation at the Model Level: Relevance Feedback

Information retrieval is usually an iterative process in which successive query re-formulations and retrievals alternate until the intended result is accomplished. A technique called *relevance feedback* is often employed in which the user is asked to rate the relevance of some of the retrieved documents in order to improve the performance of subsequent queries. Thus relevance feedback is a query alternation technique, which exploits previous retrieved results to add or modify the query terms according to user's rating of documents as relevant or not. Each step in this iterative process reduces the "distance" between the relevant documents and the reformulated query, until the intended result is accomplished. However, as the number of documents rated by the user is relatively small, smoothing techniques have to be employed in the document space. The relevance feedback algorithm described in the SMART information retrieval system [457] has been shown to substantially increase retrieval effectiveness and is used in a broad range of multimedia retrieval systems. For examples of relevance feedback algorithms for image information retrieval refer to Chapters 12 and 10.

Adaptation at the Controller Level: Spoken Dialogue Systems

Adaptation has also been applied to spoken dialogue systems at the dialogue manager (controller) level to improve on existing strategies and find optimal application control policies. For example, as noted in [235], the TOOT dialogue system [303] can appropriately adapt its dialogue strategies according to different situations. If the user's speech is poorly understood the system can adopt its strategy by acquiring just one piece of information at a time and by frequently requesting confirmation. Dialogue control for error prevention and correction is a challenging problem that can be formulated as a Markov Decision Process (MDP). Techniques such as reinforcement learning can be applied to find the optimal control policies, as described, for example, in the

RavenClaw system [68]. In practice, many multimodal systems implement two application control logics or interfaces, one for novice and one for expert users. Often the choice or novice or expert is left to the user leading to an adaptable (rather than an adaptive) system.

2.4.4 Usability Issues

One of the main concerns of adaptive interfaces is related to usability issues that may arise from adaptation. According to [235]: "some of the typical properties of user adaptive systems can lead to usability problems that may outweigh the benefits of adaptation." Some of these usability problems are outlined next.

"Predictability" refers to the extent to which a user can predict the effects of his actions. SmartMenus (refer above) can be thought as an example of lack of predictability, since the low usage of a menu item (or high usage of other items) will result in the disappearance of that item. Predictability is closely associated with "transparency" or visibility. When the adaptation mechanism is invisible (not allowing the user to understand how it works), the user will be unable to understand or explain system actions. A way to achieve "controllability", a degree of control over system actions, is to allow the user to confirm any action that may have significant consequences on the interface. Distractive or irritating system behaviors are against the goal of "unobtrusiveness". For example, the distracting ways in which the Office Assistant agent is used to pop up, violates the principles of unobtrusiveness and controllability.

Usually model level adaptation is hidden from the user and does not violate basic usability principles. However, adaptation at the interface and control level are directly observable by the user and often lead to an inconsistent look and feel of the application. For an example of how inconsistencies in adaptive interfaces can increase cognitive load and outweigh the benefits of adaptation refer to Chapter 13.

2.5 Mobile Interfaces

As mobile devices are becoming increasingly ubiquitous, mobile interface design is emerging as an important research area of human-computer interaction. Designing and implementing interfaces on mobile devices, such as PDAs and mobile phones, is a challenging task because the designer has to operate under various constraints including device size, network bandwidth and power consumption. In addition, the requirements and usage of mobile devices varies significantly among users and is situation-dependent. As a result, mobile user interface design poses unique usability challenges, but also offers new opportunities, e.g., context-aware services. Next the main differences between mobile and desktop interfaces are outlined [14]:

- **Input modality**: an important difference between mobile and desktop interfaces is that the "physical" keyboard is no longer the dominant input modality. Although keypads and mini-keyboards are still extensively used on mobile devices, alternative input modalities such as touch-screens, pen, speech, virtual keyboards are becoming increasing popular and competitive in terms of efficiency to physical keyboard input.
- **Screen size**: Mobile devices typically suffer from limited screen real estate, screen resolution and screen brightness (the later is important for achieving increased battery life). As a result, the amount of information that can be displayed using the screen is significantly decreased compared to the desktop. Alternative modalities, e.g., spoken output, or devices, e.g., augmented reality goggles, can be used to improve the system output communication efficiency for mobile interfaces.
- **Network bandwidth and device limitations**: Although the cost of network bandwidth for mobile devices is continuously decreasing, bandwidth remains an important factor when designing mobile interfaces. Mobile applications should adapt to bandwidth considerations, e.g., changing signal strength. Mobile interface design is also affected by device limitations such as processing power and energy consumption. Bandwidth and processing power considerations affect architectural design decisions, e.g., if there is not enough computing power for an application to run locally on the device a client-server architecture might be used.
- **Location**: Location information is available to an increasing number of mobile devices. Location information is obtained either from cell tower triangulation or by using a GPS receiver. This information can be a valuable feature for new services that employ the user's location as a "information filter", in essence adapting the user's list of preferences to match what is locally available. An important subset of location-aware mobile applications are geographical information systems (GIS) applications that typically use GPS-capable mobile devices.
- **Environmental conditions**: A mobile device has to face variable and often extreme environmental conditions, e.g., changing levels and patterns of background noise. Mobile interfaces should adapt to new conditions and allow the user to use appropriate input and output modalities for each condition. For example, speech might be the input modality of choice for a low-noise, hands-busy task, e.g., driving in the car, while visual input would be preferable in a "quiet" place, e.g., library.
- **Attention and cognitive load**: In contrast to the desktop, mobile users often show reduced attention (especially visual attention), because the user may be on the move or focusing on other activities. Tactile or audio feedback can be used to draw the user's attention without distracting him from his main task. In general, mobile interfaces should incur limited cognitive load, especially for applications where the user is multi-tasking, e.g., car navigation applications.

These fundamental differences between mobile and desktop interfaces call for updated design principles for mobile interface design and create new opportunities for mobile applications. Next we briefly review guidelines for mobile interface design and present examples of mobile applications.

2.5.1 Mobile Interface Design: Issues and Guidelines

"Mobile Web Best Practices" [10] is a W3C recommendation that specifies best practices for delivering Web content to mobile devices. It includes a list of 60 recommendations addressing issues such as page layout and content, navigation and links, input and overall behavior. For example, images in a web page should be properly resized and rendered for the mobile device, preferably on the server side. Alternatively, a text equivalent for every non-text element, e.g. images, should be provided so that devices with limited capabilities can display this information.

Information presentation in the limited screen displays of mobile devices is an important issue. Information should be hierarchically organized in a number of displays containing short lists of options. Displays should be properly designed to minimize clutter and navigation effort. When a large number of items is required in a list, a method to navigate efficiently between the items should be made available. To facilitate scrolling through large menu items a click wheel operated in a rotational manner can be used, e.g. iPod devices.

Another important issue is the high degree of diversity among mobile devices, which makes consistency of applications among platforms and devices a challenging task. For example, PDA devices have a miniaturized desktop-like interface with pen input and various methods of text input such as virtual/physical keyboard or graffiti recognition. Most mobile phones, on the other hand, have a list-based interface that has to be operated with just a numeric keypad for navigation among screens. One solution for the deployment of an application is to use the lower common denominator as far as device capabilities are concerned; another approach is to exploit capability profiles for groups of devices.

2.5.2 Example Applications

Despite the limitations in screen size and processing power of mobile devices, the always-on connectivity and the increased bandwidth available in 3G mobile data networks allows for the deployment of sophisticated network based applications and services. Examples include mobile browsing and map applications.

An example of a mobile phone browser is the Opera Mini micro-browser[8] that is available for a wide variety of mobile phones. The browser follows a client-server architecture to overcome the limited device capabilities. Opera

[8] http://www.operamini.com/features/

Mini requests web pages through proxy servers, which retrieve the web page, process it, compress it, and send it back to the user's mobile phone. The architecture and interface design emphasizes simplicity, speed and bandwidth conservation. Most importantly the Web page information is rendered on the server to match phone capabilities with very good results.

An example of a location-aware service is "Google Maps for mobile", a web mapping service that can be used both by GPS-enabled devices and by mobile phones (using the "My Location" feature, which exploits cell tower triangulation for approximate positioning). The service offers street maps, route planning (driving directions) and allows the user to find a variety of nearby businesses, such as theaters, restaurants and hotels. Although "Google Maps" uses a keypad and pen interface, a variety of research prototypes exist for obtaining location-aware information using a multimodal spoken dialogue interface [101].

The constraints and new opportunities that arise in mobile computing have lead to significant innovation in the research area of mobile interfaces. For a more detailed review of mobile interfaces refer to Chapter 15 of this book.

2.6 Multimedia Applications

The domain of multimedia applications is very large. One way to categorize such applications is based on their functionality, namely: multimedia search and retrieval, multimedia recommendation systems, multimedia content visualization and consumption, and multimedia content authoring. Example applications for each of these categories include web-based image search and retrieval, movie recommendation systems, music players with music maps and movie editing tools. Another way to categorize multimedia applications is based on the media that are being accessed or processed, e.g., interfaces to music, images, video, text, lectures, meetings. Applications are also categorized based on the device or mode of access, e.g., mobile applications, desktop applications or telephony applications. Finally, interfaces to multimedia can be categorized based on the main interaction modalities, e.g., spoken dialogue applications or multimodal applications. Our goal in this section is to provide example applications for each of these categories that focus on the human-computer *interaction* aspects of multimedia applications. The *multimedia processing* aspects of some of these applications have already been presented in Chapter 1.

2.6.1 Multimedia Search and Retrieval Applications

Multimedia content is hard to access unless it is organized in a way that allows for efficient browsing, search and retrieval [488, 319]. An early approach was to annotate images and videos with textual descriptions and use this information for retrieval. This approach has the disadvantage that semantic annotation of multimedia data is a complex, labor intensive task. Since the early 1990s, content-based approaches have been developed for describing and retrieving image and video using features such color, texture, shape, object and camera movements. The MPEG7 standard defines descriptors that allow users or agents to identify, filter and browse audiovisual content [488, 319].

Various studies have described and compared the most notable content based image retrieval systems, such as [450]. The first notable example is the QBIC (query by image content) system [165] that supports queries based on example images, user-constructed sketches and drawings, and selected color and texture patterns. Virage [37] supports visual queries based on color, composition (color layout), texture, and structure (object boundary information) as well as weighted combinations of the above. Other systems include VisualSeek [496] that also allows queries based on both visual features and their spatial relationships and MARS [451], which exploits relevance feedback to enhance retrieval performance. For a review of image retrieval systems refer to Chapter 12.

As noted in [357], users expect content-based retrieval systems to perform analysis at the same level of complexity and semantics that humans do. For example, 95% of queries for the VisualSeek [496] system were semantic and key-word based. In practice, however, most multimedia retrieval systems use low level features to perform search [97]. As a result, a "good" match in terms of a feature metric may yield poor results as far as the user is concerned. As defined in [495], *the semantic gap is the lack of coincidence between information that one can extract from the visual data and the interpretation that the same data have for a user on a given situation.* Although some promising efforts have emerged such as Semantic Visual Templates [97], and the probabilistic framework of multijects and multinets [357], semantic multimedia understanding is indeed the final frontier in multimedia retrieval.

2.6.2 Multimedia Recommender Systems

Recommender systems propose to the user multimedia content that is likely to be of interest. Such systems allow the user to *explore* "new" content, as opposed to multimedia search systems where the user mostly *exploits* known content. Recommender systems are based on multimedia content similarity (content-based approach) and/or user preferences similarity (collaborative filtering or social networking).

Examples of recommender systems for music are the popular Last.fm[9] and Pandora[10] services, where continuous streams of music, similar to a radio station, can be created based on the systems recommendations. StumbleUpon[11]

[9] http://www.last.fm/

[10] http://www.pandora.com/

[11] http://www.stumbleupon.com/

is a popular web discovery service that also specializes in recommending webpages containing multimedia content. These services use a simple one-click interface to rate "discovered" content and to improve on the user model. The user experience of continuously exploring (and rating) new content is very different from the traditional sequential browsing experience or the well-structured web search user experience. Exploratory interfaces to multimedia have been successful due to the large number of available content and the "semantic" gap between multimedia retrieval and user expectations. The trend is to create interfaces to multimedia that contain elements from both recommender and retrieval systems, effectively creating interfaces that balance exploration and exploitation of multimedia data.

2.6.3 Multimedia Content Consumption Applications

Traditionally content consumption refers to viewers and players of multimedia content. In addition to the basic ability of displaying images and playing back audio and video, state-of-the-art applications also contain graphical user interfaces for creating slide-shows, play-lists as well as elaborate visualization tools. Recently content consumption applications also contain rudimentary multimedia search and retrieval capabilities. Multimedia consumption on mobile devices is a important application area, especially with the advent of mobile multimedia players and multimedia phones, e.g., the iPhone.

An important area of applications is the visualization of multimedia data, often using *multimedia maps*. Maps are created by computing the pairwise similarity between multimedia content or groups of multimedia content, e.g., between two songs or two artists, and then mapping this similarity to a 2D Euclidean space. Multimedia maps can be used as a one-click search interface or for the automatic creation of play-lists, e.g., refer to Chapter 11. Automatic play-list creation is very important for music and image content where typically there are thousands of options available to the user and manual creation of play-lists is a time-consuming task. Multimedia visualization interfaces often serve the function of a personalized recommender system that uses a content-based approach to organize data.

Another important group of applications are *multimedia summarization* and *multimedia skimming* interfaces. Linear consumption of multimedia is quickly becoming inefficient, e.g., consider the amount of audio podcasts that you would like to skim through daily. The ability to summarize multimedia content, keeping the most salient information, while retaining production quality is an important emerging application area, e.g., refer to Chapter 8 on movie summarization. Interfaces to multimedia skimming that go beyond the traditional "VCR-fast forward" interface can be used in conjunction with multimedia summarization technology to significantly enhance the content consumption experience.

The future of multimedia content consumption holds an *immersive multimedia* experience. Content consumption applications will be able to model the preferences and track the behavior of the user, e.g., eye-gaze detection as described in Chapter 14. Content will then be automatically selected, rendered and played based on the wishes and the mood of the user, creating a new multimedia consumption user experience.

2.6.4 Multimedia Authoring Applications

As the Internet is quickly becoming the de facto multimedia content distribution channel, amateur content creators have created a new need for simple, easy-to-use tools for multimedia content authoring. Today there are numerous such tools available both online and offline for creating and editing web pages, text, paintings, images, movies, audio, and music. Such programs use a graphical user interface and employ multimedia signal processing technologies and templates to semi-automate the content creation process and ease the heavy work-load that multimedia authoring entails.

Two important new author creation paradigms have emerged, mostly on the Internet, namely *collaborative authoring* and *authoring by consensus*. Real-time collaborative authoring is an emerging technology that allows users to create and simultaneously edit multimedia content online, e.g., Google docs[12] allows for online editing of documents containing text and graphics in near real-time. Authoring by consensus refers to the process of allowing a (potentially large) group of non-experts to edit multimedia content until a consensus is reached, e.g., the Wikipedia paradigm[13], while in *democratic content creation* the most popular multimedia content is selected by the user group using voting or feedback aggregation, e.g., in massive online computer games. Other important directions in multimedia authoring include *interactive media*, *embedding semantics into multimedia* and the emerging area of *adaptive multimedia*, i.e., multimedia content that is automatically rendered to user preferences.

2.7 Architectures

Most multimedia and multimodal systems are very complex in terms of architecture and software design, and usually mix and exploit many software architectural styles and models like the pipe-and-filter, finite-state machine, event-based model, client-server, object-oriented and agent-based ones. For example, spoken dialogue systems are usually structured either in a pipeline fashion or use the client-server model with a central component, which facilitates the interaction between other components, like the Galaxy-II architecture [472, 473]. Multimodal systems are based on even more sophisticated architectures like [281] or agent architectures. Some of these architectures follow the MVC paradigm and separate the model from the control logic and

[12] http://docs.google.com/

[13] http://en.wikipedia.org/

the interface specification, although, in spoken dialogue systems, it is not uncommon to combine the control logic and speech interface specification into a single module, the dialogue manager. Next we briefly examine the differences in requirements between GUI and multimodal architectures, and review some typical architectures employed in multimodal input/multimedia output systems.

GUIs vs Multimodal architectures

As noted in [382], the design of multimodal/multimedia systems should address several challenging architectural issues not found in the design of GUIs. First, unlike GUI systems that assume that there is a single event stream that controls the underlying event loop, multimodal interfaces process continuous and simultaneous inputs and outputs from parallel streams. Also GUIs assume that the basic interface actions, such as selection of an item, are atomic and unambiguous events, while multimodal systems process input modes using recognition-based technologies that are designed to handle uncertainty and entail probabilistic methods of processing. Finally, multimodal interfaces that process two or more recognition-based input streams require time-stamping of input, and the development of temporal constraints on mode fusion operations.

Multimodal Architectures and Frameworks

One popular architecture among the members of the multimodal research community is the *multi-agent architecture*, exemplified by the *Open Agent Architecture* [325] and *Adaptive Agent Architecture* [281]. As described in [532, 382], multi-agent architectures provide essential infrastructure for coordinating the many complex modules needed to implement multimodal system processing, and permit doing so in a distributed manner. According to the authors, in a multi-agent architecture, the many components needed to support the multimodal system, e.g., speech recognition, gesture recognition, natural language processing, multimodal integration, may be written in different programming languages, on different machines, and with different operating systems. Agent communication languages are being developed that can handle asynchronous delivery, triggered responses, multi-casting and other concepts from distributed systems. Using a multi-agent architecture, for example, speech and gestures can arrive in parallel or asynchronously via individual modality agents, with the results recognized and passed to a *facilitator*. These results, typically an N-best list of conjectured lexical items and related time-stamp information are then routed to appropriate agents for further language processing. Next, sets of meaning fragments arrive at the multimodal integrator which decides whether and how long to wait for recognition results from other modalities, based on the system's temporal thresholds. The meaning fragments are fused into a semantically-and temporally-compatible whole interpretation before passing the results back to the facilitator. At this point, the system's final multimodal interpretation is confirmed by the interface, delivered as multimedia feedback to the user, and executed by any relevant applications.

Despite the availability of high-accuracy speech recognizers and other mature multimodal technologies such as gaze trackers, touch screens, and gesture trackers, few applications take advantage of these technologies. One reason for this is that the cost of implementing a multimodal interface is prohibitive. The system designer must usually start from scratch, implementing access to external sensors, developing ambiguity resolution algorithms, etc. However, when properly implemented, a large part of the code in a multimodal system can be reused. This aspect has been identified and many multimodal application frameworks have recently appeared such as VTT's *Jaspis* and *Jaspis2* frameworks [532, 533], Rutgers CAIP Center framework [166] and the embassi system [150].

2.8 Standards and Tools

The majority of multimedia standards refer to multimedia content encoding and description. Most notable examples of such standards are the MPEG-1,2,3 standards for video, audio and multimedia encoding, the MPEG-1 Audio Layer 3 (referred to as mp3) standard for audio encoding, the JPEG standard for image encoding, the G.xxx series of ITU standards for audio/speech, and the H.xxx series of ITU standards[14] for image/video. Recently there has been a flurry of activity on standardization of multimedia content descriptors; these standards go beyond the "physical layer" and attempt to describe the semantics of multimedia. This activity grew out of the SGML[15] and HTML[16] ISO web standards, and is championed by the semantic web research community and W3C[17] (World Wide Web Consortium), a standardization body for web activities. One outcome of these activities is RDF[18], a language based on XML that is able to express "metadata" in a standard form, and could allow machines to communicate not only at the physical level (lexical or signal sample level), but also at a higher "semantic" level. SMIL[19] (Synchronized Multimedia Integration Language) is an XML language also recommended by W3C for describing multimedia presentations. Finally the MPEG7 standard is destined to provide a multimedia content description interface (mostly for)

[14] http://www.itu.int/ITU-T/
[15] http://www.w3.org/MarkUp/SGML/
[16] http://www.w3.org/MarkUp/
[17] http://www.w3.org/
[18] http://www.w3.org/RDF/
[19] http://www.w3.org/TR/SMIL/

image/video/audio content [488, 5]. For a more detailed review of multimedia content description standards refer to Chapter 1 and [5]. Next we focus on multimedia interaction standards most notably on graphical user interface recommendations, spoken dialogue and multimodal interaction standards.

Graphical User Interfaces

In contrast to web development for which widely used standards exist, e.g., HTML, GUI development is characterized by the lack of a single dominant standard. Instead, a multitude of GUI toolkits, along with their corresponding style guides, exist for various platforms, e.g., mobile or desktop, and different desktop operating systems, e.g., MacOS, Windows, Linux. Nevertheless all these GUI toolkits are very similar in appearance and functionality. This makes the application of common design rules and guidelines easier to follow, in practice, regardless of the toolkit choice. Such guidelines, style guides, e.g., the Apple Human Interface Guidelines for desktop [1] or iPhone [2], standards, e.g., ISO 9241, and toolkits promote usability principles such as consistency and user satisfaction. However, following these guidelines is not always easy for non-HCI expert developers as reported in [175].

The appearance of cross-platform GUI toolkits and development tools that ease GUI development, e.g. automatic creation of GUI related code, helps developers and designers focus on application functionality and design principles, rather than on low-level details. The diversity of GUI toolkits is not expected to vanish any time soon, especially as new devices and platforms keep emerging. This is especially true in the mobile/embedded space where new devices and interaction paradigms appear, posing new challenges and creating new opportunities for system designers.

Spoken Dialogue Interfaces

The VoiceXML Forum[20] an organization founded by Motorola, IBM, AT&T, and Lucent to promote voice-based development, introduced the *VoiceXML* language based on the legacy of languages already promoted by these four companies. In March 2000, version 1.0 was released and in October 2001, the first working draft of the latest VoiceXML 2.0 was published as a W3C recommendation[21]. The VoiceXML standard has simplified the development of voice-based applications much like HTML did for the development of web-based applications. The main features of VoiceXML are the familiar HTML-like syntax, the logic that an application consists of a series of pages (similar to familiar GUI interface logic) and the ability to provide web content using only voice as an input modality, making web information accessible from fixed or mobile phones.

---

[20] http://www.voicexml.org/

[21] http://www.w3.org/TR/voicexml20/

VoiceXML browsers consist of an interpreter and a set of VoiceXML documents. VoiceXML supports dialogues that include menus and forms, sub-dialogues and embedded grammars. The *voice browser* renders the VoiceXML documents as a sequence of the two-way interaction between the system and the end user. Core VoiceXML interpreter and software components are used for this purpose such as *automatic speech recognition* and *text-to-speech*. Many companies build spoken dialogue development toolkits that include building blocks such as sub-dialogues and grammars. Such toolkits often introduce custom tags of objects in addition to the VoiceXML standard ones. Using such complete solutions a system designer can implement and test VoiceXML-based applications and *voice portals*, e.g., the Nuance Voice Platform[22] provides an easy-to-use, complete development environment for voice applications. Other commercial offerings include servers for deploying these applications [4], voice browsers, and VoiceXML editors and grammar development tools. There are also open source VoiceXML tools, such as Carnegie Mellon's OpenVXI interpreter[23].

Multimodal Interaction Standards

The number and diversity of devices that can access the Internet has grown tremendously in the past years. The capabilities and modes of access of these devices varies; consider for example mobile phones, smart phones, personal digital assistants, multimedia players, kiosks, automotive interfaces. The W3C *Device Independence Working Group* main focus is on standards that make the characteristics of the device available to the network and, most importantly, on standards that assist authors in creating sites and applications that can be supported on multiple devices. The group coordinates its work with the *Web Accessibility Initiative*[24] and *MultiModal Interaction Working Group*[25] activities as discussed next.

The main goal of the *Multimodal Interaction Activity* is to extend the Web user interface to multiple modes of interaction (aural, visual and tactile), offering users the means to provide input using their voice or their hands via a key pad, keyboard, mouse, or stylus. For output, users will be able to listen to spoken prompts and audio, and to view information on graphical displays. By allowing multiple modes of interaction on a variety of devices the activity aims for *accessibility to all.* The Working Group was launched in 2002 following a joint workshop between the W3C and the WAP Forum with contributions from SALT[26] (*Speech Application Language Tags*) and XHTML+Voice[27] (X+V). Major contributions of this activity include: the

[22] http://www.nuance.com/voiceplatform/

[23] http://www.speech.cs.cmu.edu/openvxi/

[24] http://www.w3.org/WAI/

[25] http://www.w3.org/2006/12/mmi-charter.html

[26] http://www.saltforum.org/

[27] http://www.voicexml.org/specs/multimodal/x+v/12/

Multimodal Interaction Use Cases, the *Multimodal Interaction Use Requirements* and the *W3C Multimodal Interaction Framework* [14]. Work has also been done on: (i) dynamic adaptation to device configurations, user preferences and environmental conditions (*System and Environment Framework*) [15], (ii) integration of composite multimodal input and modality component interfaces such as interfaces for ink and keystrokes, and (iii) context sensitive binding of gestures to semantics (note that speech and DTMF modalities are developed by the *Voice Browser Working Group*[28]).

The group's work has also stimulated the creation of mark-up languages such as EMMA, and InkML. The *Extensible MultiModal Annotation Markup Language* (EMMA) [8], is a markup language intended to represent semantic interpretations of user input (speech, keystrokes, pen input etc.) together with annotations such as confidence scores, timestamps, input medium. The interpretation of the user's input is expected to be generated by signal interpretation processes, such as speech and ink recognition, semantic interpreters, and other types of processors. InkML [9], defines an XML data exchange format for ink entered with an electronic pen or stylus as part of a multimodal system, which will enable the capture and server-side processing of handwriting, gestures, drawings and other specific notations.

Other related efforts for multimodal interaction standardization are the SALT and XHTML + Voice efforts. SALT, is a lightweight set of extensions to existing markup languages, allowing developers to embed speech enhancements in existing HTML, XHTML and XML pages. *XHTML+Voice*, by IBM, Motorola and Opera Software, is another effort exploiting the combined use of XHTML and parts of VoiceXML through *XML events* to support for visual and speech interaction.

2.9 Summary

In this review, we have presented the fundamental concepts behind interfaces to multimedia content and multimedia applications. Our brief introduction to HCI focused on the definition and principles of usability, namely learnability, flexibility and robustness. We also introduced the MVC (model-view-controller) paradigm that serves today as the basis for the architectural design of many unimodal and multimodal systems. We concluded our HCI review with the definition of the concepts of iterative design, objective and subjective evaluation and participatory design.

We then moved on to reviewing some of the input and output modalities that are involved in modern interface design, namely GUI, speech, gestures, eye-tracking, augmented reality and haptics. Much of our review focused on speech interfaces, both because of the idiosyncratic nature of the speech modality and the breadth of technologies involved in speech recognition and synthesis. Then the discussion turned to the interesting problem of

[28] http://www.w3.org/voice/

how to combine different modalities to built a multimodal input/multimedia output interface. The review focused on the problems of multimodal fusion and multimedia fission, as well as the potential rewards and pitfalls of multimodal interface design. The main advantages of multimodality are increased interface robustness and usability, especially in adverse conditions. Be warned however that the inclusion of additional modalities does not always lead to better applications.

Adaptive interfaces are especially relevant for multimedia, because the preferences and mode of access varies among users and even (over time) for the same user. In our review of adaptive multimedia systems, we followed a more formal approach that unifies much of the relevant algorithms under a single concept, the user-content preferences matrix. We showed how this matrix is both sparse and does not live in a Euclidean space, and how algorithms like collaborative filtering and relevance feedback attempt to "smooth" this sparse matrix. In our discussion, we outlined some of the pitfalls of adaptivity and explained why application designers often opt for user adaptable rather than adaptive systems.

An especially important category of multimedia interfaces were reviewed next, namely mobile interfaces and applications. Our exposition here was brief given that more details are given in Chapter 15. However, the basic differences between desktop and mobile interfaces were outlined, namely the available input and output modalities, screen size, network bandwidth, device capabilities, context, and environmental conditions. Examples applications were also given. The main categories of multimedia applications were briefly reviewed next, namely multimedia search and retrieval, recommender systems, content consumption and content authoring applications.

We concluded with a review of architectures, tools and standards. Architectures that extend the MVC paradigm and agent-based architectures were reviewed specifically for multimodal systems. Our review of standards focused on multimedia interaction rather than multimedia content description. However, as content description standards emerge that include semantic and interaction information, e.g., RDF, MPEG7, the boundaries between the two categories are becoming blurry. The review of interaction standards included VoiceXML for speech interaction; EMMA, InkML and SALT for multimodal interaction.

These are exciting times for multimedia interfaces and applications designers. The explosion of multimedia content available online, improved device capabilities, novel multimedia signal processing algorithms, new interaction modalities and interaction paradigms have created possibilities that we are only now beginning to understand. Technologies and interfaces that were up to now locked up in the research lab are slowly becoming part of our everyday life, e.g., multi-touch interfaces, zoomable interfaces, multimedia semantic descriptors, multimedia recognition and multimedia summarization. To realize the great promise that interfaces to multimedia content hold, the collaboration of many people is needed. Researchers and technologists involved in the physical (signal processing), semantic, application and interface layers of multimedia systems have to create synergies that will radically change the way that we create and consume multimedia.

Part II

INTEGRATED MULTIMEDIA ANALYSIS AND RECOGNITION

3

Stochastic Models for Multimodal Video Analysis

Manolis Delakis[1], Guillaume Gravier[2], and Patrick Gros[3]

[1] Irisa, Université de Rennes 1, Campus de Beaulieu, Rennes, France
[2] Irisa, CNRS, Campus de Beaulieu, Rennes, France
[3] Irisa, INRIA, Campus de Beaulieu, Rennes, France

Video analysis, which aims at extracting high-level information such as a structure or a genre from raw video data, is by nature multimodal as both the visual and audio modalities are used to carry the semantic meaning of a video. In addition, in some types of videos, the textual modality is also used with information displayed on screen – such as scores, statistics or player's names in sports videos – or automatic transcription of the soundtrack. Therefore, semantic analysis of videos requires multimodal analysis and, in particular, multimodal models to integrate all the sources of information available. Due to the non-deterministic nature of images and sounds, stochastic models are first choice candidates for the analysis of videos. In particular, multimodal extensions of hidden Markov models (HMM) have been extensively used for the purpose of video analysis and other multimodal applications such as audio-visual speech recognition (see *e.g.*, Chapter 4). However, as we will illustrate in this chapter, the HMM approach suffers some strong limitations, in particular due to the integration scheme which requires a perfect synchronization between the various streams of information.

This chapter presents video indexing with segment models (SM), aiming at a more efficient and versatile multimodal fusion. In segment models, synchrony constraints between modalities can be relaxed to the scene boundaries, thus enabling to process each modality with their native sampling rates and models within each scene. We illustrate the many possibilities of audiovisual integration that SM can offer in the context of tennis video structuring. We first briefly review stochastic models that have been used for multimodal video analysis. We then present the task of tennis video structuring and the cues and related features that we want to incorporate in a stochastic model. We show how HMM can be used for multimodal integration before generalizing the HMM approach based on the segment model framework. We finally show that the hierarchical structure of a tennis video can be taken into consideration in both frameworks and present a new decoding algorithm to take into account textual score information displayed on screen.

P. Maragos et al. (eds.), *Multimodal Processing and Interaction*,
DOI: 10.1007/978-0-387-76316-3_3, © Springer Science+Business Media, LLC 2008

3.1 An overview of multimodal fusion models

Hidden Markov models are widely used to exploit the temporal aspect of video data. Indeed, depending on the video genre and the production rules, video events occur with a temporal order that will finally reveal the semantics. Hidden Markov models provide a powerful statistical framework for handling sequential data and they are thus a natural candidate for learning temporal dependencies in video. Many extensions of HMM have been studied to deal with the integration of multimodal data.

A straightforward extension of HMM for multimodal integration is based on *early fusion* to generate multimodal features which are then modeled using HMM. This simple fusion scheme has been widely used for video segmentation [71, 38] and TV broadcasts classification (see, *e.g.*, [138, 148, 225]) on top of visual and audio features. Early fusion has also been widely studied in the field of audiovisual speech recognition [414]. The underlying assumption however of the early fusion scheme is that all the modalities are synchronous – in particular, the features from the different modalities in order to combine them into multimodal features – and exhibit the same model topology, which does not generally hold. A number of HMM variants have been proposed to address this problem and relax the synchrony constraints, such as multistream HMM, asynchronous HMM and layered HMM.

The idea of multistream HMM [77] is to model each modality – or stream – independently with HMM, forcing synchrony between the HMM at some predefined points. In synchronous multistream HMM, the states themselves are the synchronization points. In practice, a single HMM is used and this model does not differ from the early fusion scheme presented above, except for the explicit assumption of conditional independence of the observation streams and the possibility of introducing stream weights as discussed in Section 4.1. In asynchronous multistream HMM, the synchronization points are extended beyond the states, like the end of phonemes in audiovisual speech recognition, in order to allow different topologies for each modality. Between the synchronization points, the streams are considered independent and modeled by unimodal HMM whose likelihoods are recombined at the synchronization points. For practical reasons however, the model is often implemented as a product HMM, *i.e.*,, a synchronous multistream model where each state represents a product of state in the monomodal HMMs, where all the HMMs share the same topology.

Asynchronous HMM [53] is a special HMM architecture designed to jointly model a pair of lightly asynchronous streams containing different number of samples. The idea is to enable stretching of the shortest stream in order to meet a better match with the longer one. Viterbi decoding aims at finding out the best alignment between the two streams in addition to the best state sequence. This model has been used with success for audiovisual speech recognition and recognition of group action meetings [333].

Sharing with multistream HMM the idea of synchronization points and the use of independent models, layered architectures of HMM can be built. A video is segmented according to some fixed synchronization points, for example at the end of every second or at the shot boundaries. The respective video portion of each modality is then processed independently with some HMM. The outcomes from the HMM of the first layer are concatenated and given as input to a second layer HMM. Layered HMM were first used in a task of office activity inference [376] and has been used for recognition of group actions [588] and structure analysis of soccer videos [571].

Segment models, discussed in this chapter, unify multistream and layered HMM into a novel framework for multimodal integration and allow overcoming some of the problems related to the HMM variants presented here. Synchronization points between the modalities are part of the optimization problem as in asynchronous HMM, rather than fixed as in multistream HMM, thus enabling the use of different topologies for the different modalities. Secondly, between two synchronization boundaries, observations from the different modalities are assigned to a common "multimodal" hidden state, corresponding to a higher semantic level as in layered HMM. Finally, an explicit state duration model is added in SMs.

3.2 The framework of tennis video structuring

Before describing SMs for video analysis, we first briefly describe the task of tennis video structuring that we will use to experimentally validate SMs. In this section, we formally define the task of tennis video structuring. We first define typical scenes that occur in tennis video before discussing the relevant cues in the audio and image modalities that can be used to structure the video into scenes. We also briefly introduce the features used to represent such cues. As this chapter focuses on the model rather than the features, few details are given on the feature extraction process and the interested reader is referred to [128] for more details.

3.2.1 Tennis video parsing

Tennis videos can be described based on four major scenes, namely *missed serve plus rally*, *rally*, *replay* and *break*. The scene characteristics, in terms of audio and visual content of each scene, are mainly determined by the production style of the broadcaster. How these scenes are interleaved in the video is governed by the rules of tennis and also by the production style of the broadcaster. For example, tennis rules state that a match is composed of at least two games (three for male players), a game of at least 6 sets which contains 4 or more points. Moreover, a break occurs after the first set of a game and every two sets afterward.

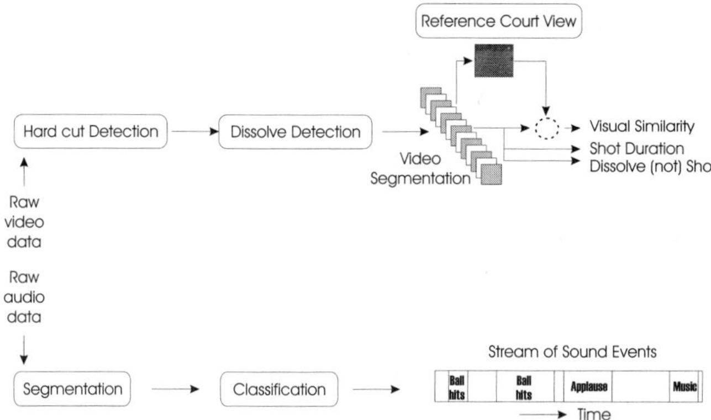

Fig. 3.1. Outline of the feature extraction process.

Video tennis parsing aims at segmenting the video according to some predefined scene-based structure. In our shot-based system, the problem is therefore to classify shots according to the structure elements and to detect the boundaries between these elements. In a first simple version of the parser, the elements are the scene themselves and the parser aims at segmenting the video according to the four previously listed scenes. A more complex version of the parser, described in Section 3.6, aims at finding out the structure of the game in terms of sets and points in addition to the scene structure.

3.2.2 Audio, visual and textual cues

There are a number of invariant characteristics that occur in every tennis video as a result of the game rules and the work of the producer. Fortunately, the producer's style vary little from one channel to another. For instance, when game action occurs, a global view of the court is displayed. It is extremely rare, although still possible, to present game action by a non global court view, like a side view. On the other hand, game idleness usually corresponds to non global court views. Special transitions, mostly dissolves, are used to delimit replays. From the audio point of view, it is obvious that sounds of ball hits are present mostly for shots representing a game action[4].

These characteristics enable the design of a system based on shots. Shot boundaries are first automatically detected based on hard cuts before detecting dissolve transitions based on the algorithm described in [528]. A special shot is defined for the latter. Simple cues as those discussed in the previous paragraph can be used to characterize each video shot. For example, the scene "*missed serve plus rally*" starts with a global court view with ball sounds where the missed serve occurs. A number of non game shots follow until a

[4] Although some advertisement broadcasted during breaks may include sounds of ball hits.

rally (or an ace) takes place, the latter being characterized by game action shots. Finally, a number of non game shots optionally appear, until a new scene begins. There is also the possibility of repetitive missed serves before the rally.

Visual cues are mostly related to production rules which state that, most of the times, global views of the tennis court are displayed while the players are playing. Shot length and the presence of dissolve transitions are also relevant cues. We therefore used three simple features to characterize the image modality for a shot: similarity to a global court view of the middle frame, duration, and dissolve. The first feature measures the distance between the middle frame of the current shot and a reference global view shot automatically extracted from each video based on dominant color. The distance feature characterizes a shot as a global court view or not. The dissolve feature is a binary feature indicating whether a shot corresponds to a dissolve or not. In the experiments described in this chapter, the visual similarity and duration features were quantized into 10 bins, where the number of bins was experimentally determined.

Audio cues are used to characterize the content of the sound track in each shot. For this purpose, we track the presence of three sound classes of interest, ball hits, applause and music. Ball hits occur during rallies while applause usually acknowledge points. Music only appears in commercials. Tracking sound classes is based on a segmentation step into small homogeneous segments followed by a classification step to detect whether a particular sound class is present or not in a segment [60]. This tracking process results in a map of the occurrences of each of the three events in the video as illustrated in Fig. 3.1.

Occasionally, points are acknowledged by scores displayed on screen. These scores constitute highly informative textual features that can be exploited for the purpose of video structuring. In this study, the displayed scores are extracted manually in the shots where they appear. Some shots have therefore an associated score label while others not. We discuss in Section 3.7 how those labels are used and the robustness to score detection errors.

3.2.3 Corpus

Experiments reported in this chapter were carried out on a corpus of 6 complete tennis videos, including an outdoor match, recorded between 1999 and 2001[5]. Every video contains a single tennis match, *i.e.*, there are no court views that are split in order to display two or more tennis matches. Even though heading and trailing events not related to tennis were manually removed, the programs still contain commercials and interviews that occasionally appear during the match. The total duration of the videos is approximately 15 hours. Three games, including the outdoor one, were used for training and three for

[5] Videos were kindly provided by the Institut National de l'Audiovisuel (INA), France.

testing. In our experiments, we did not notice significant performance variations when switching matches between the test and training sets. Each video was automatically segmented into shots before manually labeling the resulting shots according to the scene defined above and the HMM states defined in the next section. HMM state labeling is used for the purpose of parameter estimation in the various models studied in this chapter.

3.3 Structuring with hidden Markov models

As mentioned in the introduction to this chapter, state-synchronous multi-stream HMMs can be used for video structuring using the audio and video features described in the previous section. This section introduces notations for HMM applied to our video structuring problem and discusses modality integration in the HMM framework. We extend this formalism to SMs in the next section.

3.3.1 Video structure parsing

As we have discussed in Section 3.2, the four characteristic scenes can be represented as sequences of typical shots which can in turn be represented using HMMs where the observations are the shot-based feature vectors.

For example, the scene *missed serve plus rally* can be represented with a four state Markov model: the first state, representing the first serve, correspond to a global view with ball hits; the second state accounts for non global court views with neither applause nor ball hits before the player serves again; the third state represents a global court view with ball hits corresponding to the rally itself; finally, the fourth state correspond to non global court views, possibly with applause after the rally is over. Transitions represent the possible evolution of the game between these states. For example, the transition from state 2 back to state 1 accounts for multiple missed serve.

Based on this principle, we defined the topologies illustrated in Fig. 3.2 for the four scenes, with a total of 12 states. Note that the transitions depicted in the figure correspond to the most frequent transitions. However, to account for variations in the producer's style, the individual scene HMM have in fact an ergodic topology with a small probability for those transitions unobserved in the training data. Assuming an ergodic structure between the four scene HMM[6], the tennis match is therefore represented by a 12 state HMM.

Let us denote the visual feature vector for the shot i by

$$o_i^{(\mathrm{v})} = \left[o_i^{\mathrm{c}}\ o_i^{\mathrm{l}}\ o_i^{\mathrm{d}}\right] \ , \tag{3.1}$$

[6] Except for the self loops between replays and breaks. This is because, by definition, multiple repeated replays or breaks result into a larger and unique replay or break, respectively. In the same way, breaks following replays or vice versa are fused into a single break.

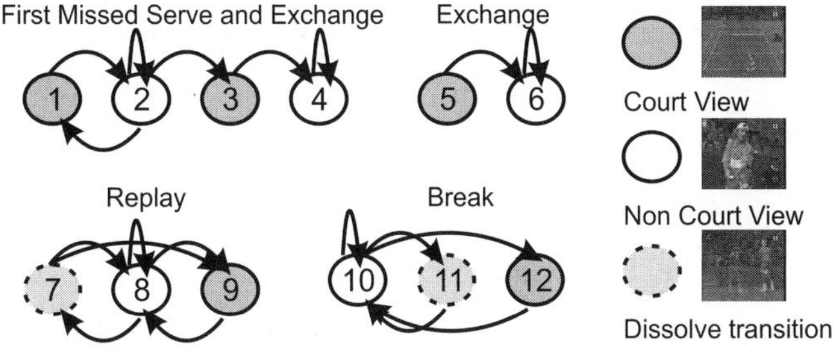

Fig. 3.2. HMM topology for the four main scenes.

where o_i^c, o_i^l, o_i^d respectively correspond to the visual similarity, the shot length and the dissolve features. Assuming the features in a feature vector are independent, segmentation into scenes of a sequence of N shot-based video feature vectors $o_{1:N}^{(\mathrm{v})}$ is classically solved by finding out the best state sequence according to

$$Q_{1:N}^* = \arg\max_{Q_{1:N}} \ln P(Q_{1:N}) + \sum_{i=1}^{N} \sum_{r \in \{c,l,d\}} \ln P(o_i^{\mathrm{r}}|Q_i) \ . \tag{3.2}$$

This baseline video only HMM based system achieves a shot classification rate of 76.3 % with recall and precision rates of respectively 73.4 % and 82.0 % (F-measure=77.5) for scene boundary detection.

3.3.2 Audiovisual integration

Audiovisual integration in the HMM framework can only be performed using the state synchronous multistream approach. To this end, three audio shot based features are extracted for each shot, based on the output of the sound class tracking algorithm. Hence, for each shot i, an audio feature vector

$$o_i^{(\mathrm{a})} = \left[o_i^{\mathrm{b}} \ o_i^{\mathrm{a}} \ o_i^{\mathrm{m}}\right] \tag{3.3}$$

is determined, where $o_i^{\mathrm{b}} = 1$ if ball hit sounds are present in the shot or 0 otherwise. The remaining features o_i^{a} and o_i^{m} represent the presence of applause and music respectively. Assuming the audio and visual features are independent, scene segmentation is carried out as previously with audiovisual feature vectors

$$o_i^{(\mathrm{av})} = \left[o_i^{(\mathrm{v})} \ o_i^{(\mathrm{a})}\right] \tag{3.4}$$

and the summation in (3.2) is extended to $r \in \{c, l, d, b, a, m\}$.

Using this state synchronous approach, a shot classification rate of 80.2 % was achieved with recall and precision rates of respectively 79.7 % and 84.7 % (F-measure=82.1).

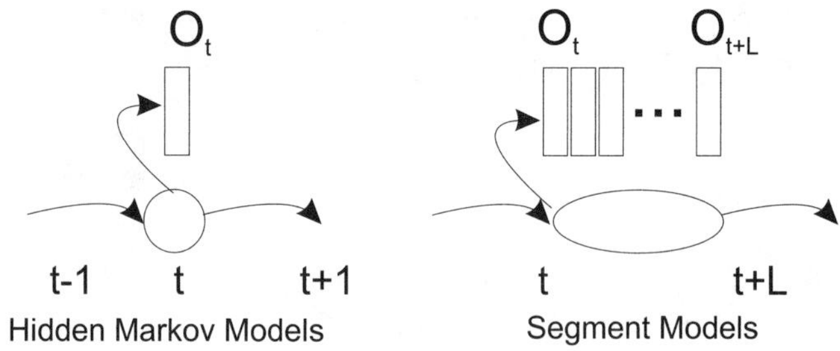

Fig. 3.3. Conceptual observation generation according to HMM (left) and to SM (right) (from [378]).

3.4 Segment models for video structuring

Apart from the fact that the audio description is rather crude and might contain errors from the sound tracking algorithm, shot based state synchronous feature fusion as introduced in the previous section has two main drawbacks. First, audio features are assumed to be synchronous with the shot boundaries. This is particularly problematic with the applause sound class since applause might start slightly before the end of a global court view. This results in $o_i^{\mathrm{a}} = 1$ for a shot which is not characterized by applause sounds that accounts for a small fraction of the shot duration. Second, and more importantly, the temporal order of the audio features cannot be taken into account. Indeed, from the audio feature vector point of view, a shot containing ball hit sounds followed by applause shares the same representation as a shot containing applause followed by ball hit sounds. Moreover, the temporal order of the audio features cannot be taken into account at the scene level.

Segment models offer a framework to overcome these limitations. We describe in this section the principle of SMs and the related decoding algorithm before discussing audiovisual integration in the following section.

3.4.1 Principle

Segment models were first introduced in speech recognition to overcome the known limitations of HMM [135, 378]. The main idea behind SMs is that a sequence of observations $o_{a:b}^{(\mathrm{v})}$, called *segment*, is associated to a state rather than a single observation $o_i^{(\mathrm{v})}$ as in HMM. This principle is illustrated in Fig. 3.3. The state conditional density is therefore defined over a segment, conditioned on the segment length l, $p(o_{a:b}^{(\mathrm{v})}|l, i)$. Associating sequences of observations with states also enables the use of a duration model $p(l|i)$ associated to each state i of a segment model. From a generative point of view, a segment model can be seen as a Markovian process where a hidden state emits a sequence of observations whose length is governed by a duration model before transiting to another state.

Decoding with SMs involves finding out the most likely state sequence *and* segmentation. Formally, the maximization problem to solve is defined as

$$(L^*_{1:M^*}, Q^*_{1:M^*}) = \arg\max_{L_{1:M}, Q_{1:M}} \ln p(Q_{1:M}) + \ln p(L_{1:M}|Q_{1:M}) + \ln p(o^{(v)}_{1:N}|L_{1:M}, Q_{1:M}) \ , \quad (3.5)$$

where N is the number of shots in the video, M^* is the number of segments found after optimization. Note that, as opposed to (3.2), the number of states – or, equivalently, segments – is also part of the optimization problem. The sequence $L^*_{1:M^*}$ represents the optimal segmentation where L_i represents the length of segment i, and $Q^*_{1:M^*}$ is the most likely state sequence. In practice, the segments are assumed to be independent conditionally to the state sequence and segmentation, as in HMM, and thus

$$\ln p(o^{(v)}_{1:N}|L_{1:M}, Q_{1:M}) = \sum_{i=1}^{M} \ln p(o^{(v)}_{s_i:e_i}|L_i, Q_i) \quad (3.6)$$

where s_i and e_i denotes the start and end shots of segment i. The maximization problem (3.5) is solved via a straightforward extension of the Viterbi algorithm to account for explicit state duration [420].

3.4.2 Modeling tennis videos with segment models

In the case of tennis videos, a scene corresponds to a segment. The segment model associated with an ergodic scene structure has therefore 4 states, each state corresponding to one of the scenes defined in Section 3.2. As in the case of HMM, there is a full ergodic scene structure, except for the non-allowed self-transitions for the *replay* and *break* scenes. This model is illustrated in Fig. 3.4 where a segment containing four shots is represented for the *missed serve plus rally* scene.

To fully define a segment model, one has to define the duration model and the state conditional probabilities. The former is straightforwardly defined on top of the segment duration in seconds, quantized into 30 bins in our experiments. For a SM with visual only attributes, one can define the state conditional probabilities $p(o^{(v)}_{a:b}|l, i)$, for a sequence $o^{(v)}_{a:b}$ of length l, using a HMM Λ_i to provide the probability of a sequence for the scene i according to

$$P(o^{(v)}_{a:b}|l, i) \equiv P(o^{(v)}_{a:b}|\Lambda_i) = \sum_{S_{1:l}} P(o^{(v)}_{a:b}, S_{1:l}|\Lambda_i) \ , \quad (3.7)$$

where the sum, carried out over all the possible state sequences in the model Λ_i, is computed using the forward-backward algorithm [420][7].

[7] For efficiency reasons during decoding, this score is computed using only the backward pass of the Baum-Welch recursion. Indeed, in SMs, one has to compute the state conditional probabilities for various segments which share the same end time. Using the backward pass, the result of the backward pass for the shortest segment can be cached and reused for the next segment and so on.

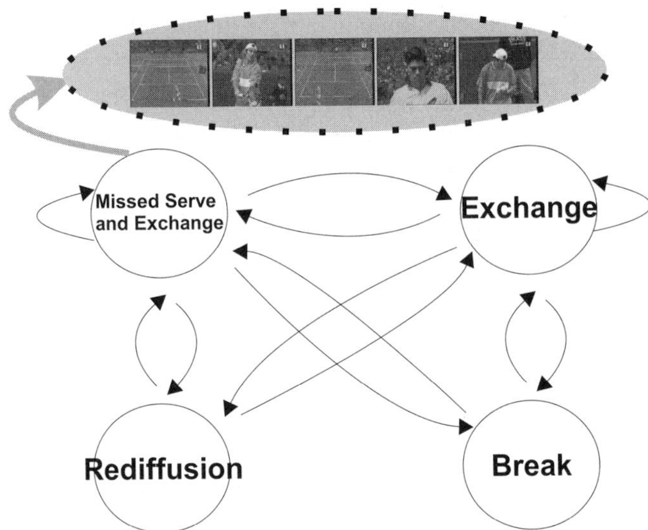

Fig. 3.4. SM-based modeling of the visual content as a succession of scenes.

It is important to note that the models Λ_i should not be confused with the HMM used in the previous section. Indeed, the models Λ_i are used essentially as observation *scorers*, *i.e.*, to provide a probability for a sequence, as opposed to the HMM used in the previous section to provide a segmentation. The first ones are used to provide a probability while the second ones provide a state sequence. However, we used the same topology for the HMM scorers in the SMs as the topology used in the HMM-based parser of Section 3.3.1. But parameter estimation is obviously different where the Baum-Welch algorithm is used in the first case while reference manual state alignments are used in the second case.

Based on this visual-only segment model, we achieved a shot classification rate of 79.7 %. The scene boundary recall and precision were respectively 74.8 % and 83.5 % (F-measure=78.9). These results are much better than the one obtained with the visual-only HMM approach which, we recall, yielded a classification rate of 76.3 % and a F-measure of 77.5. Additional experiments show that this gain is mostly due to the scene duration model in segment models.

3.5 Audiovisual integration with segment models

Now that we have defined a segment model approach for tennis structure analysis based on video only features, we present audiovisual fusion strategies in the segment model framework. In the scope of this chapter, we present only some of the possibilities that were studied to illustrate the potential of SMs for multimodal integration of loosely synchronous streams. More results and a deeper analysis of the results can be found in [128]. Results for the various approaches presented here are given at the end of the section.

A first straightforward approach for audiovisual integration in segment model implements the early fusion scheme discussed in Section 3.3.2. Indeed, rather than defining the segment models on the features $o_i^{(\mathrm{v})}$, one can directly use the feature space $o_i^{(\mathrm{av})}$ as the observation space of the SMs.

However, interestingly, SMs offer the potential of fusion at the scene level rather than at the shot level, following the multistream model paradigm with synchronization points at scene boundaries. A crucial difference with multi-stream HMM is that the synchronization points are no longer a priori fixed but left to the optimization problem. If we assume state conditional independence between the audio and visual information streams, we can recombine the conditional probabilities at the state level according to

$$p(o_{a:b}^{(\mathrm{av})}|l,i) = p(o_{a:b}^{(\mathrm{v})}|l_{\mathrm{v}},i)\; p(o_{a:b}^{(\mathrm{a})}|l_{\mathrm{a}},i) \enspace , \tag{3.8}$$

where l_{v} is the (quantized) segment length in seconds and l_{a} the number of samples in the audio stream in the segment $[a,b]$. Note that we allow the segment to have different length in each modality. Also note that, in practice, a weighted combination of log-probabilities can be used though we did not apply it in this study. The probability $p(o_{a:b}^{(\mathrm{v})}|l_{\mathrm{v}},i)$ can be defined as previously for the visual-only segment model. We present results for three models for the computation of the audio conditional probability $p(o_{a:b}^{(\mathrm{v})}|l_{\mathrm{a}},i)$ based on bigrams of audio events and on cepstral or discrete audio features HMM.

3.5.1 Scene-based discrete audio models

As discussed in the introduction to this section, one of the problems related to the early fusion scheme is the impossibility of representing the dynamics of the audio features within a scene. The fusion at the scene level enables to capture the temporal nature of the audio stream. Two models were studied for the scene-based integration of discrete audio features derived from the output of the sound class tracking algorithm.

A first approach consists in representing $p(o_{a:b}^{(\mathrm{a})}|l_{\mathrm{a}},i)$ using HMM scorers $\Lambda_i^{(\mathrm{a})}$ as for the visual modality. Basically, the models used here correspond to the audio part of the audiovisual models used for early integration, the feature vectors being defined as in (3.3). The key difference with early integration is that the audio and visual HMM are now completely independent – and thus asynchronous – within a scene.

A second approach is based on a bigram model of the sequences of audio events, where the conditional probability is given by

$$p(o_{a:b}^{(\mathrm{a})}|l_{\mathrm{a}},i) = \prod_{k=1}^{l_{\mathrm{a}}} p(o_{a:b}^{(\mathrm{a})}(k) \mid o_{a:b}^{(\mathrm{a})}(k-1), i) \enspace , \tag{3.9}$$

where $o^{(a)}_{a:b}(k)$ denotes the kth audio event in the segment $o^{(a)}_{a:b}$ and l_{a} the number of audio events. For example, if a segment contains tennis sounds followed by claps, the probability is given by

$$p(\text{tennis}, \text{claps}|l_{\text{a}}, i) = p(\text{tennis}|\text{<s>}, i)\, p(\text{claps}|\text{tennis}, i)\, p(\text{</s>}|\text{claps}, i) \ .$$

The two symbols $<s>$ and $</s>$ denotes respectively the start and end of the segment. The probabilities are estimated from the training corpus using a simple back-off scheme to avoid null probabilities for unobserved events.

3.5.2 Low-level audio models

So far, modeling the audio stream relies on the output of the sound class tracking algorithm. However, the tracking algorithm is error-prone and imprecise. First, the boundaries of the audio segments are not as clearly defined as hard cuts in the video and their detection is not precise. Second, simultaneous events, like ball hits simultaneously with speech, makes the decision process more fragile. To circumvent these problems, scene-level integration with segment models enable to directly model low-level audio features such as cepstral coefficients, thus avoiding the necessity for an error-prone pre classification step. In order to model the audio content on top of generic cepstral features, continuous density HMM are used.

Because of the fair amount of prior information embedded in the sound class detection process (see Section 3.5.3), we do not expect this approach to outperform the previous ones. However, this model illustrates the potential of SMs for the integration of asynchronous heterogeneous streams of information. Indeed, the audio stream is sampled now at 100 frames per second while the visual stream exhibits a classical shot rate. The length l_{a} of the auditory segment is now equal to the total number of audio frames within the scene boundaries.

3.5.3 Results

Results for the various audiovisual fusion approach are reported in Table 3.1. The first two lines report results obtained with HMM and SM using an early integration scheme. As previously for visual only models, SMs outperform significantly HMMs.

The results in the next two lines correspond to the scene level integration using discrete audio events using either audio HMM or a bigram model. Both approaches are roughly equivalent in terms of performance with a slight advantage to discrete audio HMM scorers. However, scene-level integration exhibits poorer results than early integration. Additional experiments demonstrated that this result is due to the fact that some important correlations at the shot level between the audio and visual features are lost in the asynchronous approaches. Indeed, the asynchrony hypothesis between the two streams does

model	%C	F	%R	%P
HMM early integration	80.2	82.1	79.7	84.7
SM early integration	84.4	82.6	79.3	86.2
SM + audio HMM	81.5	82.3	77.5	87.8
SM + audio bigram	81.7	81.7	79.4	84.1
SM + cepstral HMM	79.9	79.6	75.2	84.6
SM early int. + audio bigram	84.7	82.9	81.7	84.1

Table 3.1. Classification and segmentation results for the various audio visual integration approaches in HMM and SM. Results are given for shot classification rate (%C), F-measure (F), recall (%R) and precision (%P).

not really hold in the case of tennis videos. However, these results demonstrate that SMs provide a powerful framework for modeling asynchronous streams. Moreover, SMs allow the combination of early and late (scene-level) integration where a bigram model of audio event is combined at the scene level with the output of an audiovisual HMM scorer. Results show that an interesting performance gain can be obtained by combining early and late integration (SM early int. + audio bigram in Table 3.1).

Finally, results obtained with an audio model on low level audio features demonstrate the ability of SMs to incorporate heterogeneous information streams with different sample rates, even though the results are not as good as those obtained with a preprocessing of the audio track using the sound class tracking algorithm. Indeed, preprocessing introduces a great deal of prior information on what the useful information is, prior knowledge that is not present in the cepstral HMM approach. However, performance obtained with low level audio features are close to the performance obtained with segment models and discrete audio HMM, in spite of the loss of prior information.

3.6 Hierarchical models

On top of the scene structure that we have tried to recover so far, tennis games exhibit a highly hierarchical structure with transitions between games, sets and points, with pauses between points at regular intervals as directed by the tennis rules. This structural information can be used in both the HMM and SM framework to help scene segmentation and recover the game structure in terms of sets and points.

The hierarchical structure of a tennis match can be represented as a directed graph as depicted in Fig. 3.5, where, for sake of legibility, only one node is expanded at each level. Note that this graph is a simplified version of the true structure imposed by the tennis rules. At the highest level is the match. At the next level, a match is composed of sets, eventually followed by a *break* scene. At the third level, a set is composed of games and *break* scenes, where tennis rules instruct that there should be a break after the first game of

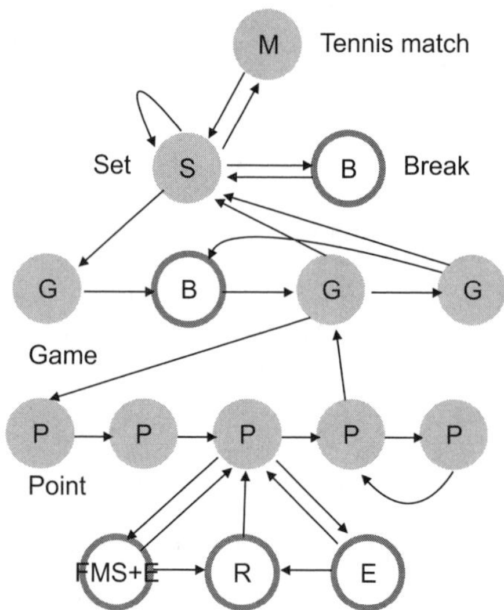

Fig. 3.5. Hierarchical structure of a tennis match in terms of game, sets and points.

the set or, subsequently, after any two consecutive games so that the players change positions. A game is composed of at least four points where a point corresponds to one of the scenes *missed serve plus rally* or *rally*, optionally followed by a *break* scene.

Based on this structural representation of the match as a graph, we can replace the scene ergodic topology that was previously used by the hierarchic one. In the HMM framework, the states corresponding to actual scenes (circled states in Fig. 3.5) are further expanded with the respective HMM as defined in Fig. 3.2. In the SM framework, these states are directly the emitting states.

Experimental results demonstrated that the hierarchical approach enables to partially recover the structure of the tennis match but does not improve the scene classification and segmentation results. For example, with SMs, we achieved a scene classification rate of 81.2 % with the hierarchical topology as opposed to 81.7 % with an ergodic scene structure whereas F measures are comparable. We believe that results with the hierarchical topology could be improved using probabilistic transitions in the hierarchical structure. Indeed, due to the limited amount of training data, we did not use stochastic transitions in the graph representing the tennis match structure.

3.7 Integrating symbolic text information

In sports videos, the score is often displayed on screen from time to time. For example, in tennis videos, the score in the current set is regularly displayed, usually – but not always – after a point. Assuming the displayed scores have

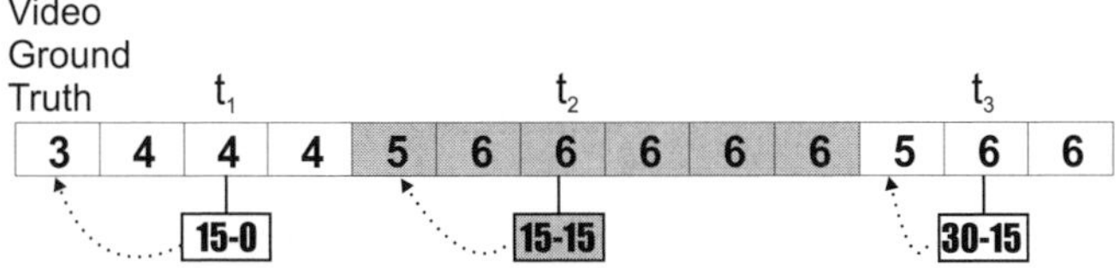

Fig. 3.6. Typical setting for the appearance of score labels w.r.t. game events and scenes. State numbers in the video ground truth refers to Fig. 3.2 where states 3 and 5 correspond to actual points. The dotted lines show the actual rally to which the score display correspond.

been recognized by some automatic optical character recognition system, the resulting symbolic stream of information provides useful hints on the game structure that we wish to exploit. However, due to the symbolic and sporadic nature of this information stream, integrating the score information in a stochastic model is not straightforward. Indeed, score labels are sporadic in the sense that they are displayed from time to time and at no particular instant.

A straightforward and somewhat naive solution to take into account score labels is to enhance the shot based audiovisual feature vectors $o_i^{(\mathrm{av})}$ with a new binary feature indicating whether a score is displayed in the shot or not. In SMs, this additional feature can be integrated at the scene level rather than at the shot level where the conditional probability (3.8) is replaced by

$$p(o_{a:b}^{(\mathrm{av})}|l,i) = p(o_{a:b}^{(\mathrm{v})}|l_{\mathrm{v}},i)\; p(o_{a:b}^{(\mathrm{a})}|l_{\mathrm{a}},i)\; p^l(o_{a:b}^{(\mathrm{s})}|l,i) \;, \tag{3.10}$$

where the probability $p(o_{a:b}^{(\mathrm{s})}|l,i)$ that a score label appears in the scene i is raised to the power l so that it scales with the segment length in the same way as the other two probabilities. Using a binary score indicator feature slightly improves the results both with HMMs and SMs. In the first case, the shot classification rate improved from 80.2 % to 80.8 % and the F measure on scene boundaries from 82.1 to 83.0, with an increase in both precision and recall while for SMs only a marginal improvement was observed.

In the previous approach, the semantic meaning of the label, *i.e.*, the score itself, is ignored and the label is merely used as an indicator that a point has been scored. We propose an algorithm, called *score-oriented Viterbi search*, to use the score labels themselves as constraints in the search for the best path in order to find a segmentation consistent with the score labels available. As it operates on the search space, this algorithm can be used both with HMM and SMs.

3.7.1 Score-oriented Viterbi search

Before proceeding to the description of the algorithm, let us examine how score labels are displayed (when they are). Score labels appear after the corresponding game event has happened and also before the next game event. A typical setting is illustrated in Fig. 3.6, where we see three score labels and the corresponding rallies. Clearly, the point acknowledged by the label appearing at $t2$ lies in $[t1, t2]$. The complete scene that contains the rally, in turn, ends somewhere in $[t1, t3]$.

The key idea of score-oriented decoding is to perform a local Viterbi forward pass between $t1$ and $t3$ with an N-best like scheme in order to keep track of the paths resulting in respectively one point, two points, up to N points. All the paths in the time interval $[t1, t3]$ that are inconsistent with the score indication are then penalized. In the example of Fig. 3.6, exactly one scoring event must occur between the labels '15-0' and '15-15'. All the paths between $t1$ and $t3$ containing zero or more than one point are therefore penalized. We refer to this first step, consisting of the local forward Viterbi pass and the penalization of the inconsistent paths, as *local search*. After performing the local search corresponding to the label occurring at time $t2$ between $t1$ and $t3$, the algorithm proceeds with the label occurring at time $t3$. The new local search relies on the best paths up to $t3$ *and* on the results of the previous local search between $t2$ and $t3$. The decoding algorithm can therefore be seen as a pipeline of local searches where the surviving paths are further developed. A formal description of the algorithm is given in [127].

Upon reaching the end of the video, backtracking is used to obtain a segmentation consistent with all the score labels available. It can be shown that this algorithm is optimal in the sense that it finds out the most likely segmentation consistent with the score labels, assuming N, the maximum allowed number of points scored between two label appearances, is large enough. We observed that a maximum of five points between two score display turned out sufficient.

In practice, the exact number of points between two labels is not deterministic[8] and the penalty depends on the estimation of the probability that n points are scored between two specific labels. These probabilities are estimated from the training corpus. It is interesting to note that if these probabilities are estimated using score labels extracted with an automatic algorithm rather than manually, then they are able to partially compensate for errors in the automatic detection algorithm. Indeed, in this case, detection errors are taken into account in the penalty function which tends to be more uniform as more errors occur.

3.7.2 Results

Table 3.2 reports the results for score-oriented Viterbi search with hierarchic and ergodic scene structure for the HMM and SMs where, in the latter, a bigram model of discrete audio events is used to model the audio stream. These results are to be compared with those of Table 3.1, rows 1 and 4 respectively. Clearly, in all the cases, a significant performance gain is obtained

[8] For example, between two consecutive occurrences of the label '*equality*', there can be two, four, six, . . . points.

	HMM				segment models			
	%C	F	%R	%P	%C	F	%R	%P
hierarchical	82.7	82.4	80.5	84.3	85.8	84.0	82.9	85.2
ergodic	82.2	82.9	82.4	83.4	86.0	84.1	83.4	84.9
error rate = 10 %	81.6	83.0	82.2	83.9	85.6	84.1	82.8	85.5
error rate = 50 %	81.1	82.5	80.7	84.4	84.2	83.5	80.2	87.0

Table 3.2. Classification and segmentation results for score-oriented Viterbi decoding.

using score information as proposed. Two interesting points are worth noting. Firstly, the improvement is larger with SMs than with HMMs. This can be explained by the fact that the positions of the occurrences of the score labels provide some rough approximations of the scene boundaries, giving some extra valuable information for Viterbi decoding in SMs. Secondly, although the results obtained with the hierarchical scene structure do not outperform those obtained with the ergodic one (for reasons discussed earlier in the chapter), the gap between the two structures is obviously reduced with score-oriented decoding, due to the additional information on the game structure carried by the score labels.

So far, we have considered error-free extraction of score labels from the video frames. The only source of uncertainty on the number of points scored between two labels is therefore due to the scoring scheme of tennis (for example between two '*equality*' labels) combined with the fact that not all labels are displayed. We therefore simulated score label recognition errors with an error rate of respectively 10 % and 50 %. Recall that the penalties applied to inconsistent paths in score-oriented decoding are re-estimated on the erroneous labeling to compensate for label recognition errors. Results reported in the last two rows of Table 3.2 show that performance slowly degrades toward those obtained with the standard Viterbi algorithm as more recognition errors occur, hence demonstrating a strong robustness of our algorithm to label recognition errors.

3.8 Discussion

This chapter has presented a new statistical framework for multimodal integration based on multistream segment models, a generalization of multistream hidden Markov models. Experimental results on a tennis video structuring task show that segment models offer an increased flexibility for audiovisual integration of loosely synchronous modalities. However, the visual and audio tracks in tennis videos are strongly synchronous and most of the gain obtained with segment models is due to the introduction of a scene duration model. Even though, we have seen that the increased flexibility offered by segment models enable to combine synchronous (early) and asynchronous (late) integration of the modalities, which resulted in the best system. In this sense, segment models unify multistream and layered approaches and are thus able to overcome most of the limits observed with hidden Markov models, in particular the need for synchronization between the information streams and the difficulty to capture information at various semantic levels.

Some sporadic and very loosely synchronized information streams, such as the score labels displayed in sport videos, are however still difficult to integrate as features in the segment model framework. The score-oriented Viterbi search discussed in this chapter addresses this problem by proposing a framework to take this information into account at the search level in a rather efficient way. We believe that this search-level integration scheme is suited for various type of sporadic information streams. For example, we have used a similar idea in [188] to drive a speech recognition Viterbi decoder with broad phonetic landmarks used as constraints on the search for the best path in the decoding graph. Clearly, integrating information as constraints on the search can be seen as a late integration fusion scheme where information obtained from a first system are used as constraints in the second system. Confidence measures associated with the decisions from the first system should be able to circumvent problems due to error propagation across systems in late integration schemes. We plan to investigate this integration scheme further in several domains.

An interesting feature of segment models is that the model can be expressed as a dynamic Bayesian network (DBN) as shown in [350]. We believe that DBN provide an interesting framework for the joint modeling of heterogeneous, loosely synchronized streams of information as arbitrary dependencies between the variables of a problem can be expressed in this framework (as long as cycles are avoided). However, the lack of generic algorithms for parameter estimation and the rapidly increasing complexity of the decoding algorithm when complex models are used has limited so far the use of DBN models for complex multimodal integration problems. We hope that segment models will provide a bridge toward DBN-based models for multimodal integration, enabling to go beyond segment models.

Finally, let us conclude this discussion by stating the obvious: the use of multistream segment models for multimodal integration is *not* limited to sport videos. Neither is multimodal fusion using information integration at the search level. In fact, segment models provide an interesting framework in many applications where limited correlation and synchrony between the streams of information is observed. A first example is audiovisual speech recognition where segment models can provide extended asynchrony at the phone or viseme boundaries thus providing a powerful framework for the integration of fast changing audio features with visual features which tends to change at a slower rate due to the inertia of the facial muscles. A second example is the use of segment models for natural language processing and integration in a multimodal multimedia application. For example, Utiyama and Isahara defined a model which can be formulated as a segment model for the segmentation of texts into topics [537]. This approach enables the integration of textual information streams into segment models, for example for spoken document segmentation and structuring based on lexical, acoustic and maybe visual cues, as illustrated in Chapter 9.

4

Adaptive Multimodal Fusion by Uncertainty Compensation with Application to Audio-Visual Speech Recognition

George Papandreou, Athanassios Katsamanis, Vassilis Pitsikalis, and Petros Maragos

National Technical University of Athens, Athens, Greece

While the accuracy of feature measurements heavily depends on changing environmental conditions, studying the consequences of this fact in pattern recognition tasks has received relatively little attention to date. In this chapter we discuss the effects of feature measurement uncertainty on classification and learning rules. Such an approach can be particularly fruitful in multimodal fusion scenarios, such as audiovisual speech recognition, where multiple streams of complementary time-evolving features are integrated. For such applications, provided that the measurement noise uncertainty for each feature stream can be estimated, this framework leads to highly adaptive multimodal fusion rules which are widely applicable and easy to implement. We further show that more traditional multimodal fusion methods relying on stream weights fall under this scheme under certain assumptions; this provides novel insights into their applicability for various tasks and suggests new practical ways for estimating the stream weights adaptively. The potential of the approach is demonstrated in audiovisual speech recognition experiments using either synchronous or asynchronous models.

4.1 Multimodal Fusion: Benefits and Challenges

Motivated by the multimodal way humans perceive their environment, complementary information sources have been successfully utilized in many applications. Such a case is audiovisual speech recognition (AV-ASR) [413], where fusing visual and audio cues can lead to improved performance in comparison to audio-only recognition, especially in the presence of audio noise.

However, successfully integrating heterogeneous information streams is challenging, mainly because multimodal schemes need to adapt to dynamic environmental conditions, which can dissimilarly affect the reliability of the separate modalities by contaminating feature measurements with noise. For

P. Maragos et al. (eds.), *Multimodal Processing and Interaction*,
DOI: 10.1007/978-0-387-76316-3_4, © Springer Science+Business Media, LLC 2008

example, the visual stream in AV-ASR should be discounted when the visual front-end momentarily mistracks the speaker's face.

A common theme in many stream integration methods is the utilization of stream weights to equalize the different modalities. These weights operate as exponents to each stream's probability density and have been employed in fusion tasks of different audio streams [344] and audiovisual integration [147, 412]. Such stream weights have been applied not only in conventional Hidden Markov Models, but also in conjunction with Dynamic Bayesian Network architectures which better account for the asynchronicity of audiovisual speech [362]. Despite its favorable experimental properties, stream weighting requires setting the weights for the different streams; although various methods have been proposed for this purpose [184], a rigorous approach to adapt the stream weights is still missing.

In this chapter, building on the recent work of [248, 404, 389], we approach the problem of adaptive multimodal fusion by explicitly taking feature measurement uncertainty of the different modalities into account, both during model training and testing. In single modality scenarios, modeling feature noise has proven fruitful for noise-robust ASR [135, 442, 577, 130] and has been further pursued in applications such as speaker verification [578] and multi-band ASR [344]. We show in a probabilistic framework how multimodal learning and classification rules should be adjusted to account for feature measurement uncertainty. Gaussian Mixture Models (GMM) and Hidden Markov Models (HMM) are discussed in detail and modified algorithms for classification and EM maximum-likelihood estimation under uncertainty are derived. Uncertainty compensation leads to adaptive multimodal fusion rules which are widely applicable and easy to implement. We demonstrate that previous stream weight-based multimodal fusion formulations can be derived from the uncertainty-aware scheme under certain assumptions; this unveils their probabilistic underpinnings and provides novel insights into their applicability for various tasks. In this context, new practical ways for estimating stream weights adaptively are suggested. Regarding audiovisual speech, we describe techniques to extract uncertainty estimates for the visual and audio features and evaluate the method in AV-ASR experiments utilizing multi-stream HMM, demonstrating improved performance. Applying the proposed technique in conjunction with Product HMMs (P-HMM) [147, 312], which better account for cross-modal asynchrony, can yield further improvements.

4.2 Feature Uncertainty and Multimodal Fusion

Let us consider a pattern classification scenario. We measure a property (feature) of a pattern instance and try to decide to which of N classes $c_i, i = 1 \dots N$ it should be assigned. The measurement is a realization x of a random variable X, whose statistics differ for the N classes. Typically, for each class we have trained a model that captures these statistics and represents the class-conditional probability functions $p(x|c_i), i = 1 \dots N$. Our decision is then based on some proper rule, *e.g.*, the Maximum A Posteriori (MAP) criterion $\hat{c} = \text{argmax}\, p(c_i|x) = \text{argmax}\, p(x|c_i)p(c_i)$.

One may identify three major sources of uncertainty that could perplex classification. First, *class overlap* due to improper modeling or limited discriminability of the feature set for the classification task. For instance, visual cues cannot discriminate between members of the same viseme class (*e.g.*, /p/, /b/) [413]. Better choice of features and modeling schemes can reduce this uncertainty. Second, *parameter estimation uncertainty* that mainly originates from insufficient training. Using the Bayesian Predictive Classification rule can possibly alleviate it [220]. Third, *feature observation uncertainty* due to errors in the measurement process or noise contamination. This is the type of uncertainty we mainly address in this chapter.

4.2.1 Feature Observation Uncertainty and its Compensation in Classification

We can formulate feature observation uncertainty considering that the actual feature measurement y is just a noisy/corrupted version of the inaccessible clean feature x. More specifically, we adopt the measurement model

$$Y = X + E\,, \tag{4.1}$$

which is graphically depicted in Fig. 4.1 and assume that the noise density $p_E(e)$ is known. This scenario of contaminated measurements corresponds to the so-called *measurement error* models in statistics [172]. Under the observation model of Eq. (4.1), classification decisions must rely on $p(c_i|y) \propto p_Y(y|c_i)p(c_i)$, and thus $p_Y(y|c_i)$ needs to be computed.

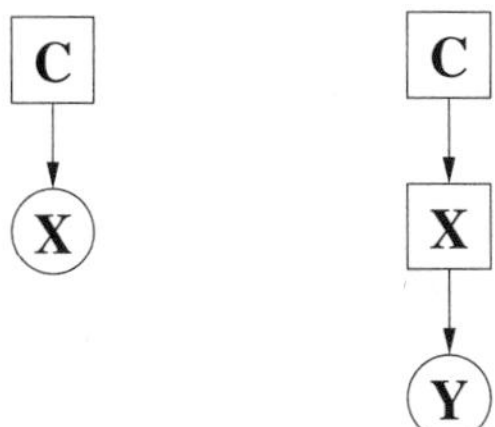

Fig. 4.1. Pictorial representation of feature measurement scenarios, with hidden variables denoted by squares and observed by circles. *Left*: Conventional case – we observe the features x directly. *Right*: Noisy measurement case – we only observe noisy features y.

To determine the desirable noisy feature probability density function $p_Y(y|c_i)$, we need to integrate out the clean feature variable x

$$p_Y(y|c_i) = \int p_X(x|c_i) p_E(y - x)\, dx. \tag{4.2}$$

Although the integral in Eq. (4.2) is in general intractable, we can obtain a closed-form solution in the important special case of Gaussian data model, $p_X(x|c_i) = N(x; \mu_i, \Sigma_i)$, with Gaussian observation noise, $p_E(e) = N(e; \mu_e, \Sigma_e)$. Then one can show that $p_Y(y|c_i)$ is given by

$$p_Y(y|c_i) = N(y; \mu_i + \mu_e, \Sigma_i + \Sigma_e), \tag{4.3}$$

implying that we can proceed by considering our features y clean, provided that we shift the model means by μ_e and increase the model covariances Σ_i by Σ_e. A similar approach has been previously followed in [442, 578, 130].

To illustrate Eq. (4.3), we discuss with reference to Fig. 4.2 how observation uncertainty influences decisions in a simple 2-class classification task. The two classes are modeled by 2D spherical Gaussian distributions, $N(\mu_1, \sigma_1^2 I)$, $N(\mu_2, \sigma_2^2 I)$ and they have equal prior probability. If our observation y contains zero mean spherical Gaussian noise with covariance matrix $\sigma_e^2 I$ then the modified decision boundary consists of those y for which $N(y; \mu_1, \sigma_1^2 I + \sigma_e^2 I) = N(y; \mu_2, \sigma_2^2 I + \sigma_e^2 I)$. When σ_e^2 is zero, the decision should be made as in the clean case. If σ_e^2 is comparable to the variances of the models, then the modified boundary significantly differs from the original one and neglecting observation uncertainty in the decision process increases misclassifications.

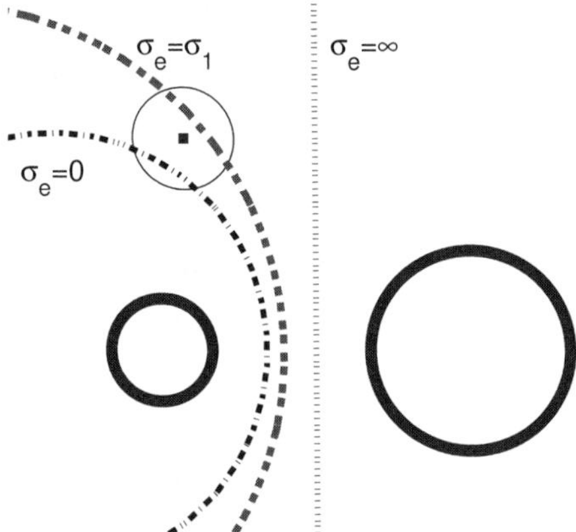

Fig. 4.2. Decision boundaries for classification of a noisy observation (square marker) in two classes, shown as circles, for various observation noise variances. Classes are modeled by spherical Gaussians of means μ_1, μ_2 and variances $\sigma_1^2 I$, $\sigma_2^2 I$ respectively. The decision boundary is plotted for three values of noise variance (a) $\sigma_e = 0$ (*i.e.*, no observation uncertainty), (b) $\sigma_e = \sigma_1$, and (c) $\sigma_e = \infty$. With increasing noise variance, the boundary moves away from its noise-free position.

4.2.2 Multimodal Fusion

For many applications one can get improved performance by exploiting complementary features, stemming from a single or multiple modalities. Let us assume that one wants to integrate S information streams which produce feature vectors $x_s, s = 1, \ldots, S$. If the features are statistically independent given the class label c, the conditional probability of the full observation vector $x_{1:S} \equiv (x_1; \ldots; x_S)$ is given by the product rule; application of Bayes' formula yields the class label probability given the features:

$$p(c|x_{1:S}) \propto p(c) \prod_{s=1}^{S} p(x_s|c) \,. \tag{4.4}$$

In an attempt to improve classification performance, several authors have introduced stream weights w_s as exponents in Eq. (4.4), resulting in the modified expression

$$b(c|x_{1:S}) = p(c) \prod_{s=1}^{S} p(x_s|c)^{w_s} \,, \tag{4.5}$$

which can be seen in a logarithmic scale as a weighted average of individual stream log-probabilities. Such schemes have been motivated by potential differences in reliability among different information streams, and larger weights are assigned to information streams with better classification performance. Using such weighting mechanisms has been experimentally proven to be beneficial for feature integration in both intra-modal (*e.g.*, multiband audio [344]) and inter-modal (*e.g.*, audiovisual speech recognition [147, 184, 362]) scenarios.

The stream weights formulation is however unsatisfactory in various respects. From a theoretical viewpoint, the weighted score b in Eq. (4.5) no longer has the probabilistic interpretation of Eq. (4.4) as class probability given the full observation vector $x_{1:S}$. Therefore it becomes unclear how to conceptually define, let alone implement, standard probabilistic operations, such as integrating-out a variable x_s (in the case of missing features), or conditioning the score on some other available information. From a more practical standpoint, it is not straightforward how to optimally select stream weights. Most authors set them discriminatively for a given set of environment conditions (*e.g.*, audio noise level in the case of audiovisual speech recognition) by minimizing the classification error on a held-out set, and then keep them constant throughout the recognition phase. However, this is insufficient, since attaining optimal performance requires that we dynamically adjust the share of each stream in the decision process, *e.g.*, to account for visual tracking failures in the AV-ASR case. Although there have been some efforts towards dynamically adjustable stream weights [184], they are not rigorously justified and are difficult to generalize.

We will now show that accounting for feature uncertainty naturally leads to a novel adaptive mechanism for fusion of different information sources. Since in our stochastic measurement framework we do not have direct access to the features x_s, our decision mechanism depends on the noisy version $y_s = x_s + e_s$ of the underlying quantity. The probability of interest is thus obtained by integrating out the hidden clean features x_s, *i.e.*,

$$p(c|y_{1:S}) \propto p(c) \prod_{s=1}^{S} \int p(x_s|c) p(y_s|x_s) dx_s \,. \tag{4.6}$$

In the common case that the clean feature emission probability is modeled as a Gaussian mixture model (GMM), *i.e.*,

$$p(x_s|c) = \sum_{m=1}^{M_{s,c}} \rho_{s,c,m} N(x_s; \mu_{s,c,m}, \Sigma_{s,c,m}), \tag{4.7}$$

and the observation noise at each stream is considered independent across streams and Gaussian, $p(y_s|x_s) = N(y_s; x_s + \mu_{e,s}, \Sigma_{e,s})$, it directly follows that

$$p(c|y_{1:S}) \propto p(c) \prod_{s=1}^{S} \sum_{m=1}^{M_{s,c}} \rho_{s,c,m} N(y_s; \mu_{s,c,m} + \mu_{e,s}, \Sigma_{s,c,m} + \Sigma_{e,s}) \,, \tag{4.8}$$

which, as in the single-stream case (4.3), involves considering our features y_s clean, while shifting the model means by $\mu_{e,s}$, and increasing the model covariances $\Sigma_{s,c,m}$ by $\Sigma_{e,s}$. Using mixtures of Gaussians for the measurement noise $p(y_s|x_s)$ is straightforward and could be useful in case of heavy-tailed noise distribution or for modeling observation outliers. Also note that, although the measurement noise covariance matrix $\Sigma_{e,s}$ of each stream is the same for all classes c and all mixture components m, noise particularly affects the most peaked mixtures, for which $\Sigma_{e,s}$ is substantial relative to the modeling uncertainty due to $\Sigma_{s,c,m}$. The adaptive fusion effect of feature uncertainty compensation in a simple 2-class classification task using two streams is illustrated in Fig. 4.3.

Although Eq. (4.8) is conceptually simple and easy to implement, given an estimate of the measurement noise variance $\Sigma_{e,s}$ of each stream, it actually constitutes a highly adaptive rule for multisensor fusion. To appreciate this, and also to show how our scheme is related to the stream weights formulation of Eq. (4.5), we examine a particularly illuminating special case of our result. We make two simplifying assumptions:

1. The measurement noise covariance is a scaled version of the model covariance, *i.e.*, $\Sigma_{es} = r_{s,c,m} \Sigma_{s,c,m}$ for some positive constant $r_{s,c,m}$ interpreted as the relative measurement error. Intuitively, as the SNR for the s-stream drops, the corresponding relative measurement error $r_{s,c,m}$ increases.
2. For every stream observation y_s the Gaussian mixture response of that stream is dominated by a single component m_0 or, equivalently, there is little overlap among different Gaussian mixtures.

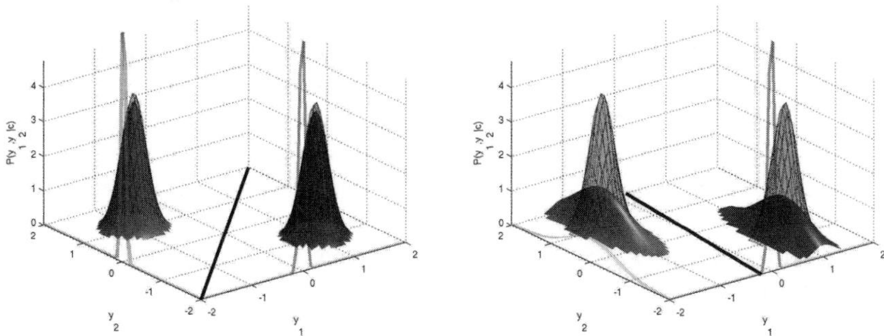

Fig. 4.3. Multimodal variance compensation leads to adaptive fusion. Figures describe a 2-class classification scenario, using two Gaussian feature streams, y_1 and y_2, with equal model covariances $\Sigma_{s,c} = \sigma^2$. The 1-D plots on the y_1 and y_2 axes represent the measurement uncertainty in the corresponding stream. *Left*: Conventional negligible measurement uncertainty scenario; the decision boundary lies on the axes' diagonal. *Right*: Significant measurement noise at the y_2 stream, $\Sigma_{e,2} \gg \Sigma_{e,1}$, in which case $p(y_S|c)$ (solid surfaces) differ significantly from $p(x_S|c)$ (transparent surfaces); the decision boundary moves and classification is mostly influenced by the reliable y_1 stream.

Under these conditions the Gaussian densities in Eq. (4.8) can be approximated by $N(y_s; \mu_{s,c,m_0}+\mu_{es}, (1+r_{s,c,m_0})\Sigma_{s,c,m_0})$; using the power-of-Gaussian identity $N(x; \mu, w^{-1}\Sigma) = (\det(w(2\pi\Sigma)^{w-1}))^{1/2} N(x; \mu, \Sigma)^w \propto N(x; \mu, \Sigma)^w$ yields

$$p(c|y_{1:S}) \propto p(c) \prod_{s=1}^{S} \left[\tilde{\rho}_{s,c,m_0} N(y_s; \mu_{s,c,m_0} + \mu_{e,s}, \Sigma_{s,c,m_0}) \right]^{w_{s,c,m_0}}, \quad (4.9)$$

where

$$w_{s,c,m_0} = 1/(1 + r_{s,c,m_0}) \quad (4.10)$$

is the *effective stream weight* and $\tilde{\rho}_{s,c,m_0}$ is a properly modified mixture weight which is independent of the observation y_s. Note that the effective stream weights are between 0 (for $r_{s,c,m_0} \gg 1$) and 1 (for $r_{s,c,m_0} \approx 0$) and discount the contribution of each stream to the final result by properly taking its relative measurement error into account; however they do not need to satisfy a sum-to-one constraint $\sum_{s=1}^{S} w_{s,c,m_0} = 1$, as is conventionally considered by other authors.

This is an appealing result. Our framework unveils the probabilistic assumptions under stream weight-based formulations; furthermore, Eq. (4.10) provides a rigorous mechanism to select for each new measurement y_s and uncertainty estimate $(\mu_{e,s}, \Sigma_{e,s})$ all involved stream weights *fully adaptively*, *i.e.*, with respect to both class label c and mixture component m.

4.3 Uncertainty in Expectation-Maximization Training

In many real-world applications requiring big volumes of training data, very accurate training sets collected under strictly controlled conditions are very difficult to gather. For example, in audiovisual speech recognition it is unrealistic to assume that a human expert annotates each frame in the training videos. A usual compromise is to adopt a semi-automatic annotation technique which yields a sufficiently diverse training set; since such a technique can introduce non-negligible feature errors in the training set, it is important to take training set feature uncertainty into account in learning procedures.

4.3.1 GMM Training Under Uncertainty

Under our feature uncertainty viewpoint, only a noisy version y of the underlying true property x can be observed. Maximum-likelihood estimation of the GMM parameters θ from a training set $\mathcal{Y} = \{y_1, \ldots, y_N\}$ under the EM algorithm [129] should thus consider the corresponding clean features $\mathcal{X}$, besides the class memberships $\mathcal{M}$, as hidden variables. The expected complete-data log-likelihood $Q(\theta, \theta') = E[\log p(\mathcal{Y}, \{\mathcal{X}, \mathcal{M}\}|\theta)|\mathcal{Y}, \theta']$ of the parameters θ in the EM algorithm's current iteration given the previous guess θ' in the **E-step** should thus be obtained by summing over discrete and integrating over continuous hidden variables. In the single stream case this translates to

$$
\begin{aligned}
Q(\theta, \theta') = \sum_{i=1}^{N} \sum_{m=1}^{M} \log \pi_m p(m|y_i, \theta') + \\
\sum_{i=1}^{N} \sum_{m=1}^{M} \int \log p(y_i|x_i) p(x_i, m|y_i, \theta') dx_i + \\
\sum_{i=1}^{N} \sum_{m=1}^{M} \int \log p(x_i|m, \theta) p(x_i, m|y_i, \theta') dx_i \,. \quad (4.11)
\end{aligned}
$$

We get the updated parameters θ in the **M-step** by maximizing $Q(\theta, \theta')$ over θ, yielding

$$
r_m = \sum_{i=1}^{N} r_{i,m}, \quad \pi_m = \frac{r_m}{N}, \quad \mu_m = \frac{1}{r_m} \sum_{i=1}^{N} r_{i,m} \hat{x}_{i,m},
$$

$$
\Sigma_m = \frac{1}{r_m} \sum_{i=1}^{N} r_{i,m} \left(\Sigma_{x_{i,m}} + (\hat{x}_{i,m} - \mu_m)(\hat{x}_{i,m} - \mu_m)^T \right), \quad (4.12)
$$

where (the prime denotes previous-step parameter estimates)

$$
r_{i,m} = p(m|y_i, \theta') \propto \pi'_m N(y_i; \mu'_m + \mu_{e,i}, \Sigma'_m + \Sigma_{e,i}) \quad (4.13)
$$

$$
\hat{x}_{i,m} = \Sigma_{x_{i,m}} \left((\Sigma'_m)^{-1} \mu'_m + (\Sigma_{e,i})^{-1} (y_i - \mu_{e,i}) \right), \quad (4.14)
$$

$$
\Sigma_{x_{i,m}} = \left((\Sigma'_m)^{-1} + (\Sigma_{e,i})^{-1} \right)^{-1}. \quad (4.15)
$$

Two important differences w.r.t. the noise-free case are notable: *first*, error-compensated scores are utilized in computing the responsibilities $r_{i,m}$ in Eq. (4.13); *second*, in updating the model's means and variances, one should replace the noisy measurements y_i used in conventional GMM training with their model-enhanced counterparts, described by the expected value $\hat{x}_{i,m}$ and variance $\Sigma_{x_{i,m}}$. Furthermore, in the multimodal case with multiple streams $s = 1, \ldots, S$, one should compute the responsibilities by $r_{i,m} \propto \pi'_m \prod_{s=1}^{S} N(y_{s,i}; \mu'_{s,m} + \mu_{s,e,i}, \Sigma'_{s,m} + \Sigma_{s,e,i})$, which generalizes Eq. (4.13) and introduces interactions among modalities.

4.3.2 HMM Training Under Uncertainty

For the HMM, similarly to the GMM case just covered, the expected complete-data log-likelihood $Q(\theta, \theta') = E[\log p(O, \{\mathcal{Q}, \mathcal{X}, \mathcal{M}\}|\theta)|O, \theta']$ of the parameters θ in the EM algorithm's current iteration, given the previous guess θ', is obtained in the E-step as:

$$
\begin{aligned}
Q(\theta, \theta') = \sum_{q \in \mathcal{Q}} \sum_{t=1}^{T} \log a_{q_{t-1} q_t} P(O, q|\theta') + \\
\sum_{q \in \mathcal{Q}} \sum_{t=1}^{T} \int \log p(o_t|x_t, q_t, \theta') P(O, q, x_t|\theta') dx_t + \\
\sum_{q \in \mathcal{Q}} \sum_{t=1}^{T} \sum_{m=1}^{M} \int \log p(x_t|m_t, q_t, \theta') P(O, q, m, x_t|\theta') dx_t + \\
\sum_{q \in \mathcal{Q}} \sum_{t=1}^{T} \sum_{m=1}^{M} p(m|q_t, \theta') P(O, q, m|\theta') + \sum_{\mathbf{q} \in \mathcal{Q}} \log \pi_{q_0} P(O, q|\theta') \, .
\end{aligned}
\tag{4.16}
$$

The responsibilities $\gamma_t(i, k) = p(q_t = i, m = k)$ are estimated via a forward-backward procedure [420] modified so that uncertainty compensated scores are utilized:

$$
a_{t+1}(j) = P(o_{1:t}, q_t = j|\theta') = \Big[\sum_{i=1}^{N} \alpha_{ij} a_t(i)\Big] b'_j(o_{t+1}) \tag{4.17}
$$

$$
\beta_t(i) = P(o_{t+1:T}|q_t = i, \theta') = \sum_{j=1}^{N} \alpha_{ij} b'_j(o_{t+1}) \beta_{t+1}(j), \tag{4.18}
$$

where $b'_j(o_t) = \sum_{m=1}^{M} \rho_m N(o_t; \mu'_{j,m} + \mu_{e_t}, \Sigma'_{j,m} + \Sigma_{e_t})$. Scoring is done similarly to the conventional case by the forward algorithm, *i.e.*, $P(O|\theta) = \sum_{i=1}^{N} a_T(i)$. The updated parameters θ are estimated using formulas similar to the GMM case in Section 4.3.1. For $\mu_{q,m}, \Sigma_{q,m}$ the filtered estimate for the observation is used as in (4.12).

4.3.3 Some Insights into Training Under Uncertainty

Focusing on the simpler GMM model and similarly to the analysis in Section 4.2, we can gain insight into the previous EM formulas by considering the special case of constant and model-aligned errors $\Sigma_{e,i} = \Sigma_e = \lambda_m \Sigma_m$. Then, after convergence, the covariance formula in Eq. (4.12) can be written as

$$\Sigma_m = \frac{1}{1+\lambda_m} \tilde{\Sigma}_m, \quad \text{or, equivalently,} \quad \Sigma_m = \tilde{\Sigma}_m - \Sigma_e \;, \tag{4.19}$$

where we just subtract from the conventional (non-compensated) covariance estimate $\tilde{\Sigma}_m = \frac{1}{r_m} \sum_{i=1}^{N} r_{i,m}(y_i - \mu_m)(y_i - \mu_m)^T$ the noise covariance Σ_e. The rule in Eq. (4.19) has been used before as heuristic for fixing the model covariance estimate after conventional EM training with noisy data (*e.g.*, [117]). We see that it is justified in the constant and model-aligned errors case; otherwise, one should use the more general rules in Eq. (4.12).

Another link of our training under uncertain measurements scenario is to neural network training with noise (or noise injection) [487], where an original training set is artificially supplemented with multiple noisy instances of it and the resulting enriched set is used for training. Monte-Carlo-based noise injection training should be contrasted to the analytic integration over the noise distribution suggested by our approach. Our interpretation thus shows that noise injection can be motivated under the noisy measurements viewpoint. Training with noise is also related to Tikhonov regularization [65] and is known to be relatively immune to over-fitting, thus leading to classifiers with improved generalization ability. Similar advantageous properties should be expected for our training under uncertain measurements technique.

4.4 Audio-Visual Speech Recognition

A challenging application domain for multimodal fusion schemes is Audio-visual Automatic Speech Recognition (AV-ASR), since it requires modeling both the relative reliability and the synchronicity of the audio and visual modalities. We demonstrate that the proposed fusion scheme can be naturally integrated with multi-stream HMMs or other multimodal sequence processing techniques and clearly improve their performance in AV-ASR.

4.4.1 Visual Front-End

Salient visual speech information can be obtained from the shape and the texture (intensity/color) of the speaker's visible articulators, mainly the lips and the jaw, which constitute the *Region Of Interest* (ROI) around the mouth [413].

We use *Active Appearance Models* (AAM) [107] of faces to accurately track the speaker's face and extract visual speech features from it, capturing both

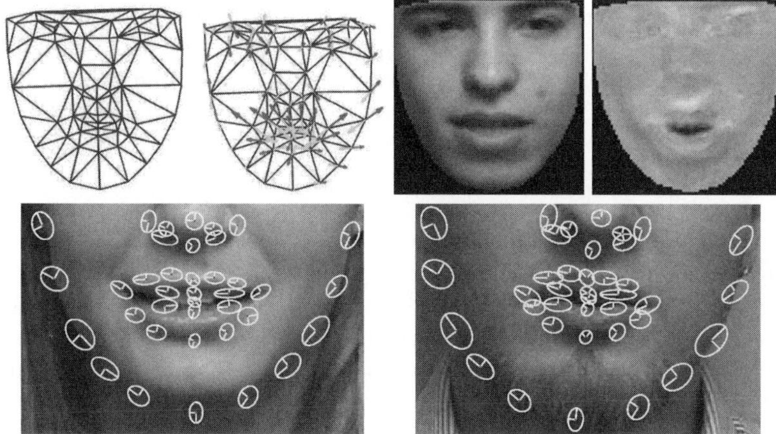

Fig. 4.4. Visual Front-End. *Upper-Left*: Mean shape s_0 and the first eigenshape s_1. *Upper-Right*: Mean texture A_0 and the first eigenface A_1. *Lower*: Tracked face shape and feature point uncertainty.

the shape and the texture of the face. AAM, which were first used for AV-ASR in [329], are generative models of object appearance and have proven particularly effective in modeling human faces for diverse applications, such as face recognition or tracking. In the AAM scheme an object's shape is modeled as a wireframe mask defined by a set of landmark points $\{x_i, i = 1 \ldots N\}$, whose coordinates constitute a shape vector s of length $2N$. We allow for deviations from the mean shape s_0 by letting s lie in a linear n-dimensional subspace, yielding $s = s_0 + \sum_{i=1}^{n} p_i s_i$. The deformation of the shape s to the mean shape s_0 defines a mapping $W(x;p)$, which brings the face exemplar on the current frame I into registration with the mean face template. After canceling out shape deformation, the face appearance (color values) registered with the mean face can be modeled as a weighted sum of "eigenfaces" $\{A_i\}$, *i.e.*, $I(W(x;p)) \approx A_0(x) + \sum_{i=1}^{m} \lambda_i A_i(x)$, where A_0 is the mean texture of faces. Both eigenshape and eigenface bases are learned during a training phase. The first few of them extracted by such a procedure are depicted in Fig. 4.4.

Given a trained AAM, model fitting amounts to finding for each video frame I_t the parameters $\tilde{p}_t \equiv \{p_t, \lambda_t\}$ which minimize the squared texture reconstruction error $I_t(W(p_t)) - A_0 - \sum_{i=1}^{m} \lambda_{t,i} A_i$; efficient iterative algorithms for this non-linear least squares problem can be found in [107]. The fitting procedure employs a face detector [158] to get an initial shape estimate for the first frame. To extract information mostly related to visual speech, we utilize a hierarchy of two AAM. The first *ROI-AAM* spans only the area around the mouth and is used to analyze in detail the ROI's shape and texture; however, the ROI-AAM covers too small an area to allow for reliable tracking. To pinpoint the ROI-AAM we use a second *Face-AAM* which spans the whole face and can reliably track the speaker in long video sequences. As visual feature vector for speech recognition we use the parameters $\tilde{p}_t$ of the fitted

ROI-AAM. We employ as uncertainty in the visual features the uncertainty in estimating the parameters of the corresponding non-linear least squares problem [415, Chapter 15]; plots of the corresponding uncertainty in localizing the landmarks on the image for two example faces are illustrated in Fig. 4.4.

4.4.2 Audio Front-End

We use the Mel Frequency Cepstral Coefficients (MFCC) to represent audio, as it is common in contemporary ASR systems. Uncertainty is considered to originate from additive noise to the audio waveform. To get estimates of the clean features we employ the speech enhancement framework proposed in [130], adapted to work with MFCCs along the lines of [186]. The enhanced features are derived from the noisy ones by iteratively improving a guess based on a prior clean speech model and Vector Taylor Series approximation [171]. The uncertainty of the resulting clean feature estimates is assumed to be zero-mean Gaussian and for each such feature estimate a rough approximation of its uncertainty is also available at the output of the enhancement module. In this way, fusion by uncertainty compensation is facilitated. Alternative enhancement procedures could equivalently be applied provided that the variance of the enhanced features could also be roughly estimated.

4.4.3 Experiments and Discussion

The novel fusion approach proposed above is evaluated via classification experiments on the Clemson University Audiovisual Experiments (CUAVE) database [391]. Experiments are performed on the section of the database comprising audiovisual recordings of 36 speakers uttering 50 isolated digits each. The speakers are standing naturally still and they are framed including their shoulders and head, as shown in Fig. 4.5. Digit models are trained on data from 30 speakers who have been randomly selected. The rest of the data is held out for testing. For the tests in noise, the audio recordings in this testing subset have been contaminated with babble noise from the NOISEX-92 database at various SNR levels.

Mel frequency cepstral coefficients (MFCC) are extracted from 25 ms Hamming windowed frames of the preemphasized (factor: 0.97) audio stream at a rate of 100 Hz. Per audio frame, 13 coefficients are extracted. A visual feature vector is estimated per video frame, consisting of 6 shape and 12 texture features and the visual feature stream is upsampled from the video frame rate (29.97 FPS) to the audio rate of 100 Hz by linear interpolation. Mean Normalization is applied to both the audio and visual features.

To demonstrate the benefits of compensating for feature uncertainty for multimodal fusion we performed a series of digit classification experiments and the results are summarized in Fig. 4.6. For these experiments, the first derivatives of the audio and visual features have also been included in the corresponding feature vectors. Uncertainty estimates for the visual features

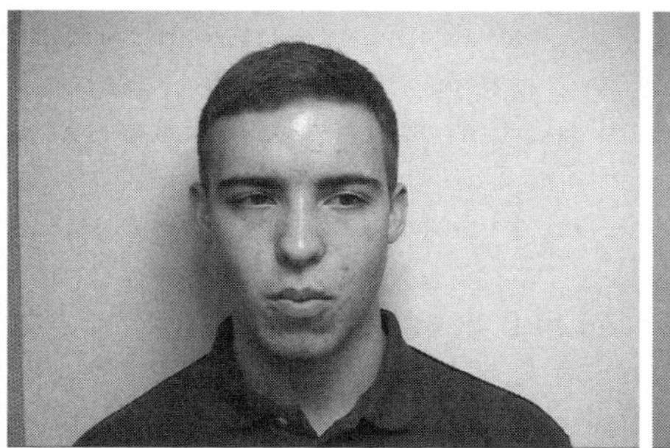

Fig. 4.5. Sample speaker images from the CUAVE database.

are acquired as discussed in Section 4.4.1. For the audio features, uncertainty is computed as the squared difference between each feature and the corresponding clean feature, which is considered to be available as well in this proof-of-concept scenario.

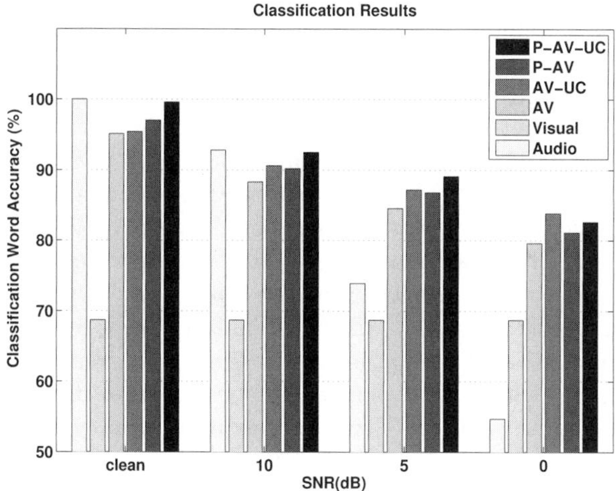

Fig. 4.6. Classification results with or without Uncertainty Compensation (UC) for fusion. Simple multistream models (AV) and product-HMMs (P-AV) have been evaluated at various SNR levels.

Audiovisual observations are modeled by digit left-right multistream Hidden Markov Models (AV), each with 8 states and with a single multidimensional Gaussian observation probability distribution per stream and per state. Single modality 8-state digit HMMs have also been evaluated for reference. Further, to better account for asynchrony between the modalities, these single-modality HMMs have been merged in product-HMMs (P-AV) as described in

[312]. Asynchrony has been limited to two states only, while stream weights are assumed to be equal to unity in all cases (multistream or product-HMMs). The multimodal models have been evaluated both with and without uncertainty compensation. Compensation has been implemented in the HMM decoder by increasing the observation variance in the modified forward algorithm described in Section 4.3.3.

Models with uncertainty compensation in general outperform those without. The best overall performance is demonstrated by the uncertainty compensated product HMMs (P-AV-UC), which at 5 dB SNR yields 89.1% accuracy, an absolute 2.3% over the conventionally decoded product HMM. The corresponding results for state-synchronous multi-stream HMMs are 87.2% for uncertainty compensated decoding and 84.5% for conventional decoding. We see that accounting for uncertainty clearly favors multimodal fusion, by approximately 2.5% absolute, and has a cumulative beneficial effect when combined with asynchrony modeling through product HMMs, which give another 2% absolute accuracy improvement. As expected, the beneficial effect of uncertainty compensation gets increasingly important for decreasing audio SNR.

In a separate series of experiments we evaluate uncertainty compensation for fusion in the training phase. The compensated models are trained on clean audio data, while for the visual training data their corresponding variances are taken into account into the modified EM algorithm of Section 4.3.3. This time, both the first and the second derivatives of the audiovisual features are also utilized. Testing with uncertainty compensation is implemented as before. In this case however we have utilized more realistic estimates of the uncertainty of the audio features following the procedure sketched in Section 4.4.2 Our experimental results summarized in Table 4.1 show that accounting for uncertainty in the case of audiovisual fusion, either solely in testing or both in training and testing, AV-UC and AV-UCT, respectively, improves AV-ASR performance in most cases. Again, for the baseline audiovisual setup we used multistream HMMs with stream weights equal to unity for both streams. The proposed approach (AV-UC, AV-UCT) seems particularly effective at lower SNRs.

4.5 Conclusions

The chapter has shown that taking the feature uncertainty into account constitutes a fruitful framework for multimodal feature analysis tasks. This is especially true in the case of multiple complementary information streams, where having a good estimate of each stream's uncertainty at a particular moment facilitates information fusion, allowing for proper training and fully adaptive stream integration schemes. In order for this approach to reach its full potential, reliable methods for dynamically estimating the feature observation uncertainty are needed. Ideally, the methods that we employ to extract

SNR	A	V	AV	AV-UC	AV-UCT
clean	99.3	75.7	90.0	-	-
15 dB	96.7	-	88.0	88.3	88.0
10 dB	91.3	-	88.3	88.7	87.7
5 dB	82.0	-	87.0	88.0	87.7
0 dB	62.7	-	84.3	87.0	87.3
-5 dB	40.3	-	81.7	82.0	83.0

Table 4.1. Word Percent Accuracy (%) of classification experiments on CUAVE database for various noise levels on the audio stream; experiments have been conducted for: Audio (A), Visual (V) and Audio-Visual (AV) features, with stream weights equal to unity, with Uncertainty Compensation in the testing phase (UC), and with Uncertainty Compensation both in the testing and training (UCT).

features in pattern recognition tasks should accompany feature estimates with their respective errorbars. Although some progress has been done in the area, further research is needed before we fully understand the quantitative behavior under diverse conditions of popular features commonly used in pattern analysis tasks such as speech recognition.

5

Action Recognition in Multimedia Streams

Rozenn Dahyot, François Pitié, Daire Lennon, Naomi Harte, and Anil Kokaram

Trinity College Dublin

It is well accepted that the rise in the proliferation of inexpensive digital media collection and manipulation devices has motivated the need to access this data by content rather than by keywords. The requirements of content based access are well understood by the digital media research community and there is no need to elaborate further here. Parsing multimedia streams by detection and classification of action implies modeling the dynamic nature of visual and audio features as they evolve in time. The Hidden Markov Model (HMM) has long been used to model dynamic behavior in audio signals. Its power to capture complex behavior in that domain has led to widespread use in visual content analysis because of the non-stationarity inherent in those signals. However, subtleties in the application of HMMs are often unclear in the use of the framework in the visual processing community and the latter portion of this chapter sets out to expose some of these. Three applications are considered to motivate the discussions: actions in sports, observational psychology and illicit video content.

Sports: Work in sports media analysis and understanding has been conducted for a decade now with clear motivation provided by the huge amount of sports media broadcasting on Internet and digital television. An overview of content analysis for sports footage in general can be found in [274]. Action recognition here involves detection of certain *plays* and *situations* as dictated by the game domain, e.g., pots, goals, wickets and aces.

Illicit Content: The distribution of pornographic materials has also benefited from the digital revolution [105]. This kind of material is illegal in the workplace and is referred to as *illicit content* in this chapter. The issue of filtering this material has been of major concern since the introduction of the web in the early 1990's. Pixalert's 'Auditor' and 'Monitor'[1], FutureSoft's 'DynaComm i:scan' [2] and Hyperdyne Software's 'Snitch'[3] all provide image and

[1] http://www.pixalert.com/product/product.htm

[2] http://www.futuresoft.com/documentation/dciscan/imagerecognition.pdf

[3] http://www.hyperdynesoftware.com/clean-porn.html

P. Maragos et al. (eds.), *Multimodal Processing and Interaction*,
DOI: 10.1007/978-0-387-76316-3_5,

text filtering for remote scanning of e-mail, hard disks and peripheral storage devices (e.g., USB memory keys). While there has been noteworthy activity in research into content-based analysis of illicit images [163, 240, 88, 557, 72, 33], there has been little work in spotting illicit activity in video streams. The need for such work has become stronger with the popularity of media sharing (via YouTube and Google Video for instance) and the requirement for host sites to police usage. Action recognition in this context requires multimodal analysis of motion and audio features.

Scientific: Observation of people occupies much of the time of the behavioral psychologist. The digital revolution has allowed video to be recorded easily enough so that behavioral assessments are in principle more scientifically recorded and analyzed. In the experiment discussed in this paper, over 300 hours of video of children undertaking specific movement therapies were recorded . Reviewing and scoring the video of each subject is therefore an arduous task made difficult by the lack of easy indexing to the key actions of interest. Action recognition in this context involves the detection and parsing of video showing rotational motion in the region of the subject's head (see Fig. 5.8). This example illustrates a little known use of HMMs, i.e., not only to classify temporal activity, but also to parse a sequence according to that activity.

Broadly speaking there are two approaches to parsing through action. In certain cases (*Direct Parsing*), specific features can be directly connected to the action of interest and a relatively *thin* inference layer then yields decisions and hence a parsed stream. In other situations (*Model Based Parsing*), the connection between features and actions is not straightforward and a *heavier* inference layer is needed to articulate the feature information in order to yield a decision. In all cases, motion of objects or the camera itself is important for action parsing, and so motion estimation and object tracking are key tools in the content analysis arsenal. In broadcast footage, where the editing itself is an indication of action, preliminary shot cut detection allows visual material in each shot to be analyzed in separate units. In scientific or surveillance type footage the actions of interest occur as impulsive events in a continuously changing stream of material.

5.1 Direct Parsing for Actions

Both sports analysis and illicit content identification contain good material for discussing Direct Parsing. When features are strong enough to yield detection directly, a useful pre-processing step is the delineation of media portions which are most likely to contain that action. In illicit content analysis, the presence of large amounts of skin colored regions is a strong indicator of video clips of interest. Skin regions occupy a relatively narrow range in the color spectrum and Dahyot et al [431] compute the posterior probability $p(\text{skin}|z)$ that each pixel z belongs to the skin class. This p.d.f. is obtained empirically using skin and non-skin reference histograms from the open-source filtering Poseia project[4]. While this formulation treats pixels independently, it is a sufficient model for the initial skin segmentation. A skin binary map is then generated by thresholding the probability map.

Sport videos usually show a finite number of different views and the actions of interest are only contained in a subset of views. View classification can be achieved in sports with either low level, direct feature manipulation or model based recognition. Since the principal actions usually take place in views that contain mostly the playing area, and the playing area is usually of a predefined high contrast color, color features from each frame allow quick identification of the shots that contain player action. This is a well established idea used to good effect by several early authors [131, 187, 256, 90, 149]. Fig. 5.1) shows example frame segmentations using color thresholding of the average frame color used to good effect in [121]. The playing area segmentation implicit in

Fig. 5.1. Top row: Tennis frame showing unsupervised segmentation of the playing areas using color information, and calibration of the playing area (far right). Bottom row: The same information for snooker.

this shot segmentation exercise then yields the geometry of the view, and the delineation of the playing area itself within the view. The Hough Transform is typically used to do this [131, 256]. See Fig. 5.1 for an example.

5.1.1 The actions

Having delineated the important video material and the active area in the frames, motion or change analysis can directly be matched to certain actions.

[4] http://www.poesia-filter.org/

For instance, Denman [131] observed that the position of the pots in the snooker table were fixed in the relevant view, and the location of the pots could be accurately determined in the calibration stage. Hence color histogram change analysis in the region around each pot could detect a ball *pot* action event. Dahyot et al [120] observed that racket hits in tennis and bat hits in cricket are unique impulsive sounds in the audio stream. Principal Component Analysis (PCA) from the audio tracks associated with relevant views, can be used to design specific filters (thresholding of the PCA feature distance from the training cluster) to perform detection of these sounds to near 100% accuracy. As the sound is associated with a specific dynamic action, this means that the action can be detected with high reliability, in effect by thresholding a single PCA-derived feature.

Motion analysis of course yields a much richer action detection process. For instance, although collision of snooker balls can be heard through the audio track, the strength of that sound is not significantly higher than the background noise and snooker ball collision through audio alone is unsuccessful. Both global/camera motion and local object motion yield information rich features. Global motion estimation (6-parameter affine motion) can be achieved with weighted least squared methods, e.g., [373, 146, 112]. Kokaram et al [273] show that global motion can be directly connected to *bowler run* up and *offside/onside shot* actions. This is because in cricket broadcasting the camera zooms in as the bowler runs in to throw the ball, and then zooms out and pans left or right to follow the ball after it is hit. The rough run of play action in soccer can also be characterized by the global translation of the camera move [294].

Local motion information contains the motion of the players and sport objects and hence is directly relevant to the play. Typically the objects of interest are first segmented from the playing area in the field of view and then tracking is instantiated in some way. Both Ekin [149] and Rea et al [430] exploit schemes based on color histograms. However, Rea et al adopt the popular (at the time) particle filter tracking approach while Ekin adopted a deterministic matching scheme that selected the matching tiles on a fixed grid over the playing area which contained the object in question. Rea et al also introduced the notion that, given the calibrated view provided from Denman et al [131], it is possible to alter the size of the bounding box containing the object to be tracked, so that it compensates for the view geometry. This is quite an important idea for sport action tracking where the view geometry will affect the size of the object and hence the ability to match any template color histogram. Nevertheless, Pitié et al [403] point out that color based segmentation in sport is able to remove much of the ambiguity inherent in many *hard* tracking problems. In other words, the regions of the playing area that are not part of the playing area color are likely to be positions of objects to be tracked. This idea leads to a Viterbi scheme for tracking that selects the best path through candidate "blobs" of interest in each frame of the sequence. This latter idea is much more computationally efficient and robust than particle filters in the sport application.

Given motion trajectories of objects it is possible to directly classify object actions in some applications. For instance, in snooker, loss of tracking "lock" near a pot in the table indicates that a ball has been potted. Loss of lock can be established by thresholding the likelihood energy of the tracker in each frame for each object [429]. In that work, a ball collision is detected by identifying changes in the ratio between the current white ball velocity and the average previous velocity. If the ball is in the vicinity of the cushion, a cushion bounce is inferred. Given that the physics of colliding bodies implies that at collision, changes in velocity in one direction are typically larger than another, a change in velocity of 50% is used to indicate of a collision. A flush collision is inferred when velocity changes in 50% in both directions.

5.1.2 Exploiting the Motion Field

In illicit content analysis the situation demands a more implicit motion feature extraction approach. The problem is that only a portion of the skin covered regions would yield information amenable to further analysis and it is not possible to easily further delineate any obvious feature for tracking on the basis of color or texture alone. Instead, local motion over the entire detected skin area can be used as a feature to segment objects or regions for further analysis. Using motion extracted from the MPEG compressed stream leads to a computationally efficient procedure.

In order to segment the local motion regions, global motion must be compensated for. Macroblocks that contain less than 30% skin pixels are cited as non-skin blocks and are used to estimate this motion. The blocks containing low texture (with low DCT coefficient energy) are removed from further analysis as they will contain unreliable motion information. The mode of the 2D motion histogram of these motion vectors yields an estimate for global motion. Segmentation using the raw MPEG vectors is likely to lead to temporally inconsistent masks because MPEG motion, based on block matching, is likely to be temporally poor. To somewhat alleviate this , the motion field is filtered with a 3D vector median operation using the ML3D filter outlined in Alp et al. [24]. Once the vectors have been compensated for global motion, they are clustered using K-means, assuming only two clusters are required for foreground/background. K-means is used because it is a computationally efficient clustering algorithm and gives satisfactory results compared to the watershed segmentation used by [113]. The region of interest is then the logical 'and' of the skin map and this foreground motion map.

Fig. 5.2 shows the binary skin image and the motion compensated segmentation with overlaid motion vectors for a still from *When Harry met Sally*. Use of motion information helps to segment relevant skin region with higher accuracy. Detecting periodic motion behavior has become increasingly popular for retrieval in video [119, 304, 156, 79]. The motion estimated here can be directly associated with periodicity of that skin region and thus a notion of *illicit video* [431].

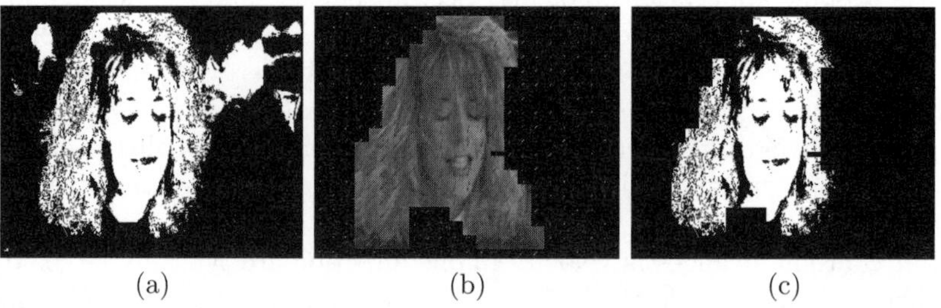

(a) (b) (c)

Fig. 5.2. (a) Binary map of the skin segmentation; (b) Motion segmentation with overlaid motion vectors; (c) Binary 'and' of motion and skin segmentations.

5.1.3 Exploiting audio

Even when not watching the video content from a multimedia stream, the nature of the stream can still be understood from the audio information alone. Examples of applications can be found in sport video indexing as discussed above. This is true also of pornographic content. Periodic audio signals can be indicative of illicit content. The famous scene from the movie *When Harry met Sally* (Sally's simulation of an orgasm, which is a series of moans and screams) serves to illustrate the point. The scene starts with a conversation between Sally and Harry. The loudness of the audio signal is computed over non-overlapping temporal windows of $0.04s$ (duration of a 25fps video frame). For analysis of periodic patterns, a 5-second period is used corresponding to 125 measurements of volume. Fig. 5.3 presents two 5 second periods and confirms that a periodic pattern is exhibited during the *illicit* extract (b) more than during the conversation (a). Periodicity in the signal is usually analyzed by autocorrelation, circular correlation or periodogram [548, 476]. Autocorrelation is used here and the autocorrelation for the two signals in Fig. 5.3 is given in Fig. 5.4. Peaks appearing in (b) show that the signal is periodic.

The key is to define a measure to discriminate autocorrelations of classes similar to (a) and (b) (cf. Fig. 5.4). A simple measure is to compute the difference between the surface defined by the minima and the maxima of the autocorrelation. This is illustrated in Fig. 5.5 for the same audio extracts (a) and (b).

Fig. 5.6 shows this periodicity measure during the whole scene of *When Harry met Sally*. The measure is low at the start as only a conversation occurs between the two main characters. Then starting at 95 seconds, the periodic pattern begins. In this case, periodic moaning and screaming appears on the

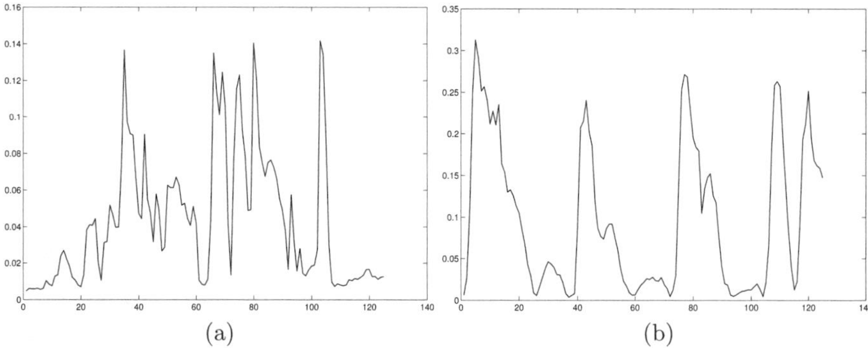

Fig. 5.3. Audio energy computed over 5s when Sally talks to Harry (a), and when Sally is simulating (b).

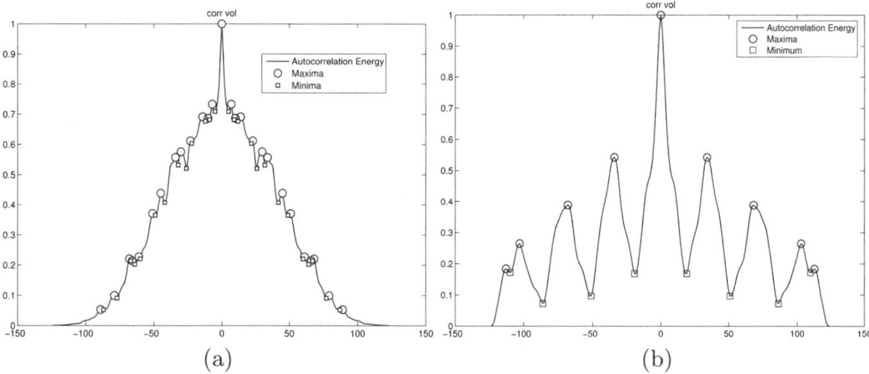

Fig. 5.4. Autocorrelation of the energy in the audio data with their maxima (circles) and minima (squares).

audio data. By the end of the scene, standard conversation takes place again and the measure of periodicity decreases.

Using a threshold of 4 to detect illicit content when the measure exceeds this value, leads to a usable action spotting algorithm. It performs a perfect segmentation in the scene of *When Harry met Sally* (cf. Fig. 5.6). The method has been assessed first on non-illicit materials (20 minutes of extracts from movies and music videos) to evaluate the false alarm rate of the method. Various audio sources was used (music, speech, explosion, scream etc.), and in all those, the false alarm rate is rather low at 2%. The detection rate is more difficult to assess as periodic sounds do not occur all the time in the audio stream. Ten minutes of eight different extracts of illicit material containing periodic sounds have been used. Five extracts corresponding to 9 minutes of the test have been properly detected. Three short extracts (representing 1 minute of recording) are missed. On those three files, a mixture of sounds is

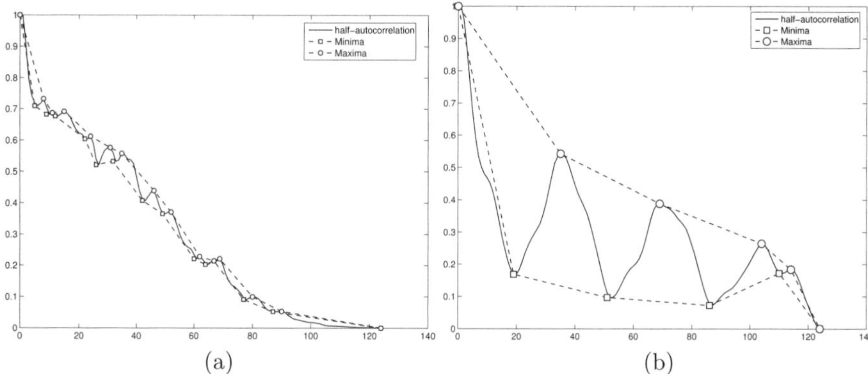

(a) (b)

Fig. 5.5. The measure of periodicity on the half-autocorrelation is computed by the surface between the dashed upper curve (defined by the maxima in Fig. 5.4) and the lower dashed curve (defined by the minima in Fig. 5.4).

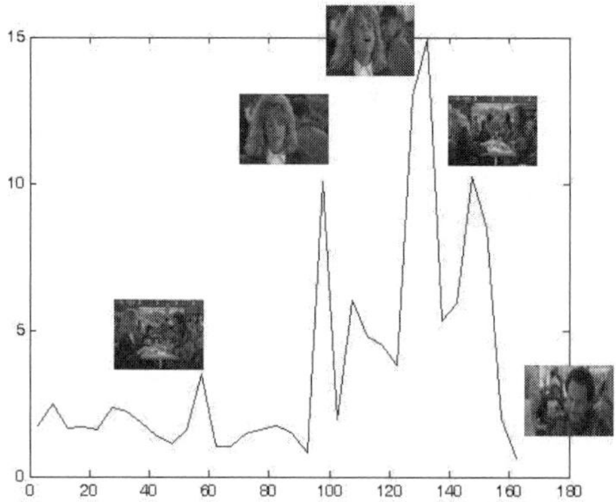

Fig. 5.6. Measure of periodicity in the scene of *When Harry met Sally* w.r.t the time (in seconds).

occurring (speech or music) masking the relevant periodicity on the loudness feature.

5.2 Model Based Parsing

To gain deeper access to action semantics some form of inference layer is needed for processing the temporal evolution of the motion feature. The HMM has been heavily exploited for this purpose. Traditionally, HMMs are well established as a means of modeling the evolution in time of spectral features in the speech envelope. The underlying IID (Independent and Identically Distributed) assumption of HMMs for audio is that there is no correlation between successive speech vectors. This has strongly motivated the use of features such as cepstrum that inherently capture the dynamic characteristics in speech. Feature vectors are generally augmented with first and second order derivatives to further improve speech recognition rates.

To clarify, the HMM is essentially a state machine describing the underlying temporal evolution of a data sequence. In the problem of temporal analysis, at each time index, the underlying (hidden) system is in some state and that state generates the observed signal or feature vector. An HMM is therefore defined through a combination of the geometry of the state machine (connectivity and number of states), transition probabilities between each state and the generating function that creates the observed signal in each state. This is a powerful idea and can be used to statistically model inhomogeneous signals through the transition between states. Discrete HMMs create observable sequences that are quantized symbols, for example a sequence of letters in a word, while continuous HMMs create observable sequences which are continuous signals, for instance speech itself. The value of HMMs as a modeling framework for content analysis is clear: it allows us to combine different phases of behavior under the same process. Adapting the use of HMMs from the audio community to the visual community is challenging.

The choice of features for visual applications is extremely diverse and in many cases ad-hoc. Visual HMM frameworks can be better designed by examining whether discrete or continuous density models are suitable for the application, whether feature sets are truly independent and hence full covariance models are not needed, and whether the HMMs are to be used for classification or recognition purposes. This is analogous to defining whether a speech recognition task is the classification of isolated units, or full recognition where both unit classification and parsing are jointly performed. To understand how HMMs can be used for action classification, consider the following two examples.

5.2.1 Action in Sports

Given the extraction of the motion trajectories of objects explained previously, it is clear that the shape of that trajectory contains information about what is happening. A simple example is the trajectory of the white ball in snooker, if it traverses the whole table and comes to rest near a cushion, which is probably a conservative play. Trajectory classification then is very similar to handwriting recognition. Analogous to the approach used for on-line handwriting recognition [286], active regions are delineated in the tennis court and on the snooker table (see Fig. 5.7). Those regions represent the discrete states on which the trajectories of the balls in snooker and the players in tennis are encoded. Hence, as the ball and players move around on the playing surface, they generate a time series of symbols.

(a) (b)

Fig. 5.7. Spatial encoding of the playing area.

Rea et al [430, 429] use a first order HMM to classify these sequences. By their nature, the sequences are discrete, and hence a discrete HMM is employed. A different model is trained using the Baum-Welch algorithm. As the actions are well understood in terms of the geometrical layout of the table, the models can be trained using user inputs or training videos with ground truth. The types of actions amenable to analysis in this fashion are as follows.

Snooker	Tennis
Break building	Aces
Conservative play	Faults
Snooker escape	Double Faults
Shot to nothing	Serve and volleys
Open table	Rallies
Foul	

5.3 Action in Psychological Assessment

Action classification using HMMs in sport relies strongly on the pre-processing mechanisms and domain specific knowledge which allow that portion of the video containing the action to be pre-segmented for analysis. In the Dysvideo project (www.dysvideo.org) [274] the video recorded is of a single view in which a stream of actions is being performed continuously. Action recognition here involves the detection and parsing of video showing rotational motion in the region of the subject's head (see Fig. 5.8). What is required here is a process not only to identify the onset of the rotation exercise, but also to qualify when the head is rotating to the right or the left. This implies recognizing the action and also using it to parse the video and it is possible to use the HMM here as well. This is a subtle variation in the use of the HMM

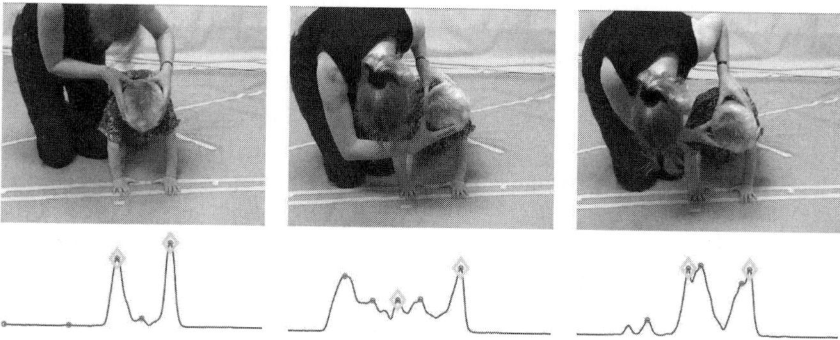

Fig. 5.8. Top row: a demonstration of a child performing the psychological exercise. Bottom row: detection of the hands positions (diamonds) [403]. The solid line shows the skin color projection and the peaks give the candidate positions (circles).

and here two **continuous** density HMMs are used - one representing rotation events, the other non-rotation events. Using classic Viterbi-based recognition, periods of rotation and non-rotation can automatically be distinguished [292].

5.3.1 Motion based features for human movement assessment

The rotation of the head is detected by analyzing features of the motion flow in the video. To avoid dealing with the movements of the instructor, the analysis is restricted to the region around the head of the child. Head tracking is thus required, and a similar technique as previously discussed in this chapter has been implemented. Skin color segmentation is first performed to isolate the child from the background. As part of the experiment, the child is required to wear T-shirt and shorts so a good part of visible skin belongs to the child. As shown in Fig. 5.8, the arms are well exposed in the view. In addition they are near vertical. Hence a vertical sum (integration) of the skin label field yields a 1D projection whose modes correspond to the horizontal position of the arms. The head position can then be found in between both arms.

As illustrated in Fig. 5.8, occlusions by the instructor can create spurious peaks in the projection. To find the correct peaks, a Bayesian approach is adopted. At every frame, all the peaks of the 1D projection are collected as candidate positions. The ensemble of these candidate positions constitutes a trellis. The positions of the hands are retrieved by imposing some prior on the motion of the hands and running the Viterbi algorithm through this trellis to extract the most likely path.

With the child head isolated, features can now be derived to model the motion of the child. These features have to be capable of determining when the head of the child is rotating. Since rotation is a unique type of motion, gradient based motion estimation was performed [275] and the motion vectors for each frame were calculated for each exercise sequence. The calculated motion vectors are only capable of showing locally translational motion. However, looking at a larger scale, the spatial variations of the vector field can be used to identify non-translational motion. In particular, the rotational component of a vector field can be obtained by measuring the curl of the motion vector field. Denote as $u(x, y)$ and $v(x, y)$ the x and y components of the motion field between frames I_n and I_{n+1}. The locally translational motion equation at pixel (x, y) is given by:

$$I_{n+1}(x + u(x, y), y + v(x, y)) = I_n(x, y) \tag{5.1}$$

The corresponding amplitude of the curl for this 2D motion field is then defined as:

$$\mathcal{C}(x, y) = \frac{dv(x, y)}{dx} - \frac{du(x, y)}{dy} \tag{5.2}$$

The curl yields an implicit measure of rotation. An example of the curl field for an head rotation exercise is displayed on Fig. 5.9. The main peak in the curl corresponds to the centre of rotation and its position remains stable during the rotation.

From the curl surface, it is possible to infer two essential features: the rotation centre and the size of the rotating object. The centre of rotation is given by the main peak in the curl. The estimation of the rotating object area requires delineating the head with a watershed segmentation on the curl surface. The set of features is completed by adding the temporal derivative of the position and the size. The reasoning behind this is that during rotation and non-rotation events, temporal variations of the object position and size are radically different. These four features are combined with two other features, which are described thoroughly in [293]. A total of six features are therefore used to characterise the rotation movement of the head.

5.3.2 Event recognition in psychological assessment

Using the feature set discussed, continuous density HMMs are trained and used in Viterbi-based recognition to parse unseen video into periods of rotation and non-rotation. The rotation model, denoted as $\mathcal{R}$, is associated with a dedicated continuous fully connected 4-state HMM (see Fig. 5.10). Other non-rotation events are modeled by another model $\overline{\mathcal{R}}$, which is also associated with a continuous fully connected 4-state HMM. For both HMMs, the likelihood of being in a particular state is defined by a single Gaussian distribution. Evaluating the Maximum A Posteriori probability (MAP) of a sequence of observations can be done using the Viterbi algorithm. To decide if a sequence is a rotation or non-rotation event, it is then sufficient to compute the MAP for each model and choose the most likely.

A naive approach would be to pre-segment the video into different shots and compare both models on these shots. In fact this is the kind of approach

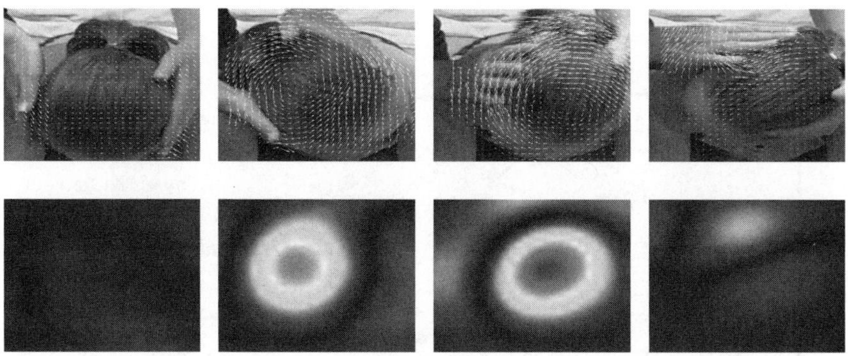

Fig. 5.9. The top four images show a selection of frames used to demonstrate a sequence of head rotation. The bottom four images show the sequence for the curl matrix. All of the above images have been zoomed in to improve clarity.

adopted for many sports action recognition tasks using the HMM. However, since both events are particularly hard to differentiate, this segmentation is not practical. A small variation in the use of the HMMs can however avoid pre-segmenting the video and allow analyzing the stream directly. Consider the layout of Fig. 5.10. By stacking both HMMs in a single network of HMMs, it becomes possible to parse for $\mathcal{R}$ and $\overline{\mathcal{R}}$ simultaneously. Now for each frame of the video, the likelihood for the eight states of both HMMs is evaluated at the same time. The extra links between exit states S_8,S_4 and entry states S_1,S_5 are the glue which allows switching between both models. They define how likely it is to switch from a rotation model to a non-rotation model, and vice-versa. Running Viterbi on this network of HMMs returns the MAP sequence of states, that, by looking at which HMM they belong to, can be simply translated in a sequence of $\mathcal{R}$ and $\overline{\mathcal{R}}$ events. Thus, this HMM framework does not simply classify previously parsed segments of video but jointly parses and classifies the events.

Twenty three exercise videos have been selected for evaluating this framework, totaling approximately 20 minutes of footage. All twenty three videos have rotational events manually noted for ground truth used in testing. Sixteen videos have been selected at random for training purposes and seven selected for testing. Both HMMs for $\mathcal{R}$ and $\overline{\mathcal{R}}$ are trained individually using the Baum-Welsh algorithm. The state transitions are reported on Fig. 5.10 and the details of the Gaussian distributions parameters are listed in [293]. The transitions between both models have been obtained by looking at the relative frequency of transitions between the models in the ground truth sequences. Note that these inter-model transitions can also be refined using an iterative Viterbi re-estimation scheme [580]. Note that different HMMs topolo-

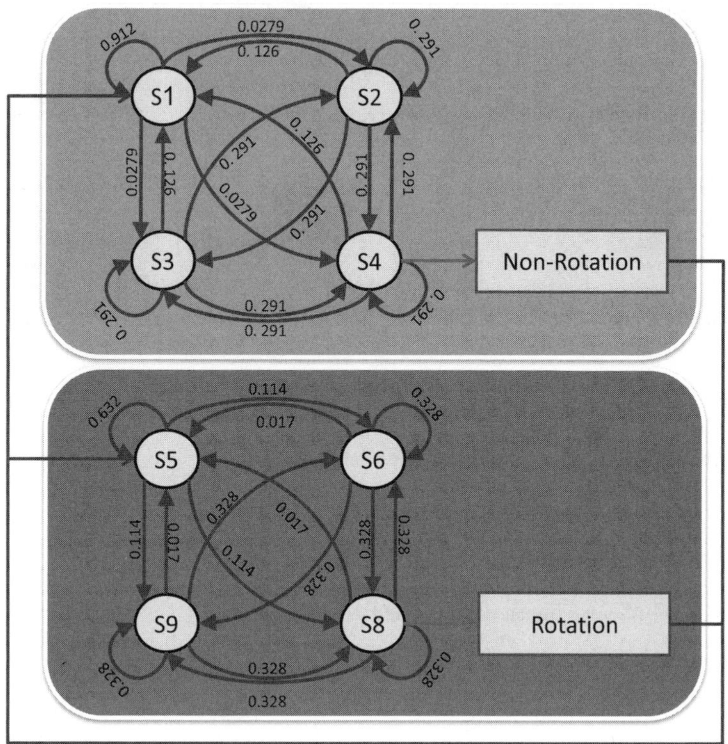

Fig. 5.10. Topology of the HMM network. On the top, the fully connected 4-state HMM for the non-rotational model, on the bottom the fully connected 4-state HMM for the rotational model. Both HMMs are linked to each other to allow a simultaneous segmentation of both models in the sequence.

gies have been examined, and it seems that the fully connected 4-state model is optimal for this application.

The Viterbi algorithm has then been run using the two trained HMMs $\mathcal{R}$ and $\overline{\mathcal{R}}$ to recognise rotation events. The comparison between the estimates calculated by the network of HMMs and the manual segmentations is presented in Table 5.1. Table 5.1 reports the average Recall and Precision as well as the standard deviation of the Recall and Precision for all 23 video sequences, the 16 training sequences alone and the 7 testing sequences. A tolerance of 14 frames, roughly half a second, is allowed between the HMM estimates and manual segmentations. This is to allow for human error in noting rotation events, as a human observer can sometimes misclassify pre-rotation head translation as rotation.

videos	Recall	Precision	Recall Standard Deviation	Precision Standard Deviation
All (23)	91.78	90.68	7.14	7.72
Training (16)	92.12	90.21	6.78	8.80
Test (7)	91	91.77	8.42	4.80

Table 5.1. Rotation/non-rotation segmentation results for psychological exercises.

Videos	Tennis	Snooker
Recall	87.89%	92.75%
Precision	94.45%	90.16%

Table 5.2. View classification results using combined shape and color features for tennis and snooker [432].

Videos	Fault	Rally
Recall	100%	100%
Precision	87.5%	89.47%

Table 5.3. Event classification results. Precision/recall for fault and rally phases in tennis, based on motion [432].

5.4 Discussion

It is generally the case that action recognition based on specific observed features is computationally cheaper than the use of HMMs for the same performance gain. This is not to say that HMMs as a framework is a poor idea, only that simple actions that can be addressed by analysis of a single feature are better addressed as such. However, more complex actions cannot be addressed simply and the HMM is the natural solution. Hence HMMs and Direct Parsing tend to be applied to different problems. Thus pot-detection with simple histograms achieves a recall/precision rate (100%/74%) comparable with the HMM framework used for tennis trajectory analysis (100%/80%), yet with a fraction of the computational load. What is interesting is that most results published in the literature show better than 80% accuracy for both Recall and Precision when using HMMs for action parsing (see for instance our results in Tennis and Snooker view and event classifications on Table 5.2 and 5.3). This is probably because the HMM framework is good at combining different features to achieve a coherent process description. In visual media, where extracting the 'key feature' is most likely impossible, this is an important strength of HMMs. For instance, in our psychological parsing example, it is surprising that even though we were clear about the important feature, the measurement process was simply too noisy for anything other than the HMM to model the process. In that example, the recall/precision of more than 90% is encouraging. Training however remains an issue, and for complex actions long training data sequences are needed. Perhaps this observation reflects what is already well acknowledged in the real world of industrial design, that it is relatively simple to get performance up to 80%, but then extremely difficult to create systems that are 100% reliable. HMMs help to approach this ceiling.

To assess how usable in general this technology is, it is possible to seek evidence of exploitation of these ideas in everyday consumer equipment. No doubt a Tivo or Sky set top box would be the ideal place to exploit action meta-data encoded into the transmitted sports bit stream, and behavioral psychologists attempting to use hundreds of hours of video would benefit from these ideas. However, right now, action spotting for the everyday consumer or scientific user is non existent. This would imply that the ideas are still new and not robust enough for operation in the marketplace. One of the main problems remains the generalizability of the algorithms. Direct Parsing seems to work well, but in much of the published work, many more hours of testing seem to be necessary. In addition, Direct Parsing requires quite a deal of domain knowledge and the ideas seem to be very good for sports, but little else.

The future of action recognition in multimedia streams must therefore lie in the proper exploitation of dynamic inference engines like the HMM. In speech recognition, the use of statistical context-free grammars is widely spread [581]. We can imagine similar visual applications in which semantic parsing of videos without shot cut detection is possible. In a sense, the community should aspire to the level of achievement of the speech recognition community. That community has benefited greatly from the discovery of features (e.g., cepstral) which give good information for speech content. In a similar way the notion of visual words (e.g., as established by Zisserman et al [493]) could be exploited in an HMM for temporal parsing. This is certainly not a simple task but one step in that direction is placing more effort in unraveling the many subtleties of the HMM. Some discussion along these lines is undertaken elsewhere in this book.

6

Surveillance Using Both Video and Audio

Yigithan Dedeoglu[1], B. Ugur Toreyin[2], Ugur Gudukbay[1], and A. Enis Cetin[2]

[1] Department of Computer Engineering, Bilkent University
[2] Department of Electrical and Electronics Engineering, Bilkent University

It is now possible to install cameras monitoring sensitive areas but it may not be possible to assign a security guard to each camera or a set of cameras. In addition, security guards may get tired and watch the monitor in a blank manner without noticing important events taking place in front of their eyes. Current CCTV surveillance systems are mostly based on video and recently intelligent video analysis systems capable of detecting humans and cars were developed for surveillance applications. Such systems mostly use Hidden Markov Models (HMM) or Support Vector Machines (SVM) to reach decisions. They detect important events but they also produce false alarms. It is possible to take advantage of other low cost sensors including audio to reduce the number of false alarms. Most video recording systems have the capability of recording audio as well. Analysis of audio for intelligent information extraction is a relatively new area. Automatic detection of broken glass sounds, car crash sounds, screams, increasing sound level at the background are indicators of important events. By combining the information coming from the audio channel with the information from the video channels, reliable surveillance systems can be built. In this chapter, current state of the art is reviewed and an intelligent surveillance system analyzing both audio and video channels is described.

6.1 Multimodal Methods for Surveillance

Multimodal methods have been successfully utilized in the literature to improve the accuracy of automatic speech recognition, human activity recognition and tracking systems [355, 595]. Multimodal surveillance techniques are discussed in a recent edited book by Zhu and Huang [595]. In [597], signals from an array of microphones and a video camera installed in a room are analyzed using a Bayesian based approach for human tracking. A speech recognition system comprising of a visual as well as a audio processing unit is proposed in [147]. A recent patent proposes a coupled hidden Markov model based method for audiovisual speech recognition [361].

P. Maragos et al. (eds.), *Multimodal Processing and Interaction*,
DOI: 10.1007/978-0-387-76316-3_6, © Springer Science+Business Media, LLC 2008

Other abnormal human activities including falling down can also be detected using multimodal analysis. In [525], an audiovisual system is proposed for fall detection. They use wavelet based features for the analysis of audio-visual content of video. Detection of the falling people is achieved by HMM based classification. An alternative method using several other sensor types is described in [526]. Audio, Passive Infrared (PIR) and vibration sensors installed in a room are used to detect falling people in [526].

Similar to background/foreground segmentation in video applications, Cristani et al. propose an adaptive method to build background and foreground models for audio signals [115]. The method is based on the probabilistic modeling of audio channel with adaptive Gaussian mixture models. In another work, authors extend their unimodal audio based background/foreground analysis and event detection system to an audiovisual (AV) based one [116]. They propose a method to detect and segment AV events based on the computation of the so-called "audio-video concurrence matrix".

Zhang et al. propose an approach to automatic segmentation and classification of audiovisual data based only on audio content analysis [591]. They use simple audio features like the energy function, the average zero-crossing rate, the fundamental frequency, and the spectral peak tracks for real-time processing. A heuristic rule-based procedure is proposed to segment and classify audio signals and built upon morphological and statistical analysis of the time-varying functions of these audio features.

Nam et al. present a technique to characterize and index violent scenes in general TV drama and movies by identifying violent signatures and localize violent events within a movie [354]. Their method detects abrupt changes in audio and video signals by computing energy entropies over time frames.

6.2 Multimodal Method for Detecting Fight among People in Unattended Places

Detecting fighting people in unattended places is an important task to save lives and protect properties. Today most of the public places are under continuous surveillance with cameras. However, the recordings are generally saved to tapes for later use only after a forensic event. With the help of low cost digital signal processing systems surveillance video can be processed online to trigger alarms in case of violent behavior and unusual events. This will help to reduce the time it takes to respond to such events that threaten public safety and will prevent casualties. Performances of the video processing algorithms generally degrade due to the inherent noise in the video data and/or camera motion due to wind etc. Hence, it is desirable to support the decision systems with other sensors such as audio to increase the success rate.

In this chapter, we present a system using both video and audio providing information about violent behavior in a scene monitored by a camera and a microphone. Both of the sensor channels are processed in real-time and

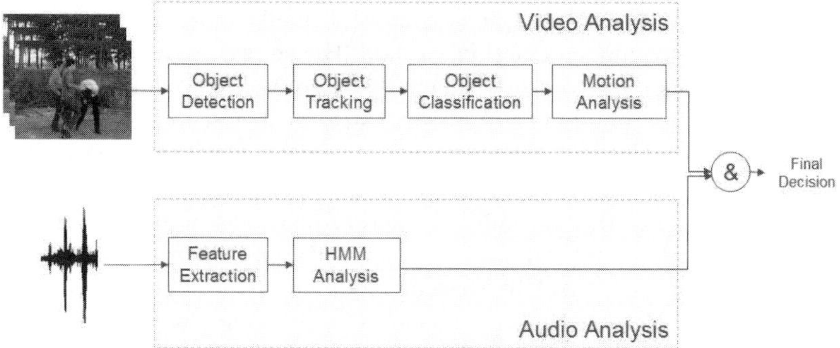

Fig. 6.1. Overview of multimodal fight detection system.

their output are fused together to give the final decision. The overview of our method is shown in Fig. 6.1. In this multimedia system video and audio is processed independently and their decision results of individual processing systems are fused to reach a final decision. In the next subsections we discuss the video processing part of the proposed system.

6.2.1 Video Analysis

Video processing unit of the system analyzes the motion characteristics of humans present in the monitored area in real-time to detect a fight event. In order to accomplish this we need fast and reliable algorithms to detect humans and analyze their actions. In our method, first, moving objects are segmented from the scene background by using an adaptive background subtraction algorithm and then segmented objects are classified into groups like vehicle, human and human group using a silhouette based feature and SVM classification method. After distinguishing humans from other objects, we analyze the motion of the human groups. In case of a fight or a violence, the limbs of the people involved in the violent action generate high frequency motion characteristic. We decide on a fight if the motion characteristic of a human group matches that of a fight action.

Learning Scene Background for Segmentation

There are various methods for segmenting moving objects in video. Background subtraction, statistical methods, temporal differencing and optical flow techniques are commonly used ones. For a discussion on the details of these methods, the reader is referred to [126]. One of the statistical methods extensively used due to its ability to robustly deal with lighting changes, repetitive motions, clutter, introducing or removing objects from the scene and slowly moving objects is presented by Stauffer et al. [505]. It uses a mixture of Gaussian models to represent each pixel on the video stream. Although this method gives good results, it is computationally more demanding than an adaptive background subtraction method. Hence, we use a combination of a background model and low-level image post-processing methods to create a foreground pixel map and extract object features at every video frame. Our implementation of adaptive background subtraction algorithm is partially inspired by the study presented in [103] and works on grayscale video imagery from a static camera. Background subtraction method initializes a reference background with the first few frames of video input. Then it subtracts the intensity value of each pixel in the current image from the corresponding value in the reference background image. The difference is filtered with an adaptive threshold per pixel to account for frequently changing noisy pixels. The reference background image and the threshold values are updated with an Infinite Impulse Response (IIR) filter to adapt to dynamic scene changes. Let $I_n(x)$ represent the gray-level intensity value at pixel position (x) and at time instance n of video image sequence I which is in the range [0, 255]. Let $B_n(x)$ be the corresponding background intensity value for pixel position (x) estimated over time from video images I_0 through I_{n-1}. As the generic background subtraction scheme suggests, a pixel at position (x) in the current video image belongs to foreground if it satisfies:

$$|I_n(x) - B_n(x)| > T_n(x) \tag{6.1}$$

where $T_n(x)$ is an adaptive threshold value estimated using the image sequence I_0 through I_{n-1}. The above equation is used to generate the foreground pixel map which represents the foreground regions as a binary array where a 1 corresponds to a foreground pixel and a 0 stands for a background pixel. The reference background $B_n(x)$ is initialized with the first video image I_0, $B_0 = I_0$, and the threshold image is initialized with some predetermined value (e.g., 15).

Since this system will be used in outdoor environments as well as indoor environments, the background model needs to adapt itself to the dynamic changes such as global illumination change (day night transition) and long term background update (parking a car in front of a building). Therefore the reference background and threshold images are dynamically updated with incoming images. The update scheme is different for pixel positions which are detected as belonging to foreground ($x \in FG$) and which are detected as part of the background ($x \in BG$):

$$B_{n+1}(x) = \begin{cases} \alpha B_n(x) + (1-\alpha)I_n(x), \ x \in BG \\ \beta B_n(x) + (1-\beta)I_n(x), \ x \in FG \end{cases} \tag{6.2}$$

$$T_{n+1}(x) = \begin{cases} \alpha T_n(x) + (1-\alpha)(\gamma \times |I_n(x) - B_n(x)|), & x \in BG \\ T_n(x), & x \in FG \end{cases} \tag{6.3}$$

Fig. 6.2. Detected regions and silhouettes. *Left*: Detected and labeled object regions. *Right*: Extracted object silhouettes.

where α, β ($\in$ [0.0, 1.0]) are learning constants which specify how much information from the incoming image is put to the background and threshold images.

The output of foreground region detection algorithm generally contains noise and therefore is not appropriate for further processing without special post-processing. Morphological operations, erosion and dilation [203], are applied to the foreground pixel map in order to remove noise that is caused by the first three of the items listed above. Our aim in applying these operations is to remove noisy foreground pixels that do not correspond to actual foreground regions and to remove the noisy background pixels near and inside object regions that are actually foreground pixels.

Calculating Object Features

After detecting foreground regions and applying post-processing operations to remove noise and shadow regions, the filtered foreground pixels are grouped into connected regions (blobs) and labeled by using a two-level connected component labeling algorithm presented in [203]. After finding individual blobs that correspond to objects, spatial features like bounding box, size, center of mass and silhouettes of these regions are calculated. In order to calculate the center of mass point, $c_m = (x_{c_m}, y_{c_m})$, of an object O, we use the following formula [463]:

$$x_{c_m} = \frac{\sum_i^n x_i}{n}, \quad y_{c_m} = \frac{\sum_i^n y_i}{n} \tag{6.4}$$

where n is the number of pixels in O. Both in offline and online steps of the classification algorithm, the silhouettes of the detected object regions are extracted from the foreground pixel map by using a contour tracing algorithm presented in [203]. Fig. 6.2 shows sample detected foreground object regions and the extracted silhouettes. Another feature extracted from the object is the silhouette distance signal. Let $S = \{p_1, p_2, \ldots, p_n\}$ be the silhouette of an object O consisting of n points ordered from top center point of the detected region in clockwise direction and c_m be the center of mass point of O. The distance signal $DS = \{d_1, d_2, \ldots, d_n\}$ is generated by calculating the distance between c_m and each p_i starting from 1 through n as follows:

$$d_i = Dist(c_m, p_i), \quad \forall\ i \in [1 \ldots n] \tag{6.5}$$

where the $Dist$ function is the Euclidean distance between two points a and b.

Different objects have different shapes in video and therefore have silhouettes of varying sizes. Even the same object has altering contour size from frame to frame. In order to compare signals corresponding to different sized objects accurately and to make the comparison metric scale-invariant we fix the size of the distance signal. Let N be the size of a distance signal DS and let C be the constant for fixed signal length. The fix-sized distance signal $\widehat{DS}$ is then calculated by sub-sampling or super-sampling the original signal DS as follows:

$$\widehat{DS}[i] = DS[i * \frac{N}{C}], \quad \forall\ i \in [1 \ldots C] \tag{6.6}$$

In the next step, the scaled distance signal $\widehat{DS}$ is normalized to have integral unit area. The normalized distance signal $\overline{DS}$ is calculated with the following equation:

$$\overline{DS}[i] = \frac{\widehat{DS}[i]}{\sum_1^n \widehat{DS}[i]} \tag{6.7}$$

Fig. 6.3 shows a sample silhouette and its original and scaled distance signals. Before using Support Vector Machine algorithm, we transformed contour signals to frequency domain in order to both reduce the amount of data for representation of objects and gaining robustness against rotation. The characteristic features of most objects are hidden in the lower frequency bands of contour signals. We used three different transformations, Discrete Cosine Transform (DCT), Fast Fourier Transform (FFT) and block wavelet. From FFT, DCT and wavelet transformations, we take the first 3-15 coefficients except the first coefficient and use these coefficients as the feature vector while training and testing an SVM.

Classifying Objects

In order to detect fight among people, we need to identify humans in a scene and especially we need to detect the formation of human groups. Categorizing the type of a detected video object is a crucial step in achieving this goal. The process of object classification method consists of two steps:

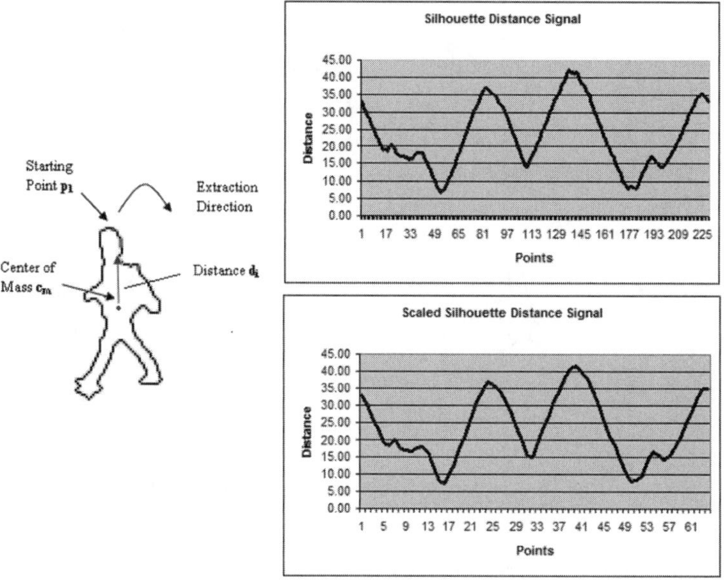

Fig. 6.3. Feature extraction from object silhouette. *Left*: Silhouette extraction. *Upper-Right*: Calculated distance signal, DS. *Lower-Right*: Scaled distance signal, $\widehat{DS}$.

- Offline step: A template database of sample object silhouettes is created by manually labeling object types (one from human, human group and vehicle) and an SVM model is created using the features obtained from the sample objects as explained in previous section.
- Online step: The silhouette of each detected object in each frame is extracted and its type is recognized by using the SVM trained using the sample objects in offline step.

Detecting Fight

During a fight and especially when a person is hitting another person, whole-body displacement is relatively small whereas motion of the limbs of the people is high. Hence, we analyze the motion track of a human group and the motion inside the moving region of the human group. Sample silhouettes of people during a fight are shown in Fig. 6.4.

For each object region R we calculate the number of moving pixels $\in R$ by using frame differencing method to approximate the motion inside the region. The pixels which satisfy the following condition are considered as moving:

$$|I_n(x) - I_{n-1}(x)| > T_n(x) \tag{6.8}$$

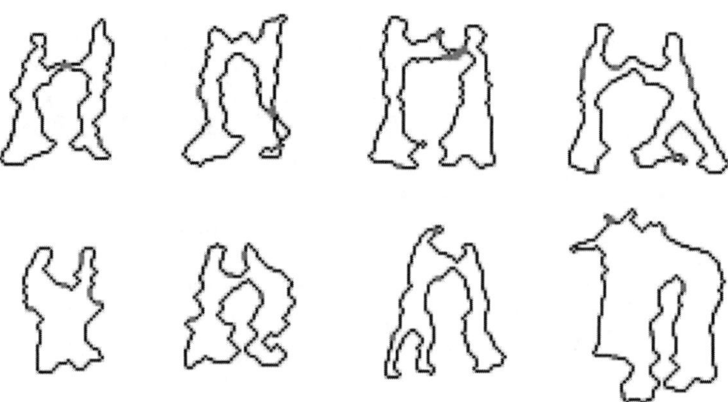

Fig. 6.4. Silhouettes of people during a fight.

where I_n and T_n correspond to image frame and adaptive threshold at time n respectively as explained in Section 6.2.1. Let α_R be the ratio of the number of moving pixels to the total number of pixels inside the region R. Then for object regions where $\alpha_R \geq \gamma$ a violent action is possible, where γ is a threshold constant obtained by tests.

6.2.2 Audio Analysis

In a typical surveillance environment, microphones can be placed near the cameras. Audio signals captured by sound sensors can be used to detect screams in audio stream as a possible indication of violent actions. Shouting has a high amplitude, non-stationary characteristic sound, whereas talking has relatively lower amplitude peakiness. Typical shouting and talking audio recording samples are shown in Fig. 6.5. In this case, the two sound waveforms are clearly different from each other. However, these waveforms may "look" similar as the distance from the sensor increases. For some other cases such as when there is background noise it may become even harder to distinguish different sound activities. In addition, the difference between these two types of signals becomes obvious after wavelet domain signal processing.

Typically audio recordings are due to regular chatting between people and background noise. When there is shouting or broken glass sounds etc this indicates an unusual event. Significantly loud voice or sound activity is detected using the Teager Energy operator based speech features originally developed by Jabloun and Cetin [229]. The sound data is divided into frames as in any speech processing method and the Teager energy based cepstral (TEOCEP) [229] feature parameters are obtained using wavelet domain signal analysis. The sound signal is divided into 21 non uniformly divided subbands

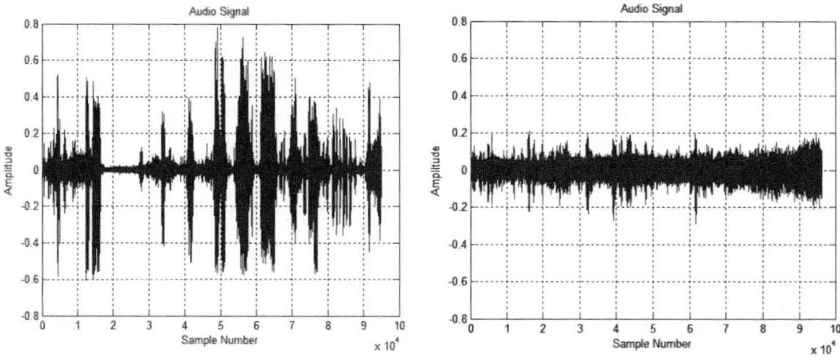

Fig. 6.5. Sample audio signals. *Left*: Shouting signal. *Right*: Talking signal.

similar to the Bark scale (or mel-scale) giving more emphasis to low-frequency regions of the sound.

To calculate the TEOCEP feature parameters, a two-channel wavelet filter bank is used in a tree structure to divide the audio signal $s(n)$ according to the mel-scale as shown in Fig. 6.6, and 21 wavelet domain sub-signals $s1(n)$, $l = 1, \ldots, L = 21$, are obtained [152]. The filter bank of a biorthogonal wavelet transform is used in the analysis [259]. The lowpass filter has the transfer function

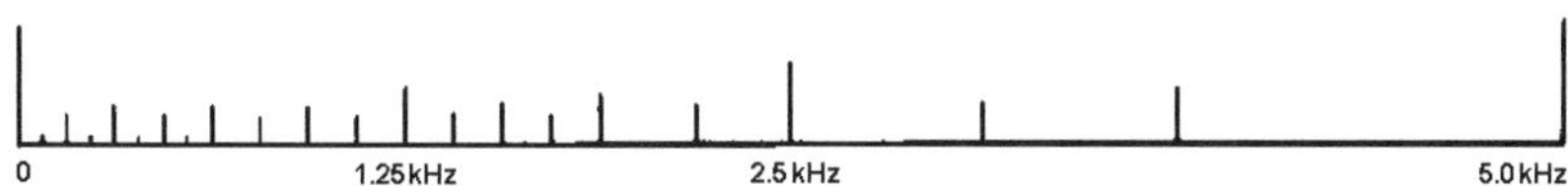

Fig. 6.6. The subband frequency decomposition of the sound signal.

$$H_l(z) = \frac{1}{2} + \frac{9}{32}(z^{-1} + z^1) - \frac{1}{32}(z^{-3} + z^3) \tag{6.9}$$

and the corresponding high-pass filter has the transfer function

$$H_h(z) = \frac{1}{2} - \frac{9}{32}(z^{-1} + z^1) + \frac{1}{32}(z^{-3} + z^3) \tag{6.10}$$

For every subsignal, the average Teager energy e_l is estimated as follows:

$$e_l = \frac{1}{N_l} \sum_{n=1}^{N_l} |\Psi[s_l(n)]| ; \qquad l = 1, \ldots, L \tag{6.11}$$

where N_l is the number of samples in the lth band, and the Teager energy operator (TEO) is defined as follows:

$$\Psi[s(n) = s^2(n) - s(n+1)s(n-1) \tag{6.12}$$

The TEO-based cepstrum coefficients are obtained after log-compression and inverse DCT computation as follows:

$$TC(k) = \sum_{l=1}^{L} \log e_l \cos\left[\frac{k(l-0.5)\pi}{L}\right]; \qquad k = 1, \ldots, N \tag{6.13}$$

The first 12 $TC(k)$ coefficients are used in the feature vector. The TEO-CEP parameters are fed to the sound activity detector algorithm described in [525] to detect significant sound activity in the environment.

When there is significant sound activity in the room, another feature parameter based on variance of wavelet coefficients and zero crossings is computed in each window. The wavelet signal corresponding to the [2.5 kHz, 5.0 kHz] frequency band is obtained after a single stage wavelet filterbank. The variance, σ_i^2 of the wavelet signal and the number of zero crossings, Z_i, in each window i is computed.

Broken glass and similar sounds are not quasi-periodic in nature. As talking is mostly quasi-periodic because of voiced sounds the zero crossing value, Z_i, is small compared to noise like sounds. When a person shouts the variance of the wavelet signal σ_i^2 increases compared to the background noise and regular chatting. So we define a feature parameter κ_i in each window i as $\kappa_i = \frac{\sigma_i^2}{Z_i}$, where the index i indicates the window number. The parameter κ_i takes non-negative values.

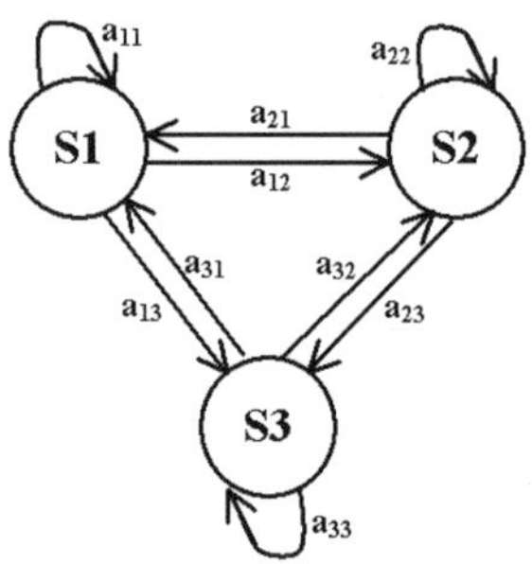

Fig. 6.7. Three state Markov model. Three Markov models are used to represent speech, walking, and fall sounds.

Activity classification based on sound information is carried out using HMMs. Three three-state Markov models are used to represent shout and talking sounds as shown in Fig. 6.7. In Markov models, S1 corresponds to the background noise or no activity. If sound activity detector (SAD) indicates that there is no significant activity, S1 is selected. If SAD detects sound activity in a sound frame, then either S2 or S3 is chosen as the current state according to the value of κ.

A non-negative threshold value, T, that is small enough to reflect the periodicity in step sounds is introduced in the κ-domain. If $|\kappa| < T$, S2; otherwise, S3 is attained as the current state. The classification performance of HMMs is based on the number of state transitions, rather than specific κ values. Hence, choice of T does not affect the values of the transition probabilities in different models.

In order to train HMMs, the state transition probabilities are estimated from 20 consecutive κ_i values corresponding to 20 consecutive 500-sample-long wavelet windows covering 125 msec of audio data.

During the classification phase a state history signal consisting of 20 κ_i values are estimated from the sound signal acquired from the audio sensor. This state sequence is fed to Markov models corresponding to shouting and talking cases in running windows. The model yielding the highest probability is determined as the result of the analysis of the sound sensor signal.

Feature parameter κ takes high values for a regular speech sound. Consequently, the value of a_{33} is higher than any other transition probabilities in the talking model. For the shout case, a relatively long noise period is followed by a sudden increase and then a sudden decrease in κ values. This results in higher a_{11} value than any other transition probabilities. In addition to that, the number of transitions within, to and from S2 are notably fewer than those of S1 and S3. The state S2 in the Markov models provides hysteresis and it prevents sudden transitions from S1 to S3 or vice versa, which is especially the case for talking.

6.2.3 Deciding on a Fight or Violent Behavior

Audio and video analysis results are combined at each frame of the video sequence in the proposed system. In order to accomplish this audio sample frames are matched to video frames by combining the video frame rate and audio signal sampling rate.

For each time frame, video processing results and audio processing results are combined with the simple AND operator and the final decision is given on the result of this operator. In other words, we require both of the processing channels to decide on fight action to raise an alarm.

6.2.4 Experimental Results

Experimental results on sample video sequences containing violent action scenarios are presented in this section. All of the tests are performed by using a video player application, vPlayer, on Microsoft Windows XP Professional operating system on a computer with an Intel Pentium dual core 3.2GHz CPU and 1 GB of RAM.

	Human	Human Group	Vehicle	Success Rate
Human	20	0	0	100 %
Human Group	1	18	1	90 %
Vehicle	0	2	18	90 %

Table 6.1. Confusion matrix for object classification.

We tested our object classification algorithm on sample video clips. After collecting sample silhouettes and applying transformations to create feature vectors, we obtained an SVM model. In support vector machine training algorithm, we used Radial Basis Function (RBF) kernel with gamma=1, and tested the performance of SVM algorithm with different types transformations (FFT, DCT and wavelet) and different coefficient numbers. In our tests, feature vectors obtained by wavelet transform slightly outperformed other transformation methods. We used three object classes in our tests: human, human group and vehicle. We used 248 random objects for training the SVM model (93 human, 102 human group and 53 vehicle pictures) and 60 different objects (20 from each group) for testing the algorithm. The confusion matrix is shown in Table 6.1.

We also tested our multi-model fight detection algorithm on sample video clips with audio. The results are shown in Tables 6.2, 6.3 and 6.4 as confusion matrices. In both audio-only and video-only processing, the success rate for detecting fight is high. However, the false alarm rate which is calling a normal action as fight is high in both cases. When we fuse the results of these two channels together we get a lower false alarm rate and thus a higher average success rate.

	Fight	Normal	Success Rate
Fight	13	2	86.7 %
Normal	8	13	61.9 %
Average			74.3 %

Table 6.2. Confusion matrix for multimodal fight detection using both Audio & Video.

6.3 Conclusion

In this chapter, we proposed a novel multimodal system for real-time violence detection. Video data and audio signals are analyzed independently with the proposed algorithms and the analysis results from these two signals are fused together to reach a final decision. The test results show that the presented

	Fight	Normal	Success Rate
Fight	14	1	93.3 %
Normal	10	11	52.3 %
Average			72.9 %

Table 6.3. Confusion matrix for multimodal fight detection using only Audio.

	Fight	Normal	Success Rate
Fight	13	2	86.7 %
Normal	9	12	57.1 %
Average			71.2 %

Table 6.4. Confusion matrix for multimodal fight detection using only Video.

method is promising and can be improved with some further work to reduce false alarms. The use of audio signals in parallel with video analysis helps us to detect violent behavior with less false alarms.

A weakness of the proposed video analysis algorithm is that it is view dependent. If the camera setup is different in training and testing, the success rate will be lower. Automating video object classification method with online learning would help to create an adaptive algorithm.

7

Movie Analysis with Emphasis to Dialogue and Action Scene Detection

Emmanouil Benetos, Spyridon Siatras, Constantine Kotropoulos, Nikos Nikolaidis, and Ioannis Pitas

Aristotle University of Thessaloniki, Greece

Movies constitute a large portion of the entertainment industry, as over 9.000 hours of video are released every year [21]. As the bandwidth available to users increases, online movie stores – the equivalent of popular digital music stores – are emerging. They provide users an opportunity to build large personal movie repositories. The convenience of digital movie repositories will be in doubt, unless multimedia data management is employed for organizing, navigating, browsing, searching, and viewing multimedia content. Semantic content-based video indexing offers a promising solution for efficient digital movie management.

Semantic video indexing aims at extracting, characterizing, and organizing video content by analyzing the visual, aural, and textual information sources of video. The need for content-based audiovisual analysis has been realized by the MPEG committee, leading to the creation of the MPEG-7 standard [16]. The current approaches for automatic movie analysis and annotation mostly focus on the visual information, while the aural information receives little or no attention. However, the integration of the aural information with the visual one can improve semantic movie content analysis.

The predominant approach to semantic movie analysis is to initially extract some low-level audiovisual features (such as color and texture from images or energy and pitch from audio), derive some mid-level entities (such as video shots, keyframes, appearance of faces and audio classes), and finally understand video semantic content by analyzing and combining these entities. A hierarchical video indexing structure is displayed in Fig. 7.1.

Movie analysis aims at obtaining a structured organization of the movie content and understanding its embedded semantics like humans do. It has been handled in different ways, depending on the analysis level and the assumptions on the film syntax described in Section 7.1. Most movie analysis efforts concentrate on movie scene or shot detection, while other works focus on the separation of dialogue and non-dialogue scenes. Several efforts have been made for dialogue scene detection, some efforts have concentrated to

P. Maragos et al. (eds.), *Multimodal Processing and Interaction*,
DOI: 10.1007/978-0-387-76316-3_7,

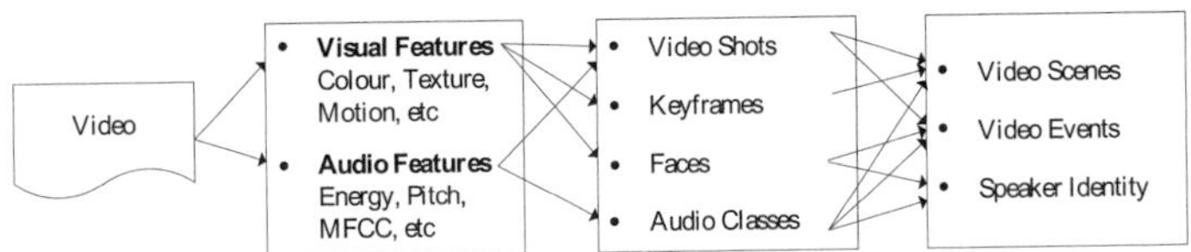

Fig. 7.1. Generic video indexing structure, where arrows between nodes indicate a causal relationship (adapted from [300]).

action scene detection, and limited work has also been performed for movie genre categorization.

In this chapter, we put emphasis on the detection of dialogue and action scenes in a video sequence using visual and aural cues. Dialogue and action scenes can be interpreted as high-level semantic features that are appropriate for inclusion in more sophisticated organization, browsing, and retrieval techniques applied to movies and television programs. Their successful detection provides significant semantic information for the video sequence, that is especially useful for managing certain classes of video content. Dialogue detection in conjunction with face or speaker identification methods could also identify the scenes where two (or more) particular persons are conversing. Furthermore, a quantitative comparison between the duration of dialogue scenes and the duration of non-dialogue scenes in a movie can be used for movie genre classification. As far as action scene detection is concerned, it can be applied to a film summarization system, where users can quickly and easily browse the content of a film. Dialogue and action scenes follow specific patterns concerning their constituent shots, a fact that makes their detection in a video sequence feasible.

The main aim of this chapter is to review the research related to dialogue and action scene detection and to assess qualitatively and quantitatively the various methods. These methods can be broadly classified as video-only, audio-only, or audiovisual ones. A second classification distinguishes them to deterministic methods and probabilistic ones.

The remainder of the chapter is organized as follows. In Section 7.1, the basic principles of film structure and video editing rules for constructing dialogue and action scenes are discussed. The most commonly employed figures of merit are defined in Section 7.2 along with the datasets utilized in movie analysis literature. Sections 7.3 and 7.4 review the basic principles and state-of-the-art algorithms for visual-only, audio-only, and audiovisual dialogue-action scene detection, respectively. Conclusions are drawn in Section 7.5.

7.1 Film Syntax Basics

A movie or television program can be divided into *shots* and *scenes*. A shot is defined as a single continuous camera recording, whereas a scene consists of a concatenation of shots, which are temporally and spatially cohesive *in the real world*, however not necessarily cohesive in the projection of the real world on film [20, 111]. Rasheed and Shah give a similar definition, stating that similar shots of a movie must be combined in order to form a scene or a *story unit* [424]. The notion of *computable scenes* (c-scenes) is proposed to characterize scenes that can be reliably computed using only low-level features [514]. They are derived by fusing information from audio and visual boundary detectors. Another term that has been proposed is the *logical story unit* (LSU) which is a high-level temporal movie segment characterized by a single event (dialog, action scene). The LSU segmentation is based on the investigation of visual information and its temporal variations in a video sequence. A movie can be modeled as a sequence of states and events, organized in space and time, by creating a *state graph* representing the film story [542].

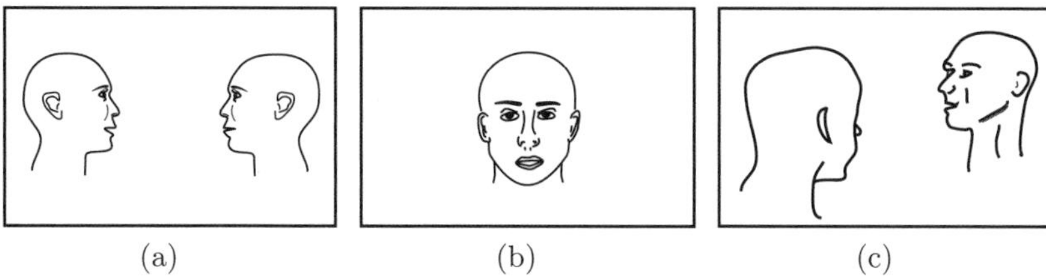

Fig. 7.2. Sample frames from shots usually employed in dialogue scenes. (a) Side view of two persons. (b) Frontal view of one person. (c) Over-the-shoulder shot (a shot of one person taken from over the shoulder of another person).

As far as dialogues are concerned, a *dialogue scene* can be defined as a set of consecutive shots, which contain conversations of people [20, 277]. In Fig. 7.2, frames from shots broadly employed in dialogue scenes are depicted. In such a scene, the persons who participate in the dialogue will be present either one at a time (Fig. 7.2(b)) or all in the same image frame, in frontal or side view (Fig. 7.2(a) and 7.2(c)). In general, a dialogue scene includes a significantly repetitious structure of shots depicting the dialogue participants. However, a dialogue scene might include shots which do not contain any conversation or do not even depict a dialogue participant. For example, shots of other persons or objects might be inserted in the dialogue scene. In addition, the shot of the speaker may depict the rear view of his head. Evidently, these shots add to the complexity of the dialogue detection problem. According to Chen and Özsu, the elements of a dialogue scene are: the people, the conversation, and the location where the dialogue takes place [94]. The basic shots in a 2-person dialogue scene are:

- Type A shot: Shot of actor A's face.
- Type B shot: Shot of actor B's face.
- Type C shot: Shot with both faces visible.

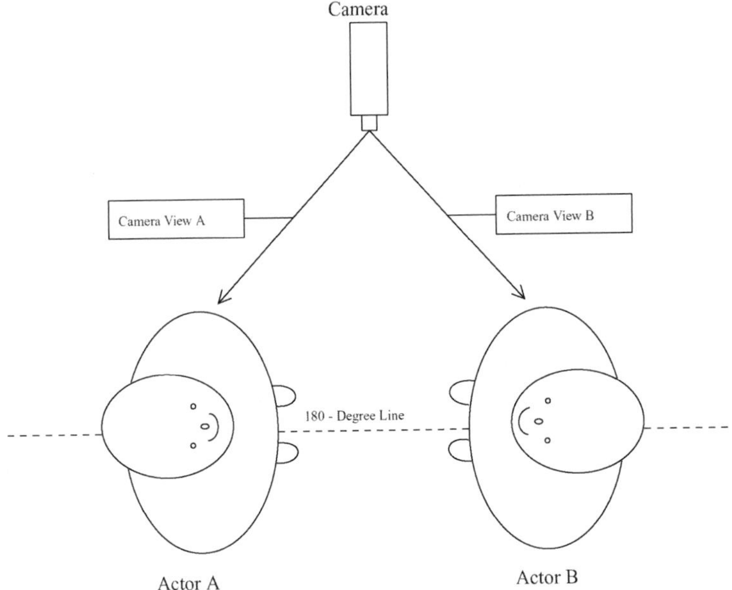

Fig. 7.3. The concept of the 180° line (adapted from [288]).

- Type # shot: Shot displaying something relevant to the dialogue, or not covered by the three previous types of shots.

Lehane et al. state that usually in a 2-person dialogue, an A-B-A-B structure of camera shots exists [288]. Moreover, the camera must remain fixed on the focus of interest. The most widely used dialogue scene convention is the concept of the 180° line. The line is set up at the start of the scene and it is typically followed in the remainder of the scene so that viewers can follow the action. Generally, this means that the camera must remain on the same side of the actors, as illustrated in Fig. 7.3.

Concerning film syntax for action sequences, Lehane et al. mention that it is a general concept meant to keep the audience's attention at all times [287]. The objective of the director is to excite the viewer by a rapid succession of shots, strong movement within shots, and variation in the length of shots. Pans, tilts, and zooms are used to follow characters moving within shots. According to Chen and Özsu, the rules governing the actor arrangement and camera placement in simple action scenes are the same to those applied to simple dialogue scenes, even though, actors move rapidly and cameras follow the actors in action scenes [94].

A 2-person dialogue scene, from the audio point of view, can be defined as a proper alternation between two speakers [277]. Dialogues in an audio framework can be detected by using the cross-correlation function between the speaker indicator functions or their respective cross-power spectra. A set of recognizable dialogue acts, according to semantic content, based on audio analysis, is proposed in [279]: (i) Statements (ii) Questions (iii) Backchannels (iv) Incomplete utterance (v) Agreements (vi) Appreciations.

In contrast with dialogue scenes, the audio channel in an action scene usually consists of less speech and more environmental sounds or music [95]. The soundtrack of an action scene is chosen in a way to create tension and suspense to the viewers. It is much different than the soundtrack of a dialogue scene, where, if music accompanies the dialogue, it is discrete and unobtrusive. Hence, action scenes exhibit a higher audio energy due to tense music, explosions, people fights, etc. A more detailed description of the basic principles of film syntax can be found in [46, 70].

7.2 Figures of merit and movie datasets

The most commonly used figures of merit in dialogue and action scene detection experiments are *recall* (R), *precision* (P), and F_1 *measure*, defined as

$$P = \frac{hits}{hits + false\ alarms}, \qquad R = \frac{hits}{hits + misses}, \qquad F_1 = \frac{2R \cdot P}{R + P}. \tag{7.1}$$

Hits are defined as correctly detected dialogue or action scenes. False alarms should not have been detected as dialogue/action scenes, but are nevertheless detected as such. Misses are defined as scenes that should have been identified as dialogue/action scenes, but were not. Other performance metrics used for the evaluation of dialogue/action scene detection algorithms are the *hit rate*, the *miss rate*, and the *false hit rate* [401]. The authors employing these figures of merit, argue that scene determination is equivalent to eliminating the shot boundaries which do not correspond to scene boundaries. The hit rate is the ratio of correctly eliminated shot boundaries plus the correctly detected scene boundaries over the number of all shot boundaries. The miss rate is the ratio of missed scene boundaries to the number of all shot boundaries. The false hit rate determines the ratio of falsely detected scene boundaries to the number of all shot boundaries. Finally, Alatan et al. [19, 20, 21] employ the *shot accuracy* measure, which is defined as the ratio of correct shot assignments to the total number of shots.

The movies and TV shows used for dialogue and action scene detection are listed in Table 7.1. It should be noted that there is no common database used for dialogue and action scene detection experiments.

7.3 Visual-only and Audio-only Dialogue and Action Scene Detection

In this section, a review of the recent advances in dialogue and action scene detection techniques, using only the visual information or the aural one, will be

Table 7.1. Movies and TV shows used in scene analysis and dialogue detection experiments.

Movie	Reference	Movie	Reference
MPEG-7 Data Set (CDs 20-22)[1]	[21][19][20]	Braveheart	[300]
Crouching Tiger, Hidden Dragon	[94][95]	When Harry Met Sally	[300]
Gladiator	[94][95]	Forrest Gump	[401]
Patch Adams	[94]	Groundhog Day	[401]
Analyze That	[277]	A Beautiful Mind	[424]
Cold Mountain	[277]	Goldeneye	[424]
Jackie Brown	[277]	Gone in 60 Seconds	[424]
Fellowship of the Ring	[277]	Terminator II	[424]
Platoon	[277]	Top Gun	[424]
Secret Window	[277]	Four Weddings and a Funeral	[514]
Dumb and Dumberer	[287][288]	Pulp Fiction	[514]
Kill Bill vol. 1	[287][288]	Sense and Sensibility	[514]
Reservoir Dogs	[287][288]	CNN Headline News	[587]
Snatch	[287][288]	Dr. No	[587]
American Beauty	[288]	Jurassic Park III	[587]
High Fidelity	[288]	Larry King Live	[587]
Shaft	[288]	Mission Impossible II	[587]
Life of Brian	[288]	Scream	[587]
Legends of the Fall	[299][300]	The Others	[587]

[1] The MPEG-7 Data Set CDs 20, 21, and 22 contain a Spanish TV movie, a Spanish TV sitcom, and a Portuguese TV sitcom, respectively.

undertaken. The features extracted from the video and audio are described, selected algorithms are examined, and their results are presented and discussed.

The proposed approaches for dialogue and action scene detection can be classified into two main categories: *deterministic* and *probabilistic* ones. Deterministic techniques exploit the repetitive structure exhibited by visually similar shots that are temporally close to each other [29, 94, 277, 287, 288, 401, 514], whereas probabilistic techniques use Hidden Markov Models (HMMs) to assign semantically meaningful scenes to model states. The video content is segmented into dialogue or action scenes using the state transitions of the HMM [161, 568].

7.3.1 Deterministic Approaches

The deterministic approaches to visual-only or audio-only dialogue and action scene detection are based on the extraction of low-level features such as color, motion, texture, silence ratio, and audio energy. Shots which exhibit similar attributes and are temporally close to one another are clustered together. The presence of a dialogue scene is revealed by a repetitious structure of similar shots or a repetitive change of speakers. However, errors emerge in methods where only low-level information is used. A scene simply exhibiting a repetitive shot structure could be classified as a dialogue scene. Furthermore, errors might appear when a speaker dominates the dialogue and the other participants are less frequently shown. Hence, most recent methods include post-processing steps in order to eliminate the errors and improve their performance. For action scene detection, dialogue detection is extended by employing the average shot length and measuring motion activity.

In [514], dialogues are detected by exploiting the local topology of an image sequence and employing statistical tests. A topological framework examining the local metric relationships between images is introduced. The analysis assumes that each shot in the video is represented by a single keyframe. The topological graph $T_G = \{V, E\}$ of a sequence of K images is a fully connected graph with vertices being the video sequence images and edges specifying the metric relationship between the images. Let T_{MAT} be the $K \times K$ adjacency matrix of T_G. An ideal dialogue is a structure, where every 2nd keyframe is alike, while adjacent keyframes differ. In such a case, T_{MAT} contains ones in the 1st off-diagonal elements, zeros in the 2nd off-diagonal elements, ones in the 3rd off-diagonal elements, and so forth. The following periodic analysis transform $\Delta(n)$ is proposed to identify the aforementioned structure in a sequence of N shot keyframes. If o_i, $i \in \{0, N-1\}$, is a time-ordered sequence of keyframes, then

$$\Delta(n) = 1 - \frac{1}{N} \sum_{i=0}^{N-1} d(o_i, o_{\mathrm{mod}(i+n,N)}), \tag{7.2}$$

where $d()$ is a color histogram-based distance function. The system detects dialogues by determining whether $\Delta(2) > \Delta(1)$ and $\Delta(2) > \Delta(3)$ are statistically significant decisions. The dialogue detection algorithm applies a sliding window to the entire video sequence. Experiments performed in three movies (cf. Table 7.1) have produced a recall rate between 80% and 91% at a precision rate fluctuating between 84% and 100%. However, the system under discussion is operating at its full potential only when the dialogue exhibits a periodic structure.

In [29], *shot interactivity* is introduced. It expresses how actively shots relate to one another in a particular time segment. The algorithm is based on the observation of repetitive appearances of similar shots. Similar shots are determined with respect to the characteristics of the included frames, such as the color histogram and the luminance layout of mosaic picture [30]. Dialogue scenes are identified by clustering groups of neighboring shots whose shot interactivity exceeds a threshold. Two parameters, *dialogue density* δ, which expresses the sum of shot durations, and *dialogue velocity* v, which expresses how frequently the speakers change, are defined:

$$\delta_{\alpha b} = \frac{\sum_{i=\alpha}^{b} \rho_{\alpha b,i} \lambda_i}{\sum_{i=\alpha}^{b} \lambda_i} \qquad \upsilon_{\alpha b} = \frac{\sum_{i=\alpha}^{b} \rho_{\alpha b,i}}{\sum_{i=\alpha}^{b} \lambda_i} \tag{7.3}$$

where λ_i is the duration of shot i, and $\rho_{\alpha b,i}$ is a binary variable which admits the value 1, when shot i contains a dialogue in the shot range $[\alpha, b]$. The shot interactivity from shot α to shot b, is the product of $\delta_{\alpha b}$ and $\upsilon_{\alpha b}$, which increases either with the increase of the length of shots which include a dialogue or when frequent transitions between the speakers occur. Experiments were conducted in 4 news shows and 3 variety shows. On average, the recall rate for news programs was 86% and the corresponding precision was 94%. For variety shows, both rates were found to be 100%.

In [288], a dialogue detection system is described, that employs low and mid-level visual features. The system is depicted in Fig. 7.4. The first level of the system involves the processing of low-level visual data, determining the shot boundaries and the motion present within each shot of a video sequence. Histogram-based shot boundary detection is applied in order to extract keyframes, whereas the motion extraction block employs the motion vectors exported from the MPEG-1 bitstream. In the second level of the system, visually similar shots, that are temporally close, are clustered together. The clustering method is based on the difference of the average color histogram between the shot keyframes [573]. At the same level, camera motion analysis is performed determining if significant motion is present in a shot. In the third level of the system, dialogue detection is performed. First, potential dialogue sequences (PDS) are identified solely from the camera motion analysis output. Hence, when a number of consecutive static shots is encountered, a PDS is declared. When non-static shots begin to dominate over the static ones, the PDS ends. After having identified all PDS, a further processing step is applied in order to verify whether these scenes are indeed dialogue scenes or not. This process involves the calculation of the so-called *cluster to shot ratio* $\varrho = C/S$ (denoted as $C : S$ in [288]) in the PDS, which determines the percentage of visually unrelated shots in the PDS. The ratio ϱ is simply the number of clusters that have shots within the PDS to the total number of shots in the PDS. The authors argue that a low value of ϱ is consistent with a dialogue scene, since it reveals a repetitive structure of similar shots. Five movies with a total of 171 manually marked-up dialogues were used to evaluate system performance (cf. Table 7.1). Scenes marked as a dialogue by the authors were sequences of five or more shots containing at least two people conversing, where the main focus of the sequence is conversation. For instance, two people conversing in the middle of a car chase would not apply to that rule, as the main focus was considered to be in the chase. The average recall and precision rates were 86% and 77.8%, respectively. However, as the authors state, an improvement in the exact start and end points of dialogues is necessary.

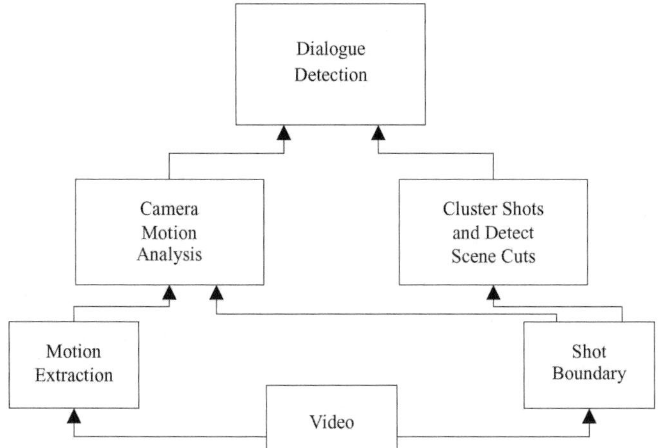

Fig. 7.4. Dialogue detection system proposed by Lehane et al. [288].

The same authors have extended the work in [288] by proposing a similar configuration for detecting action sequences in movies, where the final level of the system differs [287]. The detection of action sequences is performed by using a state machine that was created to search for sequences that match the structure of action scenes. In particular, the state machine looks for sequences in which temporally short shots with high motion activity are dominant. These potential action sequences (PAS) are either accepted or rejected as being true action sequences based on the clustering input. The authors consider that an action scene should lead to a quite high ratio ϱ. For this reason, they apply an empirically chosen threshold to this ratio. Experiments were performed in 4 movies (cf. Table 7.1), and the reported recall and precision rates exceeded 80% and 40%, respectively.

Chen and Özsu proposed a rule based model to extract simple dialogue and action scenes instead of clustering shots into scenes using image features [94]. The rules utilized the four types of shots defined in Section 7.1, which determine whether participants' faces are visible in the shot of a 2-person dialogue scene or not and define what type of shot may follow an A, B, or C-type shot. Based on these rules, a finite state machine (FSM) was developed, being able to extract simple (2-person) dialogue or one-on-one fighting scenes. More specifically, a small number of consecutive shots, used to establish a dialogue scene, was characterized as *elementary dialogue scene*. The authors empirically identified 18 different types of elementary dialogue scenes.

The concept of a *video shot string* (VSS) is introduced, in order to represent the temporal occurrence of the different shot types in a video sequence. A VSS is a set of video shots whose types belong to one of the four video shot types defined in Section 7.1. A VSS of a dialogue scene (VSSDS) is defined as a VSS whose prefix is the one for the elementary dialogue scenes expanded by appending some of the three types of shots which include the dialogue participants' faces. An elementary dialogue scene ending with a shot A can be expanded by appending either shot B or C. An elementary dialogue scene, with no additional shots appended to it, is classified as a VSSDS as well. In order to extract VSSDS, the VSS is input to a deterministic FSM. A dialogue scene is extracted when a path corresponding to a VSSDS is encountered. The differentiation between dialogue and action scenes was based on the average shot length in a scene, considering that the average shot length in action scenes is smaller than that in dialogue scenes. Experiments were conducted in 3 movies for dialogue detection and 2 movies for action detection (cf. Table 7.1). The movies were first segmented into shots and the actor appearances were manually marked and used as input to the FSM. For the three movies, the dialogue scene detection algorithm exhibited a recall rate equal to 96.6%, 90.51%, and 97.28% at precision rate of 89.47%, 80.52%, and 91.79%, respectively. Correspondingly, the action scene detection algorithm had a recall rate equal to 84% and 81.6%, at a precision rate of 84%, 76.56%, respectively.

In [401], a technique for clustering shots into settings or dialogues is described. The dialogue scenes are considered to have alternating shots of the participants with only one character displayed at any given time in frontal view. A face detector [448] and a face recognition method are also employed. Faces in neighboring frames, which exhibit similarity in position and size, are assigned to groups called *face-based classes*. In a second step, face-based classes with similar faces within the same shot are merged by the eigenfaces [393] in order to obtain the largest possible face-based classes. A sequence of at least three consecutive shots is identified as a dialogue when the following conditions apply. At least one face-based class should be present in each shot, being no more than 1 s apart from its neighbor. Additionally, the eigenface merged face-based classes should alternate within the shot sequence. Experiments performed in two movies for the determination of dialogue scene boundaries yielded hit rates equal to 80% and 86%, miss rates equal to 7% and 4%, and false hit rates 13% and 10%, respectively.

In [277], 2-person dialogue detection using audio-only information is presented. Each speaker is characterized by an indicator function that defines that he or she is present at each time instant. Two dialogue detection rules were developed and assessed. The first rule relies on the value of the cross-correlation sequence of a pair of indicator functions at zero time lag that is compared to a threshold. The second rule is based on the cross-power in a particular frequency band that is also compared to a threshold. Experiments have been carried out in order to validate the feasibility of the aforementioned dialogue detection rules by using ground-truth indicator functions determined by human observers hearing the audio channel from six different movies. A total of 25 dialogue scenes and another 8 non-dialogue scenes were employed. Experiments were performed in 6 movies, exhibiting a precision rate of 100% at a recall rate of 85.7%, yielding an F_1 measure of 0.922. Moreover, in [276] a variety of artificial neural networks has also been tested for dialogue detection on a larger set than that in [277]. This set includes 27 dialogue scenes and another 12 non-dialogue ones extracted from the same 6 movies. All artificial neural networks are fed by the entire cross-correlation sequence and the cross-power spectral density. In particular, multilayer perceptrons (MLPs), voted perceptrons, radial basis function neural networks, support vector machines (with and without application of AdaBoost and MultiBoost), and 3-layered particle swarm optimization-based MLPs were employed. The experimental results indicate that, the highest F_1 measure achieved by the three-layered particle swarm optimization-based MLP is equal to 0.934. The reported F_1 measure can be treated as an upper bound of the actual figure of merit for dialogue detection in movies that could be obtained by employing speaker turn detection, speaker clustering, and speaker tracking.

7.3.2 Probabilistic Approaches

In addition to deterministic approaches, probabilistic ones using HMMs have been proposed and implemented for the efficient characterization of dialogue scenes [420, 421]. The design of an HMM consists in defining its states, specifying its topology, and determining the parameters at each state. Then, the HMM parameters are computed using the Baum-Welch algorithm and the best state sequence for a given input is determined using the Viterbi algorithm.

HMMs were used by Ferman and Tekalp for extracting the semantic content of a video sequence [161]. The HMM models the time-varying structure of a video sequence. It is characterized in terms of its component shots, as depicted in Fig. 7.5(a) and is used to classify each shot of the sequence into one among three categories represented by HMM states. The *Dialogue* state represents self-repetitive shots that reoccur over a temporal window, while the *Progression* state encompasses the shots introducing new camera setups. The *Misc* state accounts for miscellaneous entries, not included in the two other states. The HMM used to model the dialogue state is illustrated in Fig. 7.5(b). The *Est* state represents an establishing shot, used to determine the location of the action, whereas the *Master* state refers to master shots which provide a view of all characters in the scene. The states *1-Shot* and *2-Shot* correspond to shots including the respective number of people.

Each shot of the video sequence is characterized by a single feature vector given as input to the HMMs. The necessary features include the normalized distance of the median histograms of two successive shots, the normalized pixel differences between the last frame of a shot and the first frame of its immediate successor, and the normalized distance between the direction histograms of the last few frames of a shot and the first few frames of its neighbor. The direction histogram is comprised from the orientations of the individual motion vectors. Furthermore, shot duration, shot activity, as well as shot transition type (cut, fade, or dissolve) are incorporated in the feature vector. After having computed the feature vectors for each shot, the Baum-Welch algorithm is

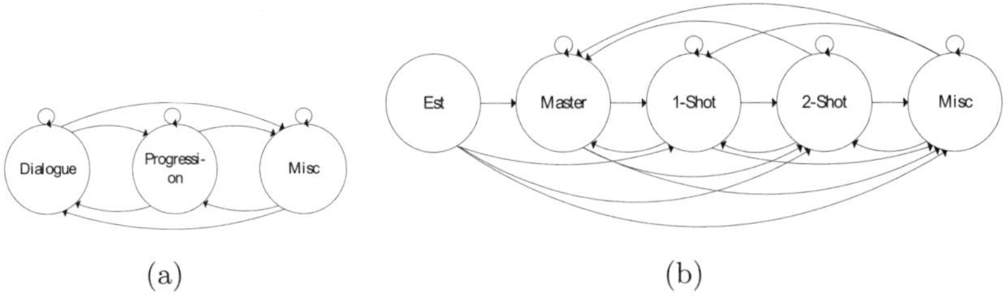

Fig. 7.5. HMMs proposed in [161]: (a) HMM for characterizing video sequences (b) HMM for dialogue sequences.

employed to train the HMMs, and shot labeling is performed using the Viterbi algorithm.

7.3.3 Performance Assessment

The results achieved for visual-only or audio-only dialogue and action scene detection techniques, we have reviewed, are summarized in Table 7.2. When the authors provide results for each movie or TV program separately, the average results, measured over the total number of dialogue and action scenes in all movies, have been included in Table 7.2. In addition, we have computed the F_1 metric for all the methods described. It should be noted however, that, since most of these results have been obtained on different test sets, they are not directly comparable and are included only to provide a rough comparison between the various methods.

Table 7.2. Results for visual-only and audio-only dialogue or action scene detection.

Reference	Recall	Precision	F_1
Aoki (dialogue detection - news) [29]	86.0%	94.0%	0.898
Aoki (dialogue detection - variety) [29]	100.0%	100.0%	1.000
Chen and Özsu (dialogue detection) [94]	94.8%	87.4%	0.909
Kotti et al. (dialogue detection) [277]	85.7%	100.0%	0.922
Lehane et al. (dialogue detection) [288]	86.0%	77.8%	0.816
Sundaram and Chang (dialogue detection) [514]	86.0%	95.0%	0.903
Chen and Özsu (action scene detection) [94]	82.3%	78.6%	0.804
Lehane et al. (action sequence detection) [287]	92.6%	59.4%	0.533

Reference	Hit Rate	Miss Rate	False Hit Rate
Pfeiffer et al. (dialogue detection) [401]	84%	12%	3.9%

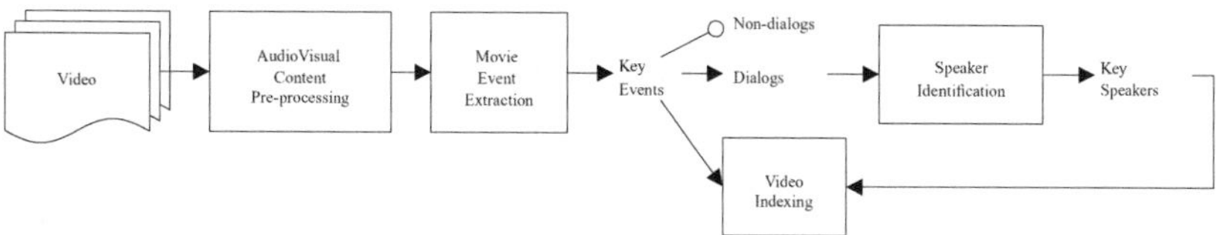

Fig. 7.6. Movie analysis framework proposed by Li et al. (adapted from [300]).

7.4 Audiovisual Dialogue and Action Scene Detection

In this section, methods are discussed, which exploit both video and audio information, for efficient detection of dialogue and action scenes. Some methods are extensions of those described in Section 7.3, incorporating the information contained in both the video and the audio channels. The techniques for audiovisual dialogue and action scene detection are classified as deterministic [95, 288, 300, 587] or probabilistic [21, 19, 20, 299, 572], like in Section 7.3. While the deterministic methods usually cluster consecutive shots by utilizing appropriate measures, most probabilistic approaches use HMMs representing the semantic events in their states. The deterministic methods are presented in Section 7.4.1, whereas the probabilistic methods are described in Section 7.4.2.

7.4.1 Deterministic Approaches

Dialogue detection using audiovisual cues is performed in [300], where three types of events are identified: *2-speaker dialogues*, *multiple-speaker dialogues*, and *hybrid events*, which are defined as events containing less speech and more visual action. The framework proposed by Li et al. is depicted in Fig. 7.6. At first, shot detection is employed using a color histogram-based method [297]. Visually related shots, that are close to each other, are grouped into *shot sinks*. The similarity between two shots is determined by the Euclidean distance or the histogram intersection between the color histograms of the two shot keyframes.

In the next stage, each sink is assigned into one of three predefined classes: *periodic*, *partly-periodic*, and *nonperiodic*. The categorization of each sink is based on the so-called *shot repetition degree*, which is determined by the distance between each pair of neighboring shots. Therefore, a *distance sequence* is determined for each sink. Intuitively, a distance sequence corresponding to a periodic class would exhibit a smaller standard deviation than the one belonging to a nonperiodic class. The k-means algorithm is employed to group all sinks into the 3 classes based on the distance sequences characteristics.

All the temporally overlapping sinks are grouped into one event. During the event grouping procedure, a boundary between two events is declared, when a *progressive scene* appears that consists of some sequential nonrepetitive shots. The events extracted are organized into 2-speaker dialogues, multiple-speaker dialogues, and hybrid events based on the number of periodic, partly-periodic, and nonperiodic shot sinks included in the event. In addition, two more features are computed for each event in order to validate the aforementioned classification: the event length, which should exceed a certain threshold, and the temporal variance, which is defined as the average variance of the color histogram of all shots within the event. The temporal variance indicates the amount of motion included in the event.

In order to reduce the errors inherent in the deterministic approaches, a post-processing step is included, where audio and face characteristics are incorporated. 5 audio features, namely the short-time energy, average short-time zero-crossing rate, fundamental frequency, energy band ratio, and silence ratio are extracted. A rule-based heuristic procedure incorporating these audio features is performed aiming at classifying the shots into one of the following classes: silence, speech, music, and environmental sounds. An event is confirmed as a dialogue, if at least 40% of its shots contain speech. The facial analysis includes the detection of frontal faces. A simple face tracking system is employed, that retains only the faces appearing in several consecutive frames. A 2-speaker dialogue is considered as not having more than one face in most of its component shots. Hence, when more faces are detected, the event is relabeled as multiple-speaker dialogue. The system was evaluated with encouraging results in three movies, containing 80 events in total. When audio and facial cues were integrated, the false alarms were eliminated yielding a precision rate of 100% and a recall rate higher than 83% in all movies. However, the amount of heuristic rules and employed thresholds requires a large validation set in addition to the test set in order to experimentally verify the rules and the corresponding thresholds associated to the rules.

A deterministic FSM for classifying video scenes is employed in [587]. Three different categories of scenes are identified: conversation, suspense, and action. The proposed method exploits the structural information of the scenes based on shot motion and audio energy as well as mid-level features, i.e., person identity based on face detection [547]. The weighted sum of the extracted low-level features constitutes the *activity intensity* parameter, which is considered to admit low values in conversation scenes. The activity intensity parameter is used as an input to the FSM. The other input, *person identity*, stems from the face detection process. The middle frame of each shot is selected as its keyframe and the face detector is applied, which is expanded in order to include the torso of the detected person. The similarity between two shots is measured by the color histogram intersection between the detected bodies. The shots are then clustered based on the body similarity using the k-means algorithm.

The FSM for classifying conversational scenes is shown in Fig. 7.7. The character having the largest cluster is denoted as *Primary Speaker* and the character with the second largest cluster is the *Secondary Speaker*. The transitions of the FSM are determined from the feature values of the shots in the scene. The state *Accept* of the FSM is reached and a *Conversation scene* is declared, when there are at least two main speakers with more than three ap-

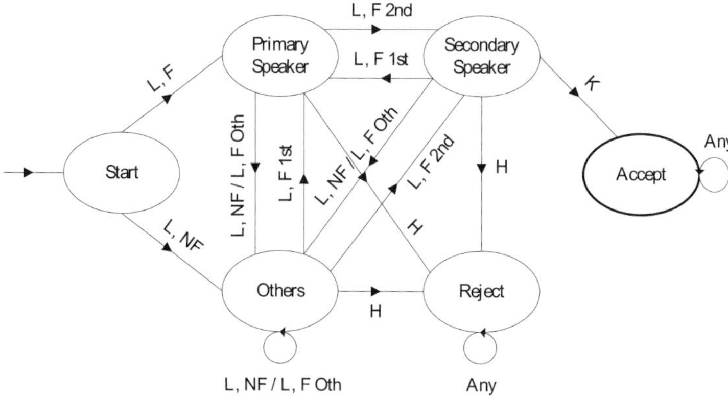

Fig. 7.7. FSM for conversational scene. L – low activity intensity; H – high activity intensity; F – facial shot; NF – non-facial shot; 1st, 2nd, Oth – speaker clusters; K – acceptance condition satisfied; Any – any shot (adapted from [587]).

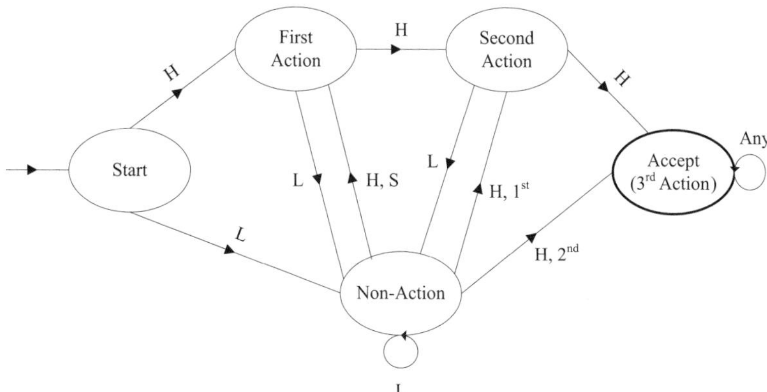

Fig. 7.8. FSM for action scene. L – low activity intensity; H – high activity intensity; S, 1st, 2nd - pre-state values to determine which transition should be taken from start 'Non-action'; Any – any shot (adapted from [587]).

pearances in the scene. Similar structures are proposed for the FSMs defining the other types of scenes. The FSM for classifying action scenes is depicted in Fig. 7.8. To classify a scene as an action scene, the scene must contain a certain number of shots with action intensity greater than a defined threshold level. The FSMs for conversational, suspense, and action scene detection have been tested in a number of movies and TV shows, where a total of 35 conversational, 16 suspense, and 33 action scenes were included. The dialogue scene detection method yielded a recall rate of 94.3% and a precision rate of 97.1%. The precision and recall rates for the suspense scenes were 100% and

93.7%, respectively, whereas the action scenes exhibited precision and recall rates equal to 91.4% and 97%, respectively.

Lehane et al. extended their work [288], described in Section 7.3, by incorporating audio analysis [288]. Low-level audio features are extracted: high zero-crossing rate, silence ratio, and short-time energy. A filter determines if an audio clip contains only silence by using the silence ratio and the short-time energy. Afterwards, in order to detect the presence of speech or music, a Support Vector Machine (SVM) that uses the zero crossing rate and the silence ratio is employed. Audio information is fed to an audio-only FSM and color and motion information is input to a video-only FSM. The output of the two FSMs is combined in order to classify the scenes. The combined system delivered a recall rate of 96.5% and a precision rate of 81.33%. The average precision using the combined audio and visual system is 3% lower than the average precision of the visual system, but there is a 12.5% improvement in recall. However, the performance evaluation assumed that a correct decision was taken, even when a part of the dialogue sequence was identified or a manually marked dialogue scene was split into two separate conversations.

Chen et al. have also extended their work [94] to dialogue and action scene extraction by incorporating audio cues in their system presented in Section 7.3 in order to improve accuracy [95]. The underlying model is an FSM coupled with audio features that are determined using an audio classifier. The audio features employed are the zero-crossing rate variance, the silence ratio, and the harmonic ratio. An SVM is trained to classify the audio channel as either speech with environmental sound or music encountered in dialogue scenes or environmental sound mixed with music encountered in action scenes. Hence, if the audio channel of a scene has more speech segments than enviromental/music segments, then the corresponding scene will be considered as a dialogue scene. The experiments performed in 2 movies (cf. Table 7.1). The dialogue scenes exhibited a recall rate equal to 96.60% and 90.51% for the 2 movies respectively, whereas the corresponding precision rates were 93.4% and 86.11%. The recall rate for action scenes was 100% in both movies and the precision rates were 86% and 81.08%, respectively.

7.4.2 Probabilistic Approaches

An approach for multimodal dialogue detection using HMMs has been proposed by Alatan et al. [19, 20, 21]. Each shot is classified into speech, silence, or music based on the audio content and at the same time face occurrences and location changes are detected by analyzing the video content. Face analysis is limited to declaring the existence or not of a face in the shot, whereas the location analysis uses histogram-based methods. Each shot is assigned a token based on the analysis of the audiovisual features, i.e., 'SFC' for *silence*, *face existence*, and *location change*. The tokens are used to identify dialogue scenes. More specifically, they are used as input, in order to obtain the state sequence that is most likely to have generated that sequence of tokens. At the output of the HMM, each shot of the input sequence is labeled according to the type of scene that best fits it. The block diagram of the system is depicted in Fig. 7.9.

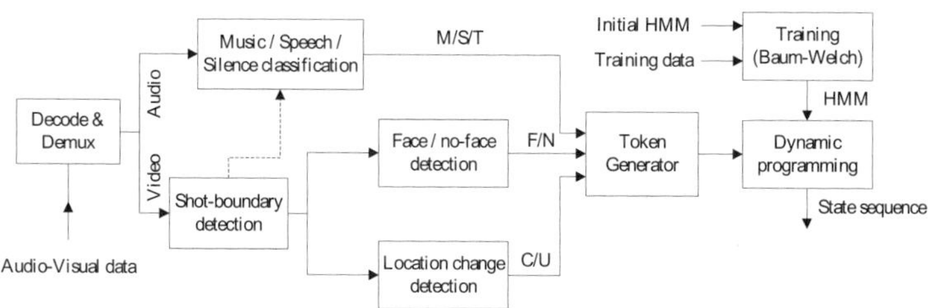

Fig. 7.9. Block diagram of the proposed system in [20]. T – speech; S – silence; M – music, F – face existence; N – no face; C – location change; U – location unchanged.

Two different topologies for the HMM are proposed, as shown in Fig. 7.10a and 7.10b. The left-to-right topology (Fig. 7.10a) includes three state types, called establishing scene, dialogue scene, and transitional scene. The circular topology (Fig. 7.10b) has only two states, the dialogue scene and the non-dialogue scene. The left-to-right topology requires the knowledge of the number of scenes in the content as a prerequisite; hence, its practical use is in doubt, since this information is not usually available a priori. The HMMs are trained by a video data set to determine the state-transition probabilities.

Two TV sitcoms and one movie were used to compare the two different HMM topologies. The ground truth was obtained by manually by assigning every shot to a scene type (establishing, dialogue, transitional, or non-dialogue), depending on the HMM topology. Furthermore, the audiovisual features, used to produce the tokens, were also manually obtained. The system performance was evaluated using the *shot accuracy* measure. The left-to-right topology performed better compared to its circular counterpart, obtaining a shot accuracy measure for each video sequence equal to 92%, 98%, 99% against 71%, 82%, 94% respectively. It is worth mentioning that the input data in the left-to-right topology had to be manually pre-segmented, so that they contained one establishing scene, one dialogue scene and one transitional scene. Otherwise, it is not possible to use the left-to-right topology. Obviously, this process is not feasible in practice.

As a next step, different observation and training sets are applied to the circular topology, in order to further examine its performance. In addition to the shot accuracy measure, a *scene accuracy* measure was introduced, which was defined as the ratio of correct scene assignments to the total number of scenes being either dialogue or non-dialogue ones. Three different sets of observation symbols were used, audio only, audio and face as well as audio, face, and location. These different data sets were also tested for different training data. The best results (scene accuracy around 91%) were obtained when face

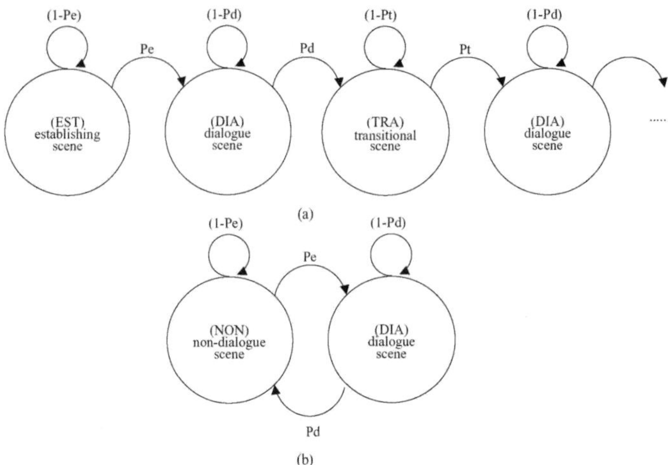

Fig. 7.10. (a) Left-to-right and (b) circular HMM state diagram for dialogue scenes in movies (adapted from [21]).

and audio were the observed features. The location change detection had no impact or even negative impact to the system. The system was unable to distinguish between dialogue and monologue scenes, since it did not incorporate any information about the occurrences of the detected face, i.e., if a face had appeared before in the sequence.

Another work on movie scene segmentation was performed by Yaşaroğlu and Alatan. [572]. In particular, an algorithm for automatic multimedia content summarization by segmenting a video into semantic scenes using HMMs was proposed. Two different content types with different properties are defined: dialogue-driven content and action-driven content. Several visual and audio descriptors are extracted, such as face detection descriptors using simple heuristics in the YUV color space and audio features including the zero-crossing rate and the autocorrelation function. In addition, location change analysis is performed using a windowed histogram comparison method. Finally, frame motion vectors are analyzed for detecting motion activity. The variance of magnitudes of these vectors is calculated for each frame and variances are averaged for each shot. The HMM, which has a 2-state topology (the states are labeled as "Dialogue" and "Non-dialogue"), is trained using the Baum-Welch algorithm and the above low-level features as input. Experiments were performed on TV series and family movies yielding recall and precision rates 95% and 80%, respectively.

7.4.3 Performance Assessment

The results obtained by the reviewed deterministic and probabilistic audiovisual dialogue detection methods are summarized in Table 7.3, along with the performance measure used. Again, since these results have been obtained on different data sets, they are not directly comparable and should be treated as such.

Table 7.3. Results for audiovisual dialogue, action scene, or suspense scene detection.

Reference	Recall	Precision	F_1
Chen et al. (dialogue detection) [95]	92.9%	88.9%	0.909
Lehane et al. (dialogue detection) [288]	96.5%	81.3%	0.882
Li et al. (dialogue detection) [300]	94.2%	100.0%	0.970
Yaşaroğlu and Alatan (dialogue detection) [572]	95.0%	80.0%	0.868
Chen et al. (action scene detection) [95]	100%	82.5%	0.904
Zhai et al. (action scene detection) [587]	97.0%	91.4%	0.941
Zhai et al. (suspense scene detection) [587]	93.7%	100%	0.967

Reference	Shot Accuracy
Alatan (dialogue detection - Left-to-Right) [21] [20]	0.96
Alatan (dialogue detection - Circular) [21][20]	0.82

7.5 Conclusions

As the amount of multimedia content available in the web, broadcast data streams or personal collections grows exponentially, multimedia data management becomes an indispensable tool for efficient and user-friendly information browsing and retrieval. Dialogue and action scene detection techniques aim at segmenting a video into semantically meaningful units with respect to these particular semantic concepts, i.e., the existence or not of either a dialogue or an action scene.

Low and mid-level features, extracted from visual and audio analysis, are exploited. The predominant approach is to classify temporally close shots that demonstrate similar low level features and search for repetitive shot patterns. However, this strategy may cause semantically unrelated shots to be clustered together, based on their low-level similarity. In addition, visually dissimilar shots that are commonly inserted in semantically coherent scenes, introduce a non-deterministic nature to these scenes. Hence, statistical models, employing HMMs, have also been applied. It has been observed that probabilistic techniques exhibit improved performance over deterministic classifiers. In addition, techniques integrating visual and audio information, using either low or mid-level features, yield more accurate dialogue and action scene detection than those employing video only or audio only information. This comes as no surprise, since both channels are rich in information in what concerns dialogue and action scene detection. Joint analysis of audio and video not only increases accuracy but also helps in resolving challenging situations, e.g., cases where the audio channel in a dialogue scene is noisy, or when shots that are not related to the dialogue are inserted between shots depicting the conversing persons.

A major problem in this area of research is that a universal and commonly accepted definition of a "dialogue scene" or an "action scene" does not exist, and most authors introduce their own perspective. Nor does a common, annotated database for the performance evaluation of the proposed methods exists. Every method is tested in a different relatively small data set, where the ground truth is subjectively defined. Hence, the comparison of the presented results can not lead to a safe conclusion. The creation of a common annotated database for scene analysis and dialogue detection experiments, that would enable comparative evaluation of different methods, is necessary. This database could include the movies and TV shows enlisted in Table 7.1. A standardization of the experimental protocols and figures of merit will also help to establish a common baseline for method comparison and evaluation.

Generally speaking, limited research has been performed so far in the fields of dialogue and action scene detection, especially when compared to other related fields, e.g., shot boundary detection or event detection in sports videos. Although the existing methods seem to achieve satisfactory performance, the rather limited test corpora used to benchmark most of the algorithms, combined with the lack of standardization mentioned above, does not allow one to reach safe conclusions on whether these algorithm would be able to perform sufficiently well on a real world application. It seems, however, that most methods would rather fail to operate consistently, efficiently and robustly in such a case. For example, most methods would definitely face difficulties in identifying dialogue scenes whose structure or style of filming does not follow the standard patterns. In addition, a large number of methods are based on information derived from other video and audio analysis tasks, such as face detection and recognition, shot boundary detection, audio classification, speaker clustering, or speaker identification. The limitations of these "auxiliary" techniques, inevitably reflect onto the performance of the corresponding dialogue or action scene detection algorithms.

As a conclusion, one can state that the problem of dialogue and action scene detection is far from being considered as solved, making it a promising research field and leaving ample room for innovative research, especially towards the direction of joint analysis of audio and visual information, which seems to be the most natural and fruitful one.

Further Reading

For further information on video content analysis techniques and their application in multimedia mining, retrieval and organization, one can consult the books [67, 173, 298, 443] or the articles in the special issue [28]. A recently proposed method for dialogue detection is presented in [280], whereas a tool for the annotation of audiovisual data (including dialogue scenes) is reported in [261].

8

Audiovisual Attention Modeling and Salient Event Detection

Georgios Evangelopoulos[1], Konstantinos Rapantzikos[1], Petros Maragos[1], Yannis Avrithis[1], and Alexandros Potamianos[2]

[1] National Technical University of Athens
[2] Technical University of Crete

Although human perception appears to be automatic and unconscious, complex sensory mechanisms exist that form the preattentive component of understanding and lead to awareness. Considerable research has been carried out into these preattentive mechanisms and computational models have been developed for similar problems in the fields of computer vision and speech analysis. The focus here is to explore aural and visual information in video streams for modeling attention and detecting salient events. The separate aural and visual modules may convey explicit, complementary or mutually exclusive information around the detected audiovisual events. Based on recent studies on perceptual and computational attention modeling, we formulate measures of attention using features of saliency for the audiovisual stream. Audio saliency is captured by signal modulations and related multifrequency band features, extracted through nonlinear operators and energy tracking. Visual saliency is measured by means of a spatiotemporal attention model driven by various feature cues (intensity, color, motion). Features from both modules mapped to one-dimensional, time-varying saliency curves, from which statistics of salient segments can be extracted and important audio or visual events can be detected through adaptive, threshold-based mechanisms. Audio and video curves are integrated in a single attention curve, where events may be enhanced, suppressed or vanished. Salient events from the audiovisual curve are detected through geometrical features such as local extrema, sharp transitions and level sets. The potential of inter-module fusion and audiovisual event detection is demonstrated in applications such as video key-frame selection, video skimming and video annotation.

8.1 Approaches and Applications

Attention in perception is formally modeled either by stimulus-driven, bottom-up processes, or by goal-driven, top-down mechanisms that require prior knowledge of the depicted scene or the important events [314]. The former,

P. Maragos et al. (eds.), *Multimodal Processing and Interaction*,
DOI: 10.1007/978-0-387-76316-3_8,

bottom-up approach is based on signal-level analysis with no prior information acquired or learning incorporated.

In analyzing the visual and aural information of video streams the main issues that arise are: i) choosing appropriate features that capture important signal properties, ii) combining the information corresponding to the different modalities to allow for interaction and iii) defining efficient salient event detection schemes. In this chapter, the potential of using and integrating aural and visual features is explored, to create a model of audiovisual attention, with application to saliency-based summarization and automatic annotation of videos. The two modalities are processed independently with the saliency of each described by features that correspond to physical changes in the depicted scene. Their integration is performed by constructing temporal indexes of saliency that reveal dynamically evolving audiovisual events.

Multimodal video analysis (i.e., analysis of various information modalities) has gained in popularity with automatic summarization being one of the main targets of research. Summaries provide the user with a short version of the video that ideally contains all important information for understanding the content. Hence, the user may quickly access and evaluate if the video is important, interesting or enjoyable. The tutorial in [574] classifies video abstraction into two main types: *key-frame selection* which yields a static small set of important video frames and *video skimming* (loosely referred to in this chapter as *video summarization*) which results in a dynamic short subclip of the original video containing important aural and visual spatiotemporal information.

Earlier works were mainly based on processing only the visual input. Zhuang et al. [596] extracted salient frames based on color clustering and global motion, while Ju et al. [242] used gesture analysis in addition to the latter low-level features. Furthermore Avrithis et al. [35] represent the video content by a high-dimensional feature curve and detect key-frames at the curvature points. Another group of methods is based on frame clustering to select representative frames [425, 536]. Features extracted from each frame of the sequence form a feature vector and are used in a clustering scheme. Frames closer to the centroids are then selected as key-frames. Other schemes based on sophisticated temporal sampling [513], hierarchical frame clustering [425, 183], where the video frames are hierarchically clustered by visual similarity, and fuzzy classification [140] have also proposed summarization schemes with encouraging results.

In an attempt to incorporate multimodal or/and perceptual features in the analysis and processing of the visual input, various systems have been designed and implemented within a variety of projects. The Informedia project and its offsprings combined speech, image, natural language understanding and image processing to automatically index video for intelligent search and retrieval [498, 201, 200]. This approach generated interesting results. In the Video Browsing and Retrieval system (VIRE) [428] a number of low-level visual and audio features are extracted and stored using MPEG-7, while MediaMill [419] provides a tool for automatic shot and scene segmentation for general content. IBMs CueVideo system [17] automatically extracts a number of low- and mid-level visual and audio features. The visually similar shots are clustered using color correlograms. Going one step further towards human perception, Ma et al. [313, 314] proposed a method for detecting the salient parts of a video that is based on user attention models. They used motion, face and camera attention along with audio attention models (audio saliency and speech/music) as cues to capture salient information and identify the audio and video segments to compose a summary.

We present a saliency-based method to detect important audiovisual segments and focus more on the potential benefits of feature-based attention modeling and multi-sensory signal integration. As content importance in a video stream is quite subjective, it is not easy to evaluate methods in the field. Hence, in an attempt to assess the proposed method both quantitatively and qualitatively, we present video summarization results on commercial videos and samples from the MUSCLE movie database[3], annotated with respect to saliency of the scene evaluated by human observers. The reference videos are clips from the movies "300" and "Lord of The Rings I". Automatic and manual annotations are studied and compared on the selected movie clips with respect to audiovisual saliency of the depicted scenes.

The remaining of the chapter is organized as follows: Section 8.2 and Section 8.3 describe the audio saliency and the visual saliency modules, respectively. Schemes for detecting salient events are proposed in Section 8.4 and experimental evaluation and applications are given in Section 8.5. Conclusions are drawn and open issues for future work are discussed in Section 8.6.

8.2 Audio Saliency

Streams of audio information may be composed from a variety of sounds, like speech, music, environmental sounds (nature, machines, noises), a result of multiple sources that correspond to natural, artificial, man-made, on purpose or randomly occurring phenomena. An audio event is a bounded region in the time continuum, in terms of a beginning and end, that is characterized by a variation or transitional state to one or more sound-producing sources. Events are "sound objects" that change dynamically with time, while retaining a set of characteristic properties that identify a single entity. Perceptually, event boundaries correspond to points of maximum quantitative or qualitative change of physical features [584].

Aural attention is triggered perceptually by changes in the involved events of an audio stream. These may be changes of the nature/source of events, newly introduced sounds, or transitions and abnormalities in the course of a specific event, in real-life or synthetic recordings. Such transitions correspond

[3] `http://poseidon.csd.auth.gr/EN/MUSCLE_moviedb`

to changes of salient audio properties, e.g. invariants, whose selection is crucial for efficient audio representations for event detection and recognition.

Biological observations indicate that one of the segregations performed by the auditory system in complex channels is in terms of temporal modulations, while according to psychophysical experiments, modulated carriers seem more salient perceptually to human observers compared to stationary signals [250, 529]. Moreover, following Gestalt theories, the salient audio signal structures constitute meaningful audio Gestalts which in turn define manifestations of audio events [342]. Thus, we formulate a curve modeling audio attention based on saliency measures of meaningful temporal modulations in multiple frequencies.

8.2.1 Audio Processing and Salient Features

Processing the audio stream of multimodal systems, involves confronting a number of subproblems that compose what may be thought of as audio understanding. In that direction, the notions of audio events and salient audio segments are the backbone of audio detection, segmentation, recognition and identification. Starting from lower and going toward higher level, i.e., more complicated problems, the subproblems of audio analysis can be roughly categorized as: a) detection, where the presence of auditory information is verified and separated from silence or background noise conditions [153]; b) attention modeling and audio saliency, where the perceptual importance is valued [313, 314]; c) source separation, where the auditory signal is decomposed to different generating sources and sound categories (e.g. speech, music, natural or synthetic sounds); d) segmentation and event labeling, where the aural activity is assigned boundaries and dynamic events are sought after [310]; and e) recognition of sources and events, where the sources and events are matched to stored lexicon representations.

Descriptive signal representations are essential for all the above subproblem categories and much work has been devoted in robust audio feature extraction for applications [421, 245, 310, 314]. Psychophysical experiments indicate the nature of features responsible for audio perception [331, 529]. These are representations both in the temporal and spectral domain, that incorporate properties and notions such as scale, structure, dimension and perceptual invariance. Well-established features for audio analysis, classification and recognition include time-frequency representations (e.g., spectrograms), temporal measurements (e.g., energy, zero-crossings rate, pitch, periodicity), spectral measurements (e.g., component or resonance position and variation, bandwidth, spectral flux) and cepstral measurements like the Mel-Frequency Cepstral Coefficients (MFCCs).

Recent advances in the field of nonlinear speech modeling relate salient features of speech signals to their inherent non-stationarity and the presence of micro-modulations in the amplitude and frequency variation of their constructing components. Experimental and theoretical indications about modulations in various scales during speech production led to proposing an AM-FM modulation model for speech in [320]. The model was then employed for extracting various "modulation-based" features like formant tracks and bandwidth, mean amplitude and frequency of the components [411] as well as the coefficients of their energy-frequency distributions (TECCs) [137].

This model can be generalized to any source producing oscillating signals and for that purpose it is used here to describe a large family of audio signals. Speech, music, noise, natural and mechanical sounds are the result of resonating sources are modeled as sums of amplitude and frequency (AM-FM) modulated components. The salient structures then are the underlying modulation signals and their properties (i.e., number, scale, importance) define the audio representation.

Audio AM-FM Modeling and Multiband Demodulation

Assume that a single audio component is modeled by a real-valued AM-FM signal of the form $x(t) = a(t)\cos\left(\int_0^t \omega(\tau)d\tau\right)$, with time-varying amplitude envelope $a(t)$ and instantaneous frequency $\omega(t)$ signals. Demodulation of $x(t)$ can be approached via the use of the Teager-Kaiser nonlinear differential energy operator $\Psi[x(t)] \equiv [\dot{x}(t)]^2 - x(t)\ddot{x}(t)$, where $\dot{x}(t) = dx(t)/dt$ [518, 244]. Applied to an AM-FM signal $x(t)$, Ψ yields the instantaneous energy of the source producing the oscillation, i.e., $\Psi[x(t)] \approx a^2(t)\omega^2(t)$, with negligible approximation error under realistic constraints [320]. The instantaneous energy is separated to its amplitude and frequency components by the *energy separation algorithm* (ESA) [320] using Ψ as its main ingredient.

In order to apply ESA for demodulating a wideband audio signal, modeled by a sum of AM-FM components, it is necessary to isolate narrow-band components in advance. Bandpass filtering decomposes the signal in frequency bands, each assumed to be dominated by a single AM-FM component in that frequency range. In the *multiband demodulation analysis* (MDA) scheme, components are isolated globally using a set of frequency-selective filters [78, 411, 153]. Here MDA is applied through a filterbank of linearly-spaced Gabor filters $h(t) = \exp(-\alpha^2 t^2)\cos(\omega_c t)$, with ω_c the central filter frequency and α its rms bandwidth. Gabor filters are chosen for being compact and smooth while attaining a minimum joint time-frequency uncertainty [174, 320, 78].

Demodulation via ESA of a single frequency band, obtained by one Gabor filter, can be seen in Fig. 8.1(b). The choice of the specific band corresponds to an energy-based dominant component selection criterion that will be further employed in the following for audio feature extraction. Postprocessing by median filtering may be used to alleviate singularities in the resulting demodulation measurements.

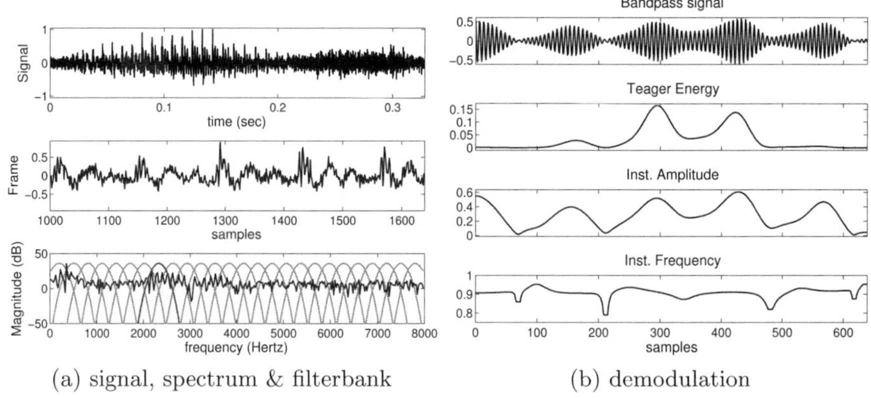

(a) signal, spectrum & filterbank (b) demodulation

Fig. 8.1. Short-time audio processing and dominant modulation extraction. (a) a vowel frame (20ms) from a speech waveform is analyzed in multiple bands (bottom) and (b) the dominant, w.r.t average source energy, band is demodulated in instantaneous amplitude and frequency (smoothed by 13-pt median) signals.

Audio Features

The AM-FM modulation superposition model for speech [320], motivated by the presence of multi-scale modulations during speech production [518], is applied here to generic audio signals. Thus an audio signal is modeled by a sum of narrowband amplitude and frequency varying, non-stationary sinusoids $s(t) = \sum_{k=1}^{K} a_k(t) \cos(\phi_k(t))$, whose demodulation in instantaneous amplitude $a_k(t)$ and frequency $\omega_k(t) = d\phi_k(t)/dt$ is obtained in the output of a set of frequency-tuned Gabor filters $h_k(t)$ using the energy operator Ψ and the ESA. The filters globally separate modulation components assuming a priori a fixed component configuration.

To model a discrete-time audio signal $s[n] = s(nT)$, we use K discrete AM-FM components whose instantaneous amplitude and frequency signals are $A_k[n] = a_k(nT)$ and $\Omega_k[n] = T\omega_k(nT)$, respectively. The model parameters are estimated from the K filtered components using a discrete-time energy operator $\Psi_d(x[n]) \equiv (x[n])^2 - x[n-1]x[n+1]$ and a related discrete ESA, which is a computationally simple and efficient algorithm with an excellent, almost instantaneous, time resolution [320]. Thus, at each sample instance n the audio signal is represented by three parameters (energy, amplitude and frequency) for each of the K components, leading to $3 \times K$ feature vector.

A representation in terms of a single component per analysis frame emerges by maximizing an energy criterion in the multi-dimensional filter response space [78, 153]. For each frame m of N samples duration, the dominant modulation component is the one with *maximum average Teager energy* (MTE):

$$\mathrm{MTE}[m] = \max_{1 \le k \le K} \frac{1}{N} \sum_{n} \Psi_d((s * h_k)[n]), \quad (m-1)N + 1 \le n \le mN \qquad (8.1)$$

where $*$ denotes convolution and h_k the impulse response of the kth filter. The filter $j = \arg\max_k(\text{MTE})$ is submitted to demodulation via ESA and the instantaneous modulating signals are averaged over a frame duration to derive the *mean instant amplitude* (MIA) and *mean instant frequency* (MIF) features:

$$j = \arg\max_{1 \leq k \leq K}(\overline{\Psi_d[(s * h_k)(n)]}),\ \text{MTE}[m] = (\overline{\Psi_d[(s * h_j)(n)]}) \tag{8.2}$$

$$\text{MIA}[m] = (\overline{|A_j[n]|})\ ,\ \text{MIF}[m] = (\overline{\Omega_j[n]}). \tag{8.3}$$

Thus, each frame yields average measurements for the source energy, instant amplitude and frequency from the filter that captures the "strongest" modulation signal component. In this context strength refers to the amount of energy required for producing component oscillations. The dominant component is the most salient signal modulation structure and energy MTE may be thought of as the salient *modulation energy*, jointly capturing essential amplitude-frequency content information.

The resulting three-dimensional feature vector of the mean dominant modulation parameters

$$\mathbf{F}_{\text{a}}[m] = [F_{\text{a}1}, F_{\text{a}2}, F_{\text{a}3}]\,[m] = [\text{MTE}, \text{MIA}, \text{MIF}]\,[m] \tag{8.4}$$

is a low dimensional descriptor, compared to the potential $3 \times K$ vector from all outputs, of the "average instantaneous" modulation structure of the audio signal involving properties such as level of excitation, rate-of-change, frequency content and source energy.

In discrete implementation, audio analysis frames usually vary between 10-25 ms. For speech signals, such a choice of window length covers all pitch duration diversities between different speakers. Sequentially, the discrete energy operator is applied to the set of filter outputs and an averaging operation is performed. Central frequency steps of the filter design varying between 200-400 Hz, yield filterbanks consisting of 20-40 filters.

An example of the short-time features extracted from a movie audio stream (1024 frames from "300") can be seen in Fig. 8.2. The chosen segment was manually annotated by a human observer, with respect to the various sources present and their boundaries. These are indicated by the vertical lines in the signal waveform. The different sources include speech (2 different speakers), music, noise, sound effects and a general "mix-sound" category. The wide-band spectrum is decomposed using 25 filters, of 400 Hz bandwidth, and the dominant modulation features are shown in (b), after median (7-point) and Hanning (5-point) post-smoothing. Features are mapped from audio-to-video temporal index by keeping maximum intraframe values. Note how a) the envelope features complement the frequency measure (i.e high-frequency sounds of low energy and the opposite), b) manual labeling matches sharp transitions to one or more features and c) frequency is characterized by longer, piece-wise constant "sustain periods."

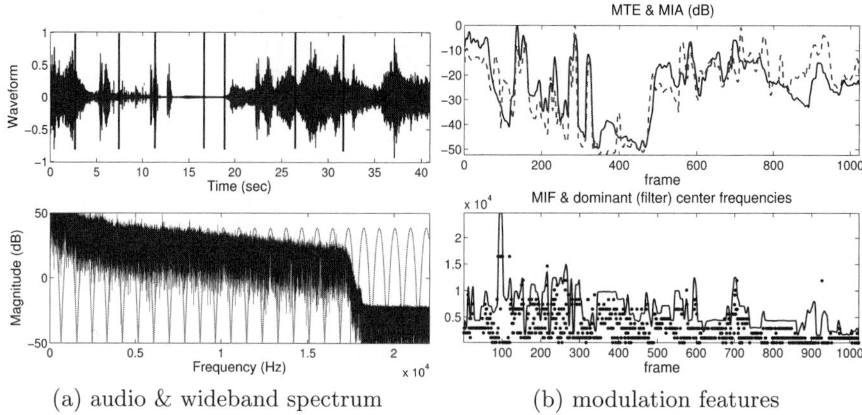

(a) audio & wideband spectrum (b) modulation features

Fig. 8.2. Feature extraction from multi-source audio stream. (a) Waveform with manual labeling of the various sources/events (vertical lines) and wideband spectrum with filterbank, (b) top: MTE (solid) and MIA (dashed), bottom: MIF with dominant carrier frequencies superimposed (1024 frames from "300" video).

This representation in terms of the salient modulation properties of sounds, is additionally supported by cognitive theories of event perception [331]. For example, rapid amplitude and frequency modulations are related to temporal acoustic micro-properties of sounds that appear to be useful for recognition of sources and events. A simplistic approach for the structure of audio events involves three parts: an onset, a relatively constant duration and an offset portion. Event onset and decay are captured by the envelope variations of the amplitude and energy measurements. On the other hand, spectral variations, retrieved perceptually from the sustain period, and variations in the main signal component are captured by the dominant frequency feature.

8.2.2 Audio Attention Curve

The attention curve for the audio signal is constructed by the saliency values, provided by the set of audio features (8.4). Conceptually, salient information is modeled through source excitation and average rate of spectral and temporal change.

The simplest scenario of an *audio saliency* curve is a weighted linear combination of the normalized audio features

$$S_{\mathrm{a}}[m] = w_1 F_{\mathrm{a}1}[m] + w_2 F_{\mathrm{a}2}[m] + w_3 F_{\mathrm{a}3}[m], \tag{8.5}$$

where $[w_1, w_2, w_3]$ is a weighting vector. Normalization is performed by least squares fit of their individual value ranges to $[0, 1]$. For this chapter we use equal weights $w_1 = w_2 = w_3 = 1/3$, which amounts to uniform linear averag-

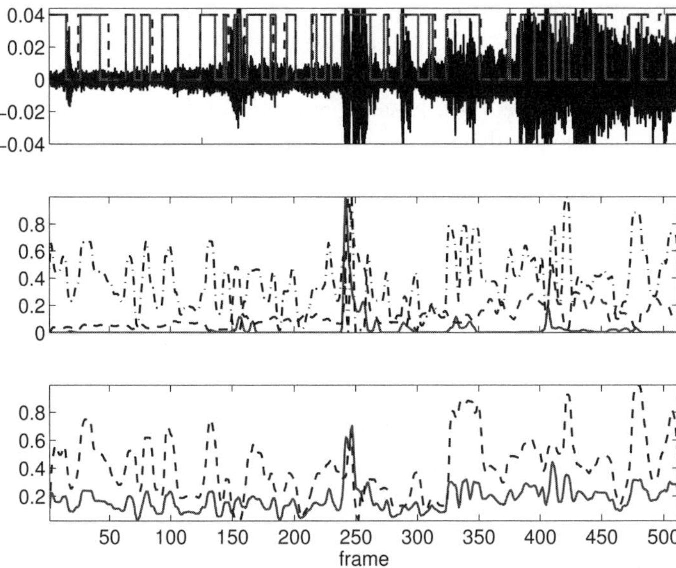

Fig. 8.3. Audio saliency curves. Top: audio waveform and threshold-based saliency indicator functions, Middle: normalized audio features, MTE (solid), MIA (dashed), MIF (dash dotted). Bottom: saliency curve (linear in solid, nonlinear in dashed). Indicator functions correspond to the two audio fusion schemes, (512 frames from the "Lord of the Rings I" stream).

ing and viewing the normalized features F_{ai} as equally important for the level of saliency and the attention provoked by the audio signal.

A different, perceptually motivated approach is a non-linear feature fusion, based on time-varying "energy weights." According to the structure and representation by the auditory system of audio events [331], temporal variation information is extracted by the onset and offset portions, while spectral change, from the intermediate sustain periods. As the energy measurement has been previously used for detecting speech event boundaries [153], we incorporate it as an index of event transitional points. Using the average source energy gradient as a weighting factor, we acquire the following *nonlinear audio-to-audio* integration scheme

$$S_{\mathrm{a}}[m] = w_{\mathrm{e}}[m]F_{\mathrm{a}2}[m] + (1 - w_{\mathrm{e}}[m])F_{\mathrm{a}3}[m], \quad w_{\mathrm{e}} = \left|\frac{dF_{\mathrm{a}1}}{dm}\right| \tag{8.6}$$

The effect of this gradient energy weighting process is that, in sharp event transitions (modeling beginning, ending or change of activity) the amplitude feature is employed more (hence, the temporal variation is more salient). The frequency is weighted more at relatively constant activity periods where the spectral variation is perceptually more important.

An example of the feature integration for saliency curve construction is presented in Fig. 8.3. Audio features, normalized and mapped to the video frame index, are combined linearly by (8.5) or nonlinearly by (8.6) to yield the corresponding saliency curves. A saliency indicator function is then obtained by applying on the resulting curves an adaptive threshold-based detection scheme.

8.3 Visual Saliency

The visual saliency computation module is based on the notion of a centralized saliency map [268] computed through a feature competition scheme. The motivation behind this scheme is the experimental evidence of a biological counterpart in the Human Visual System (interaction/competition among the different visual pathways related to motion/depth (M pathway) and gestalt/depth/color (P pathway) respectively) [246]. An overview of the visual saliency detection architecture is given in Fig. 8.4. In this framework, a video sequence is represented as a solid in the 3D Euclidean space, with time being the third dimension. Hence, the equivalent of a spatial saliency map is a spatiotemporal volume where each voxel has a certain value of saliency. This saliency volume is computed with the incorporation of feature competition by defining cliques at the voxel level and use an optimization procedure with both inter- and intra- feature constraints.

8.3.1 Visual Features

The video volume is initially decomposed into a set of feature volumes, namely intensity, color and spatiotemporal orientations. For the intensity and color features, we adopt the opponent process color theory that suggests the control of color perception by two opponent systems: a blue-yellow and a red-green mechanism. The extent to which these opponent channels attract attention of humans has been previously investigated in detail, both for biological [527] and computational models of attention [313]. According to the *opponent color* scheme, if r, g, b are the red, green and blue volumes respectively, the luminance and color volumes are obtained by

$$I = (r + g + b)/3, \quad RG = R - G, \quad BY = B - Y, \tag{8.7}$$

where $R = r - (g + b)/2$, $G = g - (r + b)/2$, $B = b - (r + g)/2$, $Y = (r + g)/2 - |r - g|/2 - b$.

Spatiotemporal orientations are computed using steerable filters [170]. A steerable filter may be of arbitrary orientation and is synthesized as a linear combination of rotated versions of itself. Orientations are obtained by measuring the filter strength along particular directions θ (the angle formed by the plane passing through the t axis and the $x - t$ plane) and ϕ (defined on

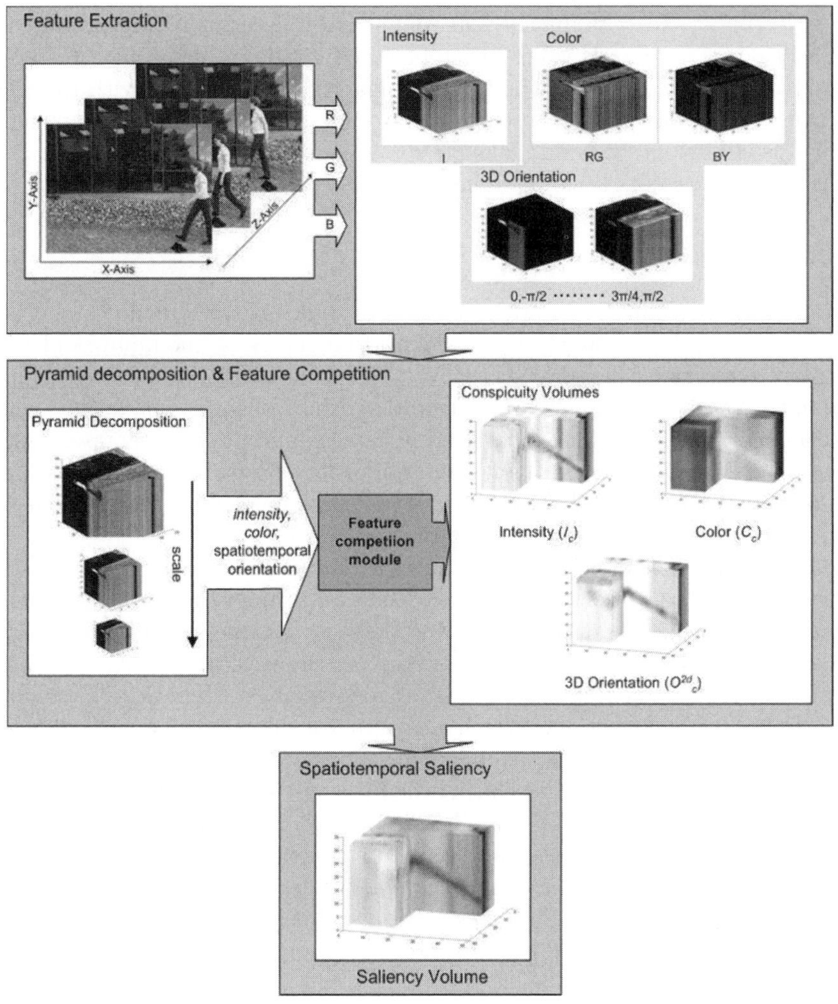

Fig. 8.4. Visual saliency module

the $x - y$ plane). The desired filtering can be implemented using the three dimensional filters $G_2^{\theta,\phi}$ (e.g. second derivative of a 3D Gaussian) and their Hilbert transforms $H_2^{\theta,\phi}$, by taking the filters in quadrature to eliminate the phase sensitivity present in the output of each filter. This is called the oriented energy:

$$E(\theta, \phi) = [G_2^{\theta,\phi} * I]^2 + [H_2^{\theta,\phi} * I]^2, \tag{8.8}$$

where

$$\theta \in \{0, \frac{\pi}{4}, \frac{\pi}{2}, \frac{3\pi}{4}\}, \quad \phi \in \{-\frac{\pi}{2}, -\frac{\pi}{4}, 0, \frac{\pi}{4}, \frac{\pi}{2}\}. \tag{8.9}$$

By selecting θ and ϕ as in (8.9), 20 volumes of different spatiotemporal orientations are produced, which must be fused together to produce a single orientation volume that will be further enhanced and compete with the rest of the feature volumes. We use an operator based on Principal Component Analysis (PCA) and generate a single spatiotemporal orientation conspicuity volume V. More details can be found in [422].

8.3.2 Visual Attention Curve

We perform decomposition of the video at a number of different scales. The final result is a hierarchy of video volumes that represent the input sequence in decreasing spatiotemporal scales. Volumes for each feature of interest, including intensity, color and 3D orientation (motion) are then formed and decomposed into multiple scales. Every volume simultaneously represents the spatial distribution and temporal evolution of the encoded feature. The pyramidal decomposition allows the model to represent smaller and larger "events" in separate subdivisions of the channels.

Feature competition is implemented in the model using an energy-based measure. In a regularization framework the first term of this energy measure may be regarded as the data term E_1 and the second as the smoothness one E_2, since it regularizes the current estimate by restricting the class of admissible solutions [423]. The energy involves voxel operations between coarse and finer scales of the volume pyramid, which means that if the center is a voxel at level $c \in \{2, ..., p-d\}$, where p is the maximum pyramid level and d is the desired depth of the center-surround scheme, then the surround is the corresponding voxel at level $h = c + \delta$ with $\delta \in \{1, 2, ..., d\}$. Hence, if we consider the intensity and two opponent color features as elements of the vector $\mathbf{F}_{\mathrm{v}} = F_{\mathrm{v}_1}, F_{\mathrm{v}_2}, F_{\mathrm{v}_3}$ and if $F^0_{\mathrm{v}_k}$ corresponds to the original volume of each of the features, each level ℓ of the pyramid is obtained by convolution with an isotropic 3D Gaussian G and dyadic down-sampling:

$$F^{\ell}_{\mathrm{v}_k} = \left(G * F^{\ell-1}_{\mathrm{v}_k}\right) \downarrow_2, \quad \ell = 1, 2, ..., p. \tag{8.10}$$

where $\downarrow_2$ denotes decimation by 2 in each dimension. For each voxel q of a feature volume F the energy is defined as

$$E_v(F^c_{\mathrm{v}_k}(q)) = \lambda_1 \cdot E_1(F^c_{\mathrm{v}_k}(q)) + \lambda_2 \cdot E_2(F^c_{\mathrm{v}_k}(q)), \tag{8.11}$$

where λ_1, λ_2 are the importance weighting factors for each of the involved terms. The first term of (8.11) is defined as

$$E_1(F^c_{\mathrm{v}_k}(q)) = F^c_{\mathrm{v}_k}(q) \cdot |F^c_{\mathrm{v}_k}(q) - F^h_{\mathrm{v}_k}(q)| \tag{8.12}$$

and acts as the center-surround operator. The difference at each voxel is obtained after interpolating $F^h_{\mathrm{v}_k}$ to the size of the coarser level. This term promotes areas that differ from their spatiotemporal surroundings and therefore attract attention. The second term is defined as

$$E_2(F^c_{\mathrm{v}_k}(q)) = F^c_{\mathrm{v}_k}(q) \cdot \frac{1}{|N(q)|} \cdot \sum_{r \in N(q)} \left(F^c_{\mathrm{v}_k}(r) + V(r) \right), \tag{8.13}$$

where V is the spatiotemporal orientation volume that may be regarded as an indication of motion activity in the scene and $N(q)$ is the 26- neighborhood of voxel q. The second energy term involves competition among voxel neighborhoods of the same volume and allows a voxel to increase its saliency value only if the activity of its surroundings is low enough. The energy is then minimized using an iterative steepest descent scheme and a *saliency volume* S is created by averaging the conspicuity feature volumes $F^1_{\mathrm{v}_k}$ at the first pyramid level:

$$S(q) = \frac{1}{3} \cdot \sum_{k=1}^{3} F^1_{\mathrm{v}_k}(q). \tag{8.14}$$

Overall, the core of the visual saliency detection module is an iterative minimization scheme that acts on 3D local regions and is based on center-surround inhibition regularized by inter- and intra- local feature constraints. A detailed description of the method can be found in [422]. Figure 8.5 depicts the computed saliency for three frames of "Lord of the Rings I" and "300" sequences. High values correspond to high salient areas (notice the shining ring and the falling elephant).

In order to create a single saliency value per frame, we use the same features involved in the saliency volume computation, namely intensity, color and motion. Each of the feature volumes is first normalized to lie in the range $[0, 1]$ and then point-to-point multiplied by the saliency one in order to suppress low saliency voxels. The weighted average is taken to produce a single *visual saliency* value for each frame:

$$S_{\mathrm{v}} = \sum_{k=1}^{3} \sum_{q} S(q) \cdot F^1_{\mathrm{v}_k}(q), \tag{8.15}$$

where the second sum is taken over all the voxels of a volume at the first pyramid level.

8.4 Audiovisual Saliency

Integrating the information extracted from audio and video channels is not a trivial task, as they correspond to different sensor modalities (aural and visual). Audiovisual fusion for modeling multimodal attention can be performed at three levels: i) *low-level* fusion (at the extracted saliency curves), ii) *middle-level* fusion (at the corresponding feature vectors), iii) *high-level* fusion (at the detected salient segments and features of the curves).

In a video stream with both aural and visual information present, audiovisual attention is modeled by constructing a temporal sequence of audiovisual saliency values. In this saliency curve, each value corresponds to a

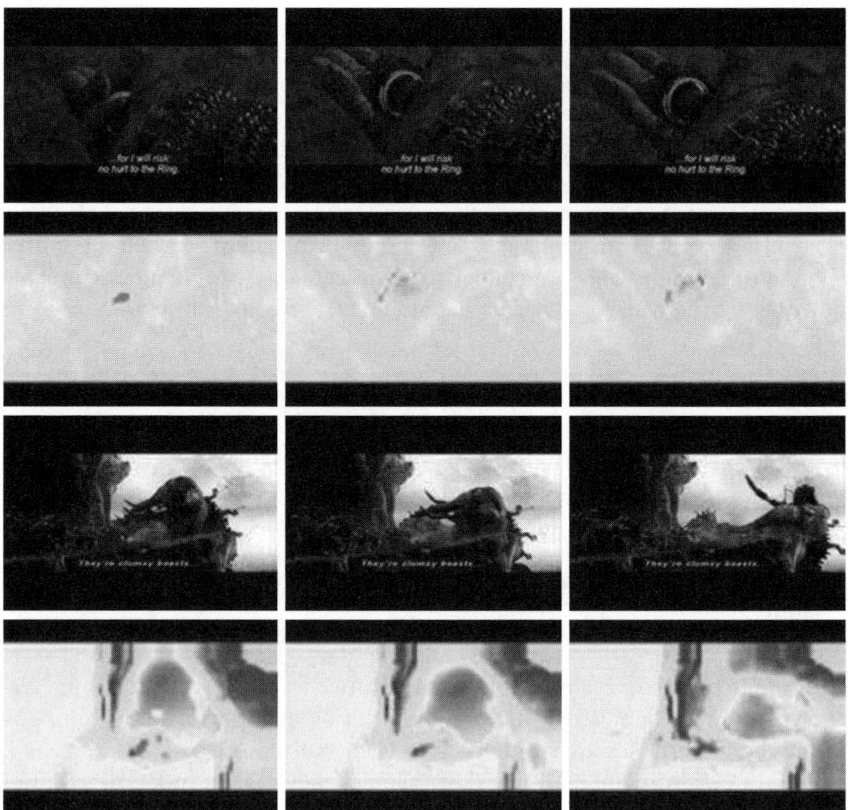

Fig. 8.5. Original frames from the movies "Lord of the Rings I" (top) and "300" (bottom) and the corresponding saliency maps (better viewed in color).

measure of importance of the multi-sensory stream at each time instance. In both modalities, features are mapped to saliency (aural and visual) curve values ($S_{\mathrm{a}}[m], S_{\mathrm{v}}[m]$), and the two curves are integrated to yield an audiovisual saliency curve

$$S_{\mathrm{av}}[m] = \mathrm{fusion}(S_{\mathrm{a}}, S_{\mathrm{v}}, m), \tag{8.16}$$

where m the frame index and fusion$(\cdot)$ is the process of combining or fusing the two modalities. This is a low-level fusion scheme. In general, this process of combining the outputs of the two saliency detection modules may be nonlinear, have memory or vary with time. For the purposes of this chapter, however, we use the following straightforward linear memoryless scheme

$$S_{\mathrm{av}}[m] = w_{\mathrm{a}} \cdot S_{\mathrm{a}}[m] + w_{\mathrm{v}} \cdot S_{\mathrm{v}}[m]. \tag{8.17}$$

Assuming that the individual audio and visual saliency curves are normalized in the range $[0, 1]$ and the weights form a convex combination, this coupled audiovisual curve serves as a continuous-valued indicator function of salient events, in the audio, the video or a common audiovisual domain. The weights can be equal, constant or adaptive depending for example on the uncertainty of the audio or video features. Actually, the above weighted linear scheme corresponds to what is called in [99] *"weak fusion"* of modalities and is optimum under the maximum a posteriori criterion, if the individual distributions are Gaussian and the weights are inversely proportional to the individual variances, as explained in Section 1.3 of Chapter 1.

The coupled audiovisual saliency curve provides the basis for subsequent detection of salient events. Audiovisual events are defined as bounded time-regions of aural and visual activity. In the proposed method, events correspond to attention-triggering signal portions or points of interest extracted from the saliency curves. The boundaries of events and the activity locus points, correspond to a maximum change in the audio and video saliency curves and the underlying features. Thus, transition and reference points in the audiovisual event stream can be tracked by analyzing the geometric features of the curve. Such geometric characteristics include:

- **Extrema points**: these are the local maxima or minima of the curve and can be detected by a 'peak-peaking' method.
- **Peaks & Valleys**: the region of support around maxima and minima, respectively. These can be extracted automatically (e.g., by a percentage to maximum) or via a user-defined scenario depending on the application (e.g., a skimming index).
- **Edges**: One-dimensional edges correspond to sharp transition points in the curve. A common approach is to detect the zero-crossings of a Derivative-of-Gaussian operator applied to the signal.
- **Level Sets**: points where the values of the curve exceed a learned or heuristic level-threshold. These sets can define indicator functions of salient activity.

Saliency-based events can be tracked at the individual saliency curves or at the integrated one. In the former case, the resulting geometric feature-events can be subjected to higher-level fusion (e.g., by logical OR, AND operators). As a result, events in one of the modalities may suppress or enhance the events present in the other. A set of audio, visual and audiovisual events can be seen in the example-application of Figs. 8.6 and 8.7. The associated movie-trailer clip contained a variety of events in both streams (soundtracks, dialogues, effects, shot-changes, motion), aimed to attract the viewer's attention. Peaks detected in the audiovisual curve revealed in many cases an agreement between peaks (events) tracked in the individual saliency curves.

8.5 Applications and Experiments

The developed audiovisual saliency curve has been applied to saliency-based video summarization and annotation. Summarization is performed in two di-

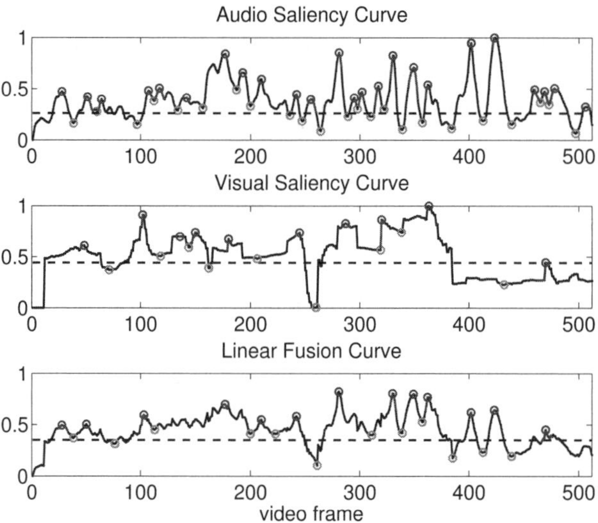

Fig. 8.6. Saliency curves and detected features (maxima, minima, lobes and levels) for audio (top), video (middle) and audiovisual streams (bottom) of the movie trailer "First Descend".

Fig. 8.7. Key-frames selection using local maxima (peaks) of corresponding audio-visual saliency curve. Selected frames correspond to the peaks in the bottom curve of Fig. 8.6 (12 out of 13 frames, peak 4 is not shown).

rections: key-frame selection for static video storyboards via local maxima detection and dynamic video skimming based on a user-defined skimming percentage. Annotation refers to labeling various video parts with respect to their attentional strength, based on sensory information solely. In order to provide statistically robust and as far as possible objective results, the results are compared to human annotation.

8.5.1 Experimental setup

The proposed method has been applied both to videos of arbitrary content and to a human annotated movie database, that consists of 42 scenes extracted from 6 movies of different genres. For demonstration purposes we selected two clips ($\simeq$10 min each) from the movies "Lord of the Rings I" and "300" and present a series of applications and experiments that highlight different aspects of the proposed method.

The clips were viewed and annotated according to the audio, visual and audiovisual saliency of their content. This means that parts of the clip were labeled as salient or non-salient, depending on the importance and the attention attracted by their content. The viewers were asked to assign a saliency factor to any part according to loose guidelines, since strict rules cannot be applied due to the high subjectivity of the procedure. The guidelines were related to the audio-only, visual-only and audiovisual changes and events, but not to semantic interpretation of the content. The output of this procedure is a saliency indicator function, corresponding to the video segments that were assigned a non-zero saliency factor. For example, Fig. 8.8 depicts the saliency curves and detected geometric features, while Fig. 8.9 the indicator functions obtained manually and automatically on a frame sequence from one movie clip.

8.5.2 Key-frame Detection

Key-frame selection to construct a static abstract of a video, was based on the local maxima, through peak detection on the proposed saliency curves. The process and the resulting key-frames are presented in Figs. 8.6 and 8.7 respectively for a film trailer ("First Descend")[4] rich in audio (music, narration, sound effects, machine sounds) and visual (objects, color, natural scenes, faces, action) events. The extracted 13 key-frames out of 512 of the original sequence (i.e., summarization percentage 2.5%) based on audiovisual saliency information, summarize the important visual scenes, some of which were selected based on the presence of important, aural attention-triggering audio events.

[4] http://www.firstdescentmovie.com

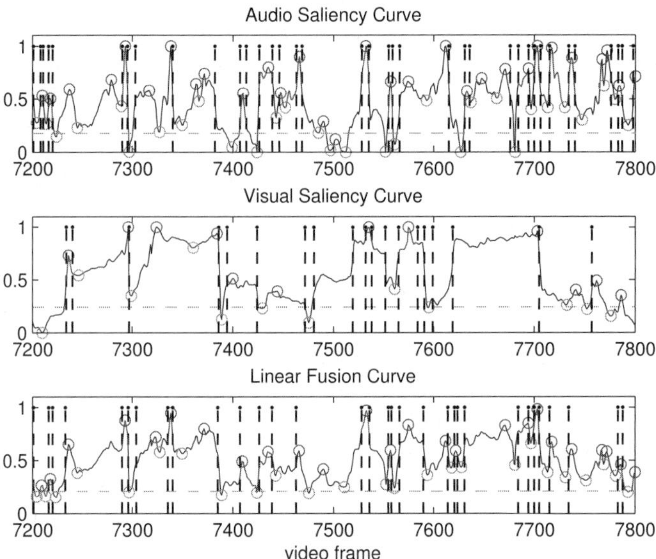

Fig. 8.8. Curves and detected features for audio saliency (top), video saliency (middle) and audiovisual saliency (bottom). The frame sequence was from the movie "Lord of the Rings I".

8.5.3 Automated Saliency-based Annotation

A method to derive automatic saliency-based annotation of audiovisual streams is by applying appropriate heuristically defined or learned thresholds on the audiovisual attention curves. The level sets of the curves thus define indicator functions of salient activity; see Fig. 8.9. A comparison against the available ground-truth is not a straight-forward task. On performing annotation, the human sensory system is able to almost automatically integrate and detect salient audiovisual information across many frames. Thus, such results are not directly comparable to the automatic annotation, since the audio part depends on the processing frame length and shift and the spatiotemporal nature of the visual part depends highly on the chosen frame neighborhood rather than on biological evidence.

Comparison against the ground-truth turns into a problem of tuning two different parameters, namely the extent (filter length) w of a smoothing operation and the threshold T that decides the salient versus the non-salient curve parts, and detecting the optimal point of operation. Perceptually, these two parameters are related, since a mildly smoothed curve (high peaks) should be accompanied by a high threshold, while a strongly smoothed curve (lower peaks) by a lower threshold. We relate these parameters using an exponential function

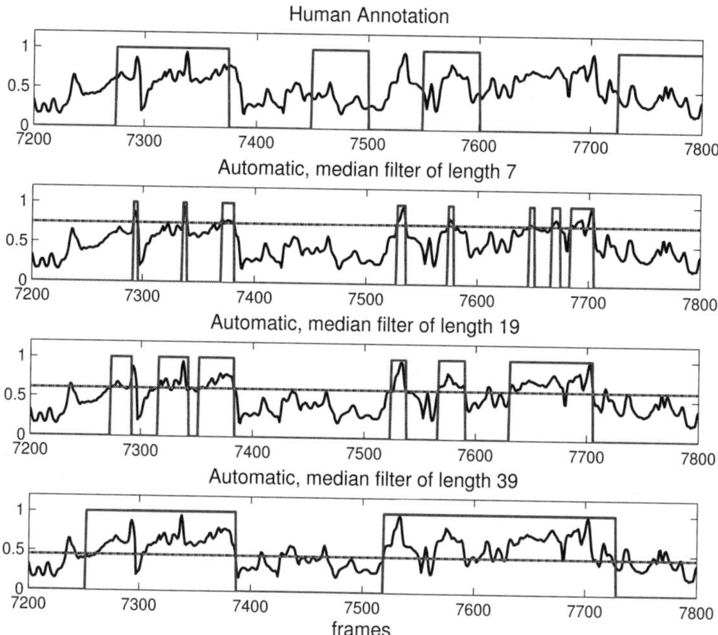

Fig. 8.9. Human and automated saliency-based annotations. Top row: Audiovisual saliency curve and manual annotation by inspection superimposed. Saliency indicator functions obtained with a median filter of variable size (7, 19, 39) in all other plots. The frame sequence was the same as in Fig. 8.8.

$$T(w) = \exp(-w/b), \tag{8.18}$$

where b is a scale factor, set to $b = 0.5$ in our experiments. Thus, a variable sized median filter is used for smoothing the audiovisual curve.

Fig. 8.9 shows a snapshot of the audiovisual curve for a sequence of 600 frames, the ground-truth, and the corresponding indicator functions and threshold levels computed by (8.18) for three different median filter lengths. We derive a precision/recall value for each filter length as shown in Fig. 8.10 for the whole duration of the two reference movie clips. Values on the horizontal x- axis relate to the size of the filter. As expected, the recall value is continuously increasing, since the thresholded, smoothed audiovisual curve tends to include an ever bigger part of the ground-truth. As already mentioned, the ability of the human eye to integrate information across time makes direct comparisons difficult. The varying smoothness imposed by the median filter simulates this integration ability in order to provide a more fair comparison. Note that although all presented experiments with the audiovisual saliency curve used the linear scheme for combining the audio features, prior to audio-

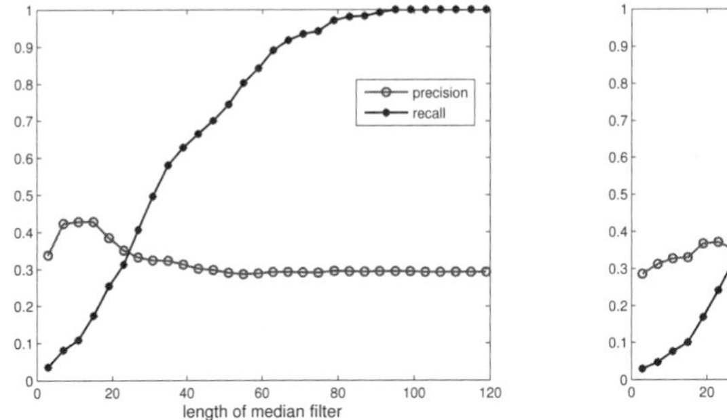

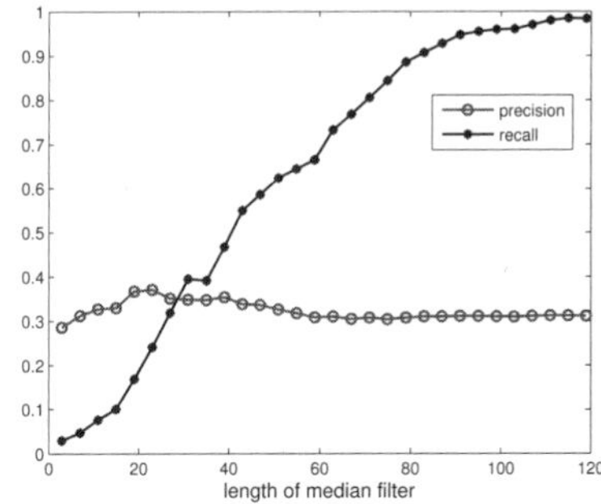

Fig. 8.10. Precision/Recall plots using human ground truth labeling on two film video segments. Left: "300", right: "Lord of the Rings I"

visual integration, preliminary experiments with the non-linear fusion scheme (8.6) for the audio saliency yielded similar performance in the precision/recall framework.

8.5.4 Video Summarization

The dynamic summarization of video sequences involves reducing the content of the initial video using a seamless selection of audio and video subclips. The selection here is based on the attentional importance given by the associated audiovisual saliency curve. In order for the resulting summary to be perceptible, informative and enjoyable by the user, the video subsegments should follow a smooth transition, the associated audio clips should not be truncated and important audiovisual events should be included. One approach to creating summaries is to select, based on a user- or application- defined skimming index, portions of video around the previously detected key frames and align the corresponding "audio sentences" [314].

Here, summaries were created using a predefined *skimming percentage* c. In effect, a smoother attention curve is created using median filtering from the initial audiovisual saliency curve, since information from key-frames or saliency boundaries is not necessary. A saliency threshold T_c is selected so that the required *percent of summarization* c is achieved. Frames m with audiovisual saliency value $S_{\text{av}}[m] > T_c$ are selected to be included in the summary. For example, for 20% summarization, $c = 0.2$, the threshold T_c is selected so that the cardinality of the set of selected frames $D = \{m : S_{\text{av}}[m] > T_c\}$ is 20% of the total number of frames. The result from this leveling step is a video frame indicator function I_c for the desired level of summarization c. The indicator function equals 1, $I_c[m] = 1$, if frame m is selected for the summary and 0 otherwise.

The resulting indicator function I_c is further processed to form contiguous blocks of video segments. This processing involves eliminating isolated segments of small duration and merging neighboring blocks in one segment. The total effect is equivalent to 1D morphological filtering operations on the binary indicator function, where the filter's length is related to the minimum number of allowed frames in a skim and the distance between skims that are to be merged.

The movie summaries, obtained by skimming 2, 3 and 5 times faster than real time, were subjectively evaluated in terms of informativeness and enjoyability by 10 naive subjects. Preliminary average results indicate that the summaries obtained by the above procedure are well informative and enjoyable. However, more work is needed to improve the "smoothness" of the summary to improve the quality and enjoyability of the created skims.

8.6 Conclusions

In this chapter we have presented efficient audio and image processing algorithms to compute audio and visual saliency curves, respectively, from the aural and visual streams of videos and explored the potential of their integration for summarization and saliency-based annotation. The involved audio and image saliency detection modules attempt to capture the perceptual human ability to automatically focus on salient events. A simple fusion scheme was employed to create audiovisual saliency curves that were applied to movie summarization (detecting static key-frames and create video skims). This revealed that successful video summaries can be formed using saliency-based models of perceptual attention. The selected key-frames described the shots or different scenes in a movie, while the formed skims were intelligible and enjoyable, when viewed by different users. In a task of saliency-based video annotation, the audiovisual saliency curve correlated adequately well with the decisions of human observers.

Future work involves mainly three directions: more sophisticated fusion methods, improved techniques to create video summarization, and incorporation of ideas from cognitive research. Fusion schemes should be explored both for intra-modality integration (audio to audio, video to video) to create the individual saliency curves and inter-modality integration for the audiovisual curve. Different techniques may proven to be appropriate for the audio and visual parts, like the non-linear audio saliency scheme described herein. To develop more efficient summarization schemes, attention should be paid to the effective segmentation and selection of the video frames, aligned with the flow of audio sentences like dialogues or music parts. Here, temporal segmentation into perceptual events is important, as there is evidence from research in cognitive neuroscience [585]. Finally, summaries can be enhanced by including other cues besides saliency, related to semantic video content.

9

Toward the Integration of Natural Language Processing and Automatic Speech Recognition: Using Morpho-Syntax and Pragmatics for Transcription

Stéphane Huet[1], Gwénolé Lecorvé[2], Guillaume Gravier[3], and Pascale Sébillot[2]

[1] IRISA, Université de Rennes 1
[2] IRISA, INSA
[3] IRISA, CNRS

In the framework of multimedia analysis and interaction, speech and language processing plays a major role. Many multimedia documents contain speech from which high level semantic information can be extracted, as in broadcast news or sports videos, with typical applications such as spoken document indexing, topic tracking and summarization. Hence, many multimedia document analysis applications require a collaboration between speech recognition and natural language processing (NLP) techniques. As NLP techniques are traditionally designed for text analysis, this combination can be seen as a multimodal fusion issue where the two modalities are audio and text. However, most of the time, both modalities are considered sequentially. A typical approach consists in automatically transcribing the audio track before analyzing the output—here considered as a regular text—with NLP methods. Independently processing the two modalities clearly seems suboptimal. This chapter focuses on recent research work toward a better integration between automatic speech recognition (ASR) and NLP for the analysis of spoken multimedia documents with the goal of achieving a better transcription of multimedia streams.

The speech processing and text processing communities have had a long history of misunderstanding, mostly due to two different approaches to natural language: a pure statistical one vs. a more symbolic, rule-based one. But the last 15 years have begun to re-appropriate the joint use of ASR and NLP. If using ASR and NLP is now a clear will, the cooperation is not that simple. First, oral output has characteristics, such as repetitions, revisions or fillers, known as disfluencies, that make it difficult. Moreover, additional difficulties come from the fact that automatic transcriptions are not segmented into sentences—the equivalents of shots for texts—, lack punctuation and, in

P. Maragos et al. (eds.), *Multimodal Processing and Interaction*,
DOI: 10.1007/978-0-387-76316-3_9, © Springer Science+Business Media, LLC 2008

the case of some ASR systems, capitalization. Finally, transcription errors might impact text processing techniques.

The problem of combining the ASR and NLP can be tackled in several ways. A popular one consists in reformatting the automatic transcription to look like a regular text using re-punctuation techniques and correcting disfluencies [306]. A second possibility is to adapt NLP techniques to take into account additional information provided by the ASR system, such as word-level confidence measures or word graphs [47]. We believe that these approaches cannot replace a better and deeper integration between ASR and NLP: for example, re-punctuation cannot help NLP recover from transcription errors. This chapter proposes a reflection and research tracks toward this goal, considering the use in ASR of linguistic knowledge that are mostly absent from current transcription systems.

Different kinds of linguistic knowledge have been considered for integration into ASR systems, namely morphological, syntactic, semantic and pragmatic, as reviewed in Section 9.2. However, most approaches consider minor changes of the ASR system (e.g., by modifying the language model) rather than a real in-depth integration. We explore in this chapter two instances of a better combination of ASR and NLP, considering morpho-syntactic information in Section 9.3 and pragmatic information for unsupervised language model adaptation in Section 9.4. Clearly, the main idea underlying this work is to take into account multimodal cues at each step of the spoken document analysis process, for example to correct transcription errors using NLP knowledge, to segment multimedia streams into topics (see Section 9.4.2) or to adapt the ASR system to the current topic.

9.1 The basic principles of automatic speech recognition

Before considering the use of linguistic information in ASR systems, we review the fundamentals of speech recognition and briefly describe the experimental framework common to the two experiments described in Sections 9.3 and 9.4.

9.1.1 General principles

Most automatic speech recognition systems rely on statistical models of speech and language to find out the best transcription, i.e., word sequence, given a (representation of the) signal y, according to

$$\widehat{w} = \arg\max_{w} p(y|w)\ P[w] \ . \tag{9.1}$$

Language models (LM), briefly described below, are used to get the prior probability $P[w]$ of a word sequence w. Acoustic models, typically continuous density hidden Markov models (HMM) representing phones, are used to compute the probability of the acoustic material for a given word sequence,

$p(y|w)$. The relation between words and acoustic models of phone-like units is provided by a pronunciation dictionary which lists the words known to the ASR system along with the corresponding pronunciations. Hence, ASR systems operate on a closed vocabulary whose typical size is between 60,000 and 100,000 words or tokens. Because of the limited size of the vocabulary, word normalization, by ignoring the case for example or by breaking compound words, is often used to limit the number of out-of-vocabulary words. The consequence is that the vocabulary of an ASR system is not necessarily suited for natural language processing.

As mentioned previously, the role of the language model is to define a probability distribution over the set of possible sentences according to the vocabulary of the system. As such, the language model is a key component for a better integration between ASR and NLP. ASR systems typically rely on N-gram based language models because of their simplicity which makes the maximization in (9.1) tractable. The N-gram model defines the probability of a sentence w_1^n as

$$P[w_1^n] = \prod_{i=1}^{n} P[w_i|w_{i-N+1}^{i-1}] \ , \tag{9.2}$$

where the probabilities of the sequences of N words $P[w_i|w_{i-N+1}^{i-1}]$ are estimated from large text corpora. Because of the large size of the vocabulary, observing all the possible sequences of N words is impossible. A first approach to circumvent the problem is based on smoothing techniques, such as discounting and back-off, to avoid null probabilities for events unobserved in the training corpus. Another approach rely on N-gram models based on classes of words [80] where a N-gram model operates on a limited set of classes, and words belong to one or several classes. The probability of a word sequence is then given by

$$P[w_1^n] = \sum_{t_1 \in \mathcal{C}(w_1) \dots t_n \in \mathcal{C}(w_n)} \prod_{i=1}^{n} P[w_i|t_i] P[t_i|t_{i-N+1}^{i-1}] \ , \tag{9.3}$$

where $\mathcal{C}(w)$ denotes the set of possible classes for a word w.

In practice, (9.1) is evaluated in the log-domain and the LM probabilities are scaled in order to be comparable to acoustic likelihoods, thus resulting in the following maximization problem

$$\widehat{w} = \arg\max_{w} \ \ln p(y|w) + \beta \ \ln P[w] + \gamma \ |w| \ , \tag{9.4}$$

where the LM scale factor β and the word insertion penalty γ are empirically set.

The ultimate output of an ASR system is obviously the transcription. However, additional information, such as confidence measures or transcription alternatives, can also be obtained. This information might prove useful for NLP as it can help to avoid error-prone hard decisions from the ASR system.

Rather than finding out the best word sequence maximizing (9.4), one can output a list of the $\mathcal{N}$-best word sequences thus keeping track of the alternative transcriptions that were discarded by the system. For a very large number of transcription hypotheses, these $\mathcal{N}$-best lists can be conveniently organized as word graphs where each arc corresponds to a word. From the set of alternative hypotheses, confidence measures can be computed for each word, where the measures reflect how confident is the system.

9.1.2 The IRENE broadcast news transcription system

The IRENE broadcast news transcription system, jointly developed by IRISA and ENST for the ESTER broadcast news transcription evaluation campaign [176], implements the basic principles described in the previous section after a partitioning step which aims at segmenting the input stream into pseudo-sentences. The system has a vocabulary of 64,000 words.

Regions containing speech are first detected before performing a further partitioning into speaker turns. Since (9.4) can only be solved for short utterances, the speech stream is finally segmented into breath-groups based on the energy profile in order to detect breath intakes[4]. Let us stress the fact this segmentation is not based on syntactic and grammatical considerations, even though breath pauses and grammar are related.

Transcription itself is carried out in three passes. A first pass with fairly simple context-independent acoustic models and a 3-gram word based LM aims at generating large word graphs. These word graphs are then rescored with more complex context-dependent acoustic models and a 4-gram LM. Rescoring word graphs is based on (9.4) where the maximization is limited to the set of word sequences encoded in the word graph, thus making the use of more complex models tractable. Finally, based on the transcription from the second pass and the speaker partition obtained in the segmentation step, the acoustic models are adapted for each speaker and final word graphs are obtained by rescoring the initial word graphs with speaker-adapted acoustic models.

Experiments reported in this chapter were carried out on the ESTER French broadcast news transcription task. A corpus of about one hundred hours of manually transcribed data was used and divided into three parts: a large part was reserved for the purpose of acoustic and language model training while two sets of four hours each, from four different broadcasters, were used as development and test sets respectively. The development set was used to tune the many parameters of the ASR system such as the language model scale factor. The language model was obtained by interpolating a LM estimated on 1 million words from the manual transcriptions of the training set with a LM estimated from 350 million words from the French newspaper *Le Monde*.

[4] To avoid problems due to segmentation errors, the entire partitioning process was done manually in the experiments reported in this chapter.

9.2 Fusion of text and speech modalities: an overview

Let us come back to the problem of combining the text and audio modalities. We review in this section the literature concerning the use of linguistic knowledge in ASR systems successively considering morphology, syntax, semantics and pragmatics.

Morphology considers the structure of words. Morphological analyzers can be used to convert words into their canonical form, e.g., a lemma or a stem. Such knowledge is incorporated in ASR systems by defining a LM over canonical forms rather than words, which is convenient in order to reduce the vocabulary size in particular for agglutinative or morphologically rich languages. Factored models[5] have been specifically developed to integrate morphological components as factors in the language model probability computation, where the factors can be stems, morphological classes or even the words themselves [544].

Syntax considers the structure of sentences and syntagms, e.g., nominal or verbal groups. A first possibility relies on part-of-speech (POS) information, i.e., grammatical classes such as noun, verb, and preposition, associated with each word, known as POS tags. A class-based LM can be defined over POS tags and combined with a word-based LM [317]. The main interest of POS-based LMs is the limited number of tags with respect to the number of words and their ability to point out ungrammatical word (actually tag) sequences. Moreover, morphological knowledge can also be included in the tags leading to morpho-syntactic information. A second use of syntactic information is to extract locutions based on the statistical study of co-occurrences [512] or the use of regular expressions [358]. Such locutions are included in the vocabulary of the ASR system as multi-word units. Finally, syntactic analysis of transcription hypotheses can also be done in order to choose the most grammatical ones. As designing generic syntactic parsers robust to transcription errors is an awfully difficult task, systems either complex [91] or limited to a specific domain [474] have been proposed.

Semantics considers the meaning of the words and the relations between words. Few works include semantic information in ASR systems but relations between words can be incorporated in long-span language models as in [521] and [49]. The idea is to put forward sentence hypotheses containing words with related meanings. Relations between words are automatically acquired either considering co-occurrences in syntagms or text windows, or considering words sharing the same neighbors. However, long-span language models are difficult to integrate in an ASR system.

Finally, pragmatics considers the context, shared by the redactor and the reader, so that the document makes sense. The topic of the document is a typical example of pragmatic knowledge which can be used in ASR systems,

[5] Factored model are similar to factorial Markov models where the state space is distributed over a set of factors.

for instance for LM and vocabulary adaptation. One approach for LM topic adaptation relies on a set of predefined domain-specific LMs [227, 182]. However, this method requires the *a priori* definition of the set of possible topics. Another solution is to gather a specific adaptation corpus for each document, either by selecting a subset of a very general corpus [263] or by collecting texts on the Internet [515].

Whatever the type of knowledge, most techniques naturally rely on an integration at the language model level. A typical approach consists in modifying the word-based N-gram LM, for example using interpolation techniques. However, this approach implies only minor modifications of the architecture of the ASR system and thus often only yield marginal improvements.

In this chapter, we report on work targeting a better integration of the text and speech modalities for two different sources of knowledge, namely morpho-syntax and pragmatics, where topic adaptation is considered in the latter. These two types of linguistic information are crucial for multimedia applications. Morpho-syntactic knowledge enables more grammatical transcriptions, thus facilitating the use of *a posteriori* NLP techniques on the output. Topic adaptation is vital for the accurate transcription of multimedia streams where various topics can be found.

9.3 Morpho-syntactic knowledge integration

In this section, we present our method to integrate morpho-syntactic information in the ASR process. As mentioned in the previous section, part-of-speech tags along with morphological knowledge about gender, number, tense, mode or case are used to convey morpho-syntactic information. Previous work combining class-based LMs and word-based ones have demonstrated a limited effectiveness [563]. In [202], a 3-gram LM is built over word/tag pairs rather than words and the recognition problem is redefined as finding the best joint word and POS tag sequences. This approach results in a significant reduction of the word error rate (WER) but requires very large amount of training data for the LM and heavily relies on smoothing techniques.

We propose a different approach where POS information is combined with the LM score in a post-processing stage of a $\mathcal{N}$-best list of hypotheses rather than integrated in the LM as in previous approaches. The basic idea is to tag the output of the ASR system in order to favor the hypotheses with correct POS sequences, like a singular noun following a singular adjective. Closely related to [202], our method does however not require a large amount of annotated training data. In this section, we demonstrate that POS tagging can be reliably applied to automatic transcriptions and that the resulting tags can actually improve the word error rate and confidence measures.

9.3.1 Morpho-syntactic tagging of automatic transcriptions

Morpho-syntactic tagging is a widely used technique in NLP and taggers are now considered as reliable enough to automatically tag a text according to POS information. However, most experiments were carried out on written text, and spoken corpora on the contrary have been seldom studied. As oral output has specificities that are likely to disturb taggers, we first demonstrate that such noisy texts can be reliably tagged.

We built a morpho-syntactic tagger based on the popular technique of HMM [336], where tagging is expressed as finding out, for each sentence, the most probable POS tag sequence, among all the possible sequences according to a lexicon. In order to adapt the model to the characteristics of oral, we used a 200,000-word training set from the manual transcriptions of the training corpus. Moreover, we removed all capital letters and punctuation marks to obtain a format similar to a transcription and segmented the set into breath-groups. We also restrained the vocabulary of the tagger to the one of our ASR system. We chose our POS tags in order to distinguish the gender and the number of adjectives and nouns, and the tense and the mood of verbs, which led to a set of 93 tags.

To quantitatively evaluate morpho-syntactic tagging, we manually tagged a one hour broadcast. We first investigated the behavior of the tagger on manually transcribed text by comparing the tag found for each word with the one of the reference. For automatic transcriptions, evaluating the tagger is more problematic than for manual transcriptions since ASR output contains misrecognized words; for the hypotheses containing grammatical errors, it becomes impossible to know which sequence of POS would be right. We therefore compute the tag rate only for the words that are correctly recognized.

Table 9.1, first line, reports results obtained on the one hour corpus with our tagger, where the WER on the transcription is 22.0 %. We achieved a tag accuracy over 95 % which is comparable to the results usually given on written corpora. Furthermore, similar performance level are obtained on both the manual and automatic transcriptions, which establishes therefore that morpho-syntactic tagging is reliable, even for text produced by an ASR system whose recognition errors are likely to jeopardize the tagging of correctly recognized words. The robustness of tagging is explained by the fact that tags are locally assigned. We compared the performances of our tagger with those of Cordial[6], one of the best taggers available for written French and which has already produced good results on a spoken corpus [538]. Results reported in the last line of Table 9.1 are comparable with our HMM-based tagger when we ignore confusion between proper names and common names. Indeed, the lack of capital letters is particularly problematic for Cordial, which relies on this information to detect proper names.

[6] Distributed by the *Synapse Développement* corporation.

transcription	manual	automatic
HMM tagger	95.7 (95.9)	95.7 (95.9)
Cordial	90.7 (95.0)	90.6 (95.2)

Table 9.1. Tag accuracy (in %), where results between parentheses are computed when confusion between common names and proper names is ignored.

9.3.2 Reranking of $\mathcal{N}$-best lists

Morpho-syntactic information is here used to post-processing $\mathcal{N}$-best sentence hypothesis lists. Although $\mathcal{N}$-best lists are not as informative as word graphs, each entry can be seen as a standard text, permitting thus POS tagging.

To combine morpho-syntactic information with the LM and acoustic scores, we first determine the most likely POS tag sequence t_1^m corresponding to a sentence hypothesis w_1^n. Based on this information, we compute the morpho-syntactic probability of the sentence hypothesis

$$P[t_1^m] = \prod_{i=1}^{m} P[t_i | t_{i-N+1}^{i-1}] \ . \tag{9.5}$$

Note that the number m of tags may differ from the number n of words as we associate a unique POS with locutions, consecutive proper names or cardinals. To take into account longer dependencies than the 4-gram word-based LM, we chose a 7-gram POS-based LM.

We propose a new global score of a sentence [219] by adding the morpho-syntactic score to the score given in (9.4) with an appropriate weight. The combined score for a sentence w_1^n, corresponding to the acoustic input y_1^t, is therefore given by

$$s(w_1^n) = \log p(y_1^t | w_1^n) + \alpha \log P[w_1^n] + \beta \log P[t_1^m] + \gamma n \ . \tag{9.6}$$

Integrating POS information at the sentence level allows us to differently tokenize sequences of words and tags and to more explicitly penalize unlikely sequences of tags like a plural noun following a singular adjective.

Based on the score function defined in (9.6), which includes all the available sources of knowledge, we can reorder $\mathcal{N}$-best lists using various criteria. We considered three criteria, namely maximum a posteriori (MAP), minimum expected word error rate [509] and consensus decoding on $\mathcal{N}$-best lists [318]. The two last criteria, often used in current systems, aim at reducing the word error rate at the expense of an increased sentence error rate (SER).

MAP criterion

The MAP criterion selects among the $\mathcal{N}$-best list generated for each breath-group the best hypothesis $w^{(i)}$ which maximizes $s(w^{(i)})$ as given by (9.6).

baseline ASR system	contextual probabilities	lexical and contextual probabilities	class-based LM
19.9	19.1	19.0	19.5

Table 9.2. WER (in %) on test data obtained with a LM limited to a word-based LM (1st column) or with an ASR system including POS according to equations (9.6), (9.7) or (9.8) (last three columns).

Results on the test corpus show that our approach achieves an absolute decrease of 0.8 % of the WER as reported in Tab. 9.2, columns 1 and 2. By taking into account lexical probabilities $P[w_i|t_i]$, which are usually included in class-based LM, we observed a minor additional decrease (Tab. 9.2, column 3) of the WER. The score in this last case is computed by linearly interpolating log-probabilities by

$$s'(w_1^n) = \log P(y_1^t|w_1^n) + \alpha \log P[w_1^n] + \beta \left(\sum_{i=1}^{n} \log P[w_i|t_i] + \log P[t_1^m] \right) + \gamma n \tag{9.7}$$

and tends to penalize words that are rarely associated with the proposed tag.

We compared our approach with class-based LM incorporated in the transcription process by linear interpolation with a word-based LM according to

$$P[w_1^n] = \prod_{i=1}^{n} \left(\lambda\, P_{\text{word}}[w_i|w_1^{i-1}] + (1-\lambda)\, P_{\text{pos}}[w_i|w_1^{i-1}]\right)$$

with

$$P_{\text{pos}}[w_i|w_1^{i-1}] = \sum_{t_{i-N+1}\dots t_i} P[w_i|t_i]\;\; P[t_i|t_{i-N+1}^{i-1}]\ . \tag{9.8}$$

We reevaluated the $\mathcal{N}$-best lists by interpolating the N-class based POS tagger and the word level language model, the interpolation factor λ being optimized on the development data. We noticed an absolute decrease of 0.4 % with respect to the baseline system, i.e., half of the decrease previously observed (Tab. 9.2, last column). The better improvement of WER with our method clearly establishes that linear interpolation of log probabilities is more effective than that of probabilities.

Word error minimization criteria

Combined scores incorporating morpho-syntactic information can be used to reorder $\mathcal{N}$-best lists using decoding criteria that aim at minimizing the word error rate, rather than the sentence error rate as the MAP criterion does. Two popular criteria can be used to explicitly minimize the WER: the first one consists in approximating the posterior expectation of the word error rate

	WER			SER		
	MAP dec.	min. WE	cons. dec.	MAP dec.	min. WE	cons. dec.
without POS	19.9	19.8	19.8	61.8	62.2	62.4
with POS	19.0	18.9	18.9	59.4	59.6	59.7

Table 9.3. Word (WER) and sentence (SER) error rates (in %) on the test data for various decoding techniques.

by comparing each pair of hypotheses in the $\mathcal{N}$-best list [509]; the second one, consensus decoding, is based on the multiple alignment of the $\mathcal{N}$-best hypotheses into a confusion network [318].

Both criteria rely on the computation of the posterior probability for each sentence hypothesis $w^{(i)}$

$$P[w^{(i)}|y_1^t] = \frac{e^{s(w^{(i)})/z}}{\sum_j e^{s(w^{(j)})/z}} \tag{9.9}$$

where the posterior probability is obtained from a score including morpho-syntactic knowledge, the one given by Eq. (9.7) in our case. The combined score is scaled by a factor z in order to avoid over-peaked posterior probabilities.

Results are reported in Tab. 9.3 for the three decoding criteria, namely MAP, WER minimization and consensus, with and without POS knowledge. In both cases, we observe a slight WER improvement when using word error minimization criteria, along with an increased SER. However, the gain observed is marginal because of the limited size of the $\mathcal{N}$-best lists ($\mathcal{N}$=100). Indeed, with $\mathcal{N}$ = 1000 the WER decreased from 19.7 % to 19.4 % without POS. A more limited gain was observed when using POS with a decrease from 18.7 % to 18.6 %.

Discussion on the results

Statistical tests were carried out to measure the significance of the WER improvement observed, assuming independence of the errors across breath-groups. For all the decoding criteria, both the paired t-test and the paired Wilcoxon test resulted in a confidence over 99.9 % that the difference of WER by using or not POS knowledge is not observed by chance. Besides, for the MAP criterion, the same tests indicate that global scores computed as (9.6) or (9.7) led to a significant improvement with respect to the interpolated class-based LM with a confidence over 99 %.

We observed that our method is robust for spontaneous speech. Indeed, we measured performance on a short extract of 3,650 words containing interviews with numerous disfluencies and observed that the baseline WER of 46.3 % is reduced to 44.5 % with (9.6) and to 44.3 % with (9.7) using the

	WER	NCE without POS	NCE with POS
decoding without POS	19.7	0.307	0.326
decoding with POS	18.7	0.265	0.288

Table 9.4. WER (in %) and normalized cross entropy for MAP decoding with and without POS score.

MAP criterion. This 4% relative improvement is consistent with the relative improvement obtained on the entire test set. Additional experiments with automatic segmentation also demonstrated the validity of our approach in that case.

Experiments reported here were carried out on the French language, whose nouns, adjectives and verbs are very often inflected for number, gender or tense into various homophone forms. However, experiments conducted to improve a hand-writing recognition system in the English language, show that morpho-syntactic knowledge still brings an WER improvement, even though English is less inflected than French.

To conclude this section, we observed that introducing morpho-syntactic knowledge in the ASR system yield more grammatically correct utterance transcriptions as indicated by the SERs reported in Tab. 9.3. In particular, we noticed several corrections of agreement or tense errors such as "*une date qui À DONNER le vertige à une partie de la France*" ("*a date which TO GIVE a part of France fever*").

9.3.3 Confidence measures

We have shown how POS knowledge can reduce transcript errors. Another interest of morpho-syntactic information for ASR systems is that it can bring new information to compute confidence measures.

Plots of the conditional probabilities $P[t_i|t_{i-N+1}^{i-1}]$ for POS sequences and $P[w_i|w_{i-M+1}^{i-1}]$ for word sequences show that $P[t_i|t_{i-N+1}^{i-1}]$ exhibits a significant decrease on erroneous words where language model may show the same behavior on correct words due to smoothing or back-off. This property is particularly interesting to compute confidence measures. As sentence posterior probabilities are commonly used to derive confidence measures from $\mathcal{N}$-best lists or lattices, we compute them as in [449].

Confidence measures are obtained from 1,000-best lists using the combined score (9.7). We limit the study to the lists obtained with MAP decoding for which the lowest SER was achieved. The scaling factors and insertion penalty used for the computation of the sentence posteriors are different from those used for reordering the $\mathcal{N}$-best lists and were optimized on the development set to maximize the normalized cross entropy (NCE), a commonly used indicator to evaluate confidence measure on the correctness of a word.

Table 9.4 summarizes the results, where the higher the NCE, the better the confidence measure. WER with and without POS information are given in the first column. The next two columns report NCE obtained when computing confidence measures respectively without and with morpho-syntactic information. Results show that POS improves confidence measures in both cases.

9.3.4 Summary

Experiments reported in this section clearly demonstrated that combining morpho-syntactic knowledge in an ASR system at the sentence level is an efficient strategy, resulting in improved transcriptions and confidence measures. It is worthwhile to note that the combined score defined in (9.6) implements a linear combination of log-scores similar to score combination in multistream HMMs as discussed in chapter 4. Moreover, we observed that the output after morpho-syntactic rescoring is more grammatical, a fact from which further NLP algorithms applied to the text resulting from the transcription should benefit.

9.4 Pragmatic knowledge integration

In this section, we present another step toward a better integration between ASR and NLP, focusing on pragmatic knowledge. In this framework, we consider topic-related information in order to adapt the LM of the ASR system in an unsupervised way.

Usually, LMs are trained once and for all on large multi-topic corpora. Every (part of the) document is then processed using the same general-purpose LM, whatever the actual topic, even though word frequencies depend on the theme. Topic-specific LMs are therefore a good way of improving ASR based on pragmatic knowledge. NLP methods precisely able to locate and characterize topics can be applied to update the vocabulary of an ASR system or its general-purpose LM [23, 62]. In this section, we focus on the adaptation of the LM, leaving the vocabulary untouched.

As presented in Fig 9.1, the basic idea of our approach is, first, to segment a broadcast transcript obtained with a baseline, general-purpose, LM into thematically coherent successive parts. For each segment, topic-specific data are then retrieved from a large collection of texts, i.e., the Internet, and used to modify the initial LM. To achieve this goal, an adaptation LM is obtained from the topic-specific data and linearly combined with the general-purpose LM thus resulting in an adapted LM. The latter is used to get a new, hopefully better, transcription for the corresponding segment. This adaptation process is repeated for each part of the document resulting from the segmentation step.

Note that for multimedia documents for which text data are already available, gathering topic-specific data can be done according to the available textual modality rather than based on a first transcription result. In the typology

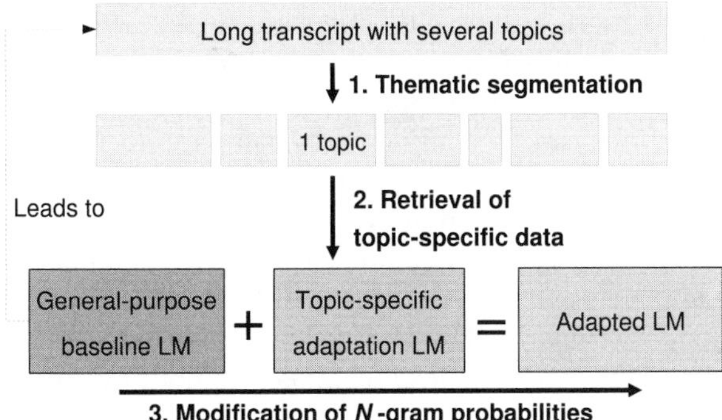

Fig. 9.1. Main scheme of a topic-based adaptation.

of fusion methods of Snoek and Worring [501], the proposed approach can be seen as an iterative fusion scheme where the audio and text modalities are considered sequentially. To achieve a better cascading of the modality, we present some adaptation of NLP algorithms to deal with the specificities of automatic transcriptions.

We first briefly review related works before presenting our approaches for the topic segmentation of transcriptions and for the creation of a topic-specific corpus from the Internet.

9.4.1 Related works

Most related works focus on only one subtask of the entire adaptation process—such as thematic segmentation, topic-specific data collecting or LM adaptation—and the combination of these subtasks as a whole topic-based LM adaptation process is still marginal [93].

The most popular indicator for the segmentation of texts into thematically consistent sections is lexical cohesion [537] which focuses on the vocabulary used in a text block and studies the numbers of word occurrences. Indeed, the frequent use of the same words in a given text section tends to demonstrate a thematic coherence of the text. This method can be enriched by the knowledge of more complex relations between words, such as synonymy. On top of lexical cohesion, other useful indicators of a topic change can be considered. For example, discourse markers [321], like "*however*" and "*furthermore*", can be used. In the case of multimedia documents, cues from the other modalities [530], e.g., shot boundaries, speaker changes or silences, provide valuable information.

Existing approaches for topic-specific data retrieval mainly differ according to the type of data collection used and the criterion chosen to select the relevant documents. Some studies are based on static sets of articles from which topic-specific texts can only be found for a restricted number of domains [263] while other, more recent, works seek to retrieve texts from the Internet [515].

This last source is more interesting, being an open resource which contains texts whose style is closer to speech than in typical written documents [543]. As for the method used to select topic-related texts, several criteria based on the word distributions can be considered to compare documents, as is classically done in the information retrieval (IR) domain [93].

Finally, language model adaptation given a topic-specific corpus of texts has been widely studied. A simple approach consists in training a LM from the corpus before interpolating the adaptation LM with the general-purpose one, either linearly or log-linearly. The N-gram probabilities of each LM are thus directly mixed. Other more complex techniques do not rely on an intermediate adaptation LM but rather search for a final N-gram distribution which minimizes an information quantity, like entropy or mutual information, according to constraints derived from the adaptation corpus. It has been shown that these methods outperform the interpolation-based ones [93].

As opposed to previous works, we study the complete adaptation process and propose a fully unsupervised approach, for which no restricting hypothesis on the domain or the number of topics is made. To this end, we first combine acoustic and text features for the segmentation of transcribed text. We then adapt NLP techniques to take into account confidence measures in order to gather topic-specific corpora from the Internet. Finally, we demonstrate that the cascaded use of NLP on transcriptions can benefit to the ASR system by providing adaptation data. The following sections describe each of these steps.

9.4.2 Transcript segmentation

Transcript segmentation is primarily based on the statistical lexical cohesion method described in [537]. In this method, a graph of all the possible segmentations is constructed where the vertex values represent the lexical cohesion for the segment represented by the vertex. Although originally designed for written documents, we observed that this method is quite robust to misrecognized words and segmentation into breath-groups [218]. However, the voluntary absence of word repetitions—for obvious stylistic reasons—limits the performance. We therefore extend semantic links between words by studying co-occurrences of lexical units in the French corpus *Le Monde*. On top of lexical cohesion, syntactic and acoustic cues were also considered. Syntactic cues are based on the sequences of words and POS tags to determine hidden boundaries between words. Moreover, as spoken documents are multimodal by nature, we take advantage of audio cues such as male/female speaker changes or jingles[7]. To accommodate the additional features, we extended the statistical lexical cohesion method by adapting the vertex weights to take into

[7] Surprisingly, pause duration turned out to be quite uninformative for the segmentation contrary to many previous studies on spoken document segmentation. This is mostly due to the nature of the documents, as radio broadcast news exhibit very few pauses.

account the syntactic and acoustic cues. To predict segment boundaries at the end of an hypothesized segment, a decision tree is used for the acoustic cues while a hidden N-gram models the syntactic information [218]. Vertex weights are modified so as to be a linear combination of the lexical cohesion, syntactic and acoustic log-scores.

Using only lexical cohesion leads to a recall of 57.4 % for a precision of 36.1 % on segment boundaries, resulting in 78.8 % of the segments containing a single topic. With the addition of semantic information plus syntactic and acoustic cues, we achieved a recall of 67.2 % with a precision of 43.2 %, yielding 83.5 % of pure segments.

To validate the other steps of our adaptation method without the bias of non thematically homogeneous segments, we consider manual topic segmentation in the rest of this section.

9.4.3 Language model adaptation

In order to train an adaptation LM for a thematically consistent section, keywords are automatically selected and submitted to a Web search engine, the resulting pages forming the adaptation corpus from which a LM is estimated. This adaptation LM is combined with the general-purpose baseline LM using linear interpolation, to obtain an adapted LM which is then used to rescore word graphs and generate a new transcription.

However, gathering an adaptation corpus from the transcription of a thematically homogeneous segment is far from trivial. First, keywords must be significant enough to fully characterize the content of the segment. On the other hand, too specific keywords are problematic as they usually result in few matches on the Internet. This remark raises questions about the "optimal" size of the adaptation corpus and its homogeneity. These many issues are discussed below.

Keyword spotting

Keywords are selected based on the well-known IR score *tf*idf*, where *tf* represents the frequency of a term w and *idf* is a value related to the inverse number of documents containing w in a text collection. Terms with the higher *tf*idf* scores are considered as characteristic terms and selected. In practice, the scores are computed on stems rather than words.

The standard *tf*idf* keyword selection method was adapted to take into account specificities of the documents at hand. First, proper names tend to result in very small and too specific adaptation corpora. A penalty is therefore applied to their *tf*idf* score which is scaled by a coefficient empirically set to 0.75. Because of the lack of cases in the transcribed texts, proper names are detected based on morpho-syntactic tags (see Section 9.3) combined with a dictionary: nouns with no definition in the dictionary are considered as proper names. Second, the *tf*idf* score of a term w is biased based on the confidence

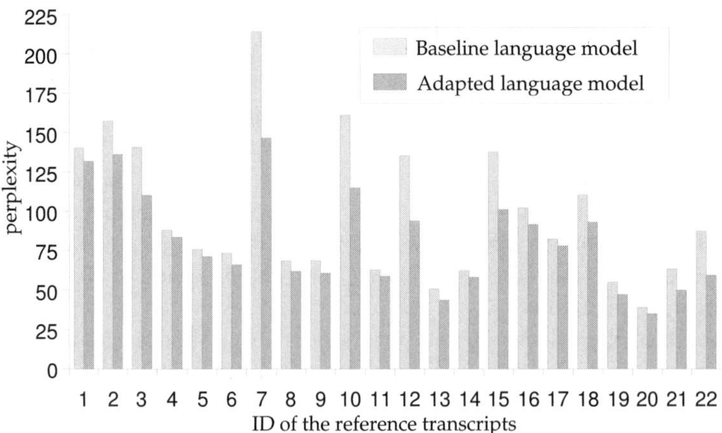

Fig. 9.2. Details of measured perplexity before and after our topic-based adaptation.

measure c of w in order to limit the impact of misrecognized words, according to

$$score(w) = tf^*idf \times \lambda + tf^*idf \times (1 - \lambda) \times c \ , \tag{9.10}$$

where λ limits the influence of c.

Adaptation corpus creation

Even if the number of selected keywords is limited to five, combining them in a single query is not relevant for the task of gathering topic-related documents. Two main problems occur: a single query often results in very small amounts of adaptation data; moreover, the impact of transcription errors is detrimental. We rather rely on a fixed number of queries combining subsets of the whole keyword set. For example, a first query can be composed of the two best-scored keywords while the second one combines the first and third keywords. This strategy maximizes the probability of having at least one relevant query, even when transcription errors are present.

As queries can return several thousands of documents, the number of matching documents must be limited. In our study, it was experimentally observed that at least fifty documents are required to get a good adaptation LM. However, increasing the number of considered documents linearly increases runtime for a limited gain. Consequently, two hundred Web pages are kept. A cosine similarity distance between the initial transcription of the segment and each Web page is used to filter out irrelevant matches.

Results

Experiments were carried out on a subset of 22 manually selected segments from our broadcast news corpus. Perplexity before and after interpolation of the baseline LM with the one obtained from the adaptation data are reported in figure 9.2 for each of these segments. Perplexity measures how well a LM can predict the next word given the word history, where the lower the perplexity, the better. These results indicate that adaptation always reduces perplexity, even for texts with a low initial perplexity (texts 13, 19 and 20).

However, due to the complex interactions between all the components of an ASR system, decreasing the perplexity of a LM does not necessarily result a decrease of the word and sentence error rates. In two out of three segments, the perplexity falls by over 10 % which translates into a global absolute WER decrease of 0.2 %. This small global WER reduction is mostly due to the fact that the WER increases in 33 % of the sections while limited WER reductions are observed in the remaining ones.

Though mitigated, these first results are encouraging as they demonstrate the validity of the proposed unsupervised adaptation scheme. A detailed analysis of the transcriptions after adaptation shows that while topic-specific terms are better recognized, more new errors appear on grammatical words (prepositions, determiners, *etc.*). This can be partially explained by the fact that the adaptation LM is poor on grammatical words due to the limited size of the training corpus. We believe that better LM adaptation techniques than interpolation should be considered to circumvent this problem.

Summary

Even if segmentation has not been yet coupled with adaptation, this section illustrates the use of pragmatic information in combination with ASR system for unsupervised topic adaptation. The proposed approach mixes information from the text and audio modalities at various levels. For example, segmentation of transcriptions rely on lexical, syntactic, semantic and acoustic cues. Acoustic based confidence measures are used in the keyword selection process which is by itself based on the text modality. The sequential use of transcription, text analysis and again transcription is another example of multimodal fusion.

9.5 Conclusion

In this chapter, we presented experiments toward a better integration between automatic speech recognition and natural language processing techniques in order to improve multimedia (or spoken) document processing techniques based on a fusion of information from the audio and text modalities. In particular, we investigated the fusion of morpho-syntactic and of pragmatic knowledge in an ASR system and demonstrated the benefits of it. We have seen that traditional multimodal fusion schemes such as the combination of log-scores or sequential processing of the modalities successfully apply to the text and audio modalities.

Many other research directions have to be investigated towards a full integration of these two modalities. For example, we have used $\mathcal{N}$-best lists at the interface between speech and natural language. This is convenient because each entry can be considered as a regular sentence thus enabling the use of standard NLP algorithms and a combination of knowledge sources at the sentence level. However, alternate transcription hypotheses are lost and NLP techniques can hardly recover from errors made by the ASR system. Using other interfaces, such as word graphs or confusion networks, might prove interesting but requires a deeper modification of standard NLP techniques. Finally, many other sources of linguistic knowledge not considered in this chapter can also benefit to ASR transcriptions, such as syntactic analysis or a more extensive use of semantic relations.

Part III

SEARCHING MULTIMEDIA CONTENT

10

Interactive Image Retrieval Using a Hybrid Visual and Conceptual Content Representation

Marin Ferecatu[1], Nozha Boujemaa[1], and Michel Crucianu[1,2]

[1] INRIA Rocquencourt
[2] Conservatoire National des Arts et Métiers

Many image databases available today have keyword annotations associated with images. State of the art low-level visual features reflect well the "physical" content and thus the visual similarity between images, but retrieval based on visual features alone is subject to the semantic gap. Alternatively, text annotations can be linked to image context or semantic interpretation but are not necessarily related to the visual appearance of the images. Keywords and visual features thus provide complementary information regarding the images. Combining these two sources of information is an advantage in many retrieval applications and recent work in this area reflects this interest.

We present here a new feature vector, based on the keyword annotations available for an image database and making use of the conceptual information extracted from an external knowledge database. We evaluate the joint use of the proposed *conceptual* feature vector and the low level visual features both in a Query By Example (QBE) context and with SVM-based Relevance Feedback (RF). Our experiments show that the use of the conceptual feature vectors can significantly improve the effectiveness of both retrieval approaches.

10.1 Hybrid search

The remarkable success of keyword-based search encouraged the extension of this paradigm from text to image retrieval. In this case, keywords are extracted either from the text found in the neighborhood of images or from the annotations explicitly provided for the images. However, the use of keywords for text retrieval has some well-known limitations: words are language dependent, words are often ambiguous and matching based on words is brittle. For image retrieval, yet other limitations add up. First, the relevant keywords associated to an image can be scarce, since the surrounding text can have little relevance, while manually providing annotations is expensive. Then, the annotations or the surrounding text seldom describe the visual aspect of images.

P. Maragos et al. (eds.), *Multimodal Processing and Interaction*,
DOI: 10.1007/978-0-387-76316-3_10,

Furthermore, they are often *inherently* incomplete with respect to the higher level semantics of the image (one can usually add new relevant keywords).

As an alternative to keyword-based image retrieval (KBIR in the following), the recent years witnessed the development of methods for image retrieval relying on automatically extracted visual features (content-based image retrieval, CBIR), see [123], [295], [76], [181] and references therein. But CBIR faces the well-known challenge of the *semantic gap* between low-level visual features and high-level semantics. Furthermore, while image analysis and recognition techniques (see Part II of this book) are in some cases able to detect the presence of specific objects or persons in an image, they cannot be expected to provide relevant information that is more related to the context than to the visual content of an image.

We note that each of the two general image retrieval paradigms mentioned above—employing keywords or employing the visual content—has specific limitations and is better adapted to a certain type of *search target*. KBIR is more adequate when the user is looking for images associated to a high-level, unambiguous concept, and the visual appearance has little relevance. CBIR performs best when the user is searching for images illustrating a concept that translates to low or intermediate level visual features (e.g., color, texture, shape). Keywords and visual features are complementary sources of information, but neither KBIR nor CBIR in their original formulations take advantage of both sources.

In many cases, the user is interested in finding images corresponding to a semantic concept that *combines* high-level descriptions and visual components. For the search to be effective, contributions from both keywords and visual features are welcome. With existing keyword-based search engines, the user relies on the engine for the higher-level component and on his own visual evaluation capabilities for the subsequent selection stage; this results in a long time spent in the search process and in a low recall rate. A simple automatic alternative, present in some prototype content-based image search engines, for performing such combined searches relies on a filtering approach. Here, the keywords in the query are employed for filtering out all the candidates that do not contain them, either before or after performing the search using the visual component; the brittleness of keyword matching has a negative impact on the recall rate.

If more appropriate representations are devised for the image annotations, *hybrid* search taking into account both visual and textual features becomes possible. Among the early proposals along this line we mention [282], [497], [590] and [593]. But these proposals do not completely meet the high expectations one has for hybrid search, mainly because of the solutions employed for representing image annotations. We consider that the descriptors of the annotations should have several desirable properties: refer to concepts rather than keywords (to avoid the ambiguousness of word-based matching), have the same type of representation as the visual features in order to enable the same retrieval mechanisms (including the use of database summaries, query by example and relevance feedback), have a relatively low dimension (to maintain the effectiveness of multidimensional index structures) and be as "interpretable" as possible (to enable other query methods).

In the following we focus on hybrid retrieval from fully annotated image databases and we put forward a new descriptor that is a convenient representation for the information provided by the set of keywords associated to an image. The design of this descriptor takes into account the fact that such annotations typically contain only a few keywords, which makes statistical descriptions unreliable. On the complementary topic of retrieval of images on the Web, an overview is presented in the chapter "Intelligent Search for Text and Image Information on the Web" of this book.

We rely on an external ontology to derive a set of semantic "key concepts" linked with the keywords employed for annotating the images in the database. We then project the keywords of each image on the selected key concepts to obtain a vector representation of fixed and rather low dimension, that has interpretable components. The resulting *conceptual* feature vector can be directly used for enhancing the results of a query by visual example or to improve retrieval with relevance feedback.

In Section 10.2 we introduce the new keyword-based feature vector and show all the stages required to obtain these feature vectors for a database of annotated images. The SVM-based active relevance feedback method we employ is described in Section. 10.3, with an emphasis on the choice of the kernel and on the selection criterion. In Section 10.4 we present the real-world annotated image database, taken from the Alinari Picture Library[3], and the visual content descriptors we employ. We then provide evaluation results obtained with query by example and with relevance feedback. We conclude by a discussion of our results and a set of promising research directions.

10.2 From keywords to conceptual feature vectors

We describe in this section a new feature vector based on keywords associated to each image in the database and taking advantage of an external ontology. Since keywords are a different source of information compared to the visual content of the images, with a higher level of semantic abstractness, this type of feature can be used to complement the visual descriptors and increase the quality of the results returned by an image search engine. By converting keywords to a standard vector feature form we reduce the impact of hybrid search on the architecture of the image search engine and on the retrieval methods. We can thus take advantage of the already existing work, especially for relevance feedback.

Our approach in building the new feature vector consists in representing the *conceptual content* associated to the keywords and in exploiting the

[3] Annotated image database kindly provided by Alinari, `http://www.alinari.com`

conceptual similarity. This allows us to avoid to a large extent the problems associated to word matching, caused by word ambiguousness, by the extensive use of synonyms or by neglecting similarities between different concepts. In order to have a reference for the concepts and to measure conceptual similarity, we rely on an external knowledge database. Such an approach, using *a priori* conceptual relations, is better adapted to the representation of image annotations than methods based on empirical corpus statistics, which can only be reliable for very large datasets and extensive annotations. We employ WordNet[4], a lexical reference system inspired by current psycholinguistic theories of human lexical memory and largely employed by many research communities.

10.2.1 Semantic knowledge database and conceptual similarity

In WordNet, English nouns, verbs, adjectives and adverbs are organized into synonym sets, each representing one underlying lexical concept. Different relations link the synonym sets. Each word has a different number of meanings depending on its morphological category (noun, verb, adjective or adverb). It is organized as a graph and offers the possibility to extract local semantic trees according to predefined semantic relations. The types of semantic relations defined in WordNet include synonymy, antonymy, hypernymy, hyponymy, holonymy, meronymy, "member of" relation, "cause to" relation, etc.

We are most interested here in hypernymy, i.e., the "X is a kind of Y" relation between words. Y is a hypernym of X if Y carries the meaning of X, that is X can be replaced by Y without a change in meaning, but the inverse is not necessarily true. For a given keyword, using hypernyms, we can build a directed graph of ascending semantic dependencies, higher levels nodes corresponding to more abstract concepts, while lower levels nodes corresponding to more specific concepts.

More detailed information on WordNet can be found in [157]. Available alternatives to WordNet as a general-purpose semantic knowledge database include Cyc [291] and ConceptNet [305], but they are not as mature as WordNet, nor as widely employed. While WordNet does not yet offer general lateral connections between any two concepts (e.g., "doctor" and "hospital"), we do obtain very good results that could certainly be improved by the use of a more complete knowledge database. Nevertheless, our method is in no way specific to WordNet and can be employed with the ontology that is most appropriate for the field of application.

Distance measures. Following Budanitsky and Hirst [81], we present a brief outline of several measures of similarity between concepts, which we employ in the definition of the keywords feature vector. The results obtained with descriptors based on these different measures are compared in Section 10.4.

[4] `http://wordnet.princeton.edu`

The evaluation of the semantic relatedness between concepts using networks such as WordNet is based on multiple aspects of the ontology, such as the length of the path, the directions of links, the relative depth or density. A number of hybrid approaches have been proposed, which combine knowledge-rich sources, such as a thesaurus, with knowledge-poor sources, such as corpus statistics (Resnik [436], Lin [302]).

Leacock and Chodorow [285] rely on the length of the shortest path, $\text{len}(c_1, c_2)$, between two synsets c_1 and c_2, to measure the semantic similarity. They use the IS-A relation and scale the path length by the overall depth D of the taxonomy: $\text{sim}_{LC}(c_1, c_2) = -\log[\text{len}(c_1, c_2)/2D]$.

Resnik [436] brings ontology and corpus together. The insight is that the similarity between two concepts can be judged by the extent they share information. They define the similarity of two concepts as the information content of their lowest super-ordinate (most specific common sub-summer), $\text{lso}(c_1, c_2)$: $\text{sim}_R(c_1, c_2) = -\log p(\text{lso}(c_1, c_2))$, where $p(c)$ is the probability of encountering an instance of a synset c in some specific corpus.

Lin [302] propose a measure inspired by the theory of similarity between arbitrary objects: $\text{dist}_L(c_1, c_2) = 2\log p(\text{lso}(c_1, c_2))/[\log p(c_1) + \log p(c_2)]$.

Wu and Palmer [570] propose a definition of the similarity related to how closely they are situated in the hierarchy: $\text{sim}(C_1, C_2) = 2N_3/(N_1+N_2+2N_3)$, where C_3 is the least common super-concept of C_1 and C_2, N_1 is the number of nodes in the path from C_1 to C_3, N_2 from C_2 to C_3 and N_3 from C_3 to the root node.

10.2.2 Hypernym graphs and semantic generalization

Directly computing the distance between the concepts corresponding to keywords is one possible approach and WordNet already provides several possibilities to determine semantic similarities. However, since we cannot store all distances for all pairs of images in the database, directly computing distances between keywords or sets of keywords requires using WordNet at query time. Accessing WordNet many times for every query would slow down the image retrieval process; while acceptable for small databases, this is computationally prohibitive for medium or large size databases. This effect tends to worsen when the number of keywords per image increase. Moreover, many algorithms used in information retrieval, such as relevance feedback, employ a vector representation of each document. Our approach is to convert the available text annotation for every image into a feature vector. We can use this vector for querying the database or for learning (as with relevance feedback). Moreover, as explained later, new images can be incrementally added to the database without having to recompute the features of all the others.

Let $B = \{I_1, I_2, \ldots, I_N\}$ be the image database. For each image $I_k \in B$, we consider the set of keywords associated to it, $\mathcal{K}(I_k)$. Our goal is to design a feature vector based on keywords: to each image I_k in the database we associate a vector in an n-dimensional vector space, $v_k \in \mathbb{R}^n$. The vector v_k

is computed from the keywords annotation of the image I_k, using a semantic generalization network extracted from WordNet.

The feature vector we propose is based on the hypernym graphs associated with every keyword that annotates some images in the database. A hypernym graph, as generated by WordNet, starts with a word and for each of its meanings, describe all paths in the ontology that lead to more general concepts. This is a directed graph in which the nodes are connected by arrows indicating a hypernymy relation between them. As an example, Fig. 10.1 shows the hypernym graph generated from WordNet starting from the word "statue".

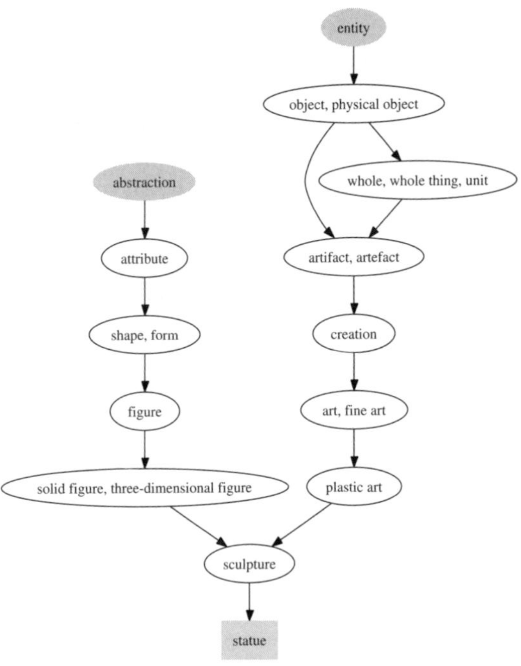

Fig. 10.1. Hypernym graph generated by WordNet for the word "statue".

Given a keyword, k, and the set of the most generic concepts linked to it as explained above, T_k, we denote by $\mathcal{C}_k$ the set of all chains connecting k and any element $e \in T_k$. The hypernym graph associated to the keyword k, denoted by G_k, is completely described by the set of chains $\mathcal{C}_k$.

Let $\mathcal{K} = \{k_1, k_2, \ldots, k_p\}$ be a set of given keywords and $\mathcal{G} = \{G_1, \ldots, G_p\}$ the corresponding set of hypernym graphs associated to them. We build the hypernym graph G for the set $\mathcal{K}$ as the union of individual graphs G_k:

$$G = \bigcup_{k=1}^{p} G_k$$

The set of chains $\mathcal{C}$ corresponding to the final graph G is the union of the set of chains, $\{\mathcal{C}_1, \ldots, \mathcal{C}_p\}$, corresponding to the individual graphs $\{G_1, \ldots, G_p\}$:

$$\mathcal{C} = \bigcup_{k=1}^{p} \mathcal{C}_k$$

Any graph $G_k \in \mathcal{G}$ is a subgraph of G, $G_k \subseteq G$, and correspondingly, any chain-set $\mathcal{C}_k$ is included in the final chain-set $\mathcal{C}$, $\mathcal{C}_k \subseteq \mathcal{C}$.

The graph corresponding to a set of keywords has several interesting properties, making it an appropriate hierarchical representation of the semantic content derived from keywords annotating an image database:

- It is a directed graph: given two nodes on the same chain, there is always one of them that can be identified as "more abstract" than the other.
- It can be viewed or organized as a pseudo-tree structure having at the lowest levels the concepts associated to the keywords used in annotation (considered as leaves) and at the highest level the most generic concepts found in the ontology.
- It can be traversed top to bottom starting from the most generic concepts, going down through intermediate level concepts and ending in the most specific concepts (corresponding to the keywords).

Associating to each image a vector where each component corresponds to a keyword may work in situations where the number of keywords is small, but it becomes quickly prohibitive for real databases, where the number of keywords is large. Having a feature vector of several thousands dimensions slows down by a large factor the speed of the queries, hinders the application of multidimensional indexing methods and also makes learning and relevance feedback very difficult. Also, since the distance between two vectors is computed component-wise, it can not reflect the fact that two different concepts (associated to two different components) may be semantically related. Our aim is to store the essential information about the keywords in an organized and easy to interpret manner, reducing the dimension of the feature vector at the same time.

We use the hypernym graph associated to all the keywords that annotate images in the database to find a set of higher level concepts, called *key concepts*, which are relevant to the annotation. Each such concept corresponds to a component of the feature vector. The selected concepts are usually different from the keywords used for annotating the the images. To build the feature vector of a image I_k, we project the set of keywords $\mathcal{K}(I_k)$ to the key concepts and obtain for each dimension a measure indicating the degree of relevance of the given set of keywords to the respective semantic concept.

When selecting the set of key concepts, a balance must be maintained with respect to the semantic coverage: nodes that are too close to the keywords do not contribute much to a reduction of the dimension of the feature vector, while nodes that correspond to too generic concepts diminish the discrimination power. The selection is a delicate task with a significant impact on the quality of the feature vector. Thus, at present we choose them by direct inspection of the hypernym graph. One of the future improvements of our method will be the definition of a robust method for the automatic selection of the key concepts. Several criteria can be used for this purpose, such as the weight (number of elements) of the subgraph of each internal node, the mean distance of a node to its children or the number of children keywords for each node.

The use of key concepts for defining the keyword-based feature vectors also makes this description relatively stable to the addition of new images to the database: the set of key concepts must be redefined (so the features of the existing images need to be recomputed) only when the existing set is no longer an appropriate representation for the annotations of the new images.

10.2.3 Computation of the conceptual feature vectors

Let $I_k \in B$ be an image, $\mathcal{K}(I_k)$ the set of keywords annotating the image and $C = (C_1, \ldots, C_p)$ the set of key concepts chosen as described above. We project the set $\mathcal{K}(I_k)$ on each concept C_i, obtaining a scalar value $\mathrm{sim}(\mathcal{K}(I_k), C_i)$ that is a measure of the semantic similarity between $\mathcal{K}(I_k)$ and C_i. This measure, more precisely described in the following, can also be seen as the degree of confidence that a user will find the concept C_i pertinent to describe the image I_k, given the set of keywords $\mathcal{K}(I_k)$.

In our experiments, we tested several methods for projecting keywords on the concepts selected for the feature vector:

- Projection only on parent key concepts: this emphasizes consistency with the hypernym graph and we put to zero all dimensions corresponding to concepts which are not parents for the keyword under focus.
- Projection on all key concepts: even if a keyword is not connected in the hypernym graph with a concept, using a semantic similarity function (previously described) may provide useful information since they are based on additional relations, such as synonymy, IS-A relation, etc.

As semantic similarities, we tested the four measures described in the previous section (Leacock and Chodorow, Lin, Resnik, Wu and Palmer). We also tested the binary measure given by:

$$\mathrm{sim}(k, C) = \begin{cases} 1, & \text{if } C \text{ is a parent of } k \\ 0, & \text{otherwise} \end{cases}$$

This measure simply turns ON the concept if an underlying keyword is present. This is motivated by the fact that sometimes the association of a concept to an image can not be modeled by a continuous variable, e.g., an image may be more or less "green", but a concept like "animal" cannot be

52% present in the image. There are also other quantification issues in the semantic description of images that make continuous variables inappropriate, see, e.g., Fig. 10.2.

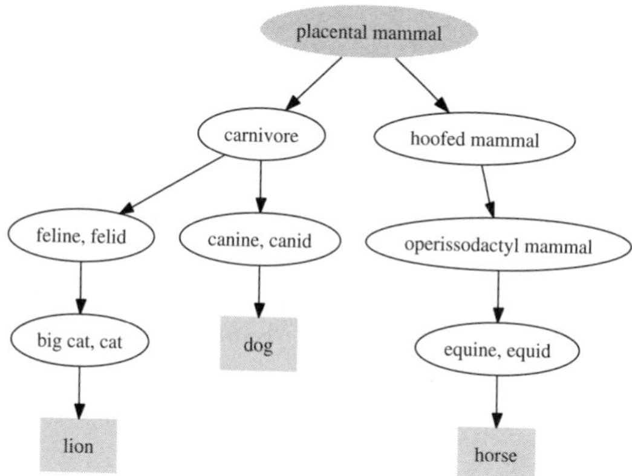

Fig. 10.2. A "dog" is not more or less a "mammal" than a "horse" just because the computed semantic similarity between the two keywords and their common parent is different.

When an image I is annotated with a set of keywords $\mathcal{K}(I)$, we define the following measure for the semantic similarity between the given image and a concept C:

$$\text{sim}(\mathcal{K}(I), C) = \max_{k \in \mathcal{K}(I)} \text{sim}(k, C) \tag{10.1}$$

Taking the maximum from the individual similarities guarantees that an image will be considered semantically close to a concept only if it is annotated with keywords semantically similar to the given concept. Conversely, suppose we take the sum of individual similarities instead of the maximum. In this case it is possible to end up with a high value for the overall similarity, even if all the individual similarities are small, which is undesirable.

10.3 SVM-based active relevance feedback

When searching generic image databases, the results are affected by the *semantic gap* which reflects the difference between the low level image signatures employed by the system and the high level descriptions expected by the users. One solution to this problem is to cut a search session into several consecutive retrieval rounds and let the user provide feedback regarding the results of every retrieval round, e.g., by qualifying images returned as either "relevant" or "irrelevant". The engine progressively learns the visual features of the "target class"; thus, relevance feedback (RF) can be used as a tool to interactively define complex visual categories that are often difficult to describe by other means (see [594] for a review).

An RF method is defined by two components, a learner and a selector. At every feedback round, the learner uses the images marked by the user to re-estimate the search target. Given an estimation of the target, the selector chooses which images the user is asked to provide feedback at the next round. The task of the learner is very difficult [89], [594] because the training set is small and heavily imbalanced and the evaluation must be performed in real time. Much recent work is based on support vector machines (SVMs, [469]) because they avoid too restrictive assumptions regarding the data (e.g., that classes should have elliptic shape), are very flexible (can be tuned by kernel engineering) and allow fast learning and evaluation.

Support Vector Machines. SVMs belong to the family of kernel methods [469], who first map the data from the original (input) space $\mathcal{I}$ to a higher-dimensional *feature space* $\mathcal{H}$ and then perform linear algorithms in $\mathcal{H}$. The nonlinear mapping $\phi : \mathcal{I} \rightarrow \mathcal{H}$ is implicitly defined by a kernel function $K : \mathcal{I} \times \mathcal{I} \rightarrow \mathbb{R}$ endowing $\mathcal{H}$ with a Hilbert space structure if the kernel is positive definite [57]. The inner product $\langle \cdot, \cdot \rangle : \mathcal{H} \times \mathcal{H} \rightarrow \mathbb{R}$ can be expressed as $\langle \phi(\mathbf{x}), \phi(\mathbf{y}) \rangle = K(\mathbf{x}, \mathbf{y})$. This "kernel trick" allows to reduce inner products in $\mathcal{H}$ to ordinary kernel computations in $\mathcal{I}$ and thus extend linear algorithms relying on inner products in $\mathcal{H}$ to nonlinear algorithms based on more ordinary computations in $\mathcal{I}$. For all the experiments presented in Section 10.4, $\mathcal{I} = \mathbb{R}^d$, but the method described here is not restricted to this case. The input space $\mathcal{I}$ does not even need to be a vector space, as long as a positive definite kernel can be defined [57]. The class of kernels for which SVM algorithms hold can actually be enlarged to the *conditionally* positive definite (CPD) kernels [468].

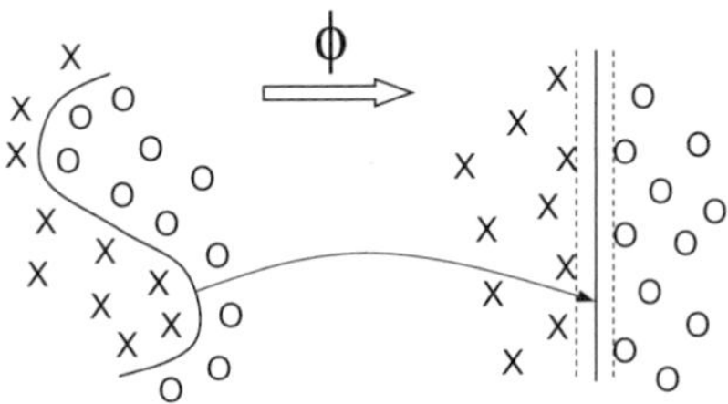

Fig. 10.3. Discrimination with 2-class SVM. ϕ maps input space (left) to feature space (right).

One-class SVM were put forward as a means to describe the domain of a data distribution having a potentially complex description in an input space $\mathcal{I}$. The data is first mapped to the feature space $\mathcal{H}$. Then, according to the first formulation [516], the smallest sphere in $\mathcal{H}$ that contains the images of the data items is taken as the feature space representation of the domain of the distribution. One-class SVM were used for relevance feedback, e.g., in [392] to model the distribution of the positive examples (images marked as "relevant") and return the unmarked items whose images in feature space are the nearest to the center of the sphere (potentially the most "relevant"); the information provided by the negative examples (items marked as "irrelevant") is ignored.

A *2-class* SVM aims to identify a frontier between two classes, based on a set of learning (labeled) examples. The 2-class SVM (Fig. 10.3) chooses as discrimination frontier the hyperplane in feature space that maximizes the *margin* to the examples from each of the 2 classes. This hyperplane is the feature space image of a usually nonlinear frontier in input space (depending on the kernel employed). The hyperplane is defined by an orthogonal vector and a position threshold. Since the orthogonal vector is in the subspace spanned by the n vectors $\phi(\mathbf{x_i})$ ($\mathbf{x_i}$ being the original data points), it is expressed as a linear combination of the "support vectors", i.e., of those vectors who are within the margin. Learning consists in identifying the support vectors and computing the linear coefficients, which is done by a fast procedure for constrained quadratic optimization.

When used for relevance feedback, a 2-class SVM learns at every feedback round to discriminate the target class from the rest of the database. The SVM learner is trained using all the available examples, both positive (items marked as "relevant" by the user) and negative (items marked as "irrelevant"). Then, the selector must choose yet unmarked items for which the user should provide feedback during the next round.

In much of the work on RF, the selector returns those images that were currently considered by the learner as (potentially) the most relevant; also, in some cases these images are randomly selected. An important step ahead was the introduction in [524] and [523] of an *active learning* framework for RF using SVMs. We present here an improved RF mechanism that tries to minimize the amount of interaction needed from the user. First, since insensitivity to the spatial scale of the data is a desirable feature for the SVMs employed as learners, we employ a specific kernel function that provides this insensitivity. Second, to optimize the transfer of information between the user and the system, we use an improved active learning selection criterion that minimizes redundancy between the candidate images shown to the user.

Scale invariance. During the study of several ground-truth databases we found that the size of the various classes often covers an important range of different scales in the space of low level descriptors. We expect yet more significant changes in scale to occur from one database to another, from one user-defined image class to another within a large database or between parts of the frontier of some classes. A too strong sensitivity of the learner to the scale of the data could then limit its applicability in an RF context.

The kernels usually employed in SVM-based RF depend on a scale parameter that makes difficult to adapt to the scale of the data. These kernels include the RBF kernel, $K(x_i, x_j) = \exp\big(-\gamma\|x_i - x_j\|^2\big)$, and the Laplace kernel,

$K(x_i, x_j) = \exp\left(-\gamma\|x_i - x_j\|\right)$. The angular kernel, $K(x_i, x_j) = -\|x_i - x_j\|$, is a *conditionally* positive definite kernel, but the convergence of SVMs remains guaranteed with this type of kernel [468]. Fleuret and Sahbi [164] show that the angular kernel makes the frontier found by SVMs invariant to the scale of the data. In real applications, the scales of the user-defined classes cannot be known a priori and the scale parameter of a kernel cannot be adjusted online. The scale-invariance obtained by the use of the angular kernel becomes then a highly desirable feature and experiments on several image databases prove this kernel to be a very good alternative. Note that for very small values of γ the Laplace kernel behaves much like the angular kernel.

Active learning. In order to maximize the ratio between the quality (or relevance) of the results and the amount of interaction between the user and the system, the selection of images for which the user is asked to provide feedback at the next round requires careful consideration. Tong and Köller [524] present several selection criteria for SVM-learners applied to content-based text retrieval with relevance feedback. The simplest criterion consists in selecting the texts whose representations (in the feature space induced by the kernel) are closest to the hyperplane currently defined by the SVM. We call this simple criterion the selection of the "most ambiguous" (MA) candidate(s). This selection criterion is justified by the fact that knowledge of the label of such a candidate halves the version-space. While the MA criterion provides a computationally effective solution to the selection of the most ambiguous images, when used for the selection of more than one candidate image it does not remove the redundancies between the candidates.

In our approach we require, for any two candidates images x_i and x_j, a low value for $K(x_i, x_j)$. If all the images of vectors in the input space have constant norm and if the kernel K is inducing a Hilbert structure on the feature space, then this condition corresponds to a requirement of quasi-orthogonality between the vectors representing the images in the feature space. We call this criterion the selection of the "most ambiguous and orthogonal" (MAO) candidates. The MAO criterion has a simple intuitive explanation for kernels $K(x_i, x_j)$ that decrease with an increase of the distance $d(x_i, x_j)$ (which is the case for most common kernels): it encourages the selection of unlabeled examples that are far from each other in input space, allowing to better explore the current frontier. To implement this criterion, we first perform an MA selection of a larger set of unlabeled examples. If S is the set of images not yet included in the current MAO selection and x_i, $i = 1 \ldots n$ are the already chosen candidates, then we choose as a new example the vector $x_j \in S$ that minimizes the highest of the values taken by $K(x_i, x_j)$: $x_j = \operatorname{argmin}_{x \in S} \max_i K(x, x_i)$. For more details and evaluation results of this RF scheme please refer to [160].

10.4 Evaluation of the hybrid representation

In this section we present an experimental evaluation of image retrieval using both visual features and the proposed conceptual image descriptor. We begin by introducing the experimental setup and the performance measures we use, after which we provide results for both query by visual example (QVBE) and for image retrieval using relevance feedback. These results show that the proposed conceptual descriptor can significantly improve the quality of the returned results when used jointly with the visual features.

10.4.1 Ground-truth database

To obtain a test database we started from an image database kindly provided by Alinari[5]. The test database has 3585 images for a total of 6664 annotations using 90 keywords. Each keyword can be viewed as defining a class of images. The image classes are coherent from a semantic perspective, but there is a high diversity in visual content for each class. Here are some examples of keywords and the corresponding number of files annotated with the respective keyword: "fresco" (274 files), "city" (206 files), "farming"(162 files), "statue" (121 files), "Gothic" (69 files). Class sizes vary between 26 and 274 images per class.

To allow a fair evaluation, we built by hand a ground truth (GT), independent from the keywords and which is not easily reduced to a combination of keywords (thus, no GT class is the union, the intersection or the difference of several initial classes). Examples of the GT classes of images include: "Madonna and child", "aerial view", "group of people", "horse statue", etc. We selected 20 classes in the GT, having between 15 and 174 images/class. The number of files included in the ground-truth is 1073 and the degree of overlapping between classes is about 10%. A certain degree of overlapping between GT classes corresponds better to real situations where an image may belong to different image classes, depending on the target of the user.

While the ground truth is smaller than the database, we perform all the tests on the entire database of 3585 images. This may bias the results, making them look worse (because of images that may belong to a GT class but were not included there), but it corresponds better to a real world situation, where the user is searching for classes of images without having prior knowledge of the image database. We build precision/recall diagrams for the query by example evaluation, and mean precision vs. iteration diagrams for retrieval with relevance feedback.

10.4.2 Content description

Visual features. To describe the visual appearance of the images we use image descriptors that take into account global characteristics such as color, texture

[5] `http://www.alinari.com`

and shape. While less precise than local descriptions, these have the advantage of being much faster to use, while offering good results with interactive retrieval based on relevance feedback.

Classical color histograms are first order statistics that do not keep spatial information: all pixels are considered equally important. However, pixels having the same color are not similar if we consider their neighborhood in the image [545], [75]. Follows the idea of weighting each color by a measure giving its importance in the local context:

$$h(\mathbf{c}) = \frac{1}{MN} \sum_{i=0}^{M-1} \sum_{j=0}^{N-1} w(i,j)\delta(f(i,j) - \mathbf{c})$$

where $h(\mathbf{c})$ is the histogram value for the color $\mathbf{c}$, M and N are the dimensions of the image (in pixels), $f(i,j)$ is the (image) color for the pixel (i,j), $w(i,j)$ is the weighting function and $\delta(\cdot)$ is the Dirac distribution. Here we use $w(i,j) = \Delta^2(i,j)$, where Δ is the Laplacian, to emphasize corners and edges in the image (*Laplacian weighted histogram*) and $w(i,j) \approx 1/p(i,j)$, where $p(i,j)$ is the probability of the current pixel in a local neighborhood, to measure the local color dominance (*probability weighted histogram*).

The texture feature vectors employed here are based on the Fourier transform, obtaining a distribution of the spectral power density along the frequency axes [75]; if the spectrum is important at high frequencies then the small scale details are relevant and there are many textured regions in the image.

To describe the shape content, a signature based on the Hough transform is employed: the gray-level image is first computed, then the direction of the gradient is found for every pixel and a reference point is considered; for every pixel, the angle of the gradient and the length of the projection of the reference point along the tangent line going through the pixel position are counted in a joint histogram that is the shape feature [159].

The visual features employed here are: the Laplacian weighted histogram, the probability weighted histogram, the Hough histogram, the Fourier histogram and a classical color histogram computed in HSV color space. The joint feature vector has more than 600 dimensions. The high number of dimensions of the joint feature vector may make relevance feedback impractical for large datasets. Also, the high dimensional feature spaces make learning more difficult (curse of dimensionality). In order to reduce the dimension of the feature vectors, we use linear principal component analysis (PCA) to obtain reduction in dimension of about 5 times, with an overall loss of quality of less than 3% for query by example.

Conceptual features. We built, as presented in Section 10.2, the hypernym graph associated with the whole database and we selected 28 representative key concepts. Examples of the chosen concepts include “vertebrate”,“religious person”, “location”, “geographical area”, etc. The keywords based feature vector has 28 dimensions, and no keyword was included as a key concept. We call the resulting feature vector WNS (WordNet Signature).

10.4.3 Evaluation for query by example

We first present the evaluation of the combined use of visual features and the keyword based WNS signature. We tested several types of WNS signatures, to have a better idea which one to use with relevance feedback:

- WNS-BINARY — this signature is the binary projection of the keywords annotating an image only on concepts linked through a chain in the hypernym graph, i.e the projection has value 1 if one of the keywords belongs to the children set of the concept, and has the value 0 otherwise. This corresponds to using the binary similarity function described in Section 10.2
- WNS-{LCH, LIN, RES, WUP} — these signatures correspond to projecting the keywords on the parent concepts, as above, but using as similarity functions Leacock and Chodorow, Lin, Resnik or Wu-Palmer.
- WNS-{LCH, LIN, RES, WUP}-ALL — the same as above, with the difference that the keywords are projected on all key concepts. For the binary similarity function this corresponds to a signature identical with WNS-BINARY, but the other similarity functions generate different signatures because they can provide fractional values for the similarity measure.

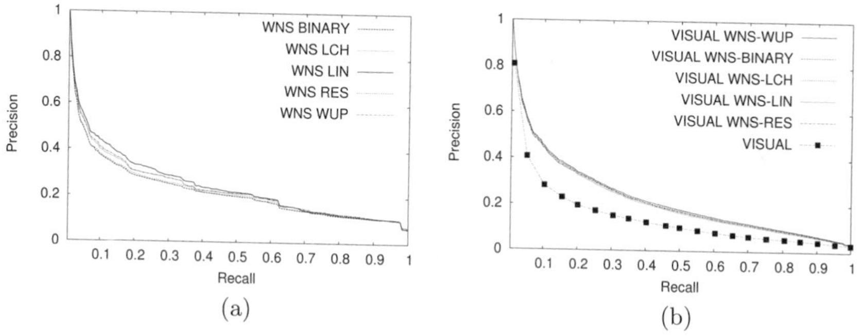

Fig. 10.4. Precision recall diagrams for the WNS signatures alone (a) and in combination with the visual features (b).

In Fig. 10.4(a) we show precision vs. recall diagrams for the WNS signatures. The binary measure is not as good as other measures for most of the recall values and the Lin measure is sometimes 3–7% better than the others on our ground truth. Fig. 10.4(b) presents the combined VISUAL–WNS signature vs. VISUAL alone. Combining the visual features with WNS signatures adjusts the differences between different similarity measures, but the overall result is most of the time 10–15% better than with visual features alone.

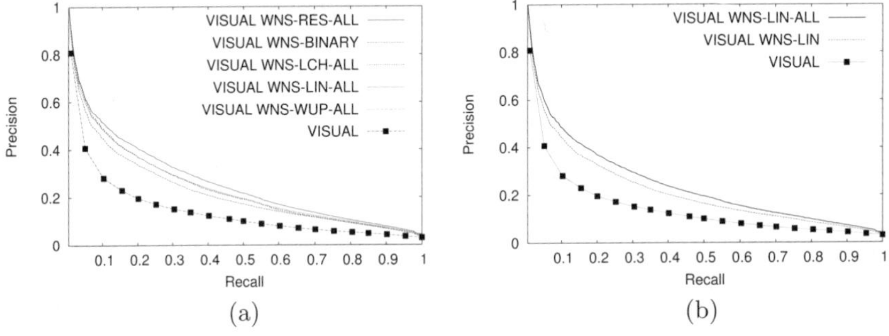

Fig. 10.5. Precision vs. recall diagrams for (a) the VISUAL and WNS-ALL signatures and (b) the VISUAL and WNS-LIN signatures.

Fig. 10.5(a) shows precision vs. recall diagrams for the combined visual–WNS-ALL signatures vs. visual alone. As we see, in this case also, the WNS signature brings large improvements in the results (on the order of 20%). In Fig. 10.5(b) we notice the difference between the WNS-ALL and WNS signatures for the Lin similarity measure. The WNS-LIN-ALL signature performs clearly better than WNS-LIN when combined with the visual features and much better than the visual alone. We obtained similar diagrams for the LCH, RES and WUP measures.

Projecting the keywords on all concepts allows the use of semantic relations in WordNet, other than hypernymy, through the similarity functions, fact which reflect positively in the results returned by the system. However, we could not obtain experimental evidence to favor any of the similarity measures presented in Section 10.2; for further tests, we employed the Lin similarity measure since in [81] it was shown to be the closest to the way human subjects judge conceptual similarity.

10.4.4 Evaluation with relevance feedback

We tested the new WNS signatures using relevance feedback on our ground-truth database. All the comparisons were performed using the MAO selection criterion, described in Section 10.3. For the SVM, we employed the angular kernel, $K(x_i, x_j) = -\|x_i - x_j\|$, because in our experiments it performed better than other kernels. Also, it produces a separating hyper-surface that is invariant to the scale of the data. This is particularly important for the classes of images in our ground-truth, which are based on a semantic definition and are very heterogeneous in their visual content.

At every feedback round the (emulated) user must label as “relevant” or “irrelevant” all the images in a window of size WS = 9. A search session is initiated by considering one “relevant” example and WS − 1 “irrelevant” examples. Our evaluation is exhaustive: every image in every class serves as the initial "relevant" example for a different RF session, while the associated initial WS-1 "irrelevant" examples are randomly selected. The MAO criterion is computed on a window of size $2 \times$ WS. Following common practice in the image retrieval literature, we pursue each relevance feedback session for 30 iterations and we measure the precision within a window of size equal to the size of the class to which the initial positive example belongs. We present in Fig. 10.6 and 10.8 the mean value of all precision vs. iteration for all feedback sessions. This provides a measure of how well relevance feedback performs, iteration by iteration, in its task of finding the target class.

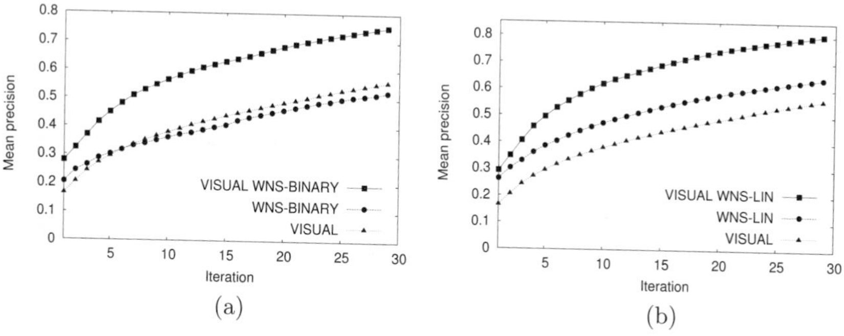

Fig. 10.6. Mean precision vs. iteration for (a) the WNS-BINARY signature and for (b) the WNS-LIN signature.

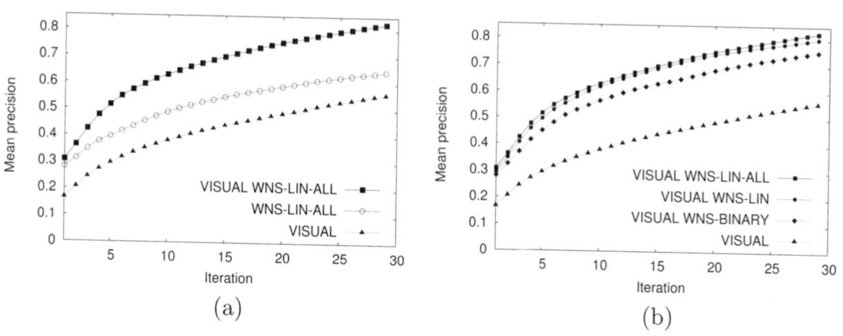

Fig. 10.7. Mean precision vs. iteration for (a) the WNS-LIN-ALL signature and for (b) the WNS-LIN(-ALL), WNS-BINARY and VISUAL features.

In Fig. 10.6(a) we can see that the visual feature vector and the WNS-BINARY signature have a similar behavior when used with relevance feedback on the proposed ground-truth. However, their joint use drastically improves the results starting from the very first iterations (sometimes with as much as

25%). A similar behavior can be seen in Fig. 10.6(b) and in Fig. 10.7(a) for the WNS-LIN and WNS-LIN-ALL signatures. Combining the visual feature vector with the keywords signature improve considerably the quality of the results in all tests we performed. This is due to the complementary nature of the information provided by the two feature vectors. Relevance feedback, as an interactive process guided at every iteration by the user, can make very good use of this complementarity.

In Fig. 10.7(b) we present results obtained using the visual feature vector in combination with WNS-BINARY, WNS-LIN and WNS-LIN-ALL vs. using visual alone. Using a similarity function instead of a binary projection improve the results, and that projection on all the coordinates instead of projecting just on parent coordinates may improve the results even further.

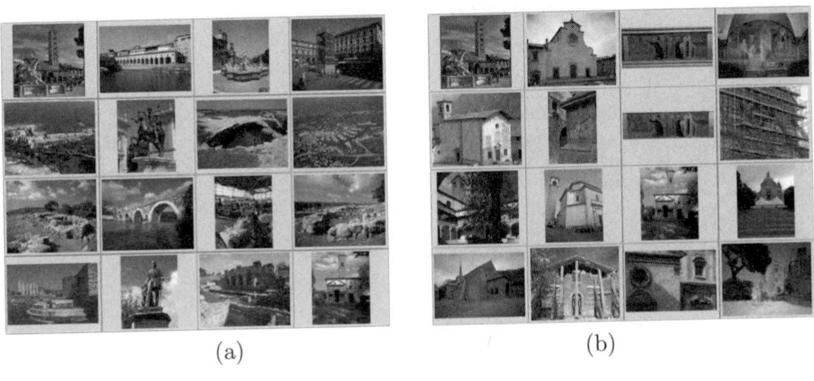

(a) (b)

Fig. 10.8. First page of QBE retrieval results with (a) the visual descriptor and (b) the conceptual descriptor.

Fig. 10.9. First page of QBE retrieval results with the combined visual and the conceptual descriptor.

As an illustration, in Fig. 10.8 and Fig. 10.9 we present some screens of results returned by our system in a QBE scenario: the query image is in the top-left corner and the user is searching for images featuring bell towers. In Fig. 10.8(a) we see the results when the system is using only the visual features; in this case the system is confused by too many images in the database having similar visual descriptors with the query image (the semantic gap). The results in Fig. 10.8(b) correspond to the use of the WNS-LIN-ALL signature alone: while the returned images are conceptually related to the query image, many of them do not represent well the query subject. Fig. 10.9 shows the results obtained when employing both the visual and concept-based descriptors. In this case, the system return many images that are not present in the previous situations and which clearly correspond better to the target class.

10.5 Conclusion

Although image retrieval using low-level visual features works well in many situations, the semantic gap limits its application to generic image databases. Alternatively, text annotations are more directly related to the high-level semantics of the images, but do not usually reflect visual similarities. Keywords and visual features thus provide complementary information and using both of them can be an advantage in retrieval applications.

We introduced here a new keyword-based feature vector that makes use of an external source of knowledge to induce a semantic generalization of the concepts corresponding to the keywords. The proposed *conceptual* feature vector can be used as a generic image feature and requires no modification in the architecture of the image search engine. Its dimension is much smaller than the number of keywords used to annotate the database and it is suitable for use with relevance feedback on large image databases. Evaluations performed on a ground truth build from a generalist database confirm that this feature vector can significantly improve the quality of the results both for query by example and with relevance feedback.

Our retrieval framework is primarily intended for datasets fully indexed with text annotations. To deal with partially annotated image databases, the solution we advocate consists in using off-line methods, such as those presented in the introduction, for extending existing annotations to the images that are not annotated. Such annotations can provide additional information coming from the use of, e.g., object detectors obtained by supervised learning on another, specific database; however, unlike user-provided annotations, these automatically generated annotations cannot bring in information that is complementary to the visual content.

Given the potential complexity of the hypernym graph, empirical selection of the key concepts is feasible for rather small databases; an automatic method is needed for large datasets. This is a difficult task: by choosing too general concepts the precision of the system will degrade, while by selecting too specific concepts the indexing set will remain large, preserving some distinction between words with rather similar meanings, with a negative impact on recall. An interesting criterion, minimum redundancy cut, was put forward in [477] and is based on information theory; the idea is to select the appropriate level of conceptual indexing by considering minimal cuts in the hypernym graph, i.e., cuts defining a well-balanced coverage of all the relevant nodes (corresponding to the keywords). While an interesting starting point, this entropy-based criterion is more appropriate for large texts than for annotations, so we pursue the investigation of alternative solutions.

11

Multimodal Analysis of Text and Audio Features for Music Information Retrieval

Robert Neumayer and Andreas Rauber

Vienna University of Technology, Austria

Multimedia content can be described in different ways as its essence is not limited to one view. For audio data those multiple views are, for instance, a song's audio features as well as its lyrics. Both of those modalities have their advantages: text may be easier to search in and could cover more of the "semantics" of a song while it does not say much about "sonic similarity". Psychoacoustic feature sets, on the other hand, provide the means to identify tracks that "sound" similar while they provide little information for semantic categorization of any kind. Discerning requirements for different types of feature sets are expressed by users' differing information needs. Particularly large collections invite users to explore them interactively in a loose way of browsing, whereas specific searches are much more feasible, if not only possible at all when supported by textual data.

This chapter describes how audio files can be treated in a multimodal way, pointing out the specific advantages of two kinds of representations. A visualization method based on audio features and lyrics data and the Self-Organizing Map is introduced. Moreover, quality metrics for such multimodal clusterings are introduced. Experiments on two audio collections show the applicability of our techniques.

11.1 Accessing and Presenting Audio Collections

Over the last decade, multimedia content has come a long way towards end users. Digital cameras, for instance, have become very common and are now used by vast numbers of people compared to just a few years ago. In addition, huge amounts of digital audio made their way into everyones life. The transition to digital media has been, and still is, progressing at high speed. The growing success of online music stores as well as the masses of users getting accustomed to digital media have been the driving force behind this development.

P. Maragos et al. (eds.), *Multimodal Processing and Interaction*,
DOI: 10.1007/978-0-387-76316-3_11,

Large amounts of audio content available in digital form pose new challenges for both private users and commercial music vendors. The main question for online shops is: "How do we present our collection to customers?" For the consumer side the main interest lies in "How do I find the music I want to listen to in an easy way?". Hierarchical meta data categories have proved to be a very efficient means of search and access – when the user knows exactly what he is looking for. Personal listening behaviors often can only be insufficiently described by predefined genre tags. Similarity search, however, essentially allows to retrieve songs similar to a given query, where similarity may be defined on several levels. Multimodal analysis of audio content may involve the following:

- Audio data (the song itself).
- Meta data.
- Web-Enriched meta data.

Whereas for the audio data itself often at least some meta data are available, additional data can be retrieved from the Web. In the course of this chapter, we will make use of audio data, provided meta data, and additional information in terms of song lyrics – partly manually assigned and partly fetched automatically from the Internet.

Personal similarity perception is not only defined by individual hearing sensation but also, to a large degree, by the users' cultural background. Particularly, song lyrics and other cultural information are feasible means for navigation within and access to audio collections. Users are often interested in songs that cover similar topics, such as "love songs", or "Christmas Carols", which are not acoustic genres per se, i.e., songs about these particular topics might cover a broad range of musical styles. In contrast with users interested in songs that "sound" similar to a given query song, similarity is herein defined differently. Even advances in audio feature extraction will not be able to overcome the fundamental limitations of this kind, i.e., overcoming the so called semantic gap between low-level features and high-level, semantically embedded, user expectations. Song lyrics therefore play an important role in music similarity. This textual information thus offers a wealth of additional information to be included in music retrieval tasks, which may be used to complement both acoustic as well as meta data information for pieces of music.

The remainder of this chapter is structured as follows. First, we introduce a range of techniques from the areas of machine learning, music information retrieval as well as user interfaces to digital libraries. Further, we introduce fundamentals as well as advanced techniques for the visualization of audio collections according to multiple dimensions. We then describe experiments performed on two test collections – one of small, one of large size – to underscore the applicability of the presented approach. Finally we conclude and give an outlook on future research in the area.

11.2 Related Work

This section summarizes related work done in the areas of Self-Organizing Map (SOM) mapping as well as in the areas of music information retrieval (MIR).

The area of MIR has been heavily researched, particularly focusing on audio feature extraction. First experiments based on and an overview of content-based MIR were reported in [168] as well as [534, 535], the focus being on automatic genre classification of music. Comprehensive overviews of MIR are given in [141, 377]. In this work the *Rhythm Patterns* features are considered, previously used within the SOMeJB system [427]. Based on that feature set, it is shown that Statistical Spectrum Descriptors (SSDs) yield relatively good results at a manageable dimensionality of 168 as compared to the original *Rhythm Patterns* that comprise 1440 feature values [301]. In the remainder of this chapter, SSDs are used as audio feature set and improvements in similarity ranking are based thereon. Another example for a set of feasible audio features is implemented in the Marsyas system [534].

In addition to features extracted from audio, several researchers have started to utilize textual information for music information retrieval (IR). A sophisticated semantic and structural analysis including language identification of songs based on lyrics is conducted in [316]. Artist similarity based on song lyrics is presented in [307]. It is pointed out that similarity retrieval using lyrics is inferior to acoustic similarity, but it is also suggested that a combination of lyrics and acoustic similarity could improve results. A powerful approach targeted at large scale recommendation engines is lyrics alignment for automatic retrieval as presented in [266]. Lyrics are fetched via the automatic alignment of the results obtained by Google queries. An evaluation of the combination of lyrics and audio information for musical genre categorization is performed in [364].

Artist similarity based on co-occurrences in Google results is studied in [465], creating prototypical artist/genre rankings, again, showing the importance of text data. Different aspects like year, genre, or tempo of a song are taken into account in [546]. Those results are then combined and a user evaluation of different weightings is presented showing that user control over the weightings can lead to easier and more satisfying playlist generation.

The importance of browsing and searching as well as the combination of both is outlined in [118]. The work presented in this chapter deals with improving those aspects, a combination approach can leverage both of them by satisfying users' information needs through offering advanced search capabilities and improving the recommendations quality.

11.2.1 Self-Organizing Maps

The Self-Organizing Map (SOM) is an unsupervised neural network that provides a mapping from a high-dimensional input space to usually two-dimensional output space [271]. The learning algorithm generally preserves topological relations. A SOM consists of a set of i units arranged in a two-dimensional grid, each attached to a weight vector $m_i \in \Re^n$. Elements from the high-dimensional input space, referred to as input vectors $x \in \Re^n$, are presented to the SOM. Then, the distance of each unit to the presented input vector is calculated (the Euclidean Distance is commonly used). The unit having the shortest distance, i.e., the best matching unit (BMU) c (for iteration t) is selected according:.

$$c(x,t) = arg\min_i\{d(x(t), m_i(t))\}. \tag{11.1}$$

In the next step, the weight vector of the BMU is moved towards the presented input signal by a certain fraction of the Euclidean distance as indicated by a time-decreasing learning rate α. Furthermore, the weight vectors of units neighboring the BMU, as described by a time-decreasing neighborhood function h_{ci}, are modified accordingly, yet to a smaller amount as compared to the BMU:

$$m_i(t+1) = m_i(t) + \alpha(t) \cdot h_{ci}(t)[x(t) - m_i(t)]. \tag{11.2}$$

Consequently, the next time the same input signal is presented, this unit's activation will be even higher. The result of this learning procedure is a topologically ordered mapping of the presented input signals in the two-dimensional space, that allows easy exploration of the given data set.

Several visualization techniques have been proposed for SOMs. These can be based on the resultant SOM grid and distances between units, on the data vectors itself, or on combinations thereof. In this chapter we make use of two kinds of visualizations, one of which are the Smoothed Data Histograms [388]. Even if it is not necessary for clustering tasks per se, class information can be used to give an overview of a clustering's correctness in terms of class-wise grouping of the data. A method to visualize class distributions on SOMs is presented in [330]. This color-coding of class assignments will later be used in the experiments to show the (dis)similarity of audio and lyrics clusterings.

SOM Based User Interfaces

Applications and user interfaces based on the SOM have been developed for a wide range of domains. Several teams have been working on user interfaces based on the SOM. This mapping technique has been extensively used to provide visualizations of and interfaces to a wide range of data, including control interfaces to industrial processing plants [272] or access interfaces for digital libraries of text documents. A SOM based interfaces for digital libraries of music was first proposed in [426], with more advanced visualizations as well as improved feature sets being presented in [388], evolving to the PlaySOM system presented in [363]. Since then, several other systems have been created based on these principles, such as the MusicMiner [343], which uses an emergent SOM. A very appealing three-dimensional user interface is presented in [265], automatically creating a three-dimensional musical landscape via a SOM for small private music collections. Navigation through the map is done via a video game pad and additional information like labeling is provided using web data and album covers.

11.2.2 Audio Features

For feature extraction from audio we rely on Statistical Spectrum Descriptors (SSDs, [301]). The approach for computing SSDs features is based on the first part of the *Rhythm Patterns* algorithm [427], namely the computation of a psycho-acoustically transformed spectrogram, i.e., a Bark-scale Sonogram. Compared to the *Rhythm Patterns* feature set, the dimensionality of the feature space is much lower (168 instead of 1440 dimensions), at a comparable performance in genre classification approaches [301]. Therefore, we employ SSD audio features, which we computed from audio tracks in standard pule code modulation (PCM) format.

SSDs are composed of statistical descriptors computed from several critical frequency bands of a psycho-acoustically transformed spectrogram. They describe fluctuations on the critical frequency bands in a more compact representation than the *Rhythm Patterns* features. In a pre-processing step the audio signal is converted to a mono signal and segmented into chunks of approximately 6 seconds. Usually, not every segment is used for audio feature extraction. For pieces of music with a typical duration of about 4 minutes, frequently the first and last one to four segments are skipped.

For each segment the audio spectrogram is computed using the Short Time Fast Fourier Transform (STFT). The window size is set to 23 ms (1024 samples) and a Hanning window is applied using 50 % overlap between the windows. The Bark scale, a perceptual scale which groups frequencies to critical bands according to perceptive pitch regions [598], is applied to the spectrogram, aggregating it to 24 frequency bands.

The Bark scale spectrogram is then transformed into the decibel scale. Further psycho-acoustic transformations are applied: Computation of the Phon scale incorporates equal loudness curves, which account for the different perception of loudness at different frequencies [598]. Subsequently, the values are transformed into the unit Sone. The Sone scale relates to the Phon scale in the way that a doubling on the Sone scale sounds to the human ear like a doubling of the loudness. This results in a Bark-scale Sonogram – a representation that reflects the specific loudness sensation of the human auditory system.

From this representation of perceived loudness a number of statistical descriptors is computed per critical band, in order to describe fluctuations within the critical bands extensively. Mean, median, variance, skewness, kurtosis, min- and max-value are computed for each of the 24 bands, and a SSD is extracted for each selected segment. The SSD feature vector for a piece of audio is then calculated as the median of the descriptors of its segments.

11.2.3 Text/Lyrics Features

In order to process the textual information of the lyrics, the documents were tokenized, no stemming was performed due to unique style features of different musical genres (e.g., word endings in colloquial terms often found in "Hip-Hop" lyrics). Stop word removal was done using the *ranks.nl*[1] stop word list. Additional stop words were removed based on their influence on the final clustering and labeling, leading to the removal of the terms: "i, he, her, she, his, and you", for they do not convey content information. Further, all lyrics were processed according to the bag-of-words model. Therein, a document is denoted by d, a term (token) by t, and the number of documents in a corpus by N. The *term frequency* $tf(t, d)$ denotes the number of times term t appears in document d. The number of documents in the collection that term t occurs in is denoted as *document frequency* $df(t)$. The process of assigning weights to terms according to their importance or significance for the classification is called "term-weighing". The basic assumptions are that terms which occur very often in a document are more important for classification, whereas terms that occur in a high fraction of all documents are less important. The weighing we rely on is the most common model of *term frequency times inverse document frequency* [456], computed as:

$$tf \times idf(t, d) = tf(d) \cdot ln(N/df(t)) \tag{11.3}$$

This results in vectors of weight values for each document d in the collection. Based on this representation of documents in vectorial form, a variety of machine learning algorithms like clustering can be applied. This representation also introduces a concept of distance, as lyrics that contain a similar vocabulary are likely to be semantically related.

11.3 SOM Clustering of Audio Collections

This section describes the test collections in use as well as the basic SOM techniques applied to both the audio and lyrics representations of the songs.

11.3.1 Test Collections

We compiled a parallel corpus of audio and song lyrics files for a music collection of 7554 titles organized into 52 genres, containing music as well as spoken documents (e.g., Shakespeare sonnets). Genres were assigned manually. Class sizes ranged from only a few songs for the "Classical" genre to about 1.900 songs for "Punk Rock", due to both the distribution across genres in the collection and difficulties in retrieving the lyrics for some genres like "Classical". The collection contains songs from 644 different artists and 931 albums.

[1] `http://www.ranks.nl/tools/stopwords.html`

Genre	Number of Songs
Christmas Carol	15
Country	17
Grunge	16
Hip-Hop	16
New Metal	16
Pop	15
Rock	16
Reggae	14
Slow Rock	15
Speech	09

Table 11.1. Composition of the test collection.

To retrieve lyrics for songs, three portals were accessed, using artist name and track title as queries. If the results from *lyrc.com.ar* were of reasonable size, these lyrics were assigned to the track. If *lyrc.com.ar* failed, *sing365lyrics.com* would be checked for validity by a simple heuristic, then *oldielyrics.com*.

For better demonstrations in initial experiments we decided to use a somewhat smaller collection that is more easily comprehensible. We selected ten genres only. Table 11.1 describes the composition of the test collection in detail. It comprises of ten genres and 149 songs in total – the number of songs per genre varies from 9 to 17. Spoken word is represented by Shakespeare sonnets mostly and therefore yields a low number of "Speech" pieces. This collection consists of songs from 20 artists and from the same number of albums. Also, for the small collection, all lyrics were manually preprocessed as to have additional markup like "[2x]", etc. removed and to include the unabridged lyrics for all songs.

11.3.2 Clustering According to Audio Features

For each song, lyrics features as well as audio features (SSD) were computed. The SOM clustering was finally performed on that data set. We then trained two SOMs of size 8×8, i.e., 64 units, one on the audio feature set, one on lyrics.

Fig. 11.1 displays the clustering of the small collection according to audio features. In this case, class distribution is of interest and we therefore make use of the Chessboard visualization to emphasize the regions covered by different classes. With this visualization different areas of the map are colored according to the dominant genre of songs mapped thereon.

Such a visualization makes it easy to comprehend the distribution of classes on the map. The "Reggae" genre (marked as circle 1) for example is located on the right lower part of the map, clustered on adjacent units only. "Christmas" songs (2), on the other hand, are spread across large parts of the map. Affected

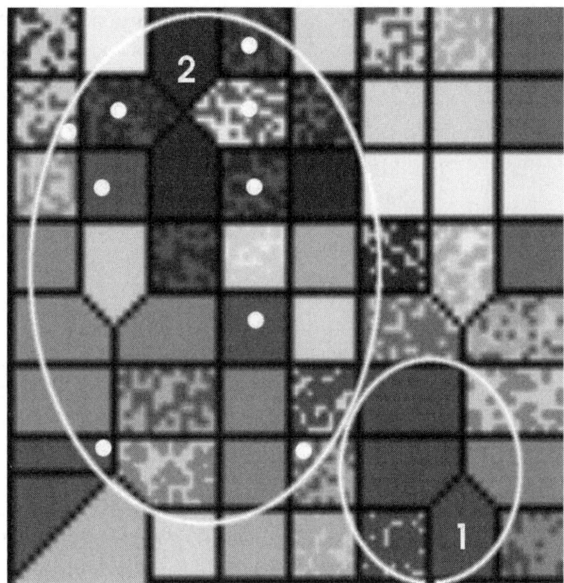

Fig. 11.1. Chessboard visualization of a clustering according to audio descriptors for the ten genres subset of the audio collection.

units within this area are marked by white dots. This corresponds to the very differently sounding nature of these two genres. “Reggae” is clearly defined by its very typical sound, whereas “Christmas” music is rather defined by its lyrics.

11.3.3 Clustering According to Lyrics Features

The same collection clustered according to song lyrics is shown in Fig. 11.2. The resultant high-dimensional feature vectors were further downscaled to 888 dimensions out of 5.942 using feature selection via document frequency thresholding, i.e., omitting of terms that occur in a very high or very low number of documents.

Among the most obvious differences are the better separation of “Hip-Hop” songs in the lower right part of the map (1). This genre is easily identified by terms like “shit”, “rap” or names of different rappers. “Christmas Carols” are clearly separated in the lower left corner of the map, exclusively covering four units (2). Tracks belonging to the genres “Grunge”, “Slow Rock”, or “New Metal” are spread across large parts of the map, reflecting the diversity of topics sung of within them (3).

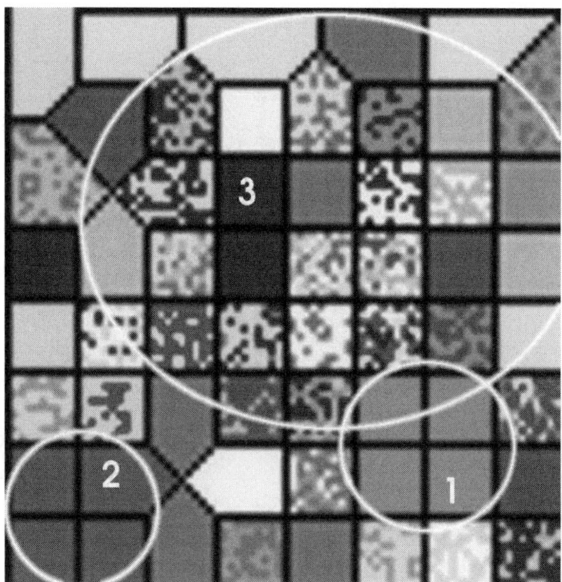

Fig. 11.2. Chessboard visualization of a lyrics clustering for the ten genres subset of the audio collection.

11.4 Visualization and Evaluation of Clusterings in Both Dimensions

This section introduces a visualization technique combining the two clusterings. The main technique used is to display both clusterings in one illustration along with links between identical songs in the two mappings.

Fig. 11.3 shows the main user interface of the prototype implementation. The right part of the application is occupied by the display of the two SOMs. The 3D display offers ways to rotate the view as well as pan and zoom in or out. Controls to select particular songs, artists or genres are located on the left side along with the palette describing the associations between colors and line counts. Selections of artists or genres automatically update the selection of songs on the left hand side.

11.4.1 Quantitative Evaluation

To quantitatively determine the quality of the resultant SOM clusterings we want to capture the scattering of instances across the maps using meta information such as artist names or genre labels as ground truth information. In general, the more units a set of songs is spread across, the more scattered and inhomogeneous this set of songs is. If the given ground truth values are accepted as reasonable, songs from ground truth sets should be clustered tightly

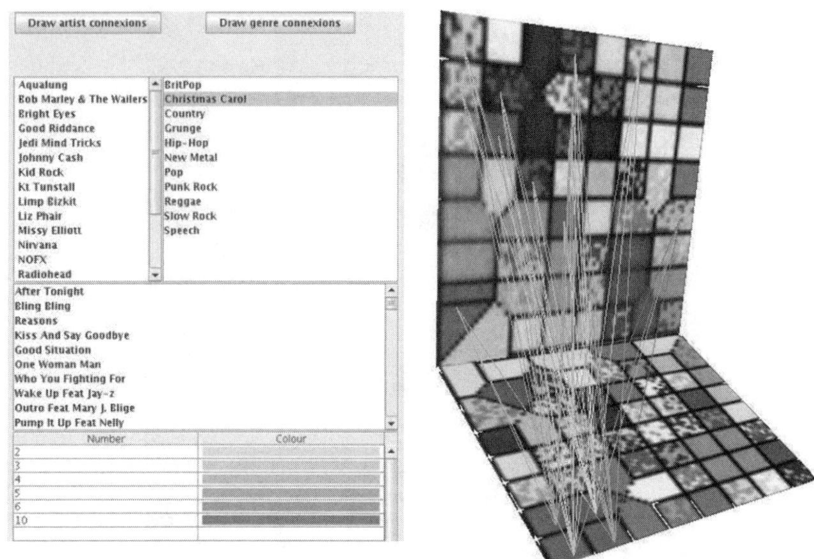

Fig. 11.3. Overview of the visualization prototype. The left part of the user interface is occupied by tools that select songs from the audio collection. The right part displays the multimodal clusterings and connections in between.

on the map. In this section, the focus lies on distances between units in terms of their position on the trained SOM. The abstraction from the high-dimensional vector descriptions of instances to the use of unit coordinates instead of unit vectors is feasible from a computational as well as a conceptual point of view. Comparison of individual vectors does not take into consideration the very nature of the SOM clustering algorithm, which is based on the preservation of topological relations across the map. This approach therefore computes the spread for genres or artists with respect to the SOMs clusterings. For distances between units the Euclidean distance is used on unit coordinates, which is also used for distances between data and unit vectors in the SOM training process. All quality measurements are computed for sets of data vectors and their two-dimensional positions on the trained SOMs. Particularly, sets of data vectors refer to all songs belonging to a certain genre or from a certain artist. Generally, a SOM consists of a number M of units ξ_i, the index i ranging from 1 to M. The distance $d(\xi_i, \xi_j)$ between two units ξ_i and ξ_j can be computed as the Euclidean distance between the units coordinates on the map, i.e., the output space of the SOM clustering. In this context, only units that have data points or songs that belong to a given category, i.e., a particular artist or genre, are considered. This holds for both maps; all quality measurements can only be calculated with respect to a class tag, i.e., for songs belonging to a particular artist or genre. The average distance between these units with respect to a SOM clustering is given as:

$$avgdist = \frac{\sum_{i=1}^{n} \sum_{j=1}^{n} d(\xi_{(i)}, \xi_{(j)})}{n^2} \tag{11.4}$$

where n denotes the number of data points or songs considered, i.e., the songs belonging to a given artist or genre. Further, the average distance ratio defines the scattering difference between a set of two clusterings $C = \{c_{audio}, c_{lyrics}\}$, c_{audio} being an audio and c_{lyrics} being a lyrics clustering, is given as the ratio of the minimum and maximum values for these clusterings.

Further, we define the ratio of the average distance across clusterings as the ratio of the respective minimum and maximum values of the average distance ratio:

$$adr_{audio,lyrics} = \frac{min(avgdist_{audio}, avgdist_{lyrics})}{max(avgdist_{audio}, avgdist_{lyrics})} \tag{11.5}$$

The closer to one the average distance ratio, the more uniformly distributed the data across the clusterings in terms of distances between units affected. However, this measure does not take into account the impact of units adjacent to each other, which definitely plays an important role. Adjacent units should rather be treated as one unit than several due to the similarity expressed by such results, i.e., many adjacent units lead to a small average distance.

Therefore, the contiguity value co for a clustering c gives an idea of how uniformly a clustering is done in terms of distances between neighboring or adjacent units. The specifics of adjacent units are taken into account, leading to different values for the minimum distances between units since distances between adjacent units are omitted in the distance calculations. If, for example, the songs of a given genre are spread across three units on the map ξ_1, ξ_2, ξ_3, where ξ_1 and ξ_2 are neighboring units, the distances between ξ_1 and ξ_2 are not taken into consideration. Currently, no difference is taken between units that are direct neighbors and units only connected via other units. The contiguity distance cd is given as:

$$cd(\xi_i, \xi_j) = \begin{cases} 0 & \text{if } \xi_i \text{ and } \xi_j \text{ are neighboring units} \\ d(\xi_i, \xi_j) & \text{otherwise} \end{cases} \tag{11.6}$$

The contiguity value co is consequently calculated similarly to the average distance ratio based on contiguity distances as:

$$co = \frac{\sum_{i=1}^{n} \sum_{j=1}^{n} cd(\xi_{(i)}, \xi_{(j)})}{n^2} \tag{11.7}$$

In the case of fully contiguous clusterings, i.e., all units that a set of songs is mapped to are neighboring units, the co value is not defined and set to one. The overall contiguity ratio for a set of clusterings is given as:

$$cr_{audio,lyrics} = \frac{min(cd_{audio}, cd_{lyrics})}{max(cd_{audio}, cd_{lyrics})} \tag{11.8}$$

This information can be used to further weigh the *adr* value from Eq. 11.5 and gives an average distance contiguity ratio value *adrcr*, i.e., the product of average distance ratio and contiguity ratio, for a set of one audio and lyrics map, as follows:

$$adrcr_{audio,lyrics} = adr_{audio,lyrics} \cdot cr_{audio,lyrics} \tag{11.9}$$

This considers both the distances between all occupied units as well as takes into account the high relevance of instances lying on adjacent units of the SOM.

Genre	AC	LC	CR	ADR	ADR × CR
Christmas Carol	.1240	1	.1240	.2982	.0370
Country	.1644	.2169	.7578	.8544	.6475
Grunge	.3162	.5442	.4714	.9791	.4616
Hip-Hop	.2425	.1961	.8086	.6896	.5576
New Metal	.1754	.1280	.7299	.9383	.6849
Pop	.1644	.1644	1	.9539	.9538
Punk Rock	.4472	.1280	.2863	.7653	.2191
Reggae	.2774	.1810	.6529	.5331	.3480
Slow Rock	.1715	.1240	.7232	.7441	.5382
Speech	.3333	.1754	.5262	.3532	.1859

Table 11.2. Genres and the corresponding spreading values across clusterings. **AC** denotes the audio contiguity, **LC** the lyrics contiguity, **CR** the contiguity ratio, **ADR** the average distance ratio, and **ADR** × **CR** the product of **ADR** and **CR**.

Table 11.2 lists these quality measures for all the genres in the small collection. Exceptionally high values for the ADR × CR were, for example, calculated for the "Pop" and "Hip-Hop" genres, meaning that these genres are rather equally distributed across clusterings. "Christmas Carol" songs have an exceptionally low value, stemming from the fact that they form a very uniform cluster on the lyrics map, the contiguity value is therefore set to one. On the audio map, "Christmas Carols" are spread well across the map. Other low values can be identified for "Punk Rock" or "Speech", both of which are more spread across the lyrics than the audio map.

Fig. 11.4 shows two examples of genre connections, the upper maps represent the audio clusterings, whereas the lower maps describe the data in the lyrics space. Fig. 11.4(a) shows the connections for all songs belonging to the "Christmas Carol" genre, clearly showing its dispersion as mentioned in the previous paragraph. Songs belonging to the "Punk Rock" genre are shown in Fig. 11.4(b). The strong dispersion of the distributions is clearly visible.

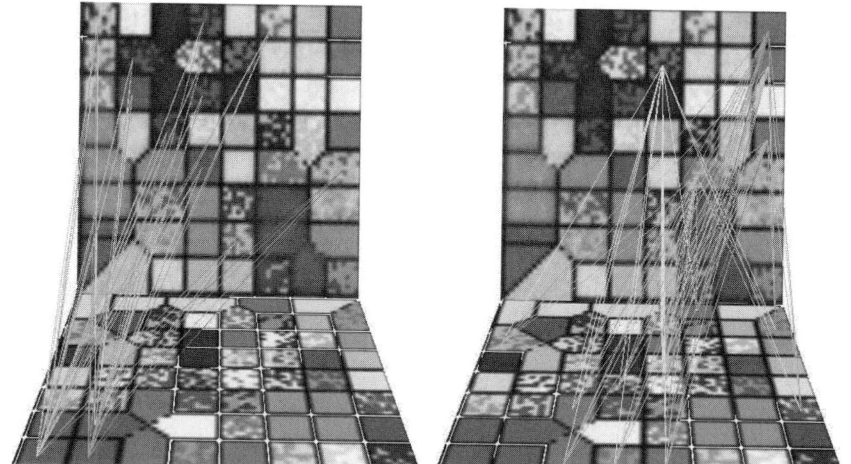

(a) Multimodal visualization of "Christmas Carols"

(b) Distribution of "Punk Rock" songs on both maps

Fig. 11.4. Distribution of selected genres across maps.

11.4.2 Application to a Large Audio Collection

To prove the applicability of the proposed methods, we performed experiments on a larger collection of digital audio, which is described in Section 11.3.1. In these experiments, we use the Smoothed Data Histograms technique to visualize the SOMs [388]. Both maps have size 20×20; dimensionality was 168 and 6579 for the audio and lyrics maps, respectively. For the lyrics experiments, the feature vectors were downscaled from 63884 original features using term selection via document frequency thresholding.

Notable Artists

Artist	AC	LC	CR	ADR	ADR × CR
Sean Paul	.3162	.1313	.4152	.4917	.2042
Good Riddance	.0403	.0485	.8299	.7448	.6181
Silverstein	.0775	.1040	.7454	.8619	.6424
Shakespeare	.2626	1.000	.2626	.3029	.0795
Kid Rock	.0894	.0862	.9640	.9761	.9410

Table 11.3. Artists belonging to the large collection having exceptionally high or low spreading values. **AC** denotes the audio contiguity, **LC** the lyrics Contiguity, **CR** the contiguity ratio, **ADR** the average distance ratio, and **ADR** × **CR** the product of **ADR** and **CR**.

Table 11.3 shows a selection of particularly interesting artists with respect to their positions on the maps. A total of 18 "Sean Paul" songs are mapped on each SOM. For the audio map, the songs are distributed among seven different units, eleven being mapped onto one unit. On the lyrics map, all songs are mapped onto two adjacent units, the first one covering 17 out of the 18 tracks.

The situation is different for "Good Riddance", a Californian "Punk Rock" band. For the lyrics map, their 27 songs are spread across 20 units. For audio, the songs lie on 18 units, but some of them are adjacent units, a fact that is represented by a rather high value for AC, the audio contiguity measure.

Shakespeare sonnets are clustered in a similar way. In terms of lyrics, the six sonnets lie on two units, whereas the audio representations are mapped on three units, none of which were adjacent (speech is read by different speakers).

"Kid Rock" songs, mainly "Country" tracks, lie on 13 units on the audio map, including two adjacent units, compared to 11 units in the lyrics space, none of which are adjacent. The spread is therefore almost identical on both maps. Fig. 11.5 shows the 3D visualization for all "Kid Rock" songs. This and the following illustration is also an example of how other techniques – in this case we use the Smoothed Data Histograms – can be used as background visualizations.

Notable Genres

Similarly to artists, we identified genres of interest in Table 11.4. "Rock" music

Genre	AC	LC	CR	ADR	ADR × CR
Speech	.0822	.0665	.8092	.3417	.2765
Christmas Carol	.0393	.0677	.5800	.7779	.4512
Reggae	.0392	.0413	.9495	.8475	.8047
Grunge	.0382	.0466	.8204	.9974	.8182
Rock	.0372	.0382	.9740	.9300	.9059

Table 11.4. Genres belonging to the large collection having exceptionally high or low spreading values. **AC** denotes the audio contiguity, **LC** the lyrics contiguity, **CR** the contiguity ratio, **ADR** the average distance ratio, and **ADR** × **CR** the product of **ADR** and **CR**.

has proved to be the most diverse genre in terms of audio features and rather diverse in terms of lyrics features alike. There were 690 songs assigned to that genre in the test collection. The overall ADR × CR measure is still rather high due to the impact of adjacent units on both maps. "Speech" as well as "Christmas Carol" are rather diverse in terms of audio similarity, but are more concentrated on the lyrics (or text) level, resulting in a low ADR × CR value. Fig. 11.6 shows the connections between all "Christmas Carols", giving an interesting idea about the differences of the distributions on the maps.

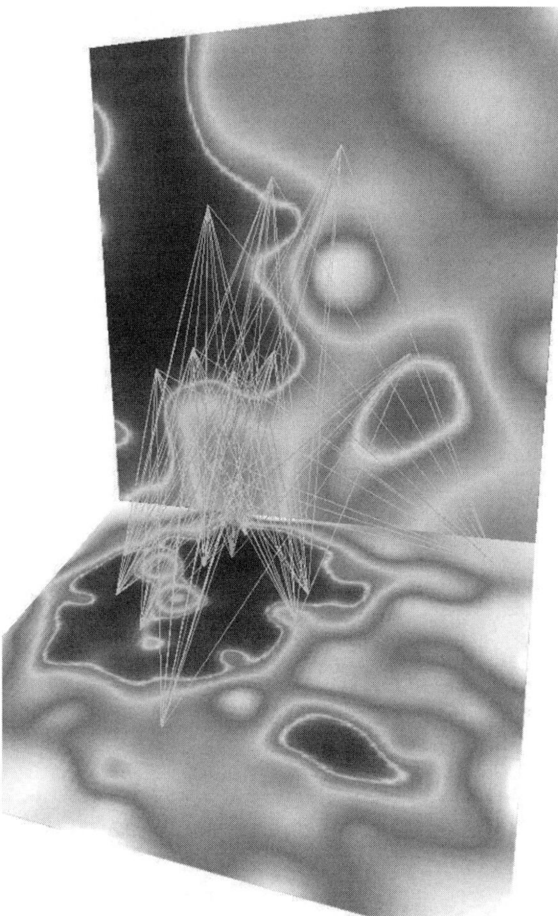

Fig. 11.5. Detailed view of connections for the almost equally distributed artist "Kid Rock". Dark lines denote a high number of connections.

The similarity of "Reggae" music is demonstrated by acoustic and lyrics features to an equal amount. This genre has rather high values for ADR and CR, caused by the many adjacent units and a low overall number of units.

A more detailed discussion about the experiments on the large collection can be found in [365].

11.5 Conclusions and Outlook

We investigated a multimodal vision of MIR, taking into account both a song's lyrics as well as its acoustic representation, as opposed to concentrating on

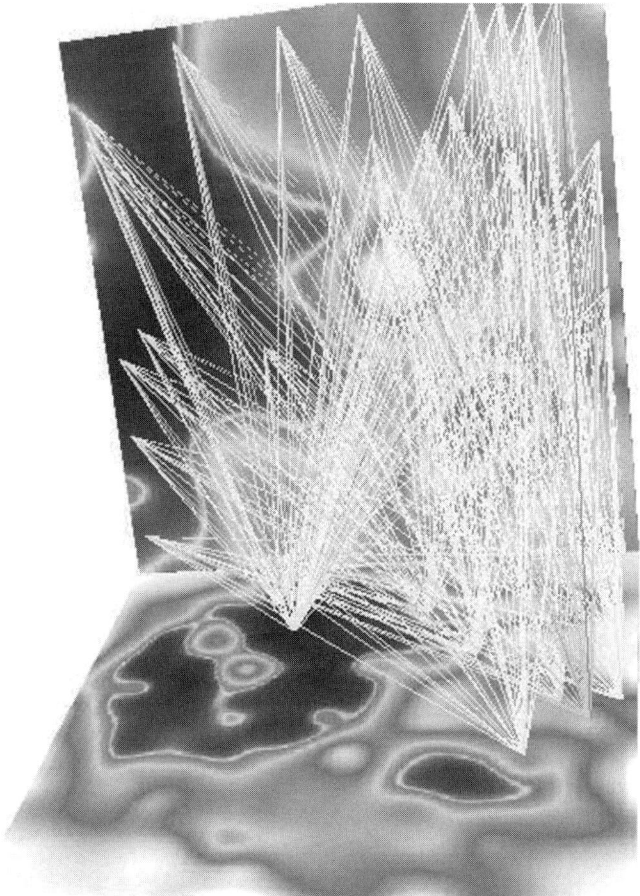

Fig. 11.6. Detailed view of connections for the genre "Christmas Carol". Dark links denote a high number of connections.

acoustic features only. We presented a novel approach to the visualization of multimodal clusterings and showed its feasibility to introspect collections of digital audio in the form of a prototype implementation for handling private music collections, emphasized by concrete examples. Evaluation was done for both a small test collection as well as a collection of larger size.

In addition, we introduced performance metrics for SOMs on a per-class level (e.g., artist or genre classes), showing differences in spreadings across maps. We introduced measurements for the comparison of multimodal clusterings and showed their application to identify genres/artists of particular interest.

Future work will mainly deal with the further exploitation of multi-faceted representations of digital audio. The impact of lyrics data on classification performance in musical genre categorization as well as possible improvements will be investigated. Further, we plan to provide a more elaborate user interface that offers sophisticated search capabilities.

12

Intelligent Search for Image Information on the Web through Text and Link Structure Analysis

Euripides G.M. Petrakis

Technical University of Crete

Searching for effective methods to retrieve information from the World Wide Web (WWW) has been in the center of many research efforts during the last few years. The relevant technology evolved rapidly thanks to advances in Web systems technology [32] and information retrieval research [418]. Image retrieval on the Web, in particular, is a very important problem in itself [254]. The relevant technology has also evolved significantly propelled by advances in image database research [495].

Several approaches to the problem of content-based image retrieval on the Web have been proposed and some have been implemented on research prototypes (e.g., ImageRover [517],WebSEEK [496]) and commercial systems. The last category of systems, includes general purpose image search engines (e.g., Google Image Search[1], Yahoo[2], Altavista[3]) as well as systems providing specific services to users such as detection of unauthorized use of images, Web and e-mail content filters, image authentication, licensing and advertising.

Image retrieval on the Web requires that content descriptions be extracted from Web pages and used to determine which Web pages contain images that satisfy the query selection criteria. The methods and systems referred to above differ in the type of content descriptions used and in the search methods applied. There are four main approaches to Web image search and retrieval.

Retrieval by text content: Typically images on the Web are described by text or attributes associated with images in `html` tags, e.g., filename, caption, alternate text. These are automatically extracted from the Web pages and are used in retrievals. Google, Yahoo, and AltaVista are example systems of this category. The importance of the various text fields in retrieving images by text content depends also on their relative location with regard to the location of the images within the Web pages [480].

[1] http://www.google.com/imghp
[2] http://images.search.yahoo.com
[3] http://www.altavista.com/image

P. Maragos et al. (eds.), *Multimodal Processing and Interaction*,
DOI: 10.1007/978-0-387-76316-3_12,

Retrieval by image annotations: The Web pages are indexed and retrieved by keywords or text descriptions, which are manually assigned to images by human experts. This approach does not scale-up easily for the entire range of image types and the huge volumes of images on the Web. Its effectiveness for general purpose retrievals on the Web is questionable due to the specificity and subjectivity of image interpretations. This approach is common to corporate systems specializing in providing visual content to diverse range of image consumers, e.g., authentication, licensing and advertising of logos, trademarks, artistic photographs.

Retrieval by image content: The emphasis is on extracting meaningful image content from Web pages and in using this content in the retrieval process. Image analysis techniques are applied to extract a variety of image features such as histograms, color, texture measurements, shape properties. This approach has been adopted mainly by research prototypes, e.g., [517, 496].

Hybrid retrieval systems These systems combine the above approaches such as systems using image analysis features in conjunction with text and attributes, e.g., [592, 551].

Effective image retrieval on the Web requires integration of text and image content information into the retrieval process. A method is successful if it retrieves the images that the user expects to see in the answers with as few errors as possible. This is a highly subjective processes, i.e., the same results may be judged differently by different users. Query uncertainty and user subjectivity may have a disastrous impact on the quality of the results. Query uncertainty depends on users' level of expertise or familiarity with the system and system functions. Most commonly, users perceive image content in terms of high or semantic level concepts while, in the system, image content is represented in terms of low level image features, e.g., color, texture features. Consequently, users cannot express their information needs in queries or, even worst, there may exist a degree of uncertainty in queries as to what the users are really looking for. Relevance feedback [589, 594] is the state-of-the-art approach for adjusting query results to the needs of the users.

Queries on the Web are issued through the user interface by specifying keywords or free text. The system returns Web pages with similar keywords or text. The highest complexity of queries is encountered in the case of queries by example, i.e., the user specifies an example image along with a set of keywords (or annotation) expressing his or her information needs. Queries by example image require that appropriate content representations be extracted from images in Web pages and matched with similar representations of the queries.

Focusing mainly on image and text content, the work referred to above does not show how to process queries by image example or how to select high quality web pages on the topic of the query. This is achieved by link analysis methods such as HITS [264] link analysis and PageRank [387]. Building upon the same idea, PicASHOW [290] retrieves high quality web images on the topic of the query. However, PicASHOW does not show how to handle image content and queries by image example. In general, existing methods and systems suffer from one or more of the following drawbacks:

- Work only on annotated image collections without explicit use of image content. Image descriptions or annotations are either manually inserted or automatically computed from image file names, image captions and surrounding text.
- Support only keyword queries as opposed to the most general case of queries by example.
- Do not capture the notion of quality of Web pages. Text or image content are the only cues for achieving high quality results.
- Do not always capture the notion of topic relevance with the users' query.
- They are capable of detecting text similarities between Web pages and queries containing lexicographically similar terms but not necessarily semantically (conceptual) similar terms.

In this chapter, we show that it is possible to exploit text and image content characteristics of images in Web pages for enhancing the performance of retrievals on the Web. Searching for important (authoritative) Web pages and images is a desirable feature of many Web search engines and is also taken into account. Also, searching by semantic similarity for discovering information related to user's requests (but not explicitly specified in the queries) is a distinguishing feature of many retrieval methods and systems. An obvious enhancement for improving the effectiveness of retrieval methods on the Web is relevance feedback. This work shows how the existing framework of image retrieval with relevance feedback on the Web can be enhanced by incorporating text and image content into the search and feedback process.

As a case study and for demonstrating the efficiency of content-based image retrieval methods, this work deals with the problem of retrieval of logo and trademark images on the Web. Logos and trademarks, in particular, are important characteristic signs of corporate Web sites or of products presented there. A recent analysis of Web content [228] reports that logos and trademarks comprise 32,6% of the total number of images on the Web. Therefore, retrieval of logo and trademarks is of significant commercial interest, e.g., Patent Offices provide services on unauthorized uses of logos and trademarks.

12.1 Web Content Representation

Typically, images are retrieved by addressing text associated with them (e.g., captions) in Web pages [551]. This is the state-of-the-art approach for achieving consistency of representation and high accuracy results. Image analysis approaches for extracting meaningful and reliable descriptions for all image types are not yet available. The adaptation of image descriptions to the different image types coexisting on the Web or to the search criteria or different interpretations of image content by different users is also very difficult.

12.1.1 Text Representation

Typically, images are described by the text surrounding them in the Web pages [551]. The following types of image descriptive text are derived based on the analysis of `html` formatting instructions:

Image filename: The `URL` entry (with leading directory names removed) in the `src` field of the `img` formatting instruction.

Alternate text: The text entry of the `alt` field in the `img` formatting instruction. This text is displayed on the browser (in place of the image), if the image fails to load. This attribute is optional, i.e., is not always present.

Page title: The title of the Web page in which the image is displayed. It is contained between the `TITLE` formatting instructions in the beginning of the document. It is optional.

Image caption: A sentence that describes the image. It usually follows or precedes the image when it is displayed on the browser. Because it does not correspond to any `html` formatting instruction it is derived either as the text within the same table cell as the image (i.e., between `td` formatting instructions) or within the same paragraph as the image (i.e., between `p` formatting instructions). If neither case applies, the caption is considered to be empty. In either case, the caption is limited to 30 words before or after the reference to the image file.

All descriptions are lexically analyzed and reduced into term (noun) vectors. First, all terms are reduced into their morphological roots, a stemming algorithm. Similarly, text queries are also transformed to term vectors and matched against image term vectors [418]. More specifically, the similarity between the query Q and the image I is computed as a weighted sum of similarities between their corresponding term vectors

$$\begin{aligned} &S_{text}(Q,T) = \\ &S_{file\_name}(Q,I) + S_{alternate\_text}(Q,I) \ + \\ &S_{page\_title}(Q,I) \ + S_{image\_caption}(Q,I). \end{aligned} \tag{12.1}$$

Each S term is computed as a weighted sum of $tf \cdot idf$ terms without normalizing by query term frequencies (it is not required for short queries). All measures above are normalized on [0,1].

12.1.2 Image Content Representation

Logo and trademark images are easier (than natural images) to describe by low level features computed from raw images. For logo and trademark images the following features are computed [502]:

Intensity histogram: Shows the distribution of intensities over the whole range of intensity values, e.g., [0..255].

Energy spectrum: Describes the image by its frequency content. It is computed as a histogram showing the distribution of average energy over 256 co-centric rings (with the largest ring fitting the largest inscribed circle of the DFT spectrum).

Moment invariants: Describes the image by its spatial arrangement of intensities. It is a vector of 7 moment coefficients.

The above representations are used to solve the following two problems:

Logo-Trademark detection: Because images on the Web are not properly categorized, filters based on machine learning by decision trees for distinguishing logo and trademark images from images of other categories (e.g., graphics, photographs, diagrams, landscapes) are designed and implemented. In our case, a five-dimensional vector is formed from each image: Each image is specified by the mean and variance of its Intensity and Energy spectrum plus a count of the number of distinct intensities per image. A set of 1000 image examples is formed consisting of 500 logo-trademark images and 500 images of other types. Images of other types can belong to more than one class: non-logo graphics, photographs, diagrams etc. Their feature vectors are fed into a decision-tree [567], which is trained to detect logo and trademark images. The estimated classification accuracy by the algorithm is 85%. For each image the decision computes an estimate of its likelihood of being logo or trademark or "Logo-Trademark Probability".

Logo-Trademark similarity: The similarity between two images Q, I (e.g., query and a Web image) is computed as

$$S_{image}(Q, I) = \\ S_{intensity\_spectrum}(Q, I) + S_{energy\_spectrum}(Q, I) + \\ S_{moment\_invariants}(Q, I). \tag{12.2}$$

The similarity between histograms is computed by their intersection whereas the similarity between their moment invariant is computed as *1 - Euclidean_vector_distance.*

All measures above are normalized to lie in the interval [0, 1]. To answer queries consisting of both text and example image, the similarity between a query Q and an image I is computed as

$$w = S_{image}(Q, I) + S_{text}(Q, I), \tag{12.3}$$

12.2 Image Information Retrieval on the Web

Image retrieval search engines for the Web supports queries by free text and keywords (the most frequent type of image queries in Web image retrieval systems) addressing text or images in Web pages. Methods for computing the text similarity between queries and Web page or image descriptions are reviewed below.

12.2.1 Vector Space Model (VSM)

Queries and texts are syntactically analyzed and reduced into term (noun) vectors. A term is usually defined as a stemmed non stop-word. Very infrequent or very frequent terms are eliminated. Each term in this vector is represented by its weight. Typically, the weight d_i of a term i in a document is computed as $d_i = tf_i \cdot idf_i$, where tf_i is the frequency of term i in the document and idf_i is the inverse frequency of i in the whole text collection. The formula is modified for queries to give more emphasis to query terms.

Traditionally, the similarity between two documents (e.g., a query Q and a document D) is computed according to the Vector Space Model (VSM) [418] as the cosine of the inner product between their vector representations

$$S(Q, D) = \frac{\sum_i q_i d_i}{\sqrt{\sum_i q_i^2} \sqrt{\sum_i d_i^2}}, \qquad (12.4)$$

where q_i and d_i are the weights in the two vector representations. Given a query, all documents (Web pages or images) are ranked according to their similarity with the query.

12.2.2 Semantic Similarity Retrieval Model (SSRM)

For queries by keywords or text, existing methods and systems (e.g., Google, Yahoo) are capable of locating Web pages that contain terms that the users specify in queries. However, the lack of common terms in Web pages and queries does not necessarily mean that they are not related. Two terms can be semantically similar (e.g., can have similar meaning) although they are lexicographically different.

SSRM [212] (Semantic Similarity Retrieval Model) works by discovering semantically similar terms using WordNet[4] to estimate the similarity between different terms. The similarity between an expanded and re-weighted query q and a text d is computed as

$$S(Q, D) = \frac{\sum_i \sum_j q_i d_j \mathrm{sim}(i, j)}{\sum_i \sum_j q_i d_j}, \qquad (12.5)$$

where i and j are terms in the query and the query Q and document D respectively and $sim(i, j)$ denotes the semantic similarity between terms i and j [296, 400]. Query terms are expanded with synonyms and semantically similar terms (i.e., hyponyms and hypernyms), while document terms d_j are computed as $tf \cdot idf$ terms (they are neither expanded nor re-weighted).

SSRM outperforms VSM, the classic information retrieval method and demonstrates promising performance improvements over other semantic information retrieval methods in Web image retrieval based on text image descriptions extracted automatically [212]. SSRM can work in conjunction with

[4] http://wordnet.princeton.edu

any taxonomic ontology and any associated document corpus. Current research is directed towards extending SSRM to work with compound terms (phrases), and more term relationships (in addition to the Is-A relationships).

12.3 Image Link Analysis Methods

Effective content-based image retrieval on the Web often requires that important (authoritative) images satisfying the query selection criteria are assigned higher ranking over other relevant images. This is achieved by exploiting the results of link analysis for re-ranking the results of retrieval. Classical link analysis methods such as HITS [264], and PageRank [387] estimate the quality of Web pages and the topic relevance between the Web pages and the query. These methods estimate the importance of Web pages as a whole. PicASHOW [290], estimates the importance of images contained within Web pages. However, PicASHOW does not show how to handle image content and queries by image example. This is solved by WPicASHOW [551] (Weighted PicASHOW) a weighted scheme for co-citation analysis that incorporates, within the link analysis method of PicASHOW, the text and image content of the queries and of the Web pages.

12.3.1 PicASHOW

Co-citation analysis is proposed as a tool for assigning importance to pages or for estimating the similarity between a query and a Web page. A link from page a to page b may be regarded as a reference from the author of a to b. The number and quality of references to a page provide an estimate of the quality of the page and also a suggestion of relevance of its contents with the contents of the pages pointing to it.

HITS [264] exploits co-citation information between pages to estimate the relevance between a query and a Web page, and ranking of this page among other relevant pages. The analysis results into pages on the topic of the query referred to as "authorities" and directory-like pages pointing to pages on the topic, referred to as "hubs". HITS computes authority and hub values by link analysis on the *query focused graph* $\mathcal{F}$, i.e., a set of pages formed by initial query results obtained by VSM expanded by backward and forward links. The page-to-page adjacency matrix W relates each page in $\mathcal{F}$ with the pages it points to. The rows and the columns in $\mathcal{W}$ are indices to pages in $\mathcal{F}$. Then, $w_{ij} = 1$ if page i points to page j; 0 otherwise. The authority and hub values of pages are computed as the principal eigenvectors of the page co-citation $W^T \cdot W$ and bibliographic matrices $W \cdot W^T$ respectively. The higher the authority value of an image the higher its likelihood of being relevant to the query.

Building upon HITS, PicASHOW [290] handles pages that link to images and to pages that contain images. PicASHOW demonstrates how to retrieve high quality Web images on the topic of a keyword-based query. It relies on the idea that images co-contained or co-cited by Web pages are likely to be related to the same topic. Fig. 12.1 illustrates examples of co-contained and co-cited images. PicAHOW computes authority and hub values by link analysis on the query focused graph $\mathcal{F}$ as in HITS. PicASHOW filters out from $\mathcal{F}$ non-informative images such as banners, logo, trademarks and "stop images" (bars, buttons, mail-boxes etc.) from the query focused graph utilizing simple heuristics such as small file size.

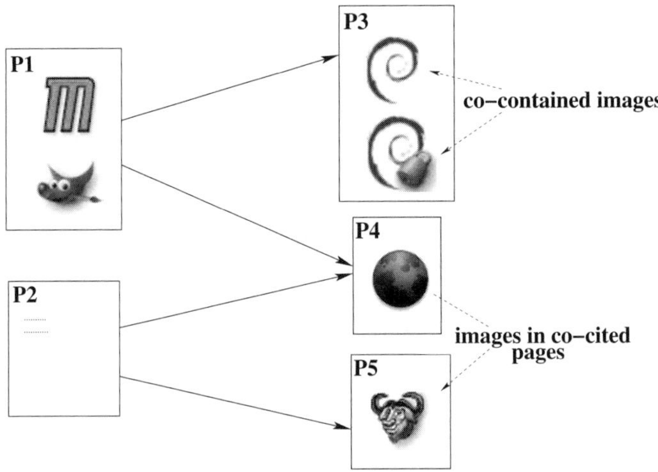

Fig. 12.1. The focused graph corresponding to query "Debian logo".

PicASHOW introduces the following adjacency matrices defined on the set of pages in the query focused graph:

$\mathcal{W}$: The page to page adjacency matrix (as in HITS) relating each page in $\mathcal{F}$ with the pages it points to. The rows and the columns in $\mathcal{W}$ are indices to pages in $\mathcal{F}$. Then, $w_{ij} = 1$ if page i points to page j; 0 otherwise.

$\mathcal{M}$: The page to image adjacency matrix relating each page in $\mathcal{F}$ with the images it contains. The rows and the columns in $\mathcal{M}$ are indices to pages and images in $\mathcal{F}$ respectively. Then, $m_{ij} = 1$ if page i points to (or contains) image j.

$(\mathcal{W} + \mathcal{I})\mathcal{M}$: The page to image adjacency matrix ($\mathcal{I}$ is the identity matrix) relating each page in $\mathcal{F}$ both, with the images it contains and with the images contained in pages it points to.

Fig. 12.2 illustrates these matrices for the pages $(P_1, P_2, \ldots P_5)$ and images of Fig. 12.1. Notice that in PicASHOW all non-zero values in $\mathcal{M}$, $\mathcal{W}$ and $(\mathcal{W} + \mathcal{I})\mathcal{M}$ matrices are 1 (non normalized weights). Fig. 12.3.1 illustrates authority and hub values computed by PicASHOW in response to query "Debian

	P_1	P_2	P_3	P_4	P_5
P_1	0	0	1	1	0
P_2	0	0	0	1	1
P_3	0	0	0	0	0
P_4	0	0	0	0	0
P_5	0	0	0	0	0

P_1	0	0	1	1	0	0
P_2	0	0	0	0	0	0
P_3	1	1	0	0	0	0
P_4	0	0	0	0	1	0
P_5	0	0	0	0	0	1

P_1	1	1	1	1	1	0
P_2	0	0	0	0	1	1
P_3	1	1	0	0	0	0
P_4	0	0	0	0	1	0
P_5	0	0	0	0	0	1

Fig. 12.2. Adjacency matrices $\mathcal{W}$, $\mathcal{M}$ and $(\mathcal{W}+\mathcal{I})\mathcal{M}$ for the focused graph of Fig. 12.1.

logo". Notice the high authority scores of pages showing logo or trademark images of "Debian Linux". Notice that the Mozilla trademark has higher authority value than the Debian trademark.

Image						
Authorities	0.492	0.492	0.339	0.339	0.519	0.117

Page	P_1	P_2	P_3	P_4	P_5
Hubs	0.519	0.0001	0.854	0.001	0

Fig. 12.3. Image authority (top) and hub values (bottom) computed by PicASHOW in response to query "Debian trademark".

Hub and Authority values of images are computed as the principal eigenvectors of the image co-citation $[(\mathcal{W}+\mathcal{I})\mathcal{M}]^T \cdot (\mathcal{W}+\mathcal{I})\mathcal{M}$ and bibliographic matrices $(\mathcal{W}+\mathcal{I})\mathcal{M}) \cdot [(\mathcal{W}+\mathcal{I})\mathcal{M}]^T$ respectively. The higher the authority value of an image the higher its likelihood of being relevant to the query.

PicASHOW can answer queries on a given topic but, similarly to HITS, it suffers from the following problems [61]:

Mutual reinforcement between hosts: Encountered when a single page on a host points to multiple pages on another host or the reverse (when multiple pages on a host point to a single page on another host).

Topic drift: Encountered when the query focused graph contains pages not relevant to the query (due to the expansion with forward and backward links). Then, the highest authority and hub pages tend not to be related to the topic of the query.

12.3.2 Weighted PicASHOW (WPicASHOW)

PicASHOW cannot handle image content or image text context. This problem is addressed by WPicASHOW [551] (or Weighted PicASHOW), a weighted scheme for co-citation analysis. WPicASHOW relies on the combination of text and visual content and on its resemblance with the query for regulating the influence of links between pages. Co-citation analysis then takes this information into account. WPicASHOW has been shown to achieve better quality answers and higher accuracy results (in terms of precision and recall) than PicASHOW using co-citation information alone [551].

WPicASHOW handles topic drift and mutual reinforcement as follows: Mutual reinforcement is handled by normalizing the weights of nodes pointing to k other nodes by $1/k$. Similarly, the weights of all l pages pointing to the same page are normalized by $1/l$. An additional improvement is to purge all intra-domain links except links from pages to their contained images. Topic drift is handled by regulating the influence of nodes by setting weights on links between pages. The links of the page-to-page relation $\mathcal{W}$ are assigned a relevance value computed by VSM and Eq. 12.6 as the similarity between the term vector of the query and the term vector of the anchor text on the link between the two pages. The weights of the page-to-image relation matrix $\mathcal{M}$ are computed by VSM and Eq. 12.7 (as the similarity between the query and the descriptive text of an image).

WPicASHOW starts by formulating the query focused graph as follows:

- An initial set R of images is retrieved. These are images contained or pointed-to by pages matching the query keywords according to Eq. 12.1.
- Stop images (banners, buttons, etc.) and images with logo-trademark probability less than 0.5 are ignored. At most T images are retained and this limits the size of the query focused graph ($T = 10000$ in *IntelliSearch*).
- The set R is expanded to include pages pointing to images in R.
- The set R is further expanded to include pages and images that point to pages or images already in R. To limit the influence of very popular sites, for each page in R, at most t (e.g., $t = 100$) new pages are included.
- The last two steps are repeated until R contains T pages and images.

WPicASHOW then builds $\mathcal{M}$, $\mathcal{W}$ and $(\mathcal{W} + \mathcal{I})\mathcal{M}$ matrices for information in R. Fig. 12.4 illustrates these matrices for the example set R of Fig. 12.1 with weights corresponding to query "Debian logo". Notice that in PicASHOW all non-zero values in $\mathcal{M}$ and $\mathcal{W}$ are 1 (non normalized weights).

Fig. 12.3.2 illustrates authority and hub values computed by WPicASHOW in response to query "Debian logo". Notice the trademark images of "Debian Linux" are assigned the highest authority values followed by the images of "Mozilla Firefox".

12.4 Relevance Feedback

Relevance feedback [589, 594, 399] is the state-of-the-art approach for adjusting query results to the needs of the users. A common assumption is that

	P_1	P_2	P_3	P_4	P_5
P_1	0	0	.6	.1	0
P_2	0	0	0	.1	.1
P_3	0	0	0	0	0
P_4	0	0	0	0	0
P_5	0	0	0	0	0

P_1	0	0	.1	.1	0	0
P_2	0	0	0	0	0	0
P_3	.8	.7	0	0	0	0
P_4	0	0	0	0	.2	0
P_5	0	0	0	0	0	.15

P_1	.48	.42	.1	.1	.02	0
P_2	0	0	0	0	.02	.015
P_3	.8	.7	0	0	0	0
P_4	0	0	0	0	.2	0
P_5	0	0	0	0	0	.15

Fig. 12.4. Adjacency matrices $\mathcal{M}$, $\mathcal{W}$ and $(\mathcal{M}+\mathcal{I})\mathcal{W}$ for the focused graph of Fig. 12.1 corresponding to query "Debian logo".

Image						
Authorities	0.751	0.657	0.0418	0.0418	0.008	0

Page	P_1	P_2	P_3	P_4	P_5
Hubs	0.519	0.0001	0.854	0.001	0

Fig. 12.5. Image authority (top) and hub values (bottom) computed by WPicASHOW in response to query "Debian logo".

there exists an ideal query (or matching method) that captures the information needs of the users. Relevance feedback attempts to guess the ideal query (or matching method) from answers that are initially obtained from the database. The users mark relevant (positive) or irrelevant (negative) examples among the retrieved answers, these examples are processed to form a new query, which is combined with the original query and is resubmitted to the system. The process is repeated until convergence, i.e., the answers do not change. A categorization of methods includes:

Query point movement methods assuming that the ideal query is a point in a multi-dimensional space that the method approximates iteratively [440].

Term re-weighting methods that adjust the relative importance (weights) of terms in image representations [452, 224]. Terms that vary less in the set of positive examples are more important and should weigh more in retrievals. The inverse of the standard deviation is usually used for re-weighting the query terms.

Query expansion methods that attempt to guess an ideal query by adding new terms into the user's query [480, 96, 311].

Similarity adaptation methods that approximate the ideal matching method by substituting the system similarity (or distance) function with one that better captures the user's notion of similarity [569].

There are also approaches combining the above ideas. MindReader [224] combines query point movement and term re-weighting and handles correlations between attributes. Weight estimation is formulated as a minimization problem. MARS [451] is a prototype image retrieval system implementing a variation of the standard term re-weighting method. iFind [311] supports keyword-based image search along with queries by image example. The main idea behind this approach is that images, which are similar to the same query represent similar semantics. Images are linked to semantics by applying data mining on user's feedback log [96].

In the following, the existing framework of image retrieval with relevance feedback on the Web is extended to handle more sophisticated queries (e.g., queries by image example), by incorporating text and image content into the image retrieval and relevance feedback processes [399]. To do so, the concepts of text and image similarity of Sec. 12.1 are generalized as follows: The text similarity between a query Q and an image I is computed as

$$S^{text}(Q,I) = \sum_{i \,\in\, representation} w_i^{text} S_i^{text}(Q,I), \tag{12.6}$$

where w_i^{text} are weights (inner weights) denoting the relative significance of the above lists. Each S_i component is computed as list similarity: The more common terms (in the same order) two term lists have in common, the more similar they are. Similarly, the image similarity between a query image Q and an image I is computed as

$$S^{image}(Q,I) = \sum_{i \,\in\, representation} w_i^{image} S_i^{image}(Q,I), \tag{12.7}$$

where w_i^{image} are weights (inner weights) denoting the relative significance of the above types of image content representations. The computation of each S_i component depends on feature type: The similarity between histograms is computed by their intersection whereas the similarity between moment invariants is computed by subtracting the Euclidean vector distance from its maximum value.

To answer queries combining text and image example, the similarity between a query Q and a Web image I is computed as

$$S(Q,I) = W^{image} S^{image}(Q,I) + W^{text} S^{text}(Q,I), \tag{12.8}$$

where W^{text} and W^{image} are weights (outer weights) denoting the relative significance of image and text descriptions. All measures above are normalized to lie in the interval [0,1].

The inner and outer weights of Eq. 12.1, Eq. 12.2 and Eq. 12.8 place different emphasis on different features or representations respectively and can be used to adapt the query results to user's preferences. Typically, the weights are user defined. However, weight definition is beyond the understanding of most users. Relevance feedback is employed to estimate good weight values. Query expansion, term re-weighting and similarity adaptation methods are considered as representatives of most important categories of methods. Query point movement methods assume vector representations and cannot be applied. In the following, the basic steps of each method are discussed. The same steps are applied iteratively until convergence (i.e., the results of the retrieval method do not change). Initial results are obtained by applying either Eq. 12.1 for text queries or Eq. 12.8 for queries combining text with image example. All weights are initialized to 1.

12.4.1 Query Expansion

The query is expanded with new terms obtained from positive examples. Two methods are evaluated. These methods work only with text.

Accumulation [480]: The most relevant image is selected from the answers and its text representation (i.e., a list of descriptive terms) is extracted. The query is matched with each term in this representation. A new query is formed by merging the query representation with the most similar terms of the most relevant image.

Integration and Differentiation [480]: Relevant and irrelevant images are selected from the answers. From each relevant image, its text representation (i.e., list of descriptive terms) is extracted and matched with the query. The most similar terms are combined to form a new "positive query". Similarly, the most dissimilar (to the query) terms are extracted from all irrelevant answers and combined to form a "negative query". The positive query is applied. Images which are more similar to the negative query rather than to the positive query are removed from the the answer.

12.4.2 Term Re-Weighting

Term re-weighting adjusts the relative importance of query terms [452]. The method is extended to accommodate for the definition of image similarity by text and image content as follows [399].

Let R be the set of the N_R most similar images, e.g., $N_R = 30$. A relevance score taking values -3 (for highly non-relevant answers) through 3 (for highly relevant answers) is assigned to each answer in R (neutral or no-opinion answers take score 0). R also denotes the query results at the beginning of each feedback cycle.

The outer weights W^j ($j \in \{text, image\}$) are dynamically updated during each feedback cycle: The database is queried by each S^j separately (using either Eq. 12.1 or Eq. 12.2) and its answer set R^j is sorted by similarity. The weights are then updated according to the following formula

$$W^j = \begin{cases} W^j + score_I & \text{if } I \in R, \\ W^j + 0 & \text{otherwise;} \end{cases} \tag{12.9}$$

where $score_I$ is the score assigned to image I in R. Initially all $W^j = 0$. After iterating over the images in each R^j all weights W_i^j are normalized by $W_{total}^j = \sum_{I \in R^j} W^j$. Negative weights are set to 0.

The inner weights $w_i^j (j \in \{text, visual\})$ for each term i of the text or image representation are also dynamically updated using the set R' of relevant answers in R ($R' \subset R$): The smaller the variance of each S_i^j the larger the significance of the i-th term (and the reverse). Therefore, $w_i^j = 1/\sigma_i^j$, where σ_i^j is the variance of the i-th feature in the j-th representation. Each weight is normalized by $w_{total}^j = \sum_{I \in R'} w_i^j$.

12.4.3 Similarity Adaptation

Falcon [569] estimates an ideal distance function $\mathcal{D}_\mathcal{G}$ that retrieves the best results. Initially, Falcon searches the database using $d(Q, I) = 1 - S(Q, I)$ as distance function and the user adds positive examples to a set $\mathcal{G}$ (initially empty). During a feedback cycle, Falcon searches the database again using a new distance function $\mathcal{D}_\mathcal{G}$ while the user adds new positive examples to $\mathcal{G}$. The distance between the query Q and a Web image I is computed as the distance of I from the current members of $\mathcal{G}$. Falcon estimates $\mathcal{D}_\mathcal{G}$ iteratively as follows

$$\mathcal{D}_\mathcal{G}(I) = \begin{cases} 0 & \text{if } \exists i : d(g_i, I) = 0, \\ \left(\frac{1}{k}\sum_{i=1}^{k} d(g_i, I)^\alpha\right)^{1/\alpha} & \text{otherwise;} \end{cases} \tag{12.10}$$

where k is the number of positive examples in $\mathcal{G}$, g_i is a member of $\mathcal{G}$ and α is a user defined constant, e.g., $\alpha = -5$.

12.5 IntelliSearch

All previously stated methods have been implemented and integrated into *IntelliSearch* [550], a complete and fully automated system for retrieving text pages and images on the Web. It provides an ideal test-bed for experimentation and training and serves as a framework for a realistic evaluation of retrieval methods for the Web. The system stores a crawl of the Web with 1,5 million Web pages with images. The system is implemented in Java and is accessible on the Web[5]. The architecture of *IntelliSearch* is illustrated in Fig. 12.6. It consists of several modules, the most important of them being the following:

Crawler module: Implemented based upon Larbin[6], the crawler assembled locally a collection of 1,5 million pages with images. The crawler started its recursive visit of the Web from a set of 14000 pages, which is assembled from the answers of Google image search to 20 queries on topics related to Linux and Linux products. The crawler worked recursively in breadth-first order and visited pages up to depth 5 links from each origin.

[5] http://www.intelligence.tuc.gr/intellisearch
[6] http://larbin.sourceforge.net

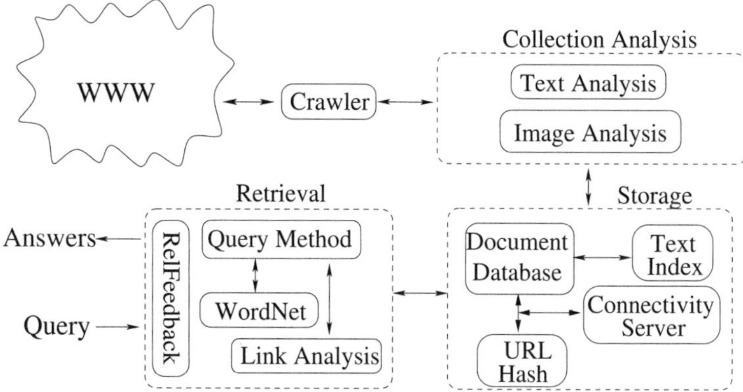

Fig. 12.6. *IntelliSearch* Architecture.

Collection analysis module: The content of crawled pages is analyzed. Text, images, link information (forward links) and information for pages that belong to the same site is extracted.

Storage module: Implements storage structures and indices providing fast access to Web pages and information extracted from Web pages, i.e., text, image descriptions and links. For each page, except from raw text and images, the following information is stored and indexed: Page URLs, image descriptive text (i.e., alternate text, caption, title, image file name), terms extracted from pages, term inter document frequencies (i.e., term frequencies in the whole collection), term intra document frequencies (i.e., term frequencies in image descriptive text parts), link structure information (i.e., backward and forward links). Image descriptions are also stored.

Retrieval module: Queries are issued by keywords or free text. The user is prompted at the user interface to select mode of operation (retrieval of text pages or image retrieval).

The Entity Relationship Diagram (ERD) of the database in Fig. 12.7 describes entities (i.e., Web pages) and relationships between entities. There are many-to-many (denoted as $N : M$) relationships between Web pages implied by the Web link structure (by forward and backward links), one-to-many (denoted as $1 : N$) relationships between Web pages and their constituent text and images and $N : M$ relationships between terms in image descriptive text parts and documents and. The ERD also illustrates properties of entities and relationships, i.e., page URLs for documents, titles for page text, image content descriptions for images, stemmed terms, inter and intra document frequencies for terms in image descriptive text parts.

The database schema is implemented in BerkeleyDB[7] Java Edition. BerkeleyDB is an embedded database engine providing a simple Application Pro-

[7] http://www.sleepycat.com

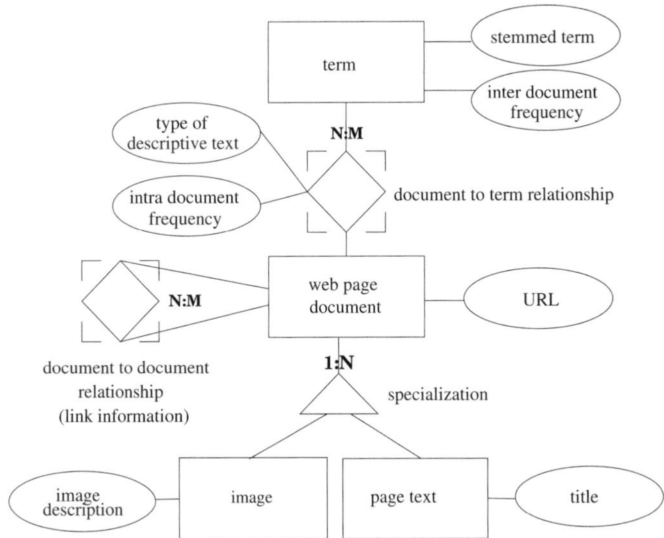

Fig. 12.7. The Entity Relational Diagram (ERd) of the database.

gramming Interface (API) supporting efficient storage and retrieval of Java objects. The mapping of the ERD of Fig. 12.7 to database files (Java objects) was implemented using the Java Collections-style interface. Apache Lucene[8] is providing mechanisms (i.e., inverted files) for indexing text and link information. There are Hash tables for URLs and inverted files for terms and link information. Two inverted files implement the connectivity server [61] and provide fast access to linkage information between pages (backward and forward links) and two inverted files associate terms with their intra and inter document frequencies and allow for fast computation of term vectors.

12.6 Conclusions

This chapter presents comparative study of several retrieval methods for the Web with emphasis on methods for retrieving images by content. Several aspects of the problem of content-based image retrieval on the Web are examined including retrieval by text, text semantics, image content features and retrieval by authority (importance) characteristics. Relevance feedback is also discussed in this context is a tool for adjusting the retrieved results to the actual needs of the users.

the query.

[8] http://lucene.apache.org

The experimental results [551] demonstrate that Web search methods utilizing content information (or combination of content and link information) perform significantly better than methods using link information alone. Link analysis improved the quality of the results but not necessarily their accuracy (at least for data sets smaller than the Web). The analysis revealed that content relevance and searching for authoritative answers can be traded-off against each other. Giving higher ranking to important pages seems to reduce the accuracy of the results, i.e., link analysis methods tend to assign higher ranking to higher quality but not necessary relevant pages. High quality pages, on the other hand, may be irrelevant to the content of the query. Weighted link analysis methods (WHITS, WPicASHOW) attempted to compromise between text and link analysis methods.

Text searching methods like Vector Space Model (VSM), the same as semantic retrieval methods are far more effective than link analysis methods implying that text is a very effective descriptor of Web content itself. Between the two, semantic retrieval methods demonstrated promising performance improvements over VSM [212]. However, text similarity methods tend to assign higher ranking even to Web pages and images pointed to by very low quality pages, e.g., pages created by individuals or small companies.

The size of the data set is also a problem. If the queries are very specific, the set of relevant answers is small and within it, the set of high quality and relevant answers are even smaller. The results may improve with the size of the data set, implying that it is plausible for the method to perform better when applied to the whole Web.

The evaluation of relevance feedback methods [399] demonstrated that term re-weighting based on text and image content is the most effective approach. The results demonstrate that term re-weighting is the most effective relevance feedback approach for all query types. Term re-weighting allows also for much smaller iteration cycles (and therefore for faster retrieval with less users effort) while maintaining good performance. All methods converge very fast, i.e., after two iteration cycles.

Future work includes experimentation with larger data sets and more elaborate detection and matching methods for more image types. Extracting semantic information from Web pages (image concepts and relationships) through automatic text analysis, combining text with image features as well as representing this information by image ontologies, is another aspect of future research. Image ontologies would not only serve as a means for bridging the semantic gap between image features and concepts, but also as a means for more effective image content representation and for supporting semantically rich query answering on the Web.

Part IV

INTERFACES TO MULTIMEDIA CONTENT

13

Design Principles for Multimodal Spoken Dialogue Systems

Alexandros Potamianos and Manolis Perakakis

Technical University of Crete

Speech is the primary form of human-human communication. In the past decades, technological progress in the areas of speech recognition, text-to-speech synthesis and natural language processing have made (the task-oriented) communication between humans and machines a reality. However, despite significant progress, speech interfaces are still very far from human capabilities, especially in the areas of robust speech recognition and semantic processing. Multimodal interfaces that combine speech input with other modalities have been hailed as the solution to the robustness problem. However, despite the advent of multimodal dialogue systems, speech interfaces have not been readily adopted by the user and their market penetration is still relatively limited. Our goal in this chapter is to help us better understand the shortcomings and challenges that are posed when the speech modality is incorporated in a multimodal interface both qualitatively and quantitatively. We also wish to understand how traditional human-computer interaction (HCI) principles should be adapted for multimodal dialogue interfaces.

A variety of efforts exist in the literature outlining the basic principles for multimodal dialogue system design and speech interfaces. These principles are motivated from technological, computer science, system design, human-factors, cognitive modeling, psychology, and other considerations [433, 353, 554, 483, 175]. Most of these recommendations, however, talk abstractly about multimodal interfaces and ignore the peculiarities of the speech modality. As we shall see in our analysis, the distinction of speech interfaces as being the "most natural" does not come "free-of-charge".

In this chapter, we review efforts in defining design principles and creating tools for building multimodal dialogue systems with emphasis on the speech modality. General design principles for architecting and building such systems are reviewed and challenges are outlined. The focus is on system architecture, interface design, data collection, and evaluation tools. We also present a multimodal system that combines pen and speech input as a design case study. Two important issues with multimodal systems design, is the selection of appropriate modalities in a given context and the exploitation of the *synergies*

P. Maragos et al. (eds.), *Multimodal Processing and Interaction*,
DOI: 10.1007/978-0-387-76316-3_13,

among the modalities in order to design a consistent and efficient interface. We introduce the concept of *modality synergy* that measures the added value from efficiently combining multiple input modalities. User behavior and system evaluation results on the prototype system demonstrate how users and multimodal systems can (and should) adapt to maximize modalities synergy and create efficient, natural, and intelligent multimodal interfaces.

The organization of this chapter is as follows. First a brief review of the most important interaction modalities and example applications of multimodal dialogue systems are given in Section 13.1. In Section 13.2, we review an iterative application-centric design process for multimodal dialogue interfaces and present some fundamental architectural principles for such systems. In Section 13.3, well-established design principles for graphical user interfaces (GUI) are reviewed and adapted to the speech modality. Our discussion focuses on how these principles should be extended for multimodal dialogue interfaces. These ideas are put to the test in a case study in Section 13.4. The main conclusions of this study are presented in Section 13.5.

13.1 Interaction modalities and applications

Speech input can be combined with different modalities on a variety of devices. The most common combination of spoken input is with keypad input on fixed and mobile phones, with keyboard and mouse input on computer desktops, and with pen input on personal digital assistants (PDAs) and mobile phones. Speech can be also combined with gestures, eye-tracking, haptic interfaces, virtual keyboards and specialized pointing devices for a variety of applications. Note that speech input can also be captured audiovisually (lip-reading). Speech input can be processed at various levels: lexical, syntactic, semantic, pragmatic, emotions/affect.

Today a variety of multimodal dialogue applications exist, most of them using speech and other modalities sequentially. Information-seeking applications on the phone and the PDA combine the speech and GUI modalities, e.g., travel reservation, stock quotes. Communication applications, such as name-dialing, are also popular, especially on next-generation mobile phones. Text-entry is an application where speech is the main input modality (combined with pen input for robustness) on portable devices in "hands-busy" situations. Dictation is the main text-entry application on desktop computers. Speech is combined with other modalities in various gaming applications running on desktop computers, home entertainment platforms and mobile devices. Finally, the car is a special mobile environment, where multimodal interaction with heavy emphasis on speech input is an effective and safe alternative to GUI interfaces.

For a brief review of the range of technologies that make spoken dialogue interfaces possible, refer to Section 2.2.2.

13.2 Multimodal Architecture and Design Process

The architecture of dialogue and multimodal systems has steadily evolved from monolithic to *modular*, with well-defined communication protocols between modules. Clearly a modular architecture is important as it adds flexibility, scalability, and robustness to the system. A good example of a highly-modular architecture built using a distributed message-based, hub-and-spoke infrastructure is the Galaxy Communicator Software Package [45]. In Galaxy, all communication between modules is delegated by a central controller, the hub. Alternatively, a peer-to-peer model can be used for communication between models, which is efficient for multimodal dialogue systems since processing modules often are arranged in a processing chain (acoustic, lexical, syntactic, semantic, pragmatic, and application processing). In practice, a combination of peer-to-peer and hub-and-spoke architectures are used in most systems, e.g., audio resources are often controlled by a separate controller in a "hub-and-spoke" like architecture, while speech multimodal input processing often follows a "peer-to-peer" architecture in a processing chain. There are also agent-based architectures that are popular especially in the research community. Communication between agents or modules can be done via a shared communication space, a blackboard. For examples of such systems, refer to [486, 554].

As discussed in Section 2.1, an interactive system consists of three main conceptual parts: (i) the *model* or *application semantics*, (ii) the *view* or *interface implementation* and (iii) the *control* or *application logic*. The separation of these three key components both architecturally and in the system design process is an important decision also supported in the latest W3C recommendations [11]. Note that selecting the appropriate communication protocol between modules, e.g., hub-and-spoke vs. peer-to-peer, does not guarantee that the Model-View-Controller (MVC) paradigm is respected (see also Section 2.1).

13.2.1 Multimodal Architecture Design Principles

There is a list of general system architecture design principles that also apply to multimodal dialogue systems namely: encapsulation, distribution, extensibility, scalability, recursiveness, modularity [11]. Next, we present two architecture design principles that are especially important for multimodal systems and extend the MVC paradigm, namely:

- **Separation of semantics, application and interface logic**: This design principle is consistent with the MVC paradigm, where model (semantics), view (interface), and control (application logic) are separated and a well defined interface is defined among the three components. However there are unimodal systems that do not follow this principle, e.g., in most spoken dialogue systems application and interface logic is combined into a single module known as the *dialogue manager*. Separation of the application and the interface is especially important for multimodal interfaces where application states and communication goals have to be implemented for multiple modalities. By separating the logic, *a single application manager can be built for all modalities* that selects the communication goals, while the implementation of these goals is separate for each modality[1].

- **Common semantic representation across modalities**: By defining an application ontology and separating the data from the interface, it is possible to build a common representation across modalities. This significantly simplifies the communication between the various input and output modalities and avoids writing filters that translate concepts between system modules. This unified semantic framework should include not only simple attribute-value pair constructs, but also more complex typed feature structures. In addition, having a common semantic representation makes unification operations or inference operations truly modality-independent. Note that it is acceptable to handle semantics that are modality-specific locally at the interface level, e.g., "repeat this" only makes sense for a speech interface.

In practice it is not always easy to impose these two important architecture principles. Multimodal systems consist of unimodal modules that do not always follow the MVC paradigm, i.e., sometimes combine semantics and application logic, or application logic and interface. In other cases, a unimodal module might not provide an interface for accessing each of the three components (model, view, control). When faced with such "monolithic" modules programmers often have to create filters that translate semantics among modules or write additional application (control) logic. However, when starting for a clean slate these maxims should be followed.

These architectural principles can be found both in research work and multimodal standards. For example, one of the six main design principles cited in the SALT multimodal standard is the "separation of the speech interface from business logic and data" [6]; the principle appears also in W3C's multimodal interaction requirements as requirement MMI-A3 [12]. Examples of dialogue and multimodal systems that have used the MVC paradigm include VxOne [251] and SmartKom [554]. For a common semantic representation across modalities refer to [25, 554].

13.2.2 Design Process

As discussed in [410], data collection and analysis form a crucial part of multimodal dialogue system development. In Fig. 13.1, the various stages of application development are shown, as the interface evolves from GUI-only to

[1] Separate, but not independent. The coordination of these modality-dependent interface implementation is known as modality fusion and fission for system input and output respectively.

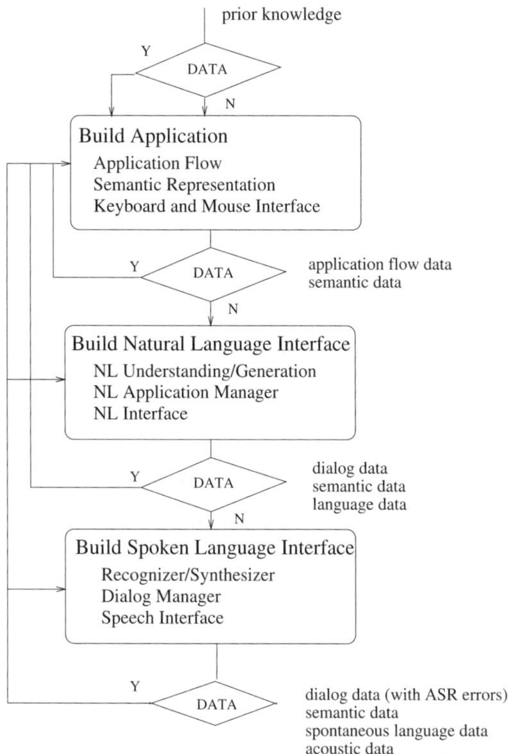

Fig. 13.1. Iterative dialogue system design using multi-stage data collection (from [410]).

include also spoken input. Data can be collected at various stages of application development either automatically or assisted by supervisors in a "Wizard of Oz" scenario. Collected data include acoustic, lexical, semantic, application/dialogue flow and user/evaluation data as shown in Fig. 13.1. The quality and coverage of the collected data is very much dependent on the system configuration and the application scenario. As a result, dialogue system development is an iterative process: collected data are used to improve the system, and more data are collected using the updated system configuration.

Designing a good application is the first step towards building a successful multimodal system. The importance of application design is often overlooked by the speech and multimodal community, where the emphasis is on the interface rather than the functionality. In Fig. 13.1, an application-, data- and user-centric approach to multimodal dialogue system design is outlined, where the application evolves as the interface is augmented with natural language and spoken language capabilities. The main advantages of this approach are increased modularity and flexible multi-stage data collection.

13.3 Design Principles for Multimodal Dialogue Systems

In this section, we review efforts in defining design principles and creating tools for building multimodal dialogue systems with emphasis on the speech modality. General design principles for architecting and building such systems are reviewed and challenges are outlined. The focus is on system architecture, application, speech interface design, and data collection.

13.3.1 Basic HCI principles

Most papers reviewing principles for designing spoken dialogue and multimodal systems follow a "tabula rasa" approach. Here instead, we reuse the experience and expertise gained (mostly) from GUI interface design, show which of these GUI-design principles apply to multimodal systems and present new principles that are specific to multimodal system design.

Here is a (self-explanatory) list of the general principles of good user interface design: aesthetically pleasing, clarity, compatibility, comprehensibility, configurability, consistency, control, directness, efficiency, familiarity, flexibility, forgiveness, predictability, recovery, responsiveness, simplicity, and transparency [175]. For a review of HCI principles see also Section 2.1.

13.3.2 Adapting HCI principles to speech interfaces

Next, we discuss how some basic HCI principles should be adapted for spoken dialogue and multimodal system design. We focus on principles that need to be modified or added for the case of multimodal dialogue systems. Specifically:

- **Control**: Traditional HCI design principles include the notion that the "user should always be in control". However, for spoken dialogue systems it has been observed that (with the exception of gaming applications) "mixed-initiative" systems ofter perform better than "user-initiative" systems, i.e., putting the user in control is not always a good idea[2]. This is probably due to worse automatic speech recognition (ASR) performance for "user-initiative" systems as well as the deviation from other basic HCI principles in spoken dialogue system (SDS) design, e.g., consistency, transparency, forgiveness. For multimodal dialogue systems this problem is somewhat alleviated and the user can once again be in control.
- **Efficiency**: Speech input and (especially) speech output are rarely the most efficient means of communication. In [175], the author reports human interaction speeds of various communication methods, as gathered by a number of research studies. The average reader can proofread at approximately 180 words per minute (wpm) and read prose at speeds over 250 wpm. The average listener can consume approximately 150-160 wpm.

[2] Note that for human-human verbal communication, initiative is also often held by the agent rather than the customer.

The average typist can type 60-70 wpm, while an experienced one over 150 wpm. Speech input can reach speeds of 105 wpm assuming that there are no speech recognition errors; with errors (and correction via a GUI interface) the speed for a dictation task can be as low as 25 wpm. Clearly speech input is less efficient compared to keyboard input in most situations; unless speech recognition accuracy is close to 100%. Speech output is almost always less efficient than text output. However, speech can compete favorably with other input modalities, e.g., pen input, in the absence of keyboard.

- **Consistency**: Speech interfaces are notorious for being inconsistent. The user ofter repeats the same input, while the speech recognizer understands two different things. Inconsistency in SDS systems is especially annoying to the user who is often confused and frustrated by system errors. For multimodal systems, this problem is less prominent, due to synergistic error correction, but does not go away. The multimodal system designer should be careful to point out these inconsistencies to the user right away, by always displaying visually the belief state of the system and if possible highlighting beliefs that are probably erroneous (have low confidence scores). Ambiguity should always be displayed visually and the user should be prompted to correct it via the GUI.
- **Familiarity and Transparency**: Human-machine spoken dialogue interaction is very different than natural human-human interaction (for good reason). Due to the "unnaturalness" of human-machine interaction, the novice user is often surprised by the design of the speech or multimodal interface and needs training to learn how to interact with the system. In addition, speech interfaces are not transparent to the user. The functionality of the speech interface, i.e., what can be recognized or understood by the system, is often a mystery to the user. To help the user become familiar with the SDS or multimodal interface, tutorial, help messages and example speech inputs should be provided to the novice user through-out the interaction. Also, provided that the multimodal interface is consistent, the user is guided by the GUI input options available to figure out what speech input options are available at any point in the interaction.
- **Forgiveness and Recovery**: Speech interfaces are usually not forgiving to the user. The inner workings of the speech recognizer produce errors that seem both unexpected and unnatural to the the user. Recovering from such errors is hard, due to the limited ability of todays spoken dialogue systems to handle clarification sub-dialogues. Again these shortcomings of SDS can be overcome by going multimodal: the GUI should be used to provide clear paths for recovering from speech recognition errors.

Two additional concepts that are especially important for speech interfaces are the notion of *turn-taking* and *persistence*. Speech communication is usually synchronous in nature, speakers take turns that are well-defined in time. In spoken dialogue systems, a turn consists of human input and corresponding machine output (or vice-versa depending on who holds the dialogue initiative). For other interaction modalities, the coupling between input and corresponding output is not as strong or obvious; in fact, for the GUI modality, input/output synchronization might occur at the event, field and/or form levels. The implementation of "turn" in multimodal dialogue systems is non-trivial; a variety of interaction styles (concurrent vs. sequential multimodality), interaction modes ("click-to-talk","open-mike") and event-handling (level of synchrony, blocking/non-blocking) have been devised to address these issues.

For GUI interfaces, there is a clear notion of a session and there are well defined ways to add, remove or clear the semantics of a session. In speech communication, the semantics of a session might persist after a session is over or be referenced in a side-conversation. For example, in a movie information system, the user might make multiple requests assuming that the city value persists from his initial query, while movie theater and title values expire after the first query. This *selective semantic persistence* makes speech interfaces harder to design. Note that for multimodal dialogue interfaces this problem is easier to solve using GUI output and input for visualization and disambiguation.

In addition to these issues, speech is a unique modality since it is the main means of communication among humans. Psychologists and cognitive scientists have outlined over the years the basic principles of human-human speech communication. For an excellent review of these principles and their implications for SDS design refer to [353]. In summary, speech is a strong correlate for gender, emotion, personality and speakers' face. People expect reciprocity, symmetry, and collaboration when they converse. People speak multimodaly and attempt to convey their message as well as affect. Finally, speech communication is a social act that implies presence, e.g., users are more cautious when interacting with a SDS than with a GUI. These principles are important to keep in mind when designing spoken dialogue systems.

It is clear from this discussion, that speech interfaces violate some basic HCI design principles, including consistency, transparency and forgiveness, as well as introduce new challenges. Given these short-comings it is not surprising that speech interfaces have not been adopted as readily as expected by users. However, as discussed next, by combing speech and GUI input/output modalities, most of these short-comings are alleviated.

13.3.3 HCI principles of multimodal dialogue systems

In addition to the aforementioned principles, there are also HCI principles that are relevant mostly or have special meaning for multimodal systems (and much less so for unimodal systems). Some of these issues are outline also in [433]. Next we present such multimodal design principles:

- **Consistency**: In addition to the traditional notion of consistency in HCI, consistency takes on new meaning for multimodal interfaces. The functionality and semantic representation of the underlying spoken dialogue and GUI systems should be identical. For example, if the speech interface can interpret "round trip" to mean a trip with two legs from city A to city B and back, the GUI should be able to handle such input (if possible have a "round trip" check-box). Providing consistency between the various input and output modes is not simple when speech input is involved. Speech input is richer than GUI input and a variety of spoken language expressions might not directly correspond to a GUI construct. In such cases, special care should be taken to inform the user of the application functionality and the speech interface functionality. Two important principles are also related to the maxim of consistency, namely:

- **Symmetric multimodality**: The principle of "symmetric" multimodality [554] requires that the same modalities are used for both input and output. Using the same modality for both input and output reduces the cognitive load and improves efficiency [353].
- **No representation without presentation**: According to [553], there should always be output presentation for internal system representations (system states) and vice versa, output should correspond to an internal semantic representation or communication act. This principle emphasizes consistency between the interface and data model of the system.

- **Efficiency and Synergy**: Synergy is a design principle that applies to systems that have more than one input or output modalities. A synergistic multimodal interface is more than the sum of its parts. To achieve high synergy it is important not only to use the appropriate modality for each part of the application, but also to allow for interplay between the modalities, e.g., speech misrecognitions should be resolved via the GUI interface. Synergistic multimodal interface design can achieve system performance that is better than the performance of individual unimodal systems, thus improving overall efficiency. Here is a short list of design principles that bring out the "best" of the speech and GUI modalities:
  a) the system semantic state is represented visually,
  b) speech prompts are short, if any,
  c) the user in prompted to correct speech recognition errors via the GUI,
  d) ambiguity is displayed and corrected via the GUI,
  e) the focus (or context) of the interaction is highlighted visually,
  f) the GUI takes full advantage of speech-interface "intelligence", and,
  g) conflicting GUI and speech input is seamlessly integrated.
- **Robustness**: Novel "modalities" are based on new technologies and interaction paradigms that might be error-prone, e.g., recognition errors for speech input. As discussed in Section 2.3.4, multimodal interfaces offer increased robustness and error correction capabilities against error-prone modalities due to both user behavior and system design. It was found [380, 382] that for multimodal dialogue systems users tend to use simpler language when interacting multimodaly. Also users tend to use the less

error-prone modality at each context (error avoidance) and switch modalities after system errors (synergistic error correction). These behaviors can be reinforced by appropriate user interfaces design, e.g., use pen input as a default modality for resolving ambiguities that arise from speech recognition errors. System support, such as multimodal ambiguity resolution via constraints or a probabilistic framework for multimodal fusion, can also help reduce ambiguity and errors resulting in a more robust interface.

- **Compositionality**: The space of possible user interface configurations increases exponentially as the number of modes increases. The same is true for the space of possible semantic representations of user input, as well as the space of possible presentations of system output. To handle this world of possibilities, the principle of compositionality can be used, e.g., assume that the meaning of multimodal input is the sum of the meaning of its parts (independent of the modality that each part comes from). The principle of compositionality reduces the complexity of the problem of optimal multimodal interface design; in essence, "linearizes" the problem. Compositionality is in most cases a good approximation and can significantly reduce the search space for the "best" multimodal system configuration. Note that the extensible multimodal annotation markup language (EMMA) proposed by W3C applies this principle to the description of data semantics by building semantic tokens bottom-up starting from the simplest conceptually token [8].

Overall, synergy, robustness, modularity, customizability and consistency are some important features of successful multimodal dialogue systems and design tools. Next we show how some of these principles are applied to the design of a speech and pen multimodal travel reservation system running on a PDA environment.

13.4 Multimodal Dialogue System Design: A Case Study

In this section, we describe a case study of a multimodal dialogue system that combines the GUI and speech modalities. The system was built using the multimodal spoken dialogue platform described in [409]. The form-filling part of the travel reservation system is studied here[3]. The multimodal interface was designed to emphasize consistency and synergies between modalities. The GUI input modalities are keyboard and mouse input in a desktop environment, or pen input in a personal digital assistant (PDA) environment. The GUI output modalities are text and graphics. Three multimodal interaction modes are presented and evaluated here namely "click to talk" (CTT), where GUI input is the default modality, "open-mike" (OM), where speech input is the default modality, and "modality-selection" (MS) where the system selects the

[3] Note that travel reservation was one of the three scenarios studied in W3C's multimodal interaction user cases document [13].

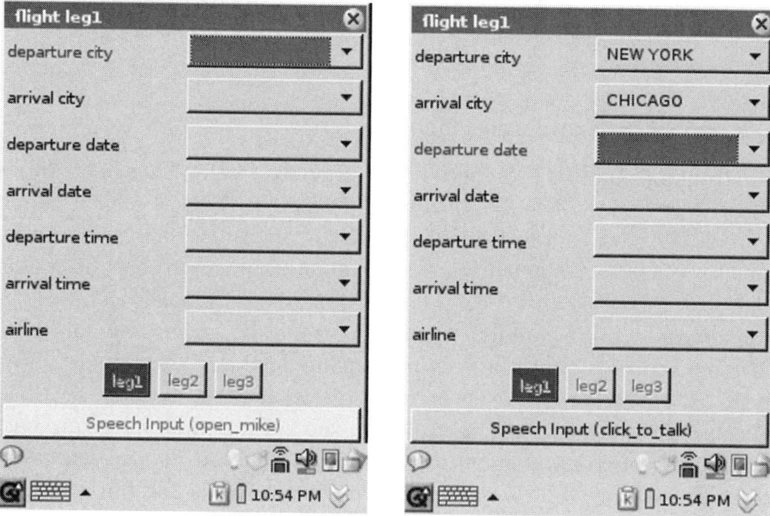

Fig. 13.2. MS interaction mode examples on a PDA. System is in OM mode in the first frame receives user input "From New York to Chicago" and switches to CTT mode in the second frame. Speech/pen default input mode is selected based the large/small number of input options in the combo-box respectively.

modality that is most efficient for the typical user at each turn [396, 395]. Note that in all three multimodal modes only one modality is active at a time, i.e., the system does not allow for concurrent multimodal input. Also, for all multimodal modes, users are free to override the system's proposed input modality, that is, use a modality other than the system's default, e.g., GUI input during OM mode.

Specifically, for CTT interaction pen is the default input; the user needs to click the "Speech Input" button to override the default input modality and use speech input. For OM interaction, speech is the default input modality; the system is always listening and a voice-activity detection event activates the recognizer. MS is a mix of CTT and OM interaction; the system switches between the two interaction modes depending on efficiency considerations (the number of input choices available for the current context). Speech input is faster compared to pen input when many input choices are available on the PDA; the threshold of 25 input choices was chosen based on the input mode efficiency of the stereotypical user. For attributes with over 25 choices the system defaulted to the OM mode, else the CTT mode was selected. In Fig. 13.2, examples from the MS mode running on a PDA are shown. At the screen-shot shown on the left, where the interaction context is "city", speech is selected as the default input modality by the system due to the large number of input choices. At the next screen-shot shown on the right of Fig. 13.2, pen is selected as the default modality due to the limited number of choices (less than 25).

13.4.1 Architecture and Interface Design

The main design principles presented in the previous section have been applied to the design of this multimodal system. Specifically there is a clear separation between the task (application states and control flow) and the interface (implementation of the application states in terms of input/output modalities). The task manager and the spoken dialogue system have been designed to be domain and modality-independent: consequently, adding new modalities to the system requires only a few enhancements that are easy to design and implement.

The semantic and pragmatic modules for the multimodal system are based on the principles of compositionality and on a common semantic representation across modalities. The semantic representation used for both the GUI and speech interfaces is identical. The semantics of the application (encoded in the domain ontology) are identical since the GUI interface has the same functionality as the speech interface (consistency). The basic semantic data structures that encode system beliefs in the form of attribute-value pairs, now encode the instantiated *joined* semantics of the GUI and speech input modalities. The speech and GUI parsers are recursive finite-state parsers used also for the unimodal systems. In addition to spoken forms the GUI parser understands abbreviations such as “2/3/08” for date or “15:00” for time [25].

The semantic/pragmatic algorithm introduced in [25] is also used in our system. The algorithm is designed to allow integration of any type of evidence for or against candidate values and thus provides a very useful framework for merging often conflicting information collected from the multiple input modalities: given multiple candidates for a given attribute, we update the pragmatic confidence score for each candidate using MYCIN style formulae as in the single modality case [485, 25]. The principle of compositionality is used: (i) the belief for the value of an attribute is computed by combining all evidence from the user-system interaction, and (ii) beliefs are the composition of attribute-values along with their corresponding pragmatic confidence.

The principles of consistency and synergy have been followed when designing the interface. Specifically, the systems state is presented visually, the GUI modality is used to correct speech recognition errors, the context (focus of the interaction) is highlighted visually as well as communicated via audio output, and all tasks (including semantic inference) that can be performed via speech can also be performed via GUI input.

13.4.2 Evaluation

Five scenarios of varying complexity were used for evaluation: one/two/three-legged flight reservations and round trip flights with hotel/car reservation.

In Table 13.1, the usage of attributes in each scenario as well as cumulative usage across scenarios are shown; attributes are ordered based on the number of available values in the grammar. We refer to the three attributes listed, namely "hotelname", "city" and "airline", that have more that 25 possible values as "long" attributes while the rest are referred to as "short". Note that the cumulative attributes usage across all scenarios is about the same for "long" and "short" attributes (20 vs 22). Eight non-native English-speaking users evaluated all systems on all five scenarios. All users had prior limited experience using a previous version of the system.

Table 13.1. Attribute usage for the five travel reservation scenarios and number of values available in the application grammar for each attribute.

attribute name	number of values	total usage
hotelname	250	1
city	135	14
airline	93	5
date	22	10
car type	15	1
car rental	10	1
time	9	10

The evaluation procedure is described next. First, users are given a short introductory document which explains the system functionality with emphasis on the modes to be evaluated. In order to familiarize users with the system before actual evaluation takes place, users are asked to complete a demo scenario using all different systems, for a maximum of 30 minutes. Finally evaluation takes place, by asking users to complete all five scenarios using all ten systems (a total of 50 sessions per user and 40 sessions per mode). Systems are evaluated in random order and logs for each session are saved for later processing by our analysis software (objective evaluation). Upon completion of all runs, an exit interview is conducted (user feedback and overall subjective evaluation). Next we present a subset of the evaluation results that are relevant for our discussion. For a full list of the evaluation results refer to [396].

13.4.3 Modality Efficiency

We measure the *modality efficiency* of multimodal systems as a function of interaction mode, interaction context and user. Modality efficiency is defined here to be proportional to the inverse of the time required by that modality to complete a task. Specifically, lets assume that T_s and T_g is the overall time spent using the speech and GUI modality respectively for a form-filling task using a multimodal interface. The number of fields (attributes) that are filled correctly using each modality is N_s and N_g respectively[4]. The relative efficiency of the speech modality (compared to the GUI modality) is defined as

$$S_s = \frac{\frac{N_s}{T_s}}{\frac{N_s}{T_s} + \frac{N_g}{T_g}} = \frac{N_s T_g}{N_s T_g + T_s N_g} \tag{13.1}$$

for a GUI and speech multimodal interface. *Thus efficiency is proportional to the number of tokens (filled fields) communicated correctly in unit time.* The quantity above can be computed as a function of the interaction mode, interaction context or user by adjusting appropriately the modality times and filled context per modality.

In Fig. 13.3, we show speech modality usage as a function of relative speech modality efficiency. There are three free variables in these plots, namely, interaction mode (CTT, OM, MS), interaction context (city, airline, date, time) and user (u1 to u8). Due to data sparsity instead of showing all 96 datapoints we show: in Fig. 13.3(a), the combined data points for all contexts and modes (12 data points) averaged over all eight users, and in Fig. 13.3(b), the combined data points for all contexts and users (30 out of possible 32 data points shown) averaged over all three modes. In both plots, there is significant correlation between modality efficiency and modality usage. It can be seen in Fig. 13.3(a), that the "average" user behavior is to select the modality which maximizes efficiency, with a switch occurring in modality usage around the 50% relative speech efficiency line. However, for the OM mode there is clearly a bias towards speech input. Thus, **interface design can bias modality usage and affect system efficiency.**

In Fig. 13.3(b), the same trends exist as in (a), however, the variability among speakers in modality usage is very significant. This is especially pronounced for relative speech efficiencies between 35% and 60%; in that region the user cannot properly gage which modality is more efficient. In [511], a longitudinal study shows that users adapt their modality usage over time and adopt more efficient strategies. In any case, the high variability in modality usage patterns and relative modality efficiency among users clearly demonstrates the importance of creating interfaces that **adapt to users needs**. However, as discussed in Section 2.4, one should be careful when designing adaptive interfaces to clearly communicate the system state to the user and to keep interface changes to a minimum to avoid increased cognitive load.

---

[4] We define as field any attribute defined in the GUI that has a label and gets filled, thus a single field might contain variable numbers of concepts or words, e.g., "date" field. Also note that there are cases where both modalities are used to correctly fill a field, e.g., concurrent multimodality or correction of speech recognition errors via the GUI, slightly biasing our estimator.

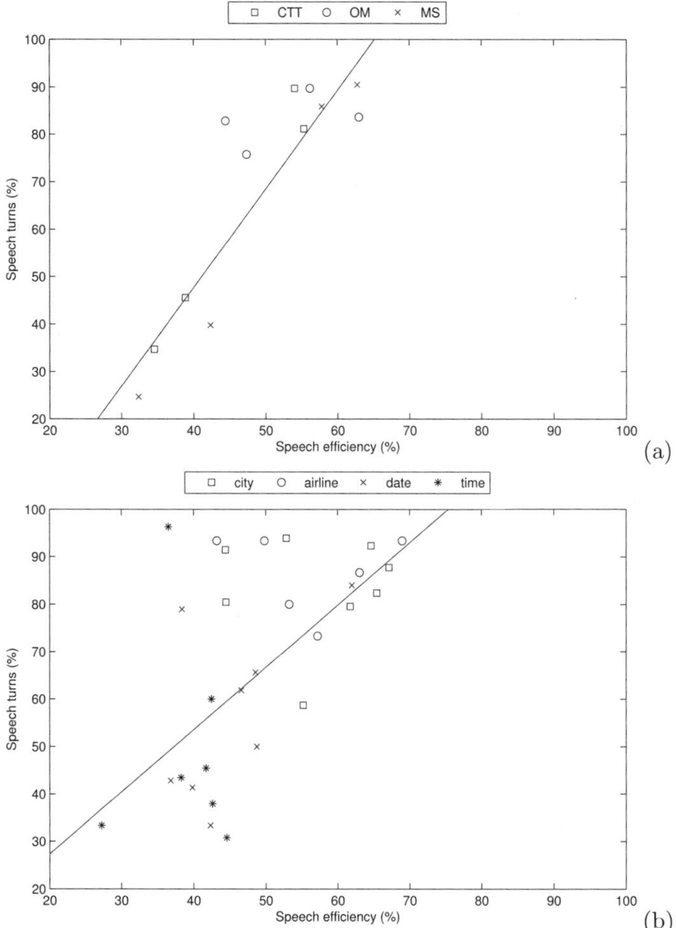

Fig. 13.3. Speech modality usage as a function of relative speech modality efficiency. Data points are shown for (a) context and interaction modes, and (b) context and users.

13.4.4 Multimodal Synergy

Next we define *modality synergy* (or multimodal synergy) as the percent improvement in terms of time-to-completion achieved by our multimodal system compared to a multimodal system that randomly combines the different modalities. In our example, for the GUI and speech modalities, time-to-completion for the "random" system is computed as the weighted linear combination of the time-to-completion of the speech-only and the GUI-only systems, with weights proportional to the usage of each modality in our actual multimodal system. Specifically, lets assume that T_s, T_g and T_m are the time-to-completion of the speech-only, GUI-only and multimodal systems, and

M_s and M_g are the relative usage of the speech and GUI modalities in the multimodal system (normalized in [0,1] and summing to 1). Then the time-to-completion of the multimodal system T_r that randomly selects a modality at each turn (respecting the a-priori probability of modality usage) is $T_r = M_s T_s + M_g T_g$. In general, $T_r = \sum_i M_i T_i$, where i sums over all available modalities. Modality synergy $S_{s,g}$ is defined as:

$$S_{s,g} = \frac{T_r - T_m}{T_r} \quad (13.2)$$

Note that modality synergy expresses the relative improvement in terms of time-to-completion achieved by multimodal interfaces over the sum-of-its unimodal parts, thus the term *synergy*. Synergy can be computed for each interaction mode, interaction context or user by using the appropriate time and modality usage measurements. As shown next, the achieved synergy is both interface design dependent, context-dependent and user-dependent.

In Table 13.2, the synergy between the speech and GUI modality is computed for the three multimodal interaction modes according to Eq. 13.2. Note that modality synergy is almost double when using an "open-mike" mode compared to a "click-to-talk" interaction mode. This is due both to different modality usage patterns in each interaction mode, as well as increased overhead related to switching between the two input modalities. Specifically for the "click-to-talk" mode, the user often overrides the default GUI input and uses speech instead. In any case, it is clear that achieved **synergy depends on interaction mode and, in general, on user interface design.** Designing interfaces that use efficiency and user preference considerations to "optimally" mix the various modalities can maximize synergy, and, in effect, the gain over unimodal interfaces.

Table 13.2. Gains from modality synergy for the three multimodal interaction modes.

Interaction Mode	click-to-talk	open-mike	modality selection
Modality Synergy (%)	11.4	21.0	17.5

In Table 13.3, the synergy between the speech and GUI modality is compared across the eight users. Note the significant differences in achieved synergy for each user, in fact, modality synergy ranges from -18% to 38%! The differences in synergy are due to user dependent input modality usage, variable speech recognition rates, variable number of concepts per utterance for speech input, variable ability/experience using pen for form-filling on a PDA, and, most-importantly, to what degree users used efficiency considerations when selecting the input modality at each part of the interaction[5]. In any

[5] This last factor is directly related to synergy, random input modality selection achieves zero synergy.

case, the fact that synergy is highly user-dependent (can be even negative for some users) clearly shows that:

(i) There is **potentially high-reward in designing multimodal interfaces that adapt to the user**. Creating multimodal interfaces that are "optimal" for a stereotypical user does not grep all the reward (in terms of synergy) over unimodal interfaces.
(ii) **Multimodal dialogue interfaces will not work for all users**. Just as is the case for unimodal spoken dialogue systems, there might be catastrophic failures for some users (these users are referred to as "goats" in the speech recognition slang). For these users, one or more modalities might not work well at all, or the ability of the user to maximize modality synergy might be limited. Some of these shortcomings might be cured over time with training, but clearly multimodal interfaces will not work for everyone, right off the bat.

Table 13.3. Gains from modality synergy for each user (over all modes).

User	user1	user2	user3	user4	user5	user6	user7	user8
Modality Synergy (%)	23.7	38.0	-18.0	8.7	19.0	10.3	29.3	10.7

We conclude with a remark about adaptive multimodal interfaces. In Table 13.2, the "modality-selection" interaction mode is compared with "click-to-talk" and "open-mike" modes in terms of modality synergy. Note that "modality-selection" is an interaction mode that has been designed to maximize efficiency (and thus synergy) for the stereotypical user; at each turn, the system selects as the default input modality the one that is the most efficient for the typical user. It is surprising to see in Table 13.2, that a multimodal interface designed to maximize synergy performs (somewhat) worse that the "open-mike" multimodal interaction mode in terms of synergy. This is due to two reasons: (i) the stereotypical user model cannot capture the user-dependent modality synergy behavior demonstrated in Table 13.3 that can yield potentially high-rewards, and (ii) adaptivity creates additional cognitive load to the user; users appear to be confused when the default input modality changes adaptively from turn to turn. As a result, the small advantage gained by using a stereotypical user model to design the multimodal interface is overshadowed by increased cognitive load. This is clearly demonstrated in [395] where "modality-selection" is shown to achieve better interaction times but worse inactivity times. Clearly adaptive interface behavior appears inconsistent to the user and can increase cognitive load. All in all, **adaptation and consistency are two conflicting maxims that have to be balanced properly in multimodal user interface design.**

13.5 Conclusions

In this chapter, we have exposed some important aspects of multimodal dialogue system design. The basic design principles of HCI design apply also in the case of multimodal dialogue systems, however, multimodal dialogue systems are special in many ways. First, speech interfaces do not respect many traditional HCI design principles, such as control, consistency, transparency and recovery. Second, multimodality forces us to introduce new design principles that are not strictly enforced in traditional HCI, such as, consistency across interaction modes, synergy between modalities, separation of task and interface, and the principle of compositionality. Finally, the design process of multimodal dialogue systems is a multi-step iterative process.

The proposed design process and principles have been put to the test: a multimodal travel reservation system was built that can handle both speech and GUI input and output. The basic design principles employed in this system include: consistency across modalities (common functionality and a common semantic representation), the principle of compositionality for semantic/pragmatic understanding, a clear separation between task and interface (where the task manager is modality-independent) and a synergistic multimodal interface design. The multimodal prototype system was evaluated on a PDA with good results. Metrics for measuring efficiency and multimodal synergy were proposed and used for evaluation of the multimodal system. ¿From the experiments it was clear that, although, on average users tended to use the most efficient modality at each turn, modality usage patterns were highly user dependent. Overall, we saw that: (i) multimodal interaction mode affects interface efficiency and modality synergy, (ii) user adaptation can potentially yield significantly higher interface efficiency and synergy, and (iii) multimodal interaction will not work for all users from the start.

Based on these observations our future work will focus on adaptive algorithms for selecting the appropriate mix of input and output modalities. It is also important to focus our analysis on the problem of multimodal error correction. Other important research areas include fusion and fission at the interface and data levels. More research is needed to better understand when and why users use one input modality over another, and how adaptive modality selection relates to interface efficiency.

14

Eye Tracking: A New Interface for Visual Exploration

Oyewole K. Oyekoya and Fred W. M. Stentiford

University College London

Widespread interest in discovering information has created a demand for tools that capture users' intentions. The popularity of search engines (such as Google and Yahoo) has highlighted users' requirements for rapid and effortless access to relevant information. But there is now increasing research activity in the categorization and retrieval of visual multimedia content for sharing and entertainment purposes, as opposed to text-based mechanisms targeted at improving access to written material.

Whereas key words form a convenient feature for characterizing documents, there is no such obvious attribute present in images and video material. In addition, there is no agreement on what might constitute a universal syntax for images that could capture the meaning that we all see in images. In fact, every user possesses a different subjective perception of the world and it is not therefore possible to capture this in a single fixed set of features and associated representations. In this way, it is not possible to guarantee to anticipate a user's perception of the visual content and indeed users may change their minds in the middle of a retrieval operation.

The mouse and the keyboard dominate the types of interfaces found in computers today. Most people are happy to use them to interact with their machines, but they present mental and physical barriers to communication. The keyboard requires knowledge of a language of interaction and a chain of events involving vision, thought and muscular movement, all of which require a judgment whether initiating the effort will be worthwhile or not. The mouse reduces keyboard interaction and enables simple visual selection, but still requires the same physical and conscious mental processes to take place. Eye tracking offers a valuable short cut in computer communications for visual tasks [231]. Gaze behavior could provide information to the machine without the essential need for extra co-ordinated muscular movement and the associated effort. Indeed, the reduced level of effort should allow users to convey more relevant factors more easily to the machine and in a shorter time. In addition, there is scope for identifying users' intentions from pre-attentive activity

P. Maragos et al. (eds.), *Multimodal Processing and Interaction*,
DOI: 10.1007/978-0-387-76316-3_14,

of which the user is not consciously aware and promises to yield extremely rapid search performances.

The following sections present a background to this work. This is followed by descriptions of our system and recent experiments in image retrieval through an eye tracking interface. The final sections discuss and present some conclusions and an indication of how eye tracking technology might enter the mass market.

14.1 Eye Tracking Technologies

The first technologies up to the 1960's were invasive and required tampering directly with the eyes. The search coil method [437] offers high accuracy and large dynamic range but requires an insertion into the eye! Non-invasive methods such as the Dual Purkinje Image eye tracker [114] require the head to be restricted and are relatively expensive. More recently systems have appeared that use video images with some using infrared cameras. The eye has several key characteristics that makes gaze direction measurable from a video camera image. Eye pointing is precise because there is a centralized region in the retina, where there is increasing image resolution towards its center.

LC Technology's Eyegaze system uses the Pupil-Centre/Corneal-Reflection method to determine the eye gaze direction. A video camera located below the computer screen remotely and unobtrusively observes the subject's eye. No attachments to the head are required in this setup. A small, low power, infrared light emitting diode (LED) located at the center of the camera lens illuminates the eye. The LED generates the corneal reflection and causes the bright pupil effect, which enhances the camera's image of the pupil. The accuracy of eye tracking systems depends in large measure on how precisely the image processing algorithms can locate the relative positions of pupil center and the corneal reflection. To achieve the bright-eye effect, light is shone into the eye along the axis of the camera lens. The eye's lens focuses the light that enters the pupil onto a point on the retina. Because the typical retina is highly reflective, a significant portion of that light emerges back through the pupil, and the eye's lens serendipitously directs that light back along the camera axis right into the camera. Thus the pupil appears to the camera as a bright disk, which contrasts very clearly with the surrounding iris. Specialized image-processing software in the Eyegaze computer identifies and locates the centers of both the pupil and corneal reflection. Trigonometric calculations project the person's gazepoint based on the positions of the pupil center and the corneal reflection within the video image.

Different eye tracking systems have variations in the design of their respective algorithms for calculating gaze positions, with little or no difference in the basic infrared technology. Some manufacturers have a head-mounted as well as a remote version of their eye tracker and prices have gone down considerably in the last few years.

Several methods have been proposed for improving the accuracy of estimating gaze direction and inferring intent from eye movement. Identification and analysis of fixations [461] and saccades in eye tracking protocols has been shown to be important for understanding visual behavior.

Privitera et al. [416] used 10 image processing algorithms to compare human identified regions of interest with regions of interest determined by an eye tracker and defined by a fixation algorithm. The comparative approach used a similarity measurement to compare two aROIs (algorithmically-detected Region of Interests), two hROIs (human-identified Region of Interests) and an aROI plus hROI. The prediction accuracy was compared to identify the best matching algorithms and different algorithms fared better under differing conditions. They concluded that aROIs cannot always be expected to be similar to hROIs in the same image because two hROIs produce different results in separate runs. This means that algorithms are unable in general to predict the sequential ordering of fixation points.

Jaimes, Pelz et al. [232] compared eye movement across categories and linked category-specific eye tracking results to automatic image classification techniques. They hypothesized that the eye movements of human observers differed for images in different semantic categories, and that this information could be effectively used in automatic content-based classifiers. The eye tracking results suggested that similar viewing patterns occur when different subjects view different images in the same semantic category. Hence, while algorithms are unable to predict the sequential ordering of points of interest, similarity in viewing patterns over images in the same category is possible.

14.2 Applications

Eye tracking equipments are used as interface devices in several diverse applications. The number of applications of eye tracking is increasing, as presented in Duchowski's review [144] of diagnostic and interactive applications based on offline and real-time analysis, respectively. Interactive applications have concentrated upon replacing and extending existing computer interface mechanisms, rather than creating a new form of interaction. The tracking of eye movements has been employed as a pointer and a replacement for a mouse [197], to vary the screen scrolling speed [372] and to assist disabled users [108]. Schnell and Wu [467] applied eye tracking as an alternative method for the activation of controls and functions in aircraft. Dasher [560] used a method for text entry that relies purely on gaze direction. Nikolov et al. proposed [370] a system for construction of gaze-contingent multi-modality displays of multi-layered geographical maps. Gaze contingent multi-resolutional displays (GCMRDs) center high-resolution information on the user's gaze position, matching the user's interest. In this system, different map information is channeled to the central and the peripheral visual fields, giving real performance advantage.

In its diagnostic capabilities, eye-tracking provides a comprehensive approach to studying interaction processes such as the placement of menus within web sites and to influence design guidelines more widely [332]. However, the imprecise nature of saccades and fixation points has prevented these approaches from yielding benefits over conventional human interfaces. Fixations and saccades are used to analyze eye movements, but it is evident that the statistical approaches to interpretation (such as clustering, summation and differentiation) are insufficient for identifying interests due to the differences in humans' perception of image content.

Although eye tracking has not yet been implemented on mobile devices, research is underway on how the detection of regions of interest that catch the eye can be used to improve the quality of images presented on small screens. In the future, eye trackers could automate this process for individual users. Xin Fan et al. [155] proposed an image viewing technique based on an adaptive attention shifting model, which enabled the browsing of large images on limited and heterogeneous screen zones of mobile phones. Xin's paper focused on facilitating image viewing on devices with limited display sizes.

Nokia [447] conducted a usability evaluation on two mobile Internet sites and identified a demand for search on mobile phones contrary to the initial hypothesis that users would be discouraged by the effort of keying inputs. The research also showed that customers preferred any interface that produced a successful search despite any extra effort required. The Collage Machine [253] is an agent of web recombination. It deconstructs web sites and re-presents them in collage form. It can be taught to bring media of interest to the user on the basis of the user's interactions. The evolving model provides an extremely flexible way of presenting relevant visual information to the user on a variety of devices.

Eye tracking experiments have been conducted to investigate the informativeness of images and the speed of eye tracking interfaces. Arising from this work an eye tracking interface has been developed which rapidly converges to target images. This work is described and discussed in the next sections.

14.3 An Eye Tracking System for Searching Image Databases

The best interfaces are natural and easy to use. They are unobtrusive and provide relevant information quickly and in ways that do not interfere with the task itself. This system has been designed to provide an interface for searching visual digital data in an image database (Fig. 14.1). A pre-computed network of similarities between image regions in an image collection is traversed using eye tracking, always assuming that the users' gaze behaviors yield suitable information about their intentions. It is reasonable to believe that users will look at the objects in which they are interested during a search and this provides the machine with the necessary information to retrieve plausible candidate target images for the user. Retrieved images will contain regions that possess similarity links with the previously gazed regions, and can be presented to the user in a variety of ways.

14.3.1 Eye Tracking Equipment

The Eyegaze System was used in the experiments to generate raw gazepoint location data at the camera field rate of 50 Hz (units of 20ms). A clamp with chin rest provided support for chin and forehead in order to minimize the effects of head movements, although the eye tracker does accommodate head movement of up to 1.5 inches (3.8cm). It was not essential to use the chin rest, but this removed a potential source of error and eliminated any variance in head movement across subjects. The system setup is shown in Fig. 14.2. Calibration is needed to measure the properties of each subject's eye before the start of the experiments. The images were displayed on a 15" LCD Flat Panel Monitor at a resolution of 1024×768 pixels.

In the second experiment, the loading of 25 images in the 5×5 grid display took an average of 110ms on a Pentium IV 2.4GHz PC with 512MB of RAM. In the third experiment, the loading of 16 images in the 4×4 grid display took an average of 100ms on the same system. Gaze data collection and measurement of variables were suspended while the system loaded the next set of images into memory. During this period the display remained unchanged and was updated instantaneously as soon as the contents of the next display had been composed.

The processing of information from the eye tracker is carried out on a 128MB Intel Pentium III system with a video frame grabber board.

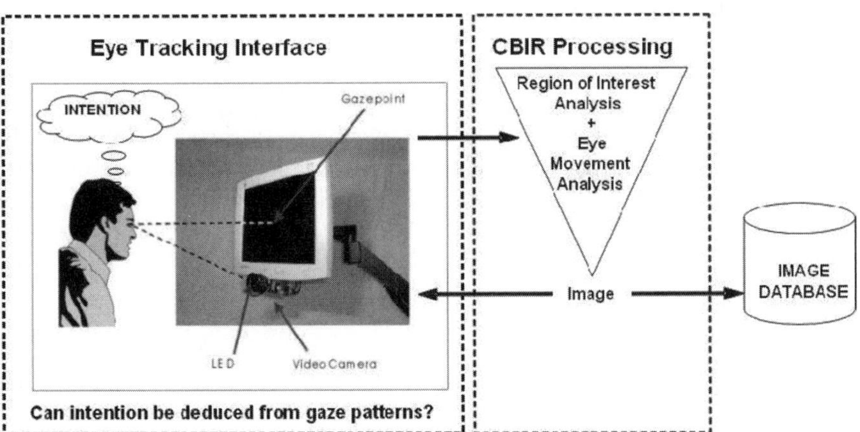

Fig. 14.1. Proposed System Architecture.

Fig. 14.2. Eyegaze Set-up.

14.3.2 Experimental Strategy

A series of experiments was devised to establish the feasibility of an eye gaze driven search mechanism. The first experiment investigated whether users looked more frequently at salient regions as determined by the attention model and whether any other eye behavior was apparent. A negative result would indicate a potential lack of information in gaze data relevant to image retrieval.

The second experiment investigated the effectiveness of an interface controlled by gaze behavior when compared with other interfaces. In this experiment, the speed of operation was compared with that of a mouse interface. Again a negative result would cast doubt on the benefits of using eye movement in such an interface.

Finally the proposed system was implemented with the aim of investigating whether eye tracking can be used to reach target images in fewer steps than by chance. The effect of the intrinsic difficulty of finding specific images and the time allowed for the consideration of successive selections were also investigated.

14.4 Gaze Behavior

It has been shown that attention mechanisms can be directly related to similarity measures [507] and affect the strength of those measures. During a search the human eye is attracted first to salient regions and those regions probably have most impact and contribute most towards recognition and user search strategies. Such regions might include anomalous objects and areas of high contrast. This work makes use of both aspects; first an attention model [507] is used to automatically identify candidate regions of interest for validation against eye tracking data where we would expect most fixations to occur; second an attention-based similarity metric is used to define visual relationships in a database of images for exploration with an eye tracking interface. The visual attention (VA) model used in this work employs an algorithm that assigns high attention scores to pixels where neighboring pixel configurations do not match identical positional arrangements in other randomly selected neighborhoods in the image. This means, for example, that high scores will be associated with anomalous objects, or edges and boundaries, providing those features do not predominate in the image. For display purposes the attention scores for each pixel are displayed as a map using a continuous spectrum of false colors with the scores being marked with a distinctive color or gray level as in Fig. 14.3 and 14.4.

The similarity measure [507] used in this work is not dependent upon intuitively selected features, but instead upon the notion that the similarity of two patterns is determined by the number of features in common. This means that the measure can make use of a virtually unlimited universe of features, rather than a tiny manually selected subset that will be unable to characterize many unseen classes of images. Moreover the features are deliberately selected from image regions that are salient according to the model and, if validated, reflect similarity as judged by a human.

14.4.1 Experiment Design

In this experiment, four participants were presented with a sequence of 6 images for 5 seconds each separated by displays of a blank screen followed for 3 seconds by a central black dot on a white background. Three of the images contained easily discernible subjects and three did not. All participants were encouraged to minimize head movement and were asked to focus on the dot before each image was displayed. The participants were not given any specific task apart from being asked simply to look at the images. All participants had normal or corrected-to-normal vision and had no knowledge of the purpose of the study. Participants included a mix of graduates and administrative staff.

14.4.2 Results

The locations of saccades and fixations performed by the subjects on each of the images were recorded by the eye tracking system. The VA score that corresponded to the pixel at each fixation point was associated with the time of the fixation and plotted for study in units of 20ms as illustrated in Fig. 14.3 and 14.4. It can be seen that there was considerable variation in behavior over the four participants, but all looked at regions with the highest VA scores early in the display period. Table 14.1 shows the total length of time in ms.

spent fixating on regions of high VA score for each participant on each image. This shows that in all cases a large proportion of the 5 seconds exposure time was spent observing the salient regions than the background, if such a salient region was present in the image. Images without obvious subjects did not give such a pronounced result. This confirmed that users' gaze was attracted by regions of high VA score, but also it showed that the eye tracking system was able to gather data related to users' interests and therefore that this information might be available for image retrieval through a suitable interface.

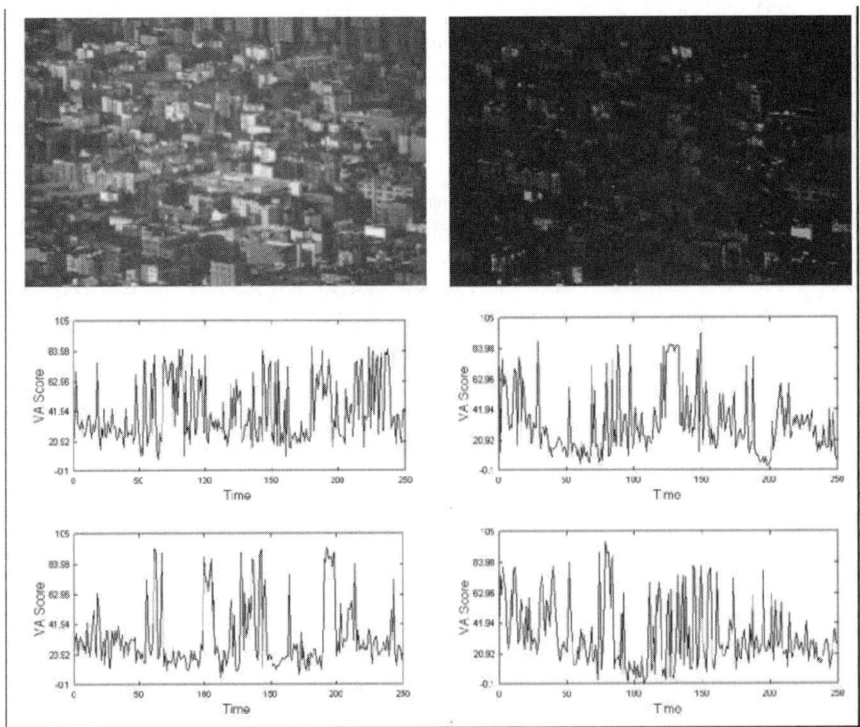

Fig. 14.3. No obvious subject image, VA map and plots.

14.5 Relative Speeds of Eye and Mouse

14.5.1 Experiment Design

A task-oriented experiment was conducted to compare the speed of the eye and the mouse as an input mode to control an interface. Participants were asked

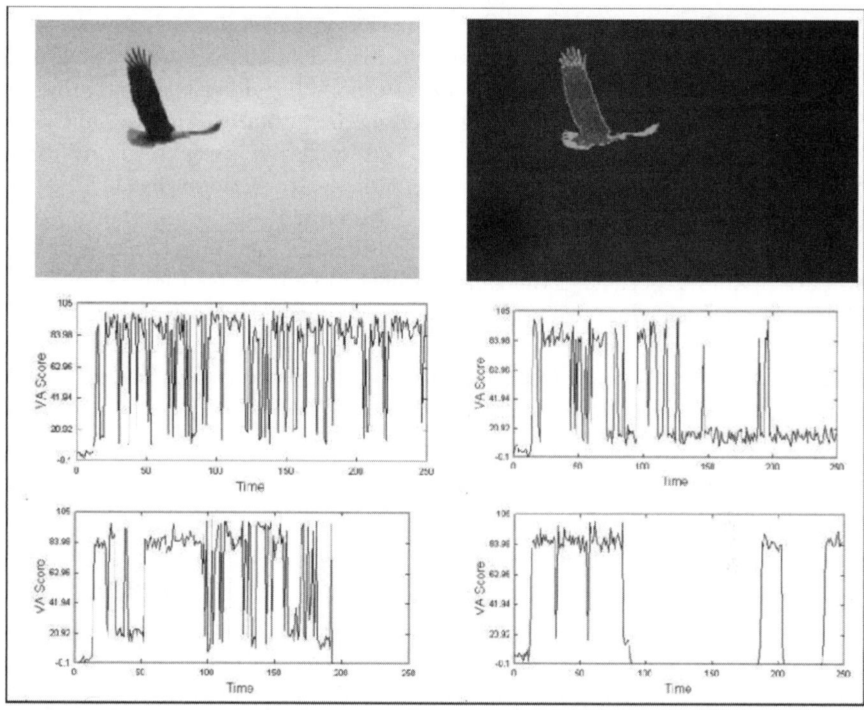

Fig. 14.4. Obvious subject image, VA map and plots.

Table 14.1. Times (ms) spent fixating on regions of high VA score.

Images		Subjects			
		1	2	3	4
Unclear ROI	1	40	60	20	140
	2 (Fig. 14.3)	580	420	500	400
	3	100	0	40	20
Obvious ROI	4	2820	2340	2420	1280
	5 (Fig. 14.4)	3680	1480	2220	1960
	6	4240	980	1620	1240

to find a target image in a series of displays with the aim of comparing the response times of searching and selecting the target image using the computer mouse and the eye under varying conditions.

A total of 12 participants took part in the experiment. Participants included a mix of students and university staff. All participants had normal or corrected-to-normal vision and provided no evidence of color blindness. Participants were asked to locate a target image in each of a series of 50 5×5 arrays of 25 thumbnail images After finding the target, the participants made a selection by clicking with the mouse or fixating on it for longer than 40ms with the eye. The array was then re-displayed with the positions of the images rearranged with the target image appearing two times in every location during the 50 displays. Participants were randomly divided into two groups; the first group used the eye tracking interface first then the mouse, and the second group used the interfaces in the reverse order. This enabled any variance arising from the ordering of the input modes to be identified. Different sequences of the 50 target positions were also employed to remove any confounding effects arising from the ordering of the individual image search tasks. All participants experienced the same sequence of target positions as well as different sequences while using the two input modes. A typical participant in the mouse first group performed four runs: mouse (target sequence 1), eye (target sequence 1), mouse (target sequence 2) and eye (target sequence 3). There was a 1 minute rest between runs.

14.5.2 Results

There was a significant main effect of input, $F(1,10) = 8.72$, $p = 0.015$ with faster response times when the eye was used as an input (2.08sec.) than when the mouse was used (2.43sec.) as shown in Table 14.2 (where F is the F test statistic and p is a rejection probability as used in analysis of variance, ANOVA). The main effect of the order was not significant with $F(1,10) = 0.43$, $p = 0.53$. The main effect of target positions was not significant, $F(1,10) = 0.58$, $p = 0.47$.

Table 14.2. Mean response times for target image identification task.

Order	Target Positions	Input Mode	Response Time	
			Mean	St Dev
Mouse First (6 participants)	Same-sequence	Mouse	2.33	0.51
		Eye	1.79	0.35
	Different-sequence	Mouse	2.43	0.38
		Eye	1.96	0.42
Eye First (6 participants)	Same-sequence	Mouse	2.35	0.82
		Eye	2.29	0.74
	Different-sequence	Mouse	2.59	1.44
		Eye	2.27	0.73

14.6 Image Retrieval

14.6.1 Experiment Design

This experiment was designed to explore the performance of an image retrieval interface driven by an eye tracker. Thirteen participants were asked to find target images in a database and their performance measured.

1000 images were selected from the Corel image library. Images of 127 kilobytes and 256 × 170 pixel sizes were loaded into the database. The categories included boats, landscapes, vehicles, aircrafts, birds, animals, buildings, athletes, people and flowers. Four easy-to-find and four hard-to-find target images were selected for the experiment by using a random gaze strategy to explore the image database. Screens of thumbnail images were displayed as 229 × 155 pixels in 4 × 4 arrays. The initial screen is shown on the left of Fig. 14.5 where the target image that the participant has to find is located at the top left.

Participants began by viewing the initial screen and endeavoring to find the target image among the other 15 images. The display automatically changed when the accumulation of all fixations greater than 80ms on a specific image position exceeded a threshold. In this way the display would change relatively quickly if the participant concentrated on a relevant image, but would take longer if the gaze was less definite. This selected image determined the next 15 thumbnails to be displayed as indicated by the highest of the pre-computed similarity scores for other images in the database. The participant was presented with a succession of such screens until the target image was retrieved whereupon the run halted and the successfully found target was highlighted with a border as shown on the right of Fig. 14.5. Each participant performed 8 runs using both easy-to-find and hard-to-find images. The maximum number of screen changes was limited to 26.

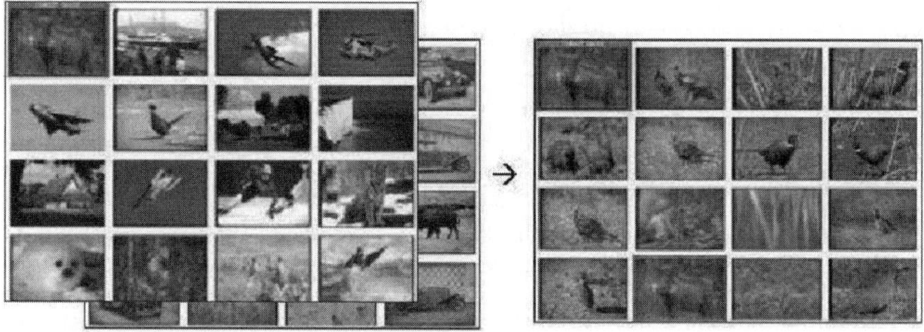

Fig. 14.5. Initial screen leading to final screen with retrieved target.

Two fixation cumulative thresholds of 400ms and 800ms were employed as a factor in the experiment. Another factor was introduced to allow the display to include either one or no randomly retrieved images. It was thought that this would reduce the likelihood of displays repeating due to occasional incorrect similarity values. In this case one of the images was retrieved randomly from the database ("Randomly-retrieved" = 1), rather than on the basis of similarity with the previously selected image. A random gaze generation strategy in which images in each screen are selected randomly was then simulated for comparison with selection by gaze.

14.6.2 Results

As measures of performance the number of steps to target, the time to target ($F1$), and the number of fixations ($F2$) of 80ms and above were monitored and recorded during the experiment (Table 14.3). The results of the ANOVA performed on the steps to target revealed a significant main effect of image type, $F(1, 12) = 23.90$, $p < 0.0004$ with fewer steps to target for easy-to-find images (14 steps) than the hard-to-find images (22 steps). The main effect of the fixation threshold was not significant with $F(1, 12) = 1.50$, $p < 0.25$. The main effect of randomly-retrieved was also not significant, $F(1, 12) = 0.17$, $p < 0.69$. The analysis of the time to target produced similar results to the analysis of the number of fixations. There was a significant main effect of image type, $F1(1, 12) = 24.11$, $p < 0.0004$, $F2(1, 12) = 21.93$, $p < 0.0005$, with shorter time to target and fewer fixations for easy-to-find images (40.5sec. and 125 fixations) than the hard-to-find images (71.3sec. and 229 fixations). The main effect of the fixation threshold was also similarly significant with $F1(1, 12) = 18.27$, $p < 0.001$ and $F2(1, 12) = 16.09$, $p < 0.002$. The main effect of randomly-retrieved was not significant, $F1(1, 12) = 1.49$, $p < 0.25$ and $F2(1, 12) = 0.76$, $p < 0.40$.

Table 14.3. Analysis of Human Eye Behavior on the Interface (rounded-off mean figures).

Image Type	Fixation Threshold	Randomly-retrieved	A	B	C	D
Easy-to-find	400ms	0	38.5%	14	34.9	99
		1	53.8%	18	36.8	109
	800ms	0	38.5%	14	55.8	153
		1	15.4%	11	51.3	140
Hard-to-find	400ms	0	69.2%	23	52.7	166
		1	84.6%	23	50.0	167
	800ms	0	92.3%	24	105.0	327
		1	69.2%	19	83.5	258

[A]Target not found (frequency); [B]Steps to target; [C]Time to Target; [D]Fixation numbers.

The same treatment combinations experienced by all participants were applied to the random gaze generation tool to obtain steps to target under same conditions (Table 14.4). In summary, the results of the ANOVA revealed a main effect of the selection mode, $F(2, 23) = 3.81$, $p < 0.037$, with fewer steps to target when the eye gaze is used (18 steps) than when random selection is used (22 steps). There was also a main effect of image type, $F(2, 23) = 28.95$, $p < 0.00001$ with fewer steps to target for easy-to-find images (16 steps) than the hard-to-find images (24 steps). Further analysis of simple main effect revealed that there was a significant difference between the modes for the hard-to-find images, $F(2,23) = 3.76$, $p < 0.039$, as opposed to the easy-to-find images, $F(2,23) = 2.02$, $p < 0.16$.

Table 14.4. Comparison of Eye and Random Selection (rounded-off mean figures).

Selection Mode	Image Type	Randomly-retrieved	A	B
Eye gaze	Easy-to-find	0	38.5%	14
		1	34.6%	15
	Hard-to-find	0	80.8%	23
		1	76.9%	21
Random selection	Easy-to-find	0	57.7%	20
		1	38.5%	16
	Hard-to-find	0	96.2%	25
		1	92.3%	26

[A]Target not found (frequency); [B]Steps to target;

14.7 Discussion

The first experiment tested whether users looked at regions declared salient by the visual attention model. The results showed that this was the case for the images and participants involved, but more images and a larger number of participants would be necessary to obtain statistical significance. This result was also indicative that users fixate on foreground material in images and that this behavior may be employed to drive a prototype search interface.

The second experiment went further to explore the speeds of visual processing involved in an image target identification task when compared with a conventional input device such as a mouse. The 25 stimuli presented to each participant and the predetermined choice of image target produced a difficult task and the experiment imposed a high cognitive load. The participant had to search for the target and then make a selection. Our results indicated slower mouse responses and was supported by the significant main effect of input ($p = 0.015$), with the eye interface having faster response times than the mouse interfaces, and was consistent with Ware and Mikaelian's conclusions [562]. When using the mouse the participant had to spend time locating both the cursor and the item to be selected, and then use the mouse to move the cursor to the item. On the other hand, the eye tracker interface was quicker because only the selected item needed to be located. However, the speed difference was not just dependent on extra mouse movement because the eye tracker required the user to fixate on the target for longer than 40ms before a screen change.

Finally, in the image retrieval experiment, the participants using the eye tracking interface found the target in fewer steps than an automated random gaze strategy ($p < 0.037$) and the analysis of the simple effect attributed the significant difference to the hard-to-find images. This meant that the probability of finding the hard-to-find images was significantly increased due to human cognitive abilities, as opposed to the indiscriminate selection by the simulated random gaze strategy using the same similarity information. The main effect of the fixation threshold was not significant which indicates that there is scope for using smaller thresholds than 400ms. Future experiments if successful, would indicate that unconscious pre-attentive vision may be playing a significant part in visual search. Additional discussion and results can be found in [384, 385, 243, 386].

14.8 Conclusions and Future Directions

An eye controlled interface can provide a more natural mode of retrieval as it requires a minimum of manual effort and cognitive load, and almost unconscious operation. It has been shown that the eye is attracted to image regions that are predicted to be salient by the attention model and that the eye tracking system was able to gather data related to users' interests. Secondly the eye tracking interface yielded a significantly better speed performance than the mouse in a target location task. In an image retrieval task users were able to successfully navigate their way to target images in a database using only eye gaze, with significantly better performance than randomly generated selections.

There is much development to be carried out before eye trackers can become as pervasive as keyboards and mice. The accuracy, cost and usability of equipment must improve before laboratory results can be reproduced on PCs, laptops, and even PDAs. We might expect cheap eye trackers to emerge in the games market where "look and shoot" would give faster gratification than painful button pressing or joystick pushing. Small cameras embedded in monitors and laptop lids or glasses would be obvious locations for the cheaper devices. Gaze contingent displays have great potential where additional information may be displayed dependent on eye movement. For example, larger scale maps may be offered at the focus of attention or additional details supplied related to an object being studied. Eye behavior may also be used to drive PTZ cameras in ways that enable people to "see" their way around remote locations. Eye trackers are already a great asset to the disabled, but only as an awkward and costly replacement for existing devices, and not as a computer interface to be used just as effectively as an able-bodied person. Further reading on eye tracking applications may be found in Duchowski [144].

The results reported here indicate that eye trackers have the potential for eliciting human intentions extremely rapidly and may be applied to certain visual search tasks. It seems reasonable that reducing costs and advancing camera technology will mean that eye trackers will appear in many more applications within the next few years.

15

User Interaction for Mobile Devices

Sanni Siltanen[1], Charles Woodward[1], Seppo Valli[1], Petri Honkamaa[1], and Andreas Rauber[2]

[1] VTT Technical Research Centre of Finland
[2] Institute of Software Technology and Interactive Systems

Smart phones have the potential to become the default physical user interface for ubiquitous mobile multimedia computing applications [40]. However, the conventional tiny keypad of a mobile phone is unsuitable for many situations; for example, typing a simple URL like http://www.google.com/ might require over 70 key presses. The fast development of mobile devices provides new possibilities for user interaction methods. Accessing large amounts of multimedia information requires specialized methods for searching and data mining. Besides direct interaction with keyboard, keypad, joystick, touchscreen or even speech recognition, interaction with mobile devices can be enhanced by analyzing the location or motion of the device. Furthermore, it is possible to fine tune the location information with the device's direction and orientation information using visual markers or various sensors. In addition, the movement of the device can be analyzed using accelerometers or analyzing optical flow of the attached camera. Augmented reality is a related technology, providing new interaction possibilities with a visual link between physical and virtual worlds.

15.1 Evolution of Mobile Multimedia

Multimedia applications have existed as long as there have been personal computers supporting the playback of audiovisual (AV) content. Especially after PCs were equipped with a network access for downloading content, the development of multimedia applications has been very rapid. After the emergence of the Internet and the world-wide-web, multimedia content has evolved towards more and more rich content including various kinds of textual, aural, and visual content.

Multimedia content includes, e.g., images, audio, music, video, films, news, documentaries, advertisements. The application types can be classified in two main categories, namely local and networked/streamed applications. PC games are a typical example of local applications, whereas video conferencing,

P. Maragos et al. (eds.), *Multimodal Processing and Interaction*,
DOI: 10.1007/978-0-387-76316-3_15,

e-commerce, e-learning, IP-telephony and IP-TV are examples of streaming applications. Various data formats and standards are being used for multimedia content, e.g., MP3 for music, MPEG4 for video, and various W3C specifications for web content.

During the time mobile phones have been on the market, various PC based applications have been ported into mobile platform, as far as it has been technically feasible. In recent years, the processing power, amount of memory, multimedia capabilities, and access speeds of mobile phones have approached that of PCs, which has made this transition easier and faster. Thus, the typical office applications, i.e., email, calendar, document viewers, editors, etc. have successfully been ported to mobile environment. Another important category are web applications, based on new mobile browsers and the increased bandwidth available for wireless data transmission.

In addition, there are several mobile applications which take the characteristics of a mobile terminal and user into account. A good example of this is SMS, which has not a direct predecessor in the PC environment. Following SMS, ring-tone downloads and image screen-savers have been surprise successes for mobile phones. As in the PC environment, local applications have been easier to implement on mobile devices, although the development goes towards real-time streaming applications.

As the display and keyboard of a mobile phone are small, mobile multimedia applications meet particular challenges for the supported content types, usability and interaction. The interaction in mobile applications has long been based on miniature versions of a mouse, joystick, and keyboard. Today, the mobile phone's camera is also increasingly used for interaction, e.g., for pointing and tracking (some mobile phones even provide an integrated accelerometer that can be used for the same purpose).

A specific opportunity in mobile applications, particularly challenged by usability issues, is providing authoring and editing functionalities for multimedia content, e.g., for either downloaded or user generated video clips. Recently, the number of location and community based mobile applications has been rapidly rising, supported for example by the integration of mobile phones with a camera and a locationing device (GPS).

A comprehensive collection of various mobile multimedia related research activities is given in [221].

15.2 Mobile Multimedia Terminals

The prerequisites for mobile multimedia solutions are the availability of: (i) suitable, e.g., powerful enough mobile terminals, (ii) intelligent, fast and reliable software, and (iii) applicable networks, i.e., modes for communication. Considerable amount of memory and computational power is required especially for capturing and processing (e.g., compressing) of images or video, displaying of 3D graphics, as well as for managing the transmission and connectivity, e.g., protocols and algorithms to cope with roaming.

Today, mobile phones, PDAs (Personal Digital Assistant) and other mobile devices are already quite capable to see, hear and sense the surrounding environment by various means. Mobile phones and other hand-held devices are advancing towards powerful communicators with multiple network access (GSM/GPRS, 3G, WLAN, Bluetooth), multimedia capabilities (digital cameras, high-resolution color displays, MMS), open platforms for applications (Java, Symbian, etc.) as well as for Internet connectivity.

The classification between the devices is becoming vague as they are providing more and more common features; for example PDAs providing in-built mobile network access and camera, and mobile phones providing larger displays and more advanced user interaction mechanisms, e.g., keyboards and input pens. Therefore we can think that in the future the different mobile device categories will merge into a *smart mobile terminal* containing all the needed functionality.

Miniaturization of tablet PCs has led to a new class of devices, nowadays called Ultra Mobile PCs (UMPC). As example of UMPCs, the recent Sony Vaio UX models is equipped with a slide-in keyboard, two built-in cameras, wireless Bluetooth, WLAN and 3G connectivity. Also, PDAs are available in a variety of models, with various operating systems, with adequate processing power, battery life, and display capabilities for mobile multimedia.

The latest smart phones, e.g., Nokia N95 and E90, have more processing power and even better 3D graphics support than super computers used to have ten or fifteen years ago. Among the different manufacturers, Samsung has been particularly active to provide the phones with new integrated functionality, such as high accuracy cameras, accelerometers and other sensors. Apple iPhone is leading the way for new interaction methods on mobile phones, with multi-touch screens and 3D visual browsing techniques.

15.3 Mobile Displays

The screens of hand held devices are obviously the most common displays for mobile multimedia applications; however there are also other options available. Besides wearable devices such as video glasses, also projector displays are developed as display extensions for mobile devices [338].

The application specifies which features are critical and the application type defines the best display type for it. On mobile phones factors, such as the small display size and resolution have to be accounted for, while on PDA and UMPC devices the screen brightness and power consumption can be more critical factors. Handheld mobile devices are generally preferred if the task does not require hands-free operation or immersive display; otherwise, head mounted or projected displays can be a better choice [64].

15.3.1 Stereo Displays

Conventional displays are monographic, but various methods are available to upgrade even standard displays to reproduce stereographic view. The standard methods can be divided into two groups named active and passive stereo. Both active and passive stereo require that the user wears special glasses meant for this purpose. With active stereo the display alternates the image meant for left and right eyes rapidly so the shutter glasses show the right image for each eye. With passive stereo, both images are shown at the same time and the glasses filter the correct image for each eye, e.g., red-green-glasses.

The third group of stereographic displays are called autostereoscopic displays that do not require any separate glasses to be worn. They usually show the left and right images for separate viewing segments, either by tracking where the viewer is located or just by offering several discrete viewing segments. Samsung has already demonstrated such stereo displays on smart phones. The primary application for stereo displays on camera phones would be mobile 3D games.

At the software level, StereoGames [576] is a solution based on anaglyph technology to enable changing originally monographic 3D applications to stereo. Besides PCs and game consoles, StereoGames works also for mobile devices like mobile phones, and it can be applied to create stereo effect for both passive and active as well as autostereoscopic displays.

15.3.2 Head Mounted Displays

Head mounted displays (HMDs) are wearable display devices ranging from helmets providing deep immersion and full field-of-view, down to miniaturized data glasses or "goggles". There are two types of HMDs, based either on video or optical see-through approach [64].

The most popular multimedia application for HMDs is watching movies on portable MP3 and DVD players. Other uses for HMDs are found in mobile games (using video glasses), and in augmented reality (using either video or optical see-through approach). Recently one of the leading HMD display companies MicroOptical changed name to MyVu and is now providing video glasses for the iPod [352].

Some visionaries and researchers are developing concepts and prototypes where the reproduced image is not shown on any display; instead the image is drawn directly to the user's retina. Thus, the technology is called virtual retinal display (VRD). However, commercial VRD products are not yet available.

15.4 Interaction Modalities

According to Foley et al. [167], input devices can be categorized by the graphics subtasks they can perform. Those tasks are: position, orient, select, path, quantify and text entry. The ability to perform these tasks and the ability to interact with the environment are essential for future ubiquitous multimedia devices. In the following, we explore various interaction modalities, starting from various methods available for text entry, up to a discussion on motion estimation for gestural interaction on camera phones.

15.4.1 Text Entry: Keyboards, Strokes and Dynamic Selection

Text entry methods with mobile devices can be divided broadly into following categories: keyboards, gestural alphabets and dynamic selection techniques. Next, we describe briefly some popular text entry methods. More detailed summaries can be found in [561, 315].

Currently the most common input method with a 12-key telephone keypad is multitap, where the user presses each key one or more times to write each letter. The 12-key input can be optimized by adding language knowledge to the system. One example is the T9 solution licensed by many phone manufacturers [109]. In T9, the keys are pressed only once for each letter and the linguistic model predicts the most probable word for the key sequence.

Touchscreen displays, e.g., on PDAs and some multimedia phones, provide the option of a screen keyboard. Some other devices, e.g. ultra mobile PCs, provide a larger keyboard that is normally hidden but can be slid or flipped out when needed. Alternatively, a full size keyboard can be a separate accessory connected using, e.g., Bluetooth. A novel approach for fitting a full QWERTY keyboard on a small device is to project the keyboard on a table with a laser beam and recognize the keyboard taps optically [309].

Keyboards and screen keyboards may also be rearranged, either to fit into smaller space or to provide faster interaction. The number of keys can be reduced either by allowing toggle operations between different letter sets, or by using key-combinations, a.k.a. chords. A good example of reduced key set is half-QWERTY keyboard which allows writing speeds up to 73% compared to writing with a full keyboard [315]. Another example is the Twiddler chord keyboard [110] which is particularly popular with wearable computing researchers.

Free-form handwriting recognition is a widely available, though not very reliable text entry method on PDA devices. An alternative to normal handwriting is the Graffiti system on Palm devices, in which each letter is written using a single stroke that is similar enough with normal hand-written characters. Another approach for gesture based writing is Quikwriting introduced in 1998. It is based on 3x3 grid where the strokes are started and ended in the center; shortest strokes need to visit only one grid position while more infrequent letters need to make a curve through several grid positions [397].

In dynamic selection techniques, the shown alphabet is changed dynamically. For example, in FOCL (Fluctuating Optimal Character Layout), the choices for the most probable next letters are always shown near the center [51]. In Dasher [561], the possible first letters are shown in a column of boxes where the box sizes reflect the letter frequency; within each of these boxes the possible next letters are presented in a similar box column, and typing is performed by moving a pointer to continuously zoom deeper and deeper in the nested boxes.

15.4.2 Joysticks

Besides the traditional keyboard or keypad, current mobile devices provide various other ways for direct interaction including joystick, trackball, touchpad, and camera. Practically all mobile phones today include four- or eight-direction navigation joysticks. Usually these navigation buttons have only binary resolution but there has also been some research using isometric joysticks [489].

15.4.3 Multi-Touch Screens

Many recent mobile devices provide a touchscreen with a natural pointing and drawing user interface. Apple has developed this idea further with the iPhone by providing a multi-touch interface. The iPhone interface is based on a capacitive touch panel and it can recognize several gestures with one or multiple touch points. The gestures are used creatively in applications for example for scaling photos, zooming in maps or for flipping through music albums or photos. The iPhone incorporates also an intelligent touchscreen keyboard that compensates the small keyboard key-size by using dictionary for favoring the more probable keys and correcting spelling mistakes on the run.

Multi-touch interfaces are currently a hot research topic as they are believed to provide more natural and more versatile interaction possibilities compared to single-touch displays. In the "non-mobile" world, interesting interaction possibilities have been presented for example by Jeff Han [195]. Also Microsoft is releasing a commercial Microsoft Surface product based on multi-touch [337]. Besides multi-touch, the upcoming Microsoft surface promises also a natural interaction with mobile devices. One presented example application includes moving photographs from your digital camera into your cell phone. In the example, this is done just by placing both devices on the multi-touch surface and dragging the photos between them.

15.4.4 Haptic Systems and Tactile Feedback

Haptic systems often refer to virtual reality input/output devices where the user can not only manipulate virtual objects directly, but also gain tactile feedback of how the virtual object feels like. With mobile devices, the most common haptic feedback is given using vibration actuator common in many phone models. This can be used for example to produce a "poor man's force feedback" in mobile games.

Several more advanced haptic systems have been presented, though less suitable for mobile use. Most typically the sense of touch is created by using mechanical or pneumatic construction, e.g., [475]. Some other methods do not restrict the motion of the user's fingers and hands, but instead they generate vibrations, e.g., using array of pins against fingertip.

15.4.5 Gesture Based Interaction

Physical manipulation of the handheld device is an integral part of an embodied user interface [162]. This may involve, e.g., moving or shaking the device, leading to interaction paradigms such as "squeeze me, hold me, tilt me" [198]. Gestures by tilting or moving the device may be used in positioning and pointing tasks or to indicate commands. For example, the user could scroll a menu on the phone's display by tilting the phone up- and downwards, select the command by shaking the phone to the left, and get to previous menu by shaking to the right.

Various sensing techniques already exist for mobile interaction, including accelerometers, touch sensors, proximity sensors, and pressure or squeezing sensors [211, 162]. In addition, the orientation of the mobile device can be analyzed in relation to earth gravity using tilt sensors, or in relation to earth magnetic field using compass. However, such sensors are seldom available as standard components on phones or other mobile devices; instead they have to be attached to the device as bulky accessories, which ordinary users have seldom available. Although this situation may change in the future (accelerometers are already integrated in some mobile phones), the most common "sensing" accessory on smart phones for the next few years will still be the camera.

15.4.6 Methods for Camera Motion Estimation

Solutions using camera image based tracking span from simple motion tracking implementations up to 3D feature tracking. The most sophisticated feature detection and tracking algorithms are able to derive 3D coordinates of the physical world from the camera view, e.g., SLAM (Simultaneous Localization and Mapping) [124]. In theory, the camera's optical flow gives enough information for 3D reconstruction of the scene and the 6 degrees-of-freedom motion path within that scene [199].

For interaction purposes, the global optical flow motion in the mobile device's camera view can be used to approximate the device's movement. Motion estimation is typically implemented by searching image blocks in various displacements within the previous image frame. As an exhaustive search is usually too tedious, the motion search process typically has to be simplified on mobile devices.

For example, the TinyMotion algorithm [558] reduces the computation complexity by using grid sampling (a multi-resolution sampling technique) for the input image before making full-search block matching algorithm. The

Projection Shift Analysis (PSA) [142] approximates 2D motion by using horizontal and vertical projection buffers of the camera image instead of image blocks.

The complexity can be reduced by tracking only "easy-to-track" features of the image. For example, Hannuksela et al. [196] propose using pixels having maximum squared differences compared to adjacent pixels. Another common feature selection method is to track corner features in the image, which in turn are found by Harris or SUSAN corner detection algorithms, or by eigenvalue methods [482].

Usually for all vision based motion or feature detection methods, horizontal and vertical camera movements are much easier to analyze than motion in the camera's depth direction; the reason being that there is not much change in the image when the camera is moved back or forth. Modern twin camera phones offer a convenient solution to partly overcome this problem: depth motion can be analyzed from the camera facing the user, having the user's face as a close target for depth comparisons.

In order to solve the motion detection problem accurately, flexibly and fast enough, a hybrid method, i.e., combination of different algorithms and sensors, is often required. A typical hybrid solution is to apply vision based camera tracking while the camera is relatively stationary, and accelerometers during fast camera movement.

15.4.7 Further Interaction Modalities

Instead of keyboard, touchpad, joystick or gestures, mobile interaction may be based also on gaze tracking, or even on user's breath [223]. These more exotic ways of interacting are suitable especially for disabled users. Spoken dialogue and multimodal interfaces are also important modes of text entry for mobile phones.

15.5 Context Aware Applications

15.5.1 Mobile Context Categories

Research for context-aware mobile applications has been reported since the early '90s. Context can be divided into four categories: computing context, user context, physical context and time context [466]. Computing context contains, e.g., network connectivity, communication bandwidth and nearby computing resources. User context includes information like user's preferences, current location and nearby people. Physical context describes physical conditions like lighting, noise levels, and temperature. Time context defines the date and time based information. Besides using the current context information, the context history is also useful for some applications. Further, context-aware applications may actively adapt their behavior based on the discovered context (active context), or leave the decision on its use to the user (passive context) [92]. Context information may be used in various ways. For example, the application font size can be made larger when the user is walking, and the mobile phone ring volume and vibrate option may be adjusted depending on the situation. One important application area for context aware services is giving guidance for the user. The location information may be used, e.g., to inform the user about nearby services, suggest routes or give more information about observed attractions. The museum visitors may be given personalized TV-like presentations depending on their location, their facing direction, device orientation and their interests during the visit [439].

Various other concepts, definitions and classifications for context exist. Next, in Section 15.5.2 we consider context aware interaction with spatially bound information. Especially, we discuss physical browsing, where the context is determined using nearby electronic or visual tags. For more thorough surveys on context-aware services see [92].

15.5.2 Spatial Information and Interaction: Physical Browsing

Spatial information consists of the physical location, orientation, and the information associated (or bound) to the respective visual view. The location can be derived either manually, by using satellites (GPS, Galileo), mobile network positioning, local network (WLAN) based methods, or short-range methods (Bluetooth, RFID , NFC , etc.). More advanced functionality can be built when taking also orientation (viewing direction) into consideration; the orientation may be derived, e.g., by electronic compasses or cameras.

In applications using spatially bound information, means are needed to search for, discover, and browse information in the environment. This is generally referred to as physical browsing, which also includes optical/camera based methods. In physical browsing, tags are typically used to provide the user with access points for available information or services. A variety of tag types are used: visual tags (e.g., barcodes and matrix codes), RFID tags (Radio Frequency Identifier), NFC (Near Field Communication) tags, Bluetooth tags, Infrared tags, etc. [18]. RFID/NFC tags typically communicate over relatively short distances.

Usually electronic tags are indicated by some visual sign as well. Pointing is perhaps the most natural user interface, and therefore the basic user paradigm in physical browsing. Children use pointing inherently in all cultures even before learning to speak. Remote controllers for home appliances are typical pointing devices at home. In addition to "point me", other user paradigms introduced in physical browsing are "sweep me", and "touch me" [406].

When noticing an access point, the user typically points at the tag with his/her mobile device to see the available information and/or make the desired action. A tag itself, either electronic or visual, may contain encoded/stored information and metadata telling what to do with the information, e.g., this is a phone number, make a phone call; this is a web address, start browser.

The user may for example establish a phone call just by pointing at a tag attached to the picture of a person [491]. A tag-based user interface can also be built to support multimodal interactions [252].

A further benefit of visual tags is that they can be used to derive additional information about the movements of the camera, including tilt, rotation, and distance in relation to the tag. Thus using visual tags for context-aware mobile applications can support free augmentation of the physical environment with spatially bound information, including efficient functionality for information detection, interaction, authoring and sharing [190].

Drag-and-drop is a paradigm where the user clicks a virtual object and drags it to different location or to another virtual object. Related to the drag-and-drop concept is the term hyper-dragging, where the user can transfer information from one computer to another (or from a mobile device to a computer), by only knowing the physical relationship between them [435].

15.6 Mobile Augmented Reality

Augmented reality (AR) is a relatively new concept within computer graphics and video processing research, yet with high potential of becoming an integral part of future mobile multimedia interfaces and services. The 2007 MIT Technology Review [241] lists mobile augmented reality (MAR) as one of the ten technologies "most likely to alter industries, fields of research, and even the way we live".

Basically, augmented reality means superimposing digital objects into the user's view of the environment [36]. The real world and a totally virtual representation are the two ends of the Mixed Reality (MR) continuum [339]; augmented reality is situated in the middle of this continuum. Besides 3D presentations, simple graphics elements such as augmented text and symbols can be applied for providing guidelines and additional information to the physical world. Instead of static content on the mobile terminal, in the future, augmented content will be increasingly provided by ubiquitous connections to Internet and local services.

The potential of wearable augmented reality has been investigated at the early stages of AR research, but until recently wearable AR systems have often been too heavy and resource demanding for practical applications. Today, the rapid development of mobile devices has lead to small devices with enough processing capacity, 3D graphics support, high resolution displays, built-in cameras and long lasting batteries to enable light-weight mobile AR systems [194]. Some examples of how tablet PCs, UMPCs, PDAs and camera phones have been successfully used in various mobile AR applications are provided by [390, 214, 207, 441]. Fig. 15.1 shows a lightweight augmented reality system [213] running on camera phone.

The most challenging task for mobile augmented reality is tracking, i.e., accurate and fast mapping of coordinates between physical and 3D virtual

Fig. 15.1. Example of augmented reality on mobile phone: virtual sofa in real environment.

worlds. The mapping is most typically done using information acquired with the mobile device's video camera. Tracking with stationary AR applications is most typically based on using visual markers; this approach can be used also with camera phones as long as the user does not move around too much [207, 441]. However, markers are generally too restrictive for mobile applications and markerless solutions are called for.

Markerless augmented reality is typically based on 3D feature tracking, using methods such as mentioned in Section 15.4.6. Additionally, the augmenting system has to be initialized with some a priori information of the view, for example, in the form of visual markers or beacons, or by having a virtual model of the scene as reference. The augmentation can also be simplified by making the process semi-automatic; using manual interaction in tasks that would be complex to automate but are easy for the user and accurate enough for the application.

Another approach for simplifying the augmenting task is to use just still images for augmenting. This enables for example the use of more sophisticated 3D mapping/tracking algorithms as speed is not a critical factor; also if required some parts of the computation and/or rendering can then be offloaded to a server machine. In many applications, the still image principle works actually more ergonomically than keeping the augmented information in real time video view. In addition, still images provide better image resolution and thus improved accuracy for augmented reality.

A good introduction to augmented reality interaction on camera phones is provided by Henrysson et al. [207]. They describe and compare several marker-based methods for interactive 3D object manipulation, e.g., selection, translation and rotation. Evaluation of markerless augmented reality interaction on mobile phones is an important topic for future research.

Different users have different preferences regarding how to interact with an augmented reality system. For example, a demo system to test multimodal user interface in AR aided assembly task is presented by [490]. This system has three input modalities (traditional keyboard, speech and gesture control) and visual feedback (output) modality. Test users favored a multimodal input interface and desired more feedback on the output side.

15.7 Example Applications

The following sections give examples of some new generation mobile multimedia applications. Gesture based interaction is discussed in Section 15.7.1, and outdoors augmented reality applications in Section 15.7.2. Section 15.7.3 presents an application of map-based music content interfaces.

15.7.1 Gesture Based Applications

SymBall [193] is a virtual table tennis game on camera phones, using the phone's movement as the sole interaction method to control the game. The movement of the phone is detected using the optical flow of the camera, which is transformed to the movement of the virtual racket in the game. The user can adjust sounds, ball speed, racket shape, etc. for the game. The game can be played in single player mode against "the wall/machine" or against another player over Bluetooth connection. The implementation has also been extended to use GPRS/3G connections. Furthermore, the game also exists as stereo version; see Fig. 15.2.

Gesture based interfaces can also be used to control external devices, for example using Bluetooth connection with mobile phones. The Phonecam-based sweep technique [41] is used to interact with large displays, making the phone act as optical mouse. Similarly, the PhoneMouse software [552] makes the camera phone work as an optical mouse for a PC: moving the phone in the air moves the cursor on PC screen, while the phone keys simulate mouse buttons and launch actions such drawing. See Fig. 15.3.

Viewing of panoramic images is a further example of multimedia applications that can be implemented intuitively based on the camera's motion detection: turning the camera phone around shows views in the panorama image accordingly. Applications for this include presentations of real estate and apartments, display of public places and related information, as well as viewing of 3D virtual architectural models of past and future.

15.7.2 Outdoors Augmented Reality

One of the earliest mobile AR implementations is the Tinmith backpack system, which since its introduction in 1998 has undergone various developments

Fig. 15.2. SymBall virtual table tennis game on camera phones[193], using StereoGames software [576] to create depth illusion.

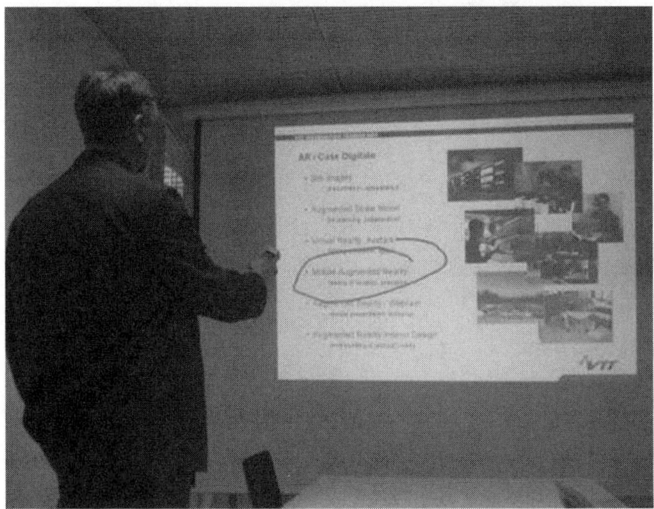

Fig. 15.3. Using PhoneMouse [552] to annotate a Powerpoint presentation over Bluetooth connection.

in both performance and size [374]. Tinmith includes various hardware devices such as immersive HMD display, GPS locationing, compass and gyrometer. As a special feature, Tinmth provides also the possibility for user interaction with the augmented data using data gloves. A well-known application example with the Tinmith system is mobile real-life implementation of the ARQuake game.

In a more recent architectural application, AROnSite [214], the virtual building's scale and orientation are deduced automatically based on its placement in Google Earth and the user's GPS coordinates. However the actual placement to the scene is done interactively by visually aligning the virtual object to the scenery. After the manual initialization, the camera's optical flow is analyzed to keep the augmented object in place. See Fig. 15.4.

Fig. 15.4. Virtual building added to Google Earth, and visualized on site with a mobile device using AROnsite [214].

An impressive hybrid tracking approach for outdoor mobile augmented reality is presented by Reitmayr et al. [434]. Their approach uses an edge-based tracker for matching the scenery with a coarse textured 3D model of the existing environment. Very good accuracy and robustness is obtained by using an additional sensor pack providing gyroscopic measurements and 3D magnetic field vector.

On mobile phones, Nokia has developed the MARA prototype system for sensor based mobile augmented reality [371]. The system consists of Nokia S60 platform phone and attached external sensor box with accelerometer, tilt compensated compass and GPS providing position and orientation information to the phone via Bluetooth connection. The application augments the camera view with graphics and text in real time, annotating the user's surroundings with location-based Internet content, e.g., tourist information.

15.7.3 Map-Based Audio Retrieval Applications

Since digital music collections are growing constantly, especially on mobile devices, it is getting more and more important to provide easy and intuitive access to these collections. Today it is possible to have thousands of songs on mobile devices but we still miss more adequate ways of accessing music than merely scrolling through directories or hierarchical structures. A possible solution to this is to use a *music map*.

To create *music maps*, first of all a feature extraction algorithm is used, in order to automatically extract semantic descriptors from the audio, which form the basis of determining similarities between pieces of music. Afterward, different clustering algorithms, e.g., a Self-Organizing Map, can be applied to the extracted feature vectors, in order to create a representation of a music collection on a map. The basic idea of clustering is the identification of coherent sub-groups of similar instances, i.e., pieces of audio. As a consequence, pieces of music will be represented on the resulting map and grouped according to acoustic similarity.

User interfaces for music based on the SOM have been researched by several teams, resulting in miscellaneous applications on the desktop [343, 265]. For mobile devices, however, interfaces have to fulfill special requirements. In addition to the size of the display itself, input possibilities for mobile devices are heavily restricted. The most difficult question, however, is how to adequately display and provide access to a large-scale dataset using these minimal interface capabilities.

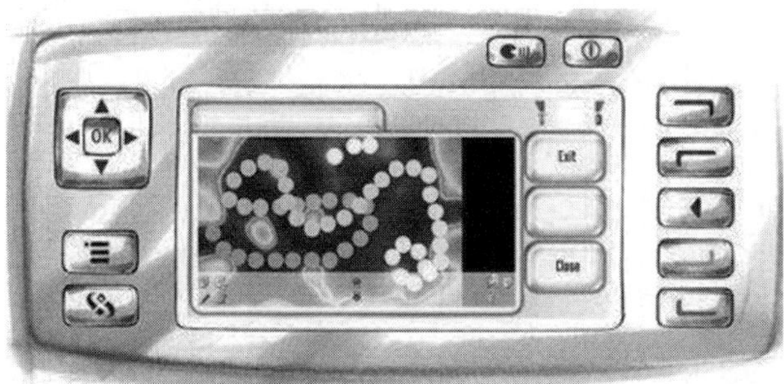

Fig. 15.5. The PocketSOM application running on a Nokia 7710 emulator.

PocketSOM is a light-weight version of the *PlaySOM* application (an overview of which is given in Section 11.2), which provides a simple but intuitive interface. The interface presents a graphical landscape with the metaphor of islands in the sea (*"Islands of Music"*). The islands represent the clusters, where music which is acoustically very similar (from the perspective of the features extracted from it) has been aggregated together. In the sea in-between the islands, music that is less strongly represented can be found, with smooth transitions in terms of genre or style from one cluster (island) to another. These music maps are generated by the *PlaySOM* application and then exported to the *PocketSOM* on the mobile device.

PocketSOM's functionality focuses on the interaction of the user with the music map to directly retrieve music and create playlists. Using the touch-screen the user can draw a path on the map, which will result in a playlist. By drawing a path from one island (cluster) to another, smooth transitions from one musical style (or genre) to another can be generated. The resulting playlist is presented to the user who can refine it by re-sorting or deleting titles, and then play it back in different ways: The music can be instantly played on the device with an audio player (if the music is stored on the device) or streamed via an Internet connection from a remote server. Alternatively, the playlist can be also exported, and opened later with a player either locally or on another device. As another possibility, PocketSOM can be used also as a remote control by sending the playlist to a player on another device, e.g., having a PC with the entire music collection playing it back.

As a conclusion, PocketSOM offers an intuitive and convenient alternative to traditional music selection by browsing and constitutes a new model of how to access a music collection on portable audio players.

15.8 Conclusions and Future Directions

Future multimedia applications and systems will evolve towards more ubiquitous, user and situation (i.e., context) aware, adaptive, proactive, and intelligent solutions. The trend is towards embedded wearable mobile computers with new displays for mobile and ubiquitous multimedia. Solutions for the perception, sensing, and modeling of the environment will be increasingly important.

As another main trend, user created content has begun to play an increasingly important role in mobile multimedia. Application platforms such as Microsoft's Photosynth will offer means for massively multi-user content creation, by augmenting of virtual worlds with photos of the real one, and fusing these into new representations such as panorama views and 3D reconstructions. Such alternative representations will in turn promote both new multimedia content and applications for augmented reality and related ubiquitous solutions.

New client-server solutions are needed taking also security and rights management issues into consideration. Reaching "beyond the SMS era" in mobile applications still requires work on new service platforms and terminal applications, especially to demonstrate and evaluate new mobile multimedia community service concepts. Software components and prototypes for enriching, managing and provisioning of mobile content must be demonstrated and promoted for these communities. User experiences and evolving usage cultures must also be analyzed, as well as suitable business models for community-based services.

Overall usability is a particularly important issue in mobile multimedia applications. This is mostly due to the restricted size of a mobile device, especially the small display and keypad. In addition, natural and intuitive gestures vary in people with different backgrounds. A lot of work is still needed to overcome these difficulties. This work includes research in human-computer interaction (HCI) technologies, user-centered studies for mobile devices, as well as user evaluations and field trials of new applications and services.

Acknowledgements

All contributors to this book would like to acknowledge the financial support by the Network of Excellence MUSCLE within the 6th Framework Program for Research of the European Commision, under contract no. FP6-507752. In addition, individual chapter acknowledgements are as follows:

Chapter 4 The authors would like to thank A. Potamianos for providing the initial experimental setup for AV-ASR, I. Kokkinos for visual front-end discussions and face detection code, K. Murphy for using his HMM toolkit, and J.N. Gowdy for the use of the CUAVE database. They are also grateful to G. Gravier for his extensive feedback on the work.

Chapter 5 The authors' work has also been supported by various agencies since 2001, including the European Union Marie Curie Programme (MOUMIR HP-99-108), Enterprise Ireland (projects MUSE-DTV, CASMS, DumpingDetective, Detection of Illicit content), Science Foundation Ireland Research Frontiers and Eureka Programmes, Adobe Systems Inc. and The Irish Research Council for Science, Engineering & Technology.

Chapter 6 The work was supported in part by the Scientific and Technical Research Council of Turkey (TUBITAK) under Grant no. EEEAG-105E065 and Ministry of Industry and Trade of Turkey under Grant no. SANTEZ-105E121.

Chapter 7 The research was co-funded by the European Union and the Hellenic Ministry of Education in the framework of program Pythagoras II of the Operational Program for Education and Initial Vocational Training within the 3rd Community Support Program.

Chapter 8 The authors would like to thank C. Kotropoulos and his group from Aristotle University of Thessaloniki for providing the annotated movie video database, A. Zlatintsi at the National Technical University of Athens (NTUA) for the annotation of the movie clips and the design and coordination of the evaluation of the movie summarizations, and all the members of the CVSP Lab at NTUA for helping as evaluators of the movie summaries.

Chapter 14 The authors acknowledge the support by EPSRC, British Telecommunications Plc, SIRA, and the Imaging Faraday Partnership for their support in this work.

References

1. "Apple Human Interface Guidelines," http://developer.apple.com/documentation/UserExperience/Conceptual/OSXHIGuidelines.
2. "Apple iPhone Human Interface Guidelines," http://developer.apple.com/documentation/iPhone/Conceptual/iPhoneHIG/iPhoneHIG.pdf.
3. "HCI term definition," http://en.wikipedia.org/wiki/Human-Computer_Interaction.
4. "IBM WebSphere Voice Server," http://www-306.ibm.com/software/pervasive/voice_server.
5. "J. Blat, A first view of multimedia standards," http://www.iua.upf.es/~jblat/material/doctorat/multimedia_standards.html.
6. "SALT forum," http://www.saltforum.org/.
7. "The NICE (Natural Interactive Communication for Edutainment) project," http://www.niceproject.com/.
8. "W3C Extensible MultiModal Annotation markup language (EMMA)," http://www.w3.org/TR/emma/.
9. "W3C Ink Markup Language," http://www.w3.org/TR/InkML/.
10. "W3C Mobile Web Best Practices," http://www.w3.org/TR/mobile-bp/.
11. "W3C Multimodal Architecture and Interfaces," http://www.w3.org/TR/mmi-arch/.
12. "W3C MultiModal Interaction Requirements," http://www.w3.org/TR/mmi-reqs/.
13. "W3C MultiModal Interaction Use Cases," http://www.w3.org/TR/mmi-use-cases/.
14. "W3C MultiModal Interaction Working Group: Multimodal Interaction Framework," http://www.w3.org/TR/mmi-framework/.
15. "W3C MultiModal Interaction Working Group: System and Environment Framework," http://www.w3.org/TR/sysenv/.
16. "Mpeg-7 overview (version 9)," ISO/IEC JTC1/SC29/WG11 N5525, Tech. Rep., March 2003.
17. B. Adams et al., "IBM research TREC-2002 video retrieval system," in *Proc. Text Retrieval Conference*, 2002.
18. H. Ailisto, I. Korhonen, T. Tuomisto, S. Siltanen, E. Strömmer, L. Pohjanheimo, J. Hyväkkä, P. Välkkynen, A. Ylisaukko-oja, and H. Keränen,

"Communications technologies. VTT's research programme 2002-2006. physical browsing for ambient intelligence (pb-ami). VTT publications 629," http://www.vtt.fi/inf/pdf/publications/2007/P629.pdf, pp. 284 – 308, 2007.

19. A. A. Alatan, "Automatic multi-modal dialogue scene indexing," in *Proc. IEEE Int'l Conf. on Image Processing*, vol. 3, 2001, pp. 374–377.
20. A. A. Alatan and A. N. Akansu, "Multi-modal dialog scene detection using hidden-markov models for content-based multimedia indexing," *Multimedia Tools and Applications*, vol. 14, pp. 137–151, 2001.
21. A. A. Alatan, A. N. Akansu, and W. Wolf, "Comparative analysis of hidden markov models for multi-modal dialogue scene indexing," in *Proc. IEEE Int'l Conf. Acous., Speech, and Signal Processing*, vol. IV, 2000, pp. 2401–2404.
22. P. Aleksic and A. Katsaggelos, "Audio-visual biometrics," *Proc. IEEE*, vol. 11, pp. 2025–2044, 2006.
23. A. Allauzen and J.-L. Gauvain, "Open vocabulary ASR for audiovisual document indexation," in *Proc. IEEE Int'l Conf. Acous., Speech, and Signal Processing*, 2005.
24. B. Alp, P. Haavisto, T. Jarske, K. Oistamo, and Y. Neuvo, "Median based algorithms for image sequence processing," in *SPIE Conf. on Visual Communications and Image Processing*, 1990, pp. 122–134.
25. E. Ammicht, E. Fosler-Lussier, and A. Potamianos, "Information seeking spoken dialogue systems - Part I: Semantics and pragmatics," *IEEE Trans. Multimedia*, vol. 9, no. 3, pp. 532–549, 2007.
26. L. Amsaleg and P. Gros, "Content-based retrieval using local descriptors: Problems and issues from a database perspective," *Pattern Analysis & Applications*, vol. 2001, no. 4, pp. 108–124, 2001.
27. E. André and T. Rist, "Presenting through performing: on the use of multiple lifelike characters in knowledge-based presentation systems," in *Proc. Int'l Conf. on Intelligent User Interfaces*, New Orleans, Louisiana, 2000, pp. 1–8.
28. D. Androutsos, L. Guan, and A. V. G. Editors), "Special issue on semantic retrieval of multimedia," *IEEE Signal Process. Mag.*, vol. 23, no. 2, March 2006.
29. H. Aoki, "High–speed dialog detection for automatic segmentation of recorded tv program," in *Proc. ACM Int'l Conference on Image and Video Retrieval*, 2005, pp. 49–58.
30. H. Aoki, S. Shimotsuji, and O. Hori, "A shot classification method of selecting effective key-frames for video browsing," in *Proc. ACM Int'l Conference on Multimedia*, 1996, pp. 1–10.
31. A. Arampatzis, T. Van Der Weide, C. Koster, and P. Van Bommel, *Linguistically Motivated Information Retrieval.* New York, New York, Etats-Unis: M. Dekker, 2000, vol. 69, pp. 201–222.
32. A. Arasu, J. Cho, H. Garcia-Molina, A. Paepke, and S. Raghavan, "Searching the web," *ACM Transactions on Internet Technology*, vol. 1, no. 1, pp. 2–43, Aug. 2001.
33. W. Arentz and B. Olstad, "Classifying offensive sites based on image content," *Computer Vision and Image Understanding*, vol. 94, pp. 295–310, 2004.
34. S. Aukstakalnis and D. Blatner, *Silicon Mirage; The Art and Science of Virtual Reality.* Berkeley, CA, USA: Peachpit Press, 1992.
35. Y. Avrithis, A. Doulamis, N. Doulamis, and S. Kollias, "Summarization of videotaped presentations: automatic analysis of motion and gesture," *Computer Vision and Image Understanding*, vol. 75, no. 12, pp. 3–24, 1998.

36. R. Azuma, Y. Baillot, R. Behringer, S. Feiner, S. Julier, and B. MacIntyre, "Recent advances in augmented reality," *IEEE Comput. Graph. Appl.*, vol. 21, no. 6, pp. 34–47, 2001.
37. J. R. Bach, C. Fuller, A. Gupta, A. Hampapur, B. Horowitz, R. Humphrey, R. C. Jain, and C. F. Shu, "Virage image search engine: an open framework for image management," in *Proc. of SPIE*, vol. 2670. SPIE, 1996, pp. 76–87.
38. T. M. Bae, S. H. Jin, and Y. M. Ro, "Video segmentation using hidden Markov model with multimodal features," in *Proc. ACM Int'l Conference on Image and Video Retrieval*, 2004, pp. 401–409.
39. R. M. Baecker, J. Grudin, W. A. S. Buxton, and S. Greenberg, *Readings in Human-Computer Interaction: Toward the year 2000.* Morgan Kaufmann Publishers, 1995.
40. R. Ballagas, J. Borchers, M. Rohs, and J. G. Sheridan, "The smart phone: a ubiquitous input device," *IEEE Pervasive Comput.*, vol. Volume 5, no. 1, pp. 70– 77, Jan-March 2006.
41. R. Ballagas, M. Rohs, and J. G. Sheridan, "Sweep and point and shoot: phonecam-based interactions for large public displays," in *Proc. ACM-SIGCHI conference on Human factors in computing systems.* New York, NY, USA: ACM Press, 2005, pp. 1200–1203.
42. J. L. Barron, D. J. Fleet, and S. S. Beauchemin, "Performance of optical flow techniques," *Int'l J. of Comp. Vis.*, vol. 12, no. 1, pp. 43–77, 1994.
43. Z. Barzelay and Y. Y. Schechner, "Harmony in motion," in *Proc. IEEE Int'l Conf. on Computer Vision and Pattern Recognition*, 2007.
44. P. W. Battaglia, R. A. Jacobs, and R. N. Aslin, "Bayesian integration of visual and auditory signals for spatial localization," *J. of the Opt. Soc. Am. (A)*, vol. 20, no. 7, pp. 1391–1397, July 2003.
45. S. Bayer, "Building a standards and research community with the Galaxy Communicator software infrastructure," in *Practical Spoken Dialog Systems*, D. A. Dahl, Ed. Kluwer Academic Publishers, 2004, pp. 167–196.
46. F. Beaver, *Dictionary of Film Terms.* Twayne Publishing, New York, 1994.
47. F. Béchet, A. L. Gorin, J. H. Wright, and D. Hakkani-Tür, "Detecting and extracting named entities from spontaneous speech in a mixed initiative spoken dialogue context: How may I help you?" *Speech Communication*, vol. 42, no. 2, pp. 207–225, 2004.
48. N. Beckmann, H.-P. Kriegel, R. Schneider, and B. Seeger, "The R*-tree: An efficient and robust access method for points and rectangles," in *ACM SIGMOD International Conference on Management of Data*, Atlantic City, New Jersey, Etats-Unis, 23-25 May 1990, pp. 322–331.
49. J. R. Bellegarda, "Large vocabulary speech recognition with multispan statistical language models," *IEEE Trans. Speech Audio Process.*, vol. 8, no. 1, pp. 76–84, 2000.
50. ——, "Statistical language model adaptation: review and perspectives," *Speech Communication*, vol. 42, no. 1, pp. 93–108, 2004.
51. T. Bellman and I. S. MacKenzie, "A probabilistic character layout strategy for mobile text entry," in *Proc. Graphics Interface*, 1998, pp. 168–176.
52. S. Belongie, J. Malik, and J. Puzicha, "Shape matching and object recognition using shape contexts," *IEEE Trans. Pattern Anal. Mach. Intell.*, vol. 24, no. 4, pp. 509–522, Apr. 2002.

53. S. Bengio, "An asynchronous hidden Markov model for audio-visual speech recognition," in *Proc. Advances in Neural Information Processing Systems*, S. Becker, S. Thrun, and K. Obermayer, Eds. MIT Press, 2003, pp. 1237–1244.
54. C. Benoit, J. C. Martin, C. Pelachaud, L. Schomaker, and B. Suhm, "Audio-visual and multimodal speech systems," in *Handbook of Standards and Resources for Spoken Language Systems*, D. Gibbon, I. Mertins, and R. Moore, Eds. Kluwer Academic Publishers, 2000.
55. J. L. Bentley, "Multidimensional binary search trees in database applications," *IEEE Trans. Softw. Eng.*, vol. 5, no. 4, pp. 333–340, 1979.
56. S. Berchtold, D. A. Keim, and H.-P. Kriegel, "The X-tree : An index structure for high-dimensional data," in *22th International Conference on Very Large Data Bases*, Mumbai (Bombay), Inde, 3-6 Sep. 1996, pp. 28–39.
57. C. Berg, J. P. R. Christensen, and P. Ressel, *Harmonic Analysis on Semigroups*. Springer-Verlag, 1984.
58. N. O. Bernsen and L. Dybkjaer, "Is speech the right thing for your application?" in *Proc. Int'l Conf. on Spoken Language Processing*, Sydney, Australia, 1998, pp. 3209–3212.
59. P. Bertelson and M. Radeau, "Cross-modal bias and perceptual fusion with auditory-visual spatial discordance," *Percept. Psychophysics*, vol. 29, pp. 578–584, 1981.
60. M. Betser and G. Gravier, "Multiple events tracking in sound tracks," in *Proc. of IEEE Int'l Conference on Multimedia and Expo*, 2004.
61. K. Bharat and M. R. Henzinger, "Improved algorithms for topic distillation in a hyperlinked environment," in *Proc. of the ACM SIGIR Conference*, Melbourne, 1998, pp. 104–111.
62. B. Bigi, Y. Huang, and R. De Mori, "Vocabulary and language model adaptation using information retrieval," in *Proc. Int'l Conf. on Spoken Language Processing*, 2004.
63. V. Bilici, E. Krahmer, S. te Riele, and R. Veldhuis, "Preferred modalities in dialogue systems," in *Proc. Int'l Conf. on Spoken Language Processing*, Beijing, China, 2000.
64. O. Bimber and R. Raskar, "Modern approaches to augmented reality," in *Proc. ACM Int'l conference on Computer Graphics and Interactive Techniques*, 2005.
65. C. Bishop, "Training with noise is equivalent to Tikhonov regularization," *Neural Computation*, vol. 7, no. 1, pp. 108–116, 1995.
66. C. M. Bishop, *Pattern Recognition and Machine Learning*. Springer, 2006.
67. H. M. Blanken, A. P. de Vries, H. E. Blok, and L. F. (Editors), *Multimedia Retrieval (Data-Centric Systems and Applications)*. Springer, 2007.
68. D. Bohus and A. I. Rudnicky, "Error handling in the RavenClaw dialog management framework," in *Human Language Technology Conference*, Vancouver, Canada, 2005, pp. 225–232.
69. R. A. Bolt, "Put-That-There : Voice and gesture at the graphics interface," in *Proc. ACM Int'l conference on Computer Graphics and Interactive Techniques*. ACM Press New York, NY, USA, 1980, pp. 262–270.
70. D. Bordwell and K. Thompson, *Film Art: An Introduction*. McGraw–Hill, Inc., 4th ed., New York, 1993.
71. J. Boreczky and L. Wilcox, "A hidden Markov model framework for video segmentation using audio and image features," in *Proc. IEEE Int'l Conf. Acous., Speech, and Signal Processing*, 1998, pp. 3741–3744.

72. A. Bosson, G. Cawley, Y. Chan, and R. Harvey, "Nonretrieval: blocking pornographic images," in *Proc. ACM Int'l Conference on Image and Video Retrieval*, 2002, pp. 50–60.
73. M. M. Bouamrane and S. Luz, "Meeting browsing: State-of-the-art review," *Multimedia Systems*, vol. 12, pp. 439–457, 2007.
74. N. Boujemaa, S. Boughorbel, and C. Vertan, "Soft color signatures for image retrieval by content," in *Eusflat'2001*, vol. 2, 2001, pp. 394–401.
75. N. Boujemaa, J. Fauqueur, M. Ferecatu, F. Fleuret, V. Gouet, B. L. Saux, and H. Sahbi, "IKONA: Interactive generic and specific image retrieval," in *Proc. Int'l Workshop on Multimedia Content-Based Indexing and Retrieval*, 2001.
76. N. Boujemaa, J. Fauqueur, and V. Gouet, "What's beyond query by example?" in *Trends and Advances in Content-Based Image and Video Retrieval*, R. V. L. Shapiro, H.P. Kriegel, Ed. Springer Verlag, 2004.
77. H. Bourlard and S. Dupont, "A new ASR approach based on independent processing and recombination of partial frequency bands," in *Proc. Int'l Conf. on Spoken Language Processing*, 1996, pp. 426–429.
78. A. Bovik, P. Maragos, and T. Quatieri, "AM-FM energy detection and separation in noise using multiband energy operators," *IEEE Trans. Signal Process.*, vol. 41, no. 12, pp. 3245–3265, Dec 1993.
79. A. Briassouli and N. Ahuja, "Extraction and analysis of multiple periodic motions in video sequences," *IEEE Trans. Pattern Anal. Mach. Intell.*, vol. 29, no. 7, pp. 1244–1261, Jul. 2007.
80. P. F. Brown, V. J. D. Pietra, P. V. de Souza, J. C. Lai, and R. L. Mercer, "Class-based n-gram models of natural language," *Computational Linguistics*, vol. 18, no. 4, pp. 467–479, 1992.
81. A. Budanitsky and G. Hirst, "Semantic distance in WordNet: An experimental, application-oriented evaluation of five measures," in *Proceedings of the Workshop on WordNet and Other Lexical Resources NAACL 2001*, 2001.
82. M. D. Byrne, "Cognitive architectures," in *The human-computer interaction handbook: Fundamentals, evolving technologies and emerging applications*, J. Jacko and A. Sears, Eds. Mahwah, NJ, USA: Lawrence Erlbaum, 2003, pp. 97–117.
83. S. K. Card, J. D. Mackinlay, and G. G. Robertson, "A morphological analysis of the design space of input devices," *ACM Transactions on Information Systems*, vol. 9, no. 2, pp. 99–122, 1991.
84. S. K. Card, A. Newell, and T. P. Moran, *The Psychology of Human-Computer Interaction.* Lawrence Erlbaum Associates, Mahwah, NJ, USA, 1983.
85. B. Carpenter, *The Logic of Typed Feature Structures.* Cambridge University Press New York, NY, USA, 1992.
86. J. Cassell, T. Bickmore, M. Billinghurst, L. Campbell, K. Chang, H. Vilhjálmsson, and H. Yan, "Embodiment in conversational interfaces: Rea," in *Proc. ACM-SIGCHI conference on Human factors in computing systems.* ACM Press New York, NY, USA, 1999, pp. 520–527.
87. L. Chaisorn, T.-S. Chua, and C.-H. Lee, "A multi-modal approach to story segmentation for news video," *World Wide Web*, vol. 6, pp. 187–208, 2003.
88. Y. Chan, R. Harvey, and J. A. Bangham, "Using colour features to block dubious images," in *Proc. European Signal Processing Conference*, 2000.
89. E. Y. Chang, B. Li, G. Wu, and K. Goh, "Statistical learning for effective visual image retrieval," in *Proc. IEEE Int'l Conf. on Image Processing*, September 2003, pp. 609–612.

90. P. Chang, M. Han, and Y. Gong, "Extract highlights from baseball game video with Hidden Markov Models," in *Proc. IEEE Int'l Conf. on Image Processing*, September 2002, pp. 609–612.
91. C. Chelba and F. Jelinek, "Structured language modeling," *Computer Speech and Language*, vol. 14, no. 4, pp. 283–332, 2000.
92. G. Chen and D. Kotz, "A survey of context-aware mobile computing research," Dept. of Computer Science, Dartmouth College, Tech. Rep. TR2000-381, November 2000.
93. L. Chen, J.-L. Gauvain, L. Lamel, and G. Adda, "Dynamic language modeling for broadcast news," in *Proc. Int'l Conf. on Spoken Language Processing*, 2004.
94. L. Chen and M. T. Özsu, "Rule-based scene extraction from video," in *Proc. IEEE Int'l Conf. on Image Processing*, vol. 2, 2002, pp. 737–740.
95. L. Chen, S. Rizvi, and M. T. Özsu, "Incorporating audio cues into dialog and action scene extraction," in *Proc. IS&T/SPIE's 15th Annual Symp. Electronic Imaging - Storage and Retrieval for Media Databases*, 2003, pp. 252–264.
96. Z. Chen, L. Wenyin, F. Zhang, M. Li, and H.-J. Zhang, "Web mining for web image retrieval," *Journal of the American Society of Information Science*, vol. 52, no. 10, pp. 831–839, 2001.
97. S. F. Cheng, W. Chen, and H. Sundaram, "Semantic visual templates: linking visual features to semantics," in *Proc. IEEE Int'l Conf. on Image Processing*, Chicago, Illinois, 1998, pp. 531–535.
98. W. Chou and B. H. Juang, *Pattern Recognition in Speech and Language Processing*. CRC Press, Boca Raton, FL, USA, 2002.
99. J. J. Clark and A. L. Yuille, *Data Fusion for Sensory Information Processing*. Kluwer Academic Publ., 1990.
100. V. Claveau, P. Sbillot, C. Fabre, and P. Bouillon, "Learning semantic lexicons from a part-of-speech and semantically tagged corpus using inductive logic programming," *Journal of Machine Learning Research*, vol. 4, pp. 493–525, Aug. 2003.
101. P. R. Cohen, M. Johnston, D. McGee, S. Oviatt, J. Pittman, I. Smith, L. Chen, and J. Clow, "Quickset: multimodal interaction for distributed applications," in *Proc. ACM Int'l Conference on Multimedia*. ACM Press New York, NY, USA, 1997, pp. 31–40.
102. P. Cohen and S. Oviatt, "The role of voice in human-machine communication," in *Voice communication between humans and machines*, D. B. Roe and J. G. Wilpon, Eds. Washington, DC, USA: National Academy Press, 1994, pp. 34–75.
103. R. Collins, A. Lipton, T. Kanade, H. Fujiyoshi, D. Duggins, Y. Tsin, D. Tolliver, N. Enomoto, and O. Hasegawa, "A system for video surveillance and monitoring," Robotics Institute, Carnegie Mellon University, Technical report CMU-RI-TR-00-12, May 2000.
104. G. F. Cooper and E. Herskovits, "A bayesian method for the induction of probabilistic networks from data," *Machine Learning*, vol. 9, pp. 309–347, 1992.
105. J. Coopersmith, "Pornography, videotape, and the internet," *IEEE Technol. Soc. Mag.*, pp. 27–34, Spring 2000.
106. T. F. Cootes, C. J. Taylor, D. H. Cooper, and J. Graham, "Active shape models – their training and application," *Computer Vision and Image Understanding*, vol. 61, no. 1, pp. 38–59, 1995.
107. T. Cootes, G. Edwards, and T. C.J., "Active appearance models," *IEEE Trans. Pattern Anal. Mach. Intell.*, vol. 23, no. 6, pp. 681–685, 2001.

108. F. L. Corno F. and S. I., "A cost effective solution for eye-gaze assistive technology," in *Proc. of IEEE Int'l Conference on Multimedia and Expo*, 2002.
109. N. Corporate, "T9 text input solutions," http://www.t9.com/.
110. H. Corporation, "Twiddler2," http://www.handykey.com/.
111. C. Cotsaces, N. Nikolaidis, and I. Pitas, "Video shot detection and condensed representation: A review," *IEEE Signal Process. Mag.*, vol. 23, no. 2, pp. 28–37, 2006.
112. R. Coudray and B. Besserer, "Global motion estimation for MPEG-encoded streams," in *Proc. IEEE Int'l Conf. on Image Processing*, 2004, pp. 3411–3414.
113. ——, "Motion based segmentation using MPEG streams and watershed method," in *International Symposium on Visual Computing*, 2005, pp. 729–736.
114. H. D. Crane and C. M. Steele, "Accurate three-dimensional eye tracker," *J. of the Opt. Soc. Am.*, vol. 17, pp. 691–705, 1978, 17, 691-705.
115. M. Cristani, M. Bicego, and V. Murino, "On-line adaptive background modelling for audio surveillance," in *Proc. Int'l Conf. on Pattern Recognition*, 2004.
116. ——, "Audio-visual event recognition in surveillance video sequences," *IEEE Trans. Multimedia*, vol. 9, pp. 257–267, Feb. 2007.
117. M. S. Crouse, R. D. Nowak, and R. G. Baraniuk, "Wavelet-based statistical signal processing using hidden Markov models," *IEEE Trans. Signal Process.*, vol. 46, no. 4, pp. 886–902, 1998.
118. S. Cunningham, N. Reeves, and M. Britland, "An ethnographic study of music information seeking: implications for the design of a music digital library," in *Proc. ACM/IEEE Joint Conference on Digital Libraries (JCDL'03)*. Houston, Texas, US: IEEE Computer Society, 2003, pp. 5–16.
119. R. Cutler and L. Davis, "Robust real-time periodic motion detection, analysis, and applications," *IEEE Trans. Pattern Anal. Mach. Intell.*, vol. 22, no. 8, pp. 781–796, August 2000.
120. R. Dahyot, A. C. Kokaram, N. Rea, and H. Denman, "Joint audio visual retrieval for tennis broadcasts," in *Proc. IEEE Int'l Conf. Acous., Speech, and Signal Processing*, April 2003.
121. R. Dahyot, N. Rea, A. Kokaram, and N. Kingsbury, "Inlier modeling for multimedia data analysis," in *Proc. of IEEE Int'l Workshop on Multimedia Signal Processing*, Siena Italy, September 2004, pp. 482–485.
122. T. Darrell, J. Fisher, P. Viola, and B. Freeman, "Audio-visual segmentation and the cocktail party effect," in *Proc. Int'l Conf. on Multimodal Interfaces*, 2000.
123. R. Datta, D. Joshi, J. Li, and J. Z. Wang, "Image retrieval: Ideas, influences, and trends of the new age," *ACM Computing Surveys*, vol. 39, 2007.
124. A. Davison, Y. Cid, and N. Kita, "Real-time 3D SLAM with wide-angle vision," in *Proceedings of the 5th IFAC/EURON Sumbosiom on Intelligent Autonomous Vehicles*, Lissabon, Portugal, July 2004.
125. "Standard international iso/iec 15836,the dublin core metadata element set," Nov. 2003.
126. Y. Dedeoglu, "Moving object detection, tracking and classification for smart video surveillance," Master's thesis, Bilkent University, Department of Computer Engineering, 2004.
127. M. Delakis, G. Gravier, and P. Gros, "Score oriented Viterbi search in sport video structuring using HMM and segment models," in *Proc. of IEEE Int'l Workshop on Multimedia Signal Processing*, 2006.

128. ——, "Audiovisual integration with segment models for tennis video parsing," *Computer Vision and Image Understanding*, 2008, in press.
129. A. P. Dempster, N. M. Laird, and D. B. Rubin, "Maximum Likelihood from incomplete data via the EM algorithm," *J. of Royal Stat. Soc. (Series B)*, vol. 39, no. 1, pp. 1–38, 1977.
130. L. Deng, J. Dropo, and A. Acero, "Dynamic compensation of HMM variances using the feature enhancement uncertainty computed from a parametric model of speech distortion," *IEEE Trans. Speech Audio Process.*, vol. 13, no. 3, pp. 412–421, 2005.
131. H. Denman, N. Rea, and A. Kokaram, "Content-based analysis for video from snooker broadcasts," *Computer Vision and Image Understanding*, vol. 92, pp. 141–306, November/December 2003.
132. M. L. Dertouzos, *The Unfinished Revolution: Making Computers Human-Centric.* HarperCollins Publishers, 2001.
133. A. Desolneux, L. Moisan, and J.-M. Morel, "Edge detection by Helmholtz principle," *J. Math. Imaging and Vision*, vol. 14, pp. 271–284, 2001.
134. A. Dielmann and S. Renals, "Automatic meeting segmentation using dynamic Bayesian networks," *IEEE Trans. Multimedia*, vol. 9, no. 1, pp. 25–36, January 2007.
135. V. Digalakis, J. Rohlicek, and M. Ostendorf, "ML estimation of a stochastic linear system with the EM algorithm and its application to speech recognition," *IEEE Trans. Speech Audio Process.*, pp. 431–442, 1993.
136. V. V. Digalakis, "Segment-based stochastic models of spectral dynamics for continuous speech recognition," Ph.D. dissertation, Speech Processing and Interpretation Laboratory, Universit de Boston, 1992.
137. D. Dimitriadis, P. Maragos, and A. Potamianos, "Auditory Teager energy cepstrum coefficients for robust speech recognition," in *Proc. Int'l Conf. on Speech Communication and Technology*, Lisboa, Portugal, Sep 2005.
138. N. Dimitrova, L. Agnihorti, and G. Wei, "Video classification based on HMM using text and faces," in *Proc. European Signal Processing Conference*, 2000.
139. A. Dix, J. Finlay, G. Abowd, and R. Beale, *Human-Computer Interaction.* Prentice Hall, 2004.
140. A. Doulamis, N. Doulamis, Y. Avrithis, and S. Kollias, "A fuzzy video content representation for video summarization and content-based," *Signal Processing*, vol. 80, no. 6, pp. 1049–1067, Jun 2000.
141. J. Downie, *Annual Review of Information Science and Technology.* Medford, NJ: Information Today, 2003, vol. 37, ch. Music Information Retrieval, pp. 295–340.
142. S. A. Drab and N. M. Artner, "Motion detection as interaction technique for games & applications on mobile devices," in *Pervasive Mobile Interaction Devices (PERMID 2005) Workshop at the Pervasive 2005*, Munich, DR, May 2005.
143. J. Driver, "Enhancement of selective listening by illusory mislocation of speech sounds due to lip-reading," *Nature*, vol. 381, pp. 66–68, May 1996.
144. A. T. Duchowski, "A breadth-first survey of eye tracking applications," *Behavior Research Methods, Instruments, and Computers*, vol. 34, no. 4, pp. 455–470, 2002.
145. R. O. Duda, P. E. Hart, and D. G. Stork, *Pattern Classification*, 2nd ed. J. Wiley & Sons, 2001.

146. F. Dufaux and J. Konrad, "Efficient, robust and fast global motion estimation for video coding," *IEEE Trans. Image Process.*, vol. 9, pp. 497–501, 2000.
147. S. Dupont and J. Luettin, "Audio-visual speech modeling for continuous speech recognition," *IEEE Trans. Multimedia*, vol. 2, no. 3, pp. 141–151, 2000.
148. S. Eickeler and S. Muller, "Content-based video indexing of TV broadcast news using hidden Markov models," in *Proc. IEEE Int'l Conf. Acous., Speech, and Signal Processing*, 1999, pp. 2997–3000.
149. A. Ekin, A. M. Tekalp, and R. Mehrotra, "Automatic soccer video analysis and summarization," *IEEE Trans. Image Process.*, vol. 12, no. 7, pp. 796–807, July 2003.
150. C. Elting, S. Rapp, G. Möhler, and M. Strube, "Architecture and implementation of multimodal plug and play," in *Proc. Int'l Conf. on Multimodal Interfaces.* ACM Press New York, NY, USA, 2003, pp. 93–100.
151. R. Engel and N. Pfleger, "Modality fusion," in *SmartKom: Foundations of Multimodal Dialogue Systems*, W. Wahlster, Ed. Springer-Verlag, New York, NY, 2006, pp. 223–236.
152. E. Erzin, A. Cetin, and Y. Yardimci, "Subband analysis for robust speech recognition in the presence of car noise," in *Proc. IEEE Int'l Conf. Acous., Speech, and Signal Processing*, 1995.
153. G. Evangelopoulos and P. Maragos, "Multiband modulation energy tracking for noisy speech detection," *IEEE Trans. Audio, Speech, and Language Processing*, vol. 14, no. 6, pp. 2024–2038, Nov 2006.
154. R. Fagin, R. Kumar, and D. Sivakumar, "Efficient similarity search and classification via rank aggregation," in *ACM SIGMOD International Conference on Management of Data*, San Diego, Californie, Etats-Unis, 9-12 Jun. 2003, pp. 301–312.
155. X. Fan, X. Xie, W.-Y. Ma, H.-J. Zhang, and H.-Q. Zhou, "Visual attention based image browsing on mobile devices," in *Proc. of IEEE Int'l Conference on Multimedia and Expo*, vol. I, 2003, pp. 53–56.
156. C. Fangxiang, W. Christmas, and J. Kittler, "Periodic human motion description for sports video databases," in *Proc. Int'l Conf. on Pattern Recognition*, vol. 3, 2004, pp. 870 – 873.
157. C. Fellbaum, Ed., *WordNet: An Electronic Lexical Database.* The MIT Press, 1998.
158. P. Felzenszwalb and D. Huttenlocher, "Pictorial structures for object recognition," *Int'l J. of Comp. Vis.*, vol. 61, no. 1, pp. 55–79, 2005.
159. M. Ferecatu, "Image retrieval with active relevance feedback using both visual and keyword-based descriptors," Ph.D. dissertation, INRIA—University of Versailles Saint Quentin-en-Yvelines, France, 2005.
160. M. Ferecatu, M. Crucianu, and N. Boujemaa, "Retrieval of difficult image classes using svm-based relevance feedback," in *Proc. ACM Int'l Workshop on Multimedia Information Retrieval*, October 2004, pp. 23 – 30.
161. M. Ferman and A. M. Tekalp, "Probabilistic analysis and extraction of video content," in *Proc. IEEE Int'l Conf. on Image Processing*, vol. 2, 1999, pp. 91–95.
162. K. P. Fishkin, A. Gujar, B. L. Harrison, T. P. Moran, and R. Want, "Embodied user interfaces for really direct manipulation," *Communications of the ACM*, vol. 43, no. 9, pp. 74–80, 2000.
163. M. M. Fleck, D. A. Forsyth, and C. Bregler, "Finding Naked People," in *Proc. European Conf. on Computer Vision*, vol. 2, 1996, pp. 593–602.

164. F. Fleuret and H. Sahbi, "Scale-invariance of support vector machines based on the triangular kernel," in *3rd International Workshop on Statistical and Computational Theories of Vision*, October 2003.
165. M. S. Flickner, H. Niblack, W. Ashley, J. Q. H. Dom, B. Gorkani, M. Hafner, J. Lee, D. Petkovic, D. Steele, and D. Yanker, "Query by image and video content: the QBIC system," *IEEE Computer*, vol. 28, no. 9, pp. 23–32, 1995.
166. F. Flippo, A. Krebs, and I. Marsic, "A framework for rapid development of multimodal interfaces," in *Proc. Int'l Conf. on Multimodal Interfaces.* ACM Press New York, NY, USA, 2003, pp. 109–116.
167. J. D. Foley, V. L. Wallace, and P. Chan, "The human factors of computer graphics interaction techniques," *IEEE Comput. Graph. Appl.*, vol. 4, no. 11, pp. 13–48, 1984.
168. J. Foote, "An overview of audio information retrieval," *Multimedia Systems*, vol. 7, no. 1, pp. 2–10, 1999.
169. G. Forney, "The Viterbi algorithm," *Proc. IEEE*, vol. 61, no. 3, pp. 268–277, 1973.
170. W. T. Freeman and E. Adelson, "The design and use of steerable filters," *IEEE Trans. Pattern Anal. Mach. Intell.*, no. 9, pp. 891–906, 1991.
171. B. Frey, T. Kristjansson, L. Deng, and A. Acero, "Learning dynamic noise models from noisy speech for robust speech recognition," in *Proc. Advances in Neural Information Processing Systems*, vol. 8, 2001, pp. 472–478.
172. W. A. Fuller, *Measurement Error Models.* Wiley, 1987.
173. B. Furht and O. M. (Editors), *Handbook of Video Databases: Design and Applications.* CRC Press, Boca Raton, FL, 2003.
174. D. Gabor, "Theory of communication," *Journal Inst. of Elec. Eng. London*, vol. 93, no. III, pp. 429–457, 1946.
175. W. O. Galitz, *The Essential Guide to User Interface Design: An Introduction to GUI Design Principles and Techniques.* John Wiley & Sons, 2002.
176. S. Galliano, E. Geoffrois, D. Mostefa, K. Choukri, J.-F. Bonastre, and G. Gravier, "The ESTER phase II evaluation campaign for the rich transcription of French broadcast news," in *Proc. Int'l Conf. on Speech Communication and Technology*, 2005.
177. E. Gamma, R. Helm, R. Johnson, and J. Vlissides, *Design Patterns: Elements of Reusable Object-Oriented Software.* Addison-Wesley Longman Publishing Co., Boston, MA, USA, 1995.
178. C. Garcia and M. Delakis, "Convolutional face finder: A neural architecture for fast and robust face detection," *IEEE Trans. Pattern Anal. Mach. Intell.*, vol. 26, no. 11, pp. 1408–1423, 2004.
179. S. Gauch, J. Wang, and S. Rachakonda, "A Corpus Analysis Approach for Automatic Query Expansion and its Extension to Multiple Databases," *ACM Transactions on Information Systems*, vol. 17, no. 3, pp. 250–269, 1999.
180. S. Geman and D. Geman, "Stochastic relaxation, gibbs distributions, and the bayesian restoration of images," *IEEE Trans. Pattern Anal. Mach. Intell.*, vol. 6, no. 6, pp. 721–741, 1984.
181. T. Gevers and A. W. M. Smeulders, "Content-based image retrieval: An overview," in *Emerging Topics in Computer Vision*, G. Medioni and S. B. Kang, Eds. Prentice Hall, 2004, ch. 8.
182. D. Gildea and T. Hofmann, "Topic-based language models using EM," in *Proc. European Conf. on Speech Communication and Technology*, 1999.

183. A. Girgensohn, J. Boreczky, and L. Wilcox, "Keyframe-based user interfaces for digital video," *IEEE Computer*, vol. 34, no. 9, pp. 61–67, Sep 2001.
184. H. Glotin, D. Vergyri, C. Neti, G. Potamianos, and J. Luettin, "Weighting schemes for audio-visual fusion in speech recognition," in *Proc. IEEE Int'l Conf. Acous., Speech, and Signal Processing*, 2001.
185. E. B. Goldstein, *Sensation and Perception.* California: Wadsworth Publ. Co., 1984.
186. Y. Gong, "A method of joint compensation of additive and convolutive distortions for speaker-independent speech recognition," *IEEE Trans. Speech Audio Process.*, vol. 13, no. 5, pp. 975–983, 2005.
187. Y. Gong, L. T. Sin, C. H. Chuan, H. Zhang, and M. Sakauchi, "Automatic parsing of TV soccer programs," in *Proc. of IEEE Int'l Conference on Multimedia Computing and Systems*, vol. 7, May 1995, pp. 167–174.
188. G. Gravier and D. Moraru, "Towards phonetically-driven hidden Markov models: Can we incorporate phonetic landmarks in HMM-based ASR?" in *Proc. ISCA Tutorial and Research Workshop on Non Linear Speech Processing*, ser. Lecture Notes in Artificial Intelligence, M. C. et al., Ed., vol. 4885. Springer Verlag, 2007, pp. 161–168.
189. U. Grenander, *Elements of Pattern Theory.* The Jonhs Hopkins Univ. Press, 1996.
190. W. G. Griswold, P. Shanahan, S. W. Brown, R. Boyer, M. Ratto, R. B. Shapiro, and T. M. Truong, "ActiveCampus: Experiments in community-oriented ubiquitous computing," *Communications of the ACM*, vol. 43, no. 9, pp. 74–80, 2000.
191. J. Gustafson, "Developing multimodal spoken dialogue systems. empirical studies of human-computer interaction," Ph.D. dissertation, Department of Speech, Music and Hearing, KTH, 2002.
192. A. Guttman, "R-trees: A dynamic index structure for spatial searching," in *ACM SIGMOD International Conference on Management od Data*, Boston, Massachusetts, Etats-Unis, 18-21 Jun. 1984, pp. 47–57.
193. M. Hakkarainen and C. Woodward, "Symball - camera driven table tennis for mobile phones," in *ACM SIGCHI International Conference on Advances in Computer Entertainment Technology, ACE 2005*, 2005, pp. 15 – 17.
194. M. Haller, M. Billinghurst, and B. H. Thomas, *Emerging Technologies of Augmented Reality.* Hershey, PA, USA: IGI Publishing, 2006.
195. J. Y. Han, "Low-cost multi-touch sensing through frustrated total internal reflection," in *UIST '05: Proceedings of the 18th annual ACM symposium on User interface software and technology.* New York, NY, USA: ACM Press, 2005, pp. 115–118.
196. J. Hannuksela, P. Sangi, and J. Heikkilä, "A vision-based approach for controlling user interfaces of mobile devices," in *Proc. of IEEE Workshop on Vision for Human-Computer Interaction (V4HCI)*, 2005.
197. J. P. Hansen, A. W. Anderson, and P. Roed, *Symbiosis of Human and Artifact.* Elsevier Science, 1995, vol. 20A, ch. Eye gaze control of multimedia systems, pp. 37–42.
198. B. L. Harrison, K. P. Fishkin, A. Gujar, C. Mochon, and R. Want, "Squeeze me, hold me, tilt me! an exploration of manipulative user interfaces," in *Proc. ACM-SIGCHI conference on Human factors in computing systems.* New York, NY, USA: ACM Press/Addison-Wesley Publishing Co., 1998, pp. 17–24.

199. R. Hartley and A. Zisserman, *Multiple View Geometry in Computer Vision.* New York, NY, USA: Cambridge University Press, 2003.
200. A. Hauptmann, "Lessons for the future from a decade of Informedia video analysis research," in *Proc. ACM Int'l Conference on Image and Video Retrieval*, vol. 3568, 2005, pp. 1–10.
201. A. Hauptmann, R. Yan, T. Ng, W. Lin, R. Jin, D. Christel, M. Chen, and R. Baron, "Video classification and retrieval with the Informedia digital video library system," in *Proc. Text Retrieval Conference*, Gaithersburg, MD, USA, Nov 2002.
202. P. A. Heeman, "POS tags and decision trees for language modeling," in *Proc. the Joint SIGDAT Conf. on Empirical Methods in Natural Language Processing and Very Large Corpora*, 1999.
203. F. Heijden, *Image Based Measurement Systems: Object Recognition and Parameter Estimation.* WILEY, Jan. 1996.
204. H. Helmholtz, *Physiological Optics, Vol.III: The Perceptions of Vision (J. P. Southall, Trans.).* Rochester, NY: Optical Soc. Amer., 1910, 1925.
205. M. Hennecke, D. Stork, and K. Prasad, "Visionary speech: Looking ahead to practical speechreading systems," in *Speechreading by Humans and Machines*, D. Stork and M. Hennecke, Eds. Berlin, Germany: Springer, 1996, pp. 331–349.
206. A. Henrich, "The lsd^{h}-tree: An access structure for feature vectors," in *14th International Conference on Data Engineering*, Orlando, Floride, Etats-Unis, 23-27 Feb. 1998, pp. 362–369.
207. A. Henrysson, M. Billinghurst, and M. Ollila, "Virtual object manipulation using a mobile phone," in *ICAT '05: Proceedings of the 2005 international conference on Augmented tele-existence.* New York, NY, USA: ACM Press, 2005, pp. 164–171.
208. H. Hermansky, M. Pavel, and S. Tibrewala, "Towards ASR using partially corrupted speech," in *Proc. Int'l Conf. on Spoken Language Processing*, Oct. 1996, pp. 458–461.
209. J. Hershey and J. Movellan, "Audio-vision: Using audio-visual synchrony to locate sounds," in *Proc. Advances in Neural Information Processing Systems*, 1999.
210. J. M. Hillis, M. O. Ernst, M. S. Banks, and M. S. Landy, "Combining sensory information: Mandatory fusion within, but not between, senses," *Science*, vol. 298, pp. 1627–1630, 2002.
211. K. Hinckley, J. Pierce, M. Sinclair, and E. Horvitz, "Sensing techniques for mobile interaction," in *UIST '00: Proceedings of the 13th annual ACM symposium on User interface software and technology.* New York, NY, USA: ACM Press, 2000, pp. 91–100.
212. A. Hliaoutakis, G. Varelas, E. Voutsakis, E. G. Petrakis, and E. Milios, "Information retrieval by semantic similarity," *Intern. Journal on Semantic Web and Information Systems (IJSWIS)*, vol. 3, no. 3, pp. 55–73, July/Sept. 2006, special Issue of Multimedia Semantics.
213. P. Honkamaa, J. Jäppinen, and C. Woodward, "Interactive outdoor mobile augmentation using markerless tracking and gps," in *Proc. Mobile Ubiquitous Multimedia (MUM2007), Oulu, Finland*, December 2007.
214. P. Honkamaa, S. Siltanen, J. Jäppinen, C. Woodward, and O. Korkalo, "A lightweight approach for augmented reality on camera phones using 2d images

to simulate 3d," in *Proc. Virtual Reality International Conference (VRIC), Laval, France*, April 2007, pp. 285–288.

215. B. K. Horn, *Robot Vision.* Cambridge, Massachusetts: MIT Press, 1986.
216. E. Horvitz, J. Breese, D. Heckerman, D. Hovel, and K. Rommelse, "The Lumiere Project: Bayesian user modeling for inferring the goals and needs of software users," in *Proc. Int'l Conf. on Uncertainty in Artificial Intelligence*, Madison, Wisconsin, 1998, pp. 256–265.
217. X. Huang, A. Acero, and H. W. Hon, *Spoken Language Processing: A Guide to Theory, Algorithm, and System Development.* Upper Saddle River, NJ, USA: Prentice Hall PTR, 2001.
218. S. Huet, "Informations morpho-syntaxiques et adaptation thématique pour améliorer la reconnaissance de la parole," Ph.D. dissertation, Université de Rennes 1, Rennes, France, dec 2007.
219. S. Huet, G. Gravier, and P. Sébillot, "Morphosyntactic processing of N-best lists for improved recognition and confidence measure computation," in *Proc. Int'l Conf. on Speech Communication and Technology*, 2007.
220. Q. Huo and C. Lee, "A bayesian predictive approach to robust speech recognition," *IEEE Trans. Speech Audio Process.*, pp. 200–204, 2000.
221. I. K. Ibrahim, *Handbook of Research on Mobile Multimedia.* Hershey, PA, USA: IGI Publishing, 2006.
222. F. Idris and S. Panchanathan, "Review of image and video indexing techniques," *Journal of Visual Communication and Image Representation*, vol. 8, no. 2, pp. 146–166, 1997.
223. C. Inferense Group, Cavendish Laboratory, "Dasher developments," http://www.inference.phy.cam.ac.uk/dasher/development/.
224. Y. Ishikawa, R. Subramanya, and C. Faloutsos, "Mindreader: Query databases through multiple examples," in *Proc. Int'l Conf. on Very Large Data Bases*, New York. USA, 1998, pp. 218–227.
225. U. Iurgel, R. Meermeier, S. Eickeler, and G. Rigoll, "New approaches to audio-visual segmentation of TV news for automatic topic retrieval," in *Proc. IEEE Int'l Conf. Acous., Speech, and Signal Processing*, 2001, pp. 1397–1400.
226. H. Iwata, "Haptic interfaces," in *The human-computer interaction handbook: Fundamentals, evolving technologies and emerging applications*, J. Jacko and A. Sears, Eds. Mahwah, NJ, USA: Lawrence Erlbaum, 2003, pp. 206–219.
227. R. Iyer and M. Ostendorf, "Modeling long distance dependence in language: Topic mixtures *versus* dynamic cache models," *IEEE Trans. Speech Audio Process.*, vol. 7, no. 1, pp. 30–39, 1999.
228. J.-Hu and A. Bagga, "Identifying story and preview images in news web pages," in *Proc. 7th Int'l Conf. on Document Analysis and Recognition (ICDAR'2003)*, Edinburgh, Scotland, Aug. 2003, pp. 640–644.
229. F. Jabloun and A. E. Cetin, "The teager energy based feature parameters for robust speech recognition in car noise," in *Proc. IEEE Int'l Conf. Acous., Speech, and Signal Processing.* Washington, DC, USA: IEEE Computer Society, 1999, pp. 273–276.
230. R. J. K. Jacob, "The use of eye movements in human-computer interaction techniques: what you look at is what you get," *ACM Transactions on Information Systems*, vol. 9, no. 2, pp. 152–169, 1991.
231. R. Jacob, "Eye movement-based human-computer interaction techniques: Toward non-command interfaces," *Advances in Human-Computer Interaction*, vol. 4, pp. 150–190, 1993.

232. A. Jaimes, J. B. Pelz, T. Grabowski, J. Babcock, and S. F. Chang, "Using human observers' eye movements in automatic image classifiers," in *Proceedings of SPIE Human Vision and Electronic Imaging VI, San Jose, CA*, 2001.
233. A. Jain, K. Nandakumar, and A. Ross, "Score normalization in multimodal biometric systems," *Pattern Recognition*, vol. 38, no. 12, pp. 2270–2285, December 2005.
234. A. K. Jain and A. Ross, "Multibiometric systems," *Communications of the ACM*, vol. 47, no. 1, pp. 34–40, January 2004.
235. A. Jameson, "Adaptive interfaces and agents," in *The human-computer interaction handbook: Fundamentals, evolving technologies and emerging applications*, J. Jacko and A. Sears, Eds. Mahwah, NJ, USA: Lawrence Erlbaum, 2003, pp. 305–330.
236. F. Jensen, S. Lauritzen, and K. Olsen, "Bayesian updating in recursive graphical models by local computations," *Computational Statistics Quarterly*, vol. 4, pp. 269–282, 1990.
237. M. Johnston, "Unification-based multimodal parsing," in *Proc. of the 36th annual meeting on Association for Computational Linguistics*, Montreal, Canada, 1998, pp. 624–630.
238. M. Johnston and S. Bangalore, "Finite-state multimodal integration and understanding," *Natural Language Engineering*, vol. 11, no. 2, pp. 159–187, 2005.
239. M. Johnston, P. R. Cohen, D. McGee, S. L. Oviatt, J. A. Pittman, and I. Smith, "Unification-based multimodal integration," in *Proc. of the 8th conference of European chapter of the Association for Computational Linguistics*, Madrid, Spain, 1997, pp. 281–288.
240. M. J. Jones and J. M. Rehg, "Statistical color models with application to skin detection." *Int'l J. of Comp. Vis.*, vol. 46, no. 1, pp. 81–96, 2002.
241. E. Jonietz, "Augmented reality: Special issue 10 emerging technologies 2007, MIT technology review," 2007.
242. S. X. Ju, M. J. Black, S. Minneman, and D. Kimber, "Summarization of videotaped presentations: automatic analysis of motion and gesture," *IEEE Trans. Circuits Syst. Video Technol.*, vol. 8, no. 5, pp. 686–696, 1998.
243. O. O. K. and S. F. W. M., "Perceptual image retrieval using eye movements," in *Proceedings of International Workshop on Intelligent Computing in Pattern Analysis/Synthesis*, 2007, xi'an, China, 26-27 August.
244. J. Kaiser, "On a simple algorithm to calculate the 'energy' of a signal," in *Proc. IEEE Int'l Conf. Acous., Speech, and Signal Processing*, Albuquerque N.M., Apr 1990, pp. 381–384.
245. ——, "Construction and evaluation of a robust multifeature speech/music discriminator," in *Proc. IEEE Int'l Conf. Acous., Speech, and Signal Processing*, 1997, pp. 1331–1334.
246. E. Kandel, J. Schwartz, and T. Jessell, *Principles of Neural Science.* Stamford, Connecticut: McGraw-Hill, 4 edition, 2000.
247. A. Katsamanis, G. Papandreou, and P. Maragos, "Audiovisual-to-articulatory speech inversion using active appearance models for the face and hidden markov models for the dynamics," in *Proc. IEEE Int'l Conf. Acous., Speech, and Signal Processing*, 2008.
248. A. Katsamanis, G. Papandreou, V. Pitsikalis, and P. Maragos, "Multimodal fusion by adaptive compensation for feature uncertainty with application to audiovisual speech recognition," in *Proc. European Signal Processing Conference*, 2006.

249. M. Kay, "Functional grammar," in *Proc. of the 5th Annual Meeting of the Berkeley Linguistics Society*, 1979, pp. 142–158.
250. C. Kayser, C. Petkov, M. Lippert, and N. Logothetis, "Mechanisms for allocating auditory attention: an auditory saliency map," *Current Biology*, vol. 15, no. 21, pp. 1943–1947, 2005.
251. R. Keiller, "Using VoiceXMl 2.0 in the VxOne unified messaging application," in *Practical Spoken Dialog Systems*, D. A. Dahl, Ed. Kluwer Academic Publishers, 2004, pp. 143–163.
252. H. Keränen, L. Pohjanheimo, and H. Ailisto, "Tag manager: a mobile phone platform for physical selection services," in *IEEE International Conference on Pervasive Services 2005 (ICPS'05)*, 2005, pp. 405 – 412.
253. A. Kerne, "Collage machine: an interactive agent of web recombination," *Leonardo*, vol. 33, no. 5, pp. 347–350, 2000.
254. M. Kherfi, D. Ziou, and A. Bernardi, "Image retrieval from the world wide web: Issues, techniques, and systems," *ACM Computing Surveys*, vol. 36, no. 1, pp. 35–67, March 2004.
255. E. Kidron, Y. Y. Schechner, and M. Elad, "Cross-modal localization via sparsity," *IEEE Trans. Signal Process.*, vol. 55, no. 4, pp. 1390–1404, Apr. 2007.
256. E. Kijak, G. Gravier, P. Gros, L. Oisel, and F. Bimbot, "Hmm based structuring of tennis videos using visual and audio cues," in *Proc. of IEEE Int'l Conference on Multimedia and Expo*, vol. 3, July 2003, pp. 309–312.
257. E. Kijak, G. Gravier, L. Oisel, and P. Gros, "Audiovisual integration for sport broadcast structuring," *Multimedia Tools and Applications*, vol. 30, pp. 289–312, 2006.
258. A. Kilgarriff and M. Palmer, "Special Issue on Senseval," *Computers and the Humanities*, vol. 34, no. 1/2, Apr. 2000.
259. C. W. Kim, R. Ansari, and A. E. Cetin, "A class of linear-phase regular biorthogonal wavelets," in *Proc. IEEE Int'l Conf. Acous., Speech, and Signal Processing*, 1992, pp. 673–676.
260. J. Kim and J. Peal, "A computational model for causal and diagnostic reasoning in inference systems," in *Proc. Int'l Joint Conf. on Artificial Intel.*, 1983, pp. 190–193.
261. M. Kipp, "ANVIL - A generic annotation tool for multimodal dialogue," in *Proc. European Conf. on Speech Communication and Technology*, 2001, pp. 1367–1370.
262. J. Kittler, M. Hatef, R. Duin, and J. Matas, "On combining classifiers," *IEEE Trans. Pattern Anal. Mach. Intell.*, vol. 20, no. 3, pp. 226–239, Mar. 1998.
263. D. Klakow, "Selecting articles from the language model training corpus," in *Proc. IEEE Int'l Conf. Acous., Speech, and Signal Processing*, 2000.
264. J. M. Kleinberg, "Authoritative sources in a hyperlinked environment," *Journal of the ACM*, vol. 46, no. 5, pp. 604–632, 1999.
265. P. Knees, M. Schedl, T. Pohle, and G. Widmer, "An innovative three-dimensional user interface for exploring music collections enriched with meta-information from the web," in *Proc. ACM Int'l Conference on Multimedia*, Santa Barbara, California, USA, October 23-26 2006, pp. 17–24.
266. P. Knees, M. Schedl, and G. Widmer, "Multiple lyrics alignment: Automatic retrieval of song lyrics," in *Proc. Int'l Conf. on Music Information Retrieval*, London, UK, September 11-15 2005, pp. 564–569.

267. D. C. Knill, D. Kersten, and A. L. Yuille, *Perception as Bayesian Inference.* Cambridge Univ. Press, 1996, ch. Introduction: A Bayesian Formulation of Visual Perception, pp. 1–21.
268. C. Koch and S. Ullman, "Shifts in selective visual attention: towards the underlying neural circuitry," *Human Neurobiology*, vol. 4, no. 4, pp. 219–227, Jun 1985.
269. K. Koffka, *Principles of Gestalt Psychology.* Routledge, 1935, 1999.
270. W. Köhler, *Gestalt Psychology.* New York: Liveright Publish. Corp., 1947, 1970.
271. T. Kohonen, *Self-Organizing Maps*, 3rd ed., ser. Springer Series in Information Sciences. Berlin: Springer, 2001, vol. 30.
272. T. Kohonen, E. Oja, O. Simula, A. Visa, and J. Kangas, "Engineering applications of the self-organizing map," *Proc. IEEE*, vol. 84, no. 10, pp. 1358–1384, October 1996.
273. A. Kokaram and P. Delacourt, "On the motion-based diagnosis of video from cricket broadcasts," in *Irish Signals and Systems Conference*, June 2002.
274. A. Kokaram, N. Rea, R. Dahyot, A. M. Tekalp, P. Bouthemy, P. Gros, and I. Sezan, "Browsing sports video," *IEEE Signal Process. Mag.*, vol. 23, no. 2, pp. 47–58, March 2006.
275. A. C. Kokaram, *Motion Picture Restoration: Digital Algorithms for Artefact Suppression in Degraded Motion Picture Film and Video.* Springer Verlag, 1998.
276. M. Kotti, E. Benetos, C. Kotropoulos, and I. Pitas, "A neural network approach to audio-assisted movie dialogue detection," *Neurocomputating*, vol. 71, pp. 157–166, 2007.
277. M. Kotti, C. Kotropoulos, B. Ziolko, I. Pitas, and V. Moschou, "A framework for dialogue detection in movies," *Lecture Notes in Computer Science*, vol. 4105, pp. 371–378, 2006.
278. W. Kraaij and R. Pohlmann, "Comparing the Effect of Syntactic vs. Statistical Phrase Indexing Strategies for Dutch," in *2nd European Conference on Research and Advanced Technology for Digital Libraries*, C. Nicolaou and C. Stephanides, Eds. Lecture Notes in Computer Science, Springer Verlag, 1998, vol. 1513, pp. 605–614.
279. P. Král, C. Cerisara, and J. Klečková, "Automatic dialog acts recognition based on sentence structure," in *Proc. Int'l Conf. on Speech Communication and Technology*, 2005, pp. 825–828.
280. B. Kroon, J. Nesvadba, and A. Hanjalic, "Dialog detection in narrative video by shot and face analysis," in *Proc. IS&T/SPIE's 19th Annual Symp. Electronic Imaging -Multimedia Content Access: Algorithms and Systems*, vol. 6506, 2007, pp. 315–325.
281. S. Kumar and P. R. Cohen, "Towards a fault-tolerant multi-agent system architecture," in *Proc. International Conference on Autonomous Agents.* ACM Press New York, NY, USA, 2000, pp. 459–466.
282. M. La Cascia, S. Sethi, and S. Sclaroff, "Combining textual and visual cues for content-based image retrieval on the world wide web," in *IEEE Workshop on Content-Based Access of Image and Video Libraries*, 1998, pp. 24–28.
283. J. Lai and N. Yankelovich, "Conversational speech interfaces," in *The human-computer interaction handbook: Fundamentals, evolving technologies and emerging applications*, J. Jacko and A. Sears, Eds. Mahwah, NJ, USA: Lawrence Erlbaum, 2003, pp. 698–713.

284. M. S. Landy, L. T. Maloney, E. B. Johnston, and M. Young, "Measurement and modeling of depth cue combination: in defense of weak fusion," *Vision Research*, vol. 35, no. 3, pp. 389–412, 1995.
285. C. Leacock, M. Chodorow, and G. A. Miller, "Using corpus statistics and WordNet relations for sense identification," *Computational Linguistics*, vol. 24, no. 1, pp. 147–165, 1998.
286. J. J. Lee, J. Kim, and J. H. Kim, "Data-driven design of HMM topology for on-line handwriting recognition," *International Journal of Pattern Recognition and Artificial Intelligence*, vol. 15, no. 1, 2001.
287. B. Lehane, N. O'Connor, and N. Murphy, "Action sequence detection in motion pictures," in *Proc. European Workshop Integration of Knowledge, Semantics and Digital Media Technology*, 2004.
288. ——, "Dialogue scene detection in movies using low and mid-level visual features," in *Proc. ACM Int'l Conference on Image and Video Retrieval*, 2004, pp. 286–296.
289. H. Lejsek, F. H. Asmundsson, B. Thor-Jonsson, and L. Amsaleg, "Scalability of local image descriptors: A comparative study," in *Proc. ACM Int'l Conference on Multimedia*, Oct. 2006.
290. R. Lempel and A. Soffer, "PicASHOW: Pictorial authority search by hyperlinks on the web," *ACM Transactions on Information Systems*, vol. 20, no. 1, pp. 1–24, Jan. 2002.
291. D. Lenat, "Cyc: A large-scale investment in knowledge infrastructure," *Communications of the ACM*, vol. 38, no. 11, pp. 33–38, 1995.
292. D. Lennon, N. Harte, and A. Kokaram, "A HMM framework for motion based parsing for video from observational psychology," in *Irish Machine Vision and Image Processing Conference*, DCU, Dublin, Ireland, August 2006, pp. 110–117.
293. D. Lennon, "Motion based parsing," Master's thesis, Trinity College Dublin, 2007.
294. R. Leonardi, P. Migliorati, and M. Prandini, "Semantic indexing of soccer audio-visual sequences: A multimodal approach based on controlled markov chains," *IEEE Trans. Circuits Syst. Video Technol.*, vol. 14, no. 5, May 2004.
295. M. Lew, N. Sebe, C. Djeraba, and R. Jain, "Content-based multimedia information retrieval: State-of-the-art and challenges," *ACM Transactions on Multimedia Computing, Communications, and Applications*, vol. 2, no. 1, pp. 1–19, 2006.
296. Y. Li, Z. A. Bandar, and D. McLean, "An approach for measuring semantic similarity between words using multiple information sources," *IEEE Trans. Knowl. Data Eng.*, vol. 15, no. 4, pp. 871–882, July/Aug. 2003.
297. Y. Li and C. C. J. Kuo, "Real-time segmentation and annotation of MPEG video based on multimodal content analysis I & II," Univ. Southern California, Los Angeles, Technical Report, Tech. Rep., 2000.
298. ——, *Video Content Analysis Using Multimodal Information.* Springer, 2003.
299. Y. Li, S. Narayanan, and C. C. J. Kuo, "Identification of speakers in movie dialogues using audiovisual cues," in *Proc. IEEE Int'l Conf. Acous., Speech, and Signal Processing*, vol. 2, 2002, pp. 2093–2096.
300. ——, "Content-based movie analysis and indexing based on audiovisual cues," *IEEE Trans. Circuits Syst. Video Technol.*, vol. 14, no. 8, pp. 1073–1085, 2004.

301. T. Lidy and A. Rauber, "Evaluation of feature extractors and psycho-acoustic transformations for music genre classification," in *Proc. Int'l Conf. on Music Information Retrieval*, London, UK, September 11-15 2005, pp. 34–41.
302. D. Lin, "An information-theoretic definition of similarity," in *Proc. Int'l Conf. on Machine Learning*, 1998, pp. 296–304.
303. D. J. Litman and S. Pan, "Predicting and adapting to poor speech recognition in a spoken dialogue system," in *Proc. National Conference on Artificial Intelligence and Conference on Innovative Applications of Artificial Intelligence*. AAAI Press / The MIT Press, 2000, pp. 722–728.
304. C.-B. Liu and N. Ahuja, "Motion based retrieval of dynamic objects in videos," in *Proc. ACM Int'l Conference on Multimedia*, 2004, pp. 288–291.
305. H. Liu and P. Singh, "Conceptnet: a practical commonsense reasoning toolkit," *BT Technology Journal*, vol. 22, no. 4, pp. 211–226, 2004.
306. Y. Liu, E. Shriberg, A. Stolcke, and M. P. Harper, "Using machine learning to cope with imbalanced classes in natural speech: Evidence from sentence boundary and disfluency detection," in *Proc. Int'l Conf. on Spoken Language Processing*, 2004.
307. B. Logan, A. Kositsky, and P. Moreno, "Semantic analysis of song lyrics," in *Proc. of IEEE Int'l Conference on Multimedia and Expo*. Taipei, Taiwan: IEEE Computer Society, June 27-30 2004, pp. 827–830.
308. D. G. Lowe, "Distinctive image features from scale-invariant keypoints," *Int'l J. of Comp. Vis.*, vol. 60, no. 2, pp. 91–110, 2004.
309. P. P. G. P. Ltd, "Virtual laser keyboard," http://www.virtual-laser-keyboard.com/.
310. L. Lu, H. Zhang, and H. Jiang, "Content analysis for audio classification and segmentation," *IEEE Trans. Speech Audio Process.*, vol. 10, no. 7, pp. 504–516, 2002.
311. Y. Lu, C. Hu, X. Zhu, H.-J. Zhang, and Q. Yang, "A unified framework for semantic and feature based relevance feedback in image retrieval systems," in *Proc. ACM Int'l Conference on Multimedia*, Los Angeles CA, USA, 2000, pp. 31–37.
312. J. Luettin, G. Potamianos, and C. Neti, "Asynchronous stream modeling for large vocabulary audio-visual speech recognition," in *Proc. IEEE Int'l Conf. Acous., Speech, and Signal Processing*, 2001.
313. Y. Ma, L. Lu, H. Zhang, and M. Li, "A user attention model for video summarization," in *Proc. ACM Int'l Conference on Multimedia*, 2002.
314. Y.-F. Ma, X.-S. Hua, L. Lu, and H.-J. Zhang, "A generic framework of user attention model and its application in video summarization," *IEEE Trans. Multimedia*, vol. 7, pp. 907–919, 2005.
315. I. S. MacKenzie and R. W. Soukoreff, "Text entry for mobile computing: models and methods, theory and practice," *Human-Computer Interaction*, vol. 17, no. 2, pp. 147–198, 2002.
316. J. P. G. Mahedero, Á. Martínez, P. Cano, M. Koppenberger, and F. Gouyon, "Natural language processing of lyrics," in *Proc. ACM Int'l Conference on Multimedia*. New York, NY, USA: ACM Press, 2005, pp. 475–478.
317. G. Maltese and F. Mancini, "An automatic technique to include grammatical and morphological information in a trigram-based statistical language model," in *Proc. IEEE Int'l Conf. Acous., Speech, and Signal Processing*, 1992.

318. L. Mangu, E. Brill, and A. Stolcke, "Finding consensus in speech recognition: Word error minimization and other applications of confusion networks," *Computer Speech and Language*, vol. 14, no. 4, pp. 373–400, 2000.
319. B. S. Manjunath, P. Salembier, and T. Sikora, *Introduction to MPEG-7: Multimedia Content Description Interface.* Wiley, 2002.
320. P. Maragos, J. Kaiser, and T. Quatieri, "Energy separation in signal modulations with application to speech analysis," *IEEE Trans. Signal Process.*, vol. 41, no. 10, pp. 3024–3051, Oct 1993.
321. D. Marcu, "The rhetorical parsing of unrestricted texts: A surface-based approach," *Computational Linguistics*, vol. 26, no. 3, pp. 395–448, 2000.
322. K. V. Mardia, J. T. Kent, and J. M. Bibby, *Multivariate Analysis.* Acad. Press, 1979.
323. J. Marroquin, S. Mitter, and T. Poggio, "Probabilistic solutions of ill-posed problems in computational vision," *J. of the Amer. Stat. Assoc.*, vol. 82, no. 37, pp. 76–89, March 1987.
324. I. Marsic, A. Medl, and J. Flanagan, "Natural communication with information systems," *Proc. IEEE*, vol. 88, no. 8, pp. 1354–1366, 2000.
325. D. L. Martin, "The Open Agent Architecture: A framework for building distributed software system," *Applied Artificial Intelligence*, vol. 13, no. 1, pp. 91–128, 1999.
326. J. Martinez, "Standards - mpeg-7 overview of mpeg-7 description tools, part 2," *IEEE Multimedia*, vol. 9, no. 3, pp. 83–93, Jul-Sep 2002.
327. R. Mason, R. Gunst, and J. Hess, *Statistical Design and Analysis of Experiments.* Wiley, 1989.
328. D. Massaro and D. Stork, "Speech recognition and sensory integration," *American Scientist*, vol. 86, no. 3, pp. 236–244, 1998.
329. I. Matthews, T. F. Cootes, J. A. Bangham, S. Cox, and R. Harvey, "Extraction of visual features for lipreading," *IEEE Trans. Pattern Anal. Mach. Intell.*, vol. 24, no. 2, pp. 198–213, 2002.
330. R. Mayer, T. A. Aziz, and A. Rauber, "Visualising class distribution on self-organising maps," in *Proc. Int'l Conf. on Artificial Neural Networks.* Porto, Portugal: Springer, September 9 - 13 2007, pp. 359–368.
331. S. McAdams, "Recognition of auditory sound sources and events," in *Thinking in Sound:The Cognitive Psychology of Human Audition.* Oxford University Press, 1993.
332. J. McCarthy, M. A. Sasse, and R. J., "Could I have the menu please?: An eye tracking study of design conventions," in *Proc. Annual Conf. on Human-Computer Interaction*, 2003, 8-12 Sep 2003, Bath, UK.
333. I. McCowan, D. Gatica-Perez, S. Bengio, G. Lathoud, M. Barnard, and D. Zhang, "Automatic analysis of multimodal group actions in meetings," *IEEE Trans. Pattern Anal. Mach. Intell.*, vol. 27, pp. 305–317, 2005.
334. H. McGurk and J. MacDonald, "Hearing lips and seeing voices," *Nature*, vol. 264, pp. 746–748, 1976.
335. M. F. McTear, "Spoken dialogue technology: enabling the conversational user interface," *ACM Computing Surveys*, vol. 34, no. 1, pp. 90–169, 2002.
336. B. Merialdo, "Tagging English text with a probabilistic model," *Computational Linguistics*, vol. 20, no. 2, pp. 155–171, 1994.
337. Microsoft, "Microsoft surface," http://www.microsoft.com/surface/.
338. MicroVision, "Microvision, inc." http://www.microvision.com/.

339. P. Milgram and F. Kishino, "Taxonomy of mixed reality virtual displays," *Institute of Electronics, Information, and Communication Engineers Trans. Information and Systems*, vol. E77-D, no. 12, pp. 1321–1239, 1994.
340. G. A. Miller, "The magical number seven, plus or minus two: Some limits on our capacity for information processing," *Psychological Review*, vol. 63, no. 2, pp. 81–97, 1956.
341. M. Minksy, "A framework for representing knowledge," in *The Psychology of Computer Vision*, P. Winston, Ed. McGraw-Hill, 1977, pp. 211–277.
342. G. Monaci and P. Vandergheynst, "Audiovisual Gestalts," in *Proc. IEEE Int'l Conf. on Computer Vision and Pattern Recognition Workshop*. New York, NY: IEEE Computer Society, 2006, p. 200.
343. F. Mörchen, A. Ultsch, M. Nöcker, and C. Stamm, "Databionic visualization of music collections according to perceptual distance," in *Proc. Int'l Conf. on Music Information Retrieval*, London, UK, September 11-15 2005, pp. 396–403.
344. A. Morris, A. Hagen, H. Glotin, and H. Bourlard, "Multi-stream adaptive evidence combination for noise robust ASR," *Speech Communication*, vol. 34, pp. 25–40, 2001.
345. "Standard international iso/iec 21000 information technology – "multimedia framework"."
346. "MPEG-7 requirements document v.15, iso/iec jtc1/sc29/wg11, mpeg01/n4320," Jul. 2001.
347. S. V. Mulken, E. André, and J. Müller, "The persona effect: How substantial is it?" in *Proc. of HCI on People and Computers*. Springer-Verlag, London, UK, 1998, pp. 53–66.
348. D. Mumford, *Perception as Bayesian Inference*. Cambridge Univ. Press, 1996, ch. Pattern Theory: A unifying perspective, pp. 25–61.
349. D. Mumford and J. Shah, "Optimal approximations by piecewise smooth functions and associated variational problems," *Commun. Pure & Appl. Math.*, vol. XLII, no. 4, 1989.
350. K. Murphy, "Dynamic Bayesian networks: Representation, inference and learning," Ph.D. dissertation, Univ. of California, Berkeley, 2002.
351. J. Myers and A. Well, *Research Design and Statistical Analysis*. Lawrence Erlbaum Associates, 2003.
352. MyVu, "Myvu corp." http://www.myvu.com/.
353. C. Naas and L. Gong, "Ten principles for designing Human-Computer dialog systems," in *Practical Spoken Dialog Systems*, D. A. Dahl, Ed. Kluwer Academic Publishers, 2004, pp. 25–40.
354. J. Nam, M. Alghoniemy, and A. Tewfik, "Audio-visual content-based violent scene characterization," in *Proc. IEEE Int'l Conf. on Image Processing*, 1998, pp. 353–357.
355. J. Nam, A. E. Çetin, and A. H. Tewfik, "Speaker identification and video analysis for hierarchical video shot classification." in *Proc. IEEE Int'l Conf. on Image Processing*, vol. 2, 1997, pp. 550–553.
356. K. Nandakumar, Y. Chen, S. C. Dass, and A. K. Jain, "Likelihood ratio based biometric score fusion," *IEEE Trans. Pattern Anal. Mach. Intell.*, vol. 30, no. 2, February 2008.
357. M. R. Naphade and T. S. Huang, "Extracting semantics from audio-visual content: the final frontier in multimedia retrieval," *IEEE Trans. Neural Netw.*, vol. 13, no. 4, pp. 793–810, 2002.

358. A. Nasr, Y. Estève, F. Béchet, T. Spriet, and R. de Mori, "A language model combining N-grams and stochastic finite state automata," in *Proc. European Conf. on Speech Communication and Technology*, 1999.
359. X. Naturel, G. Gravier, and P. Gros, "Fast structuring of large television streams using program guides," in *Proceedings of the 4th International Workshop on Adaptive Multimedia Retrieval (AMR), Geneva, Switzerland*, ser. Lecture Notes in Computer Science, vol. 4398, Jul. 2006, pp. 223–232.
360. J. G. Neal and S. C. Shapiro, "Intelligent multi-media interface technology," *ACM-SIGCHI Bulletin*, vol. 20, no. 1, pp. 75–76, 1988.
361. A. V. Nefian, "Coupled hidden markov model for audiovisual speech recognition," *US Patent No. 7,165,029*, Jan. 2007.
362. A. Nefian, L. Liang, X. Pi, X. Liu, and K. Murphy, "Dynamic bayesian networks for audio-visual speech recognition," *EURASIP Journal on Applied Signal Processing*, vol. 11, pp. 1–15, 2002.
363. R. Neumayer, M. Dittenbach, and A. Rauber, "PlaySOM and PocketSOM-Player: Alternative interfaces to large music collections," in *Proc. Int'l Conf. on Music Information Retrieval.* London, UK: Queen Mary, University of London, September 11-15 2005, pp. 618–623.
364. R. Neumayer and A. Rauber, "Integration of text and audio features for genre classification in music information retrieval," in *Proc. European Conf. on Information Retrieval*, Rome, Italy, April 2-5 2007, pp. 724–727.
365. ——, "Multi-modal music information retrieval - visualisation and evaluation of clusterings by both audio and lyrics," in *Proceedings of the 8th Conference Recherche d'Information Assistée par Ordinateur (RIAO'07).* Pittsburgh, PA, USA: ACM, May 29th - June 1 2007.
366. J. Nielsen, *Usability Engineering.* Academic Press, 1993.
367. ——, "Alert Box: F-Shaped pattern for reading web content," http://www.useit.com/alertbox/reading_pattern.html, 2006.
368. J. Nielsen and R. Molich, "Heuristic evaluation of user interfaces," in *Proc. ACM-SIGCHI conference on Human factors in computing systems.* ACM Press New York, NY, USA, 1990, pp. 249–256.
369. L. Nigay and J. Coutaz, "A design space for multimodal systems: concurrent processing and data fusion," in *Proc. ACM-SIGCHI conference on Human factors in computing systems.* ACM, New York, NY, USA, 1993, pp. 172–178.
370. S. G. Nikolov, D. R. Bull, and I. D. Glichrist, "Gaze-contingent multi-modality displays of multi-layered geographical maps," in *Proc. of the 5th Intl. Conf. on Numerical Methods and Applications (NM&A02)*, 2002, symposium on Numerical Methods for Sensor Data Processing, Borovetz, Bulgaria.
371. Nokia, "Mara - the mobile augmented reality applications project," http://research.nokia.com/research/projects/mara/index.html.
372. T. Numajiri, A. Nakamura, and Y. Kuno, "Speed browser controlled by eye movements," in *Proc. of IEEE Int'l Conference on Multimedia and Expo*, 2002, august 26-29, Lausanne, 2002.
373. J.-M. Odobez and P. Bouthemy, "Robust multiresolution estimation of parametric motion models," *Journal of Visual Communication and Image Representation*, vol. 6, no. 4, December 1995.
374. U. of South Australia, "Tinmith ar system," http://www.tinmith.net/.
375. K. Ohtsuki, K. Bessho, Y. Matsuo, S. Matsunaga, and Y. Hayashi, "Automatic multimedia indexing," *IEEE Signal Process. Mag.*, vol. 23, no. 2, pp. 69–78, 2006.

376. N. Oliver, A. Garg, and E. Horvitz, "Layered representations for learning and inferring office activity from multiple sensory channels," *Computer Vision and Image Understanding*, vol. 96, no. 2, pp. 163–180, 2004.
377. N. Orio, "Music retrieval: A tutorial and review," *Foundations and Trends in Information Retrieval*, vol. 1, no. 1, pp. 1–90, September 2006.
378. M. Ostendorf, V. Digalakis, and O. Kimball, "From HMMs to segment models: A unified view of stochastic modeling for speech recognition," *IEEE Trans. Speech Audio Process.*, vol. 4, no. 5, pp. 360–378, 1996.
379. M. Ostendorf, "From HMMs to Segment Models," in *Automatic Speech and Speaker Recognition - Advanced Topics.* Kluwer Academic Publishers, 1996, ch. 8.
380. S. Oviatt, "Mutual disambiguation of recognition errors in a multimodal architecture," in *Proc. ACM-SIGCHI conference on Human factors in computing systems.* ACM Press, New York, NY, USA, 1999, pp. 576–583.
381. ——, "Ten myths of multimodal interaction," *Communications of the ACM*, vol. 42, no. 11, pp. 74–81, 1999.
382. ——, "Multimodal interfaces," in *The human-computer interaction handbook: Fundamentals, evolving technologies and emerging applications*, J. Jacko and A. Sears, Eds. Mahwah, NJ, USA: Lawrence Erlbaum, 2003, pp. 286–304.
383. S. Oviatt, R. Coulston, S. Tomko, B. Xiao, R. Lunsford, M. Wesson, and L. Carmichael, "Toward a theory of organized multimodal integration patterns during human-computer interaction," in *Proc. Int'l Conf. on Multimodal Interfaces.* ACM Press, New York, NY, USA, 2003, pp. 44–51.
384. O. K. Oyekoya and F. W. M. Stentiford, "Exploring human eye behaviour using a model of visual attention," in *Proc. Int'l Conf. on Pattern Recognition*, 2004, cambridge UK, August.
385. ——, "A performance comparison of eye tracking and mouse interfaces in a target image identification task," in *2nd European Workshop on the Integration of Knowledge, Semantics & Digital Media Technology (EWIMT)*, 2005, london, 30th Nov - 1st Dec, 2005.
386. O. Oyekoya, "Eye tracking: A perceptual interface for content based image retrieval," Ph.D. dissertation, University College London, UK, 2007.
387. L. Page, S. Brin, R. Motwani, and T. Winograd, "The PageRank citation ranking: Bringing order to the web," Computer Systems Laboratory, Stanford Univ., CA, Tech. Rep., 1998.
388. E. Pampalk, A. Rauber, and D. Merkl, "Content-based Organization and Visualization of Music Archives," in *Proc. ACM Int'l Conference on Multimedia.* Juan les Pins, France: ACM, December 1-6 2002, pp. 570–579.
389. G. Papandreou, A. Katsamanis, V. Pitsikalis, and P. Maragos, "Multimodal fusion and learning with uncertain features applied to audiovisual speech recognition," in *Proc. of IEEE Int'l Workshop on Multimedia Signal Processing*, 2007, pp. 264–267.
390. W. Pasman and C. Woodward, "Implementation of an augmented reality system on a pda," in *Proc. IEEE/ACM Int'l Symposium on Mixed and Augmented Reality*, October 2003, pp. 276–277.
391. E. K. Patterson, S. Gurbuz, Z. Tufekci, and J. N. Gowdy, "CUAVE: A new audio-visual database for multimodal human-computer interface research," in *Proc. IEEE Int'l Conf. Acous., Speech, and Signal Processing*, 2002.

392. J. Peng and D. R. Heisterkamp, "Kernel indexing for relevance feedback image retrieval," in *Proc. IEEE Int'l Conf. on Image Processing*, Barcelona, Spain, 2003.
393. A. Pentland, B. Moghaddam, and T. Starner, "View–based and modular eigenspaces for face recognition," in *Proc. IEEE Int'l Conf. on Computer Vision and Pattern Recognition*, 1994, pp. 84–91.
394. A. Pentland, R. W. Picard, and S. Sclaroff, "Photobook: Content-based manipulation of image databases," *Int'l J. of Comp. Vis.*, vol. 18, no. 3, pp. 233–254, 1996.
395. M. Perakakis and A. Potamianos, "The effect of input mode on inactivity and interaction times of multimodal systems," in *Proc. Int'l Conf. on Multimodal Interfaces.* ACM New York, NY, USA, 2007, pp. 102–109.
396. ——, "A study in efficiency and modality usage in multimodal form filling systems," *IEEE Trans. Audio, Speech, and Language Processing*, 2008, to appear.
397. K. Perlin, "Quikwriting: continuous stylus-based text entry," in *UIST '98: Proceedings of the 11th annual ACM symposium on User interface software and technology.* New York, NY, USA: ACM Press, 1998, pp. 215–216.
398. E. Petajan, "Automatic lipreading to enhance speech recognition," Ph.D. dissertation, Univ. of Illinois, Urbana-Campaign, 1984.
399. E. G. Petrakis, K. Kontis, E. Voutsakis, and E. Milios, "Relevance feedback methods for logo and trademark image retrieval on the web," in *ACM Symposium on Applied Computing (ACM SAC'2006)*, Dijon, France, April 23-27 2006, pp. 1084–1088, special Track on Information Access and Retrieval (IAR).
400. E. G. Petrakis, G. Varelas, A. Hliaoutakis, and P. Raftopoulou, "X-similarity: Computing semantic similarity between concepts from different ontologies," *Journal of Digital Information Management*, vol. 4, no. 4, pp. 233–238, December 2006.
401. S. Pfeiffer, R. Lienhart, and W. Effelsberg, "Scene determination based on video and audio features," *Multimedia Tools and Applications*, vol. 15, pp. 59–81, 2001.
402. A. Pikrakis, T. Giannakopoulos, and S. Theodoridis, "A dynamic programming approach to speech/music discrimination of radio recordings," in *Proc. European Signal Processing Conference*, 2007.
403. F. Pitié, S.-A. Berrani, R. Dahyot, and A. Kokaram, "Off-line multiple object tracking using candidate selection and the viterbi algorithm," in *Proc. IEEE Int'l Conf. on Image Processing*, Genoa, Italy, 2005.
404. V. Pitsikalis, A. Katsamanis, G. Papandreou, and P. Maragos, "Adaptive multimodal fusion by uncertainty compensation," in *Proc. Int'l Conf. on Spoken Language Processing*, 2006, pp. 2458–2461.
405. T. Poggio, V. Torre, and C. Koch, "Computational vision and regularization theory," *Nature*, vol. 317, pp. 314–319, 1985.
406. L. Pohjanheimo, H. Keränen, and H. Ailisto, "Implementing touchme paradigm with a mobile phone," in *Proceedings of the 2005 joint conference on Smart objects and ambient intelligence.* New York, NY, USA: ACM Press, 2005, pp. 87–92.
407. J.-P. Poli and J. Carrive, "Modeling television schedules for television stream structuring, Singapour," in *Proceedings of ACM MultiMedia Modeling*, Jan. 2007, pp. 680–689.

408. P. Poller and V. Tschernomas, "Multimodal fission and media design," in *SmartKom: Foundations of Multimodal Dialogue Systems*, W. Wahlster, Ed. Springer-Verlag, New York, NY, 2006, pp. 379–400.
409. A. Potamianos, E. Fosler-Lussier, E. Ammicht, and M. Perakakis, "Information seeking spoken dialogue systems - Part II: Multimodal dialogue," *IEEE Trans. Multimedia*, vol. 9, no. 3, pp. 550–566, 2007.
410. A. Potamianos, H. Kuo, A. Pargellis, A. Saad, and Q. Zhou, "Design principles and tools for multimodal dialog systems," in *Proc. ESCA Workshop Interact. Dialog. Multi-Modal Syst.*, Kloster Irsee, Germany, Jun. 1999.
411. A. Potamianos and P. Maragos, "Speech formant frequency and bandwidth tracking using multiband energy demodulation," *J. of the Acous. Soc. Am.*, vol. 99, no. 6, pp. 3795–3806, Jun 1996.
412. A. Potamianos, E. Sanchez-Soto, and K. Daoudi, "Stream weight computation for multi-stream classifiers," in *Proc. IEEE Int'l Conf. Acous., Speech, and Signal Processing*, 2006.
413. G. Potamianos, C. Neti, G. Gravier, and A. Garg, "Automatic recognition of audio-visual speech: Recent progress and challenges," *Proc. IEEE*, vol. 91, no. 9, pp. 1306–1326, 2003.
414. G. Potamianos, C. Neti, G. Gravier, A. Garg, and A. W. Senior, "Recent advances in the automatic recognition of audio-visual speech," *Proc. IEEE*, vol. 91, no. 9, pp. 1–18, 2003.
415. W. Press, S. Teukolsky, W. Vetterling, and B. Flannery, *Numerical Recipes.* Cambridge Univ. Press, 1992.
416. C. M. Privitera and L. W. Stark, "Algorithms for defining visual regions of interest: Comparison with eye fixations," *IEEE Trans. Pattern Anal. Mach. Intell.*, vol. 22, no. 9, pp. 970–982, 2000.
417. S. Quackenbush and A. Lindsay, "Overview of MPEG-7 audio," *IEEE Trans. Circuits Syst. Video Technol.*, vol. 11, no. 6, pp. 725–729, 2001.
418. E. R. Baeza-Yates, *Modern Information Retrieval.* Addison Wesley, 1999.
419. S. Raaijmakers, J. Den Hartog, and J. Baan, "Multimodal topic segmentation and classification of news video," in *Proc. Text Retrieval Conference*, vol. 2, 2002, pp. 33–36.
420. L. Rabiner, "A tutorial on Hidden Markov Models and selected applications in speech recognition," *Proc. IEEE*, vol. 77, no. 2, pp. 257–286, 1989.
421. L. Rabiner and B.-H. Juang, *Fundamentals of Speech Recognition.* NJ, USA: Prentice-Hall, 1993.
422. K. Rapantzikos, N. Tsapatsoulis, Y. Avrithis, and S. Kollias, *Signal Processing: Image Communication*, 2007, submitted for publication.
423. K. Rapantzikos and M. Zervakis, "Robust optical flow estimation in MPEG sequences," in *Proc. IEEE Int'l Conf. Acous., Speech, and Signal Processing*, Mar 2005.
424. Z. Rasheed and M. Shah, "Scene detection in hollywood movies and tv shows," in *Proc. IEEE Int'l Conf. on Computer Vision and Pattern Recognition*, vol. 2, 2003, pp. 343–348.
425. K. Ratakonda, M. Sezan, and R. Crinon, "Hierarchical video summarization," in *Proc. SPIE, Visual Comm. and Image Proc.*, vol. 3653, Dec 1998, pp. 1531–1541.
426. A. Rauber and M. Frühwirth, "Automatically analyzing and organizing music archives," in *Proceedings of the 5th European Conference on Research and Ad-*

vanced Technology for Digital Libraries (ECDL'01), ser. LNCS. Darmstadt, Germany: Springer, September 4-8 2001, pp. 402–414.

427. A. Rauber, E. Pampalk, and D. Merkl, "Using psycho-acoustic models and self-organizing maps to create a hierarchical structuring of music by musical styles," in *Proc. Int'l Conf. on Music Information Retrieval*, Paris, France, October 13-17 2002, pp. 71–80.
428. M. Rautiainen et al., "TREC 2002 video track experiments at MediaTeam Oulu and VTT," in *Proc. Text Retrieval Conference*, 2002.
429. N. Rea, R. Dahyot, and A. Kokaram, "Semantic event detection in sports through motion understanding," in *Proc. ACM Int'l Conference on Image and Video Retrieval*, Dublin, Ireland, July 2004.
430. ——, "Classification and representation of semantic content in broadcast tennis videos," in *Proc. IEEE Int'l Conf. on Image Processing*, Genoa, Italy, 2005.
431. N. Rea, C. Lambe, G. Lacey, and R. Dahyot, "Multimodal periodicity analysis for illicit content detection in videos," in *IET European Conference on Visual Media Production (CVMP)*, London, UK, November 2006, pp. 106–114.
432. N. Rea, "High-level event detection in broadcast sports video," Ph.D. dissertation, Trinity College Dublin, 2005.
433. L. M. Reeves, J. C. Martin, M. McTear, T. V. Raman, K. M. Stanney, H. Su, Q. Y. Wang, J. Lai, J. A. Larson, and S. Oviatt, "Guidelines for multimodal user interface design," *Communications of the ACM*, vol. 47, no. 1, pp. 57–59, 2004.
434. G. Reitmayr and T. Drummond, "Going out: robust, model-based tracking for outdoor augmented reality," in *Proc. IEEE/ACM Int'l Symposium on Mixed and Augmented Reality*, 2006.
435. J. Rekimoto and M. Saitoh, "Augmented surfaces: a spatially continuous work space for hybrid computing environments," in *Proc. ACM-SIGCHI conference on Human factors in computing systems*, 1999, pp. 378–385.
436. P. Resnik, "Using information content to evaluate semantic similarity in a taxonomy," in *Proc. Int'l Joint Conf. on Artificial Intel.*, C. S. Mellish, Ed. San Mateo: Morgan Kaufmann, Aug. 1995, pp. 448–453.
437. D. A. Robinson, "A method of measuring eye movement using a scleral search coil in a magnetic field," *IEEE Trans. Bio-Med. Electron.*, vol. BME-10, pp. 137–145, 1963.
438. J. T. Robinson, "The K-D-B-tree: A search structure for large multidimensional dynamic indexes," in *ACM SIGMOD International Conference on Management of Data*, Ann Arbor, Michigan, Etats-Unis, 29 Apr. - 1 May 1981, pp. 10–18.
439. C. Rocchi, O. Stock, M. Zancanaro, M. Kruppa, and A. Krüger, "The museum visit: generating seamless personalized presentations on multiple devices," in *Proc. Int'l Conf. on Intelligent User Interfaces*. New York, NY, USA: ACM Press, 2004, pp. 316–318.
440. J. Rocchio, "Relevance feedback in information retrieval," in *The SMART Retrieval System - Experiments in Automatic Document Processing*, G. Salton, Ed. Prentice Hall, Englewood Cliffs, 1971, pp. 313–323.
441. M. Rohs, "Marker-based embodied interaction for handheld augmented reality games," *Journal of Virtual Reality and Broadcasting*, vol. 4, no. 5, Mar. 2007, `urn:nbn:de:0009-6-7939`, ISSN 1860-2037.

442. R. C. Rose, E. M. Hofstetter, and D. A. Reynolds, "Integrated models of signal and background with application to speaker identification in noise," *IEEE Trans. Speech Audio Process.*, vol. 2, no. 2, pp. 245–257, 1994.
443. A. Rosenfeld, D. Doermann, and D. D. (Editors), *Video Mining.* Springer, 2003.
444. A. Ross and A. Jain, "Information fusion in biometrics," *Pattern Recognition Letters*, vol. 24, no. 13, pp. 2115–2125, September 2003.
445. A. Ross, K. Nandakumar, and A. K. Jain, *Handbook of Multibiometrics.* Springer-Verlag, 2006.
446. L. Rothrock, R. Koubek, F. Fuchs, M. Haas, and G. Salvendy, "Review and reappraisal of adaptive interfaces: toward biologically inspired paradigms," *Theoretical Issues in Ergonomics Science*, vol. 3, no. 1, pp. 47–84, 2002.
447. V. Roto, "Best practices and future visions for search user interfaces: A workshop," in *Proc. ACM-SIGCHI conference on Human factors in computing systems*, 2003.
448. H. A. Rowley, S. Baluja, and T. Kanade, "Human face detection in visual scenes," *Proc. Advances in Neural Information Processing Systems*, vol. 8, pp. 875–881, 1996.
449. B. Rueber, "Obtaining confidence measures from sentence probabilities," in *Proc. European Conf. on Speech Communication and Technology*, 1997.
450. Y. Rui, T. S. Huang, and S.-F. Chang, "Image retrieval: Current techniques, promising directions, and open issues," *Journal of Visual Communication and Image Representation*, vol. 10, pp. 39–62, 1999.
451. Y. Rui, T. S. Huang, and S. Mehrotra, "Content-based image retrieval with relevance feedback in MARS," in *Proc. IEEE Int'l Conf. on Image Processing*, vol. 2, Washington, DC, 1997.
452. Y. Rui, T. S. Huang, M. Ortega, and S. Mehrotra, "Relevance feedback: a power tool for interactive content-based image retrieval," *IEEE Trans. Circuits Syst. Video Technol.*, vol. 8, no. 5, pp. 644–655, 1998.
453. B. Russell, *A History of Western Philosophy.* New York: Simon & Schuster, 1945.
454. S. Sagayama, K. Shinoda, M. Nakai, and H. Shimodaira, "Analytic methods for acoustic model adaptation: a review," in *Proc. of ISCA Workshop on Adaptation Methods*, Sophia-Antipolis France, 2001, pp. 67–76.
455. P. Salembier and J. R. Smith, "MPEG-7 multimedia description schemes," *IEEE Trans. Circuits Syst. Video Technol.*, vol. 11, no. 6, pp. 748–759, 2001.
456. G. Salton and C. Buckley, "Term-Weighting Approaches in Automatic Text Retrieval," *Information Processing and Management*, vol. 24, no. 5, pp. 513–523, 1988.
457. G. Salton and M. J. McGill, "The SMART and SIRE experimental retrieval systems," in *Readings in Information Retrieval*, K. S. Jones and P. Willett, Eds. Morgan Kaufmann Publishers, San Francisco, CA, USA, 1997, pp. 381–399.
458. G. Salton, *Automatic Text Processing.* Addison-Wesley, 1989.
459. G. Salton, C. Yang, and C. Yu, "A Theory of Term Importance in Automatic Text Analysis," *Journal of the American Society for Information Science*, vol. 26, no. 1, pp. 33–44, 1975.
460. G. Salvendy, *Handbook of Human Factors and Ergonomics.* John Wiley & Sons, New York, NY, USA, 2005.

461. D. D. Salvucci and G. J. H., "Identifying fixations and saccades in eye-tracking protocols," in *Proceedings of the Eye Tracking Research and Applications Symposium.* New York: ACM Press, 2000, pp. 71–78.
462. M. Sargin, Y. Yemez, E. Erzin, and A. Tekalp, "Audiovisual synchronization and fusion using canonical correlation analysis," *IEEE Trans. Multimedia*, vol. 9, no. 7, pp. 1396–1403, Nov. 2007.
463. E. Saykol, U. Gudukbay, and O. Ulusoy, "A histogram-based approach for object-based query-by-shape-and-color in multimedia databases," Bilkent University, Technical Report BUCE-0201, 2002.
464. L. L. Scharf and J. K. Thomas, "Wiener filters in canonical coordinates for transform coding, filtering, and quantizing," vol. 46, no. 3, pp. 647–654, 1998.
465. M. Schedl, P. Knees, and G. Widmer, "Discovering and visualizing prototypical artists by web-based co-occurrence analysis," in *Proc. Int'l Conf. on Music Information Retrieval*, London, UK, September 11-15 2005, pp. 21–28.
466. B. Schilit and M. Theimer, "Disseminating active map information to mobile hosts," *IEEE Netw.*, vol. 8, no. 5, pp. 22–32, 1994.
467. T. Schnell, T. Wu, "Applying eye tracking as alternative approach for activation of controls and functions in aircraft," in *Proceedings of the 5th International Conference On Human Interaction with Complex Systems (HICS)*, 2000, p. 113.
468. B. Schölkopf, "The kernel trick for distances," in *Proc. Advances in Neural Information Processing Systems*, vol. 12. MIT Press, 2000, pp. 301–307.
469. B. Schölkopf and A. Smola, *Learning with Kernels.* MIT Press, 2002.
470. R. B. Segal and J. O. Kephart, "Swiftfile: An intelligent assistant for organizing e-mail," in *Proc. of AAAI 2000 Spring Symposium on Adaptive User Interfaces*, 2000, pp. 107–112.
471. T. K. Sellis, N. Roussopoulos, and C. Faloutsos, "The R+-tree: A dynamic index for multi-dimensional objects," in *Proc. Int'l Conf. on Very Large Data Bases*, Brighton, Royaume-Uni, 1-4 Sep. 1987, pp. 507–518.
472. S. Seneff, E. Hurley, R. Lau, C. Pao, P. Schmid, and V. Zue, "GALAXY-II: A reference architecture for conversational system development," in *Proc. Int'l Conf. on Spoken Language Processing*, vol. 3, Sydney, Australia, 1998, pp. 931–934.
473. S. Seneff, R. Lau, and J. Polifroni, "Organization, communication, and control in the GALAXY-II conversational system," in *Proc. European Conf. on Speech Communication and Technology*, Budapest, Hungary, 1999, pp. 1271–1274.
474. S. Seneff, M. McCandless, and V. Zue, "Integrating natural language into the word graph search for simultaneous speech recognition and understanding," in *Proc. European Conf. on Speech Communication and Technology*, 1995.
475. SensAble, "Sensable technologies," http://www.sensable.com/.
476. W. A. Sethares and T. W. Staley, "Periodicity transforms," *IEEE Trans. Signal Process.*, vol. 47, no. 11, November 1999.
477. F. Seydoux and J.-C. Chappelier, "Semantic indexing using minimum redundancy cut in ontologies," in *Proc. of International Conference on Recent Advances in Natural Language Processing (RANLP 2005)*, September 2005, pp. 486–492.
478. A. Shaikh, S. Juth, A. Medl, I. Marsic, C. Kulikowski, and J. Flanagan, "An architecture for multimodal information fusion," in *Proc. of the Workshop on Perceptual User Interfaces*, Banf, Canada, 1997, pp. 91–93.

479. R. Sharma, V. I. Pavlovic, and T. S. Huang, "Toward multimodal human-computer interface," *Proc. IEEE*, vol. 86, no. 5, pp. 853–869, 1998.
480. H.-T. Shen, B.-C. Ooi, and K.-L. Tan, "Giving meanings to www images," in *Proc. ACM Int'l Conference on Multimedia*, Marina del Rey, CA, 2000, pp. 39–47.
481. S. Sherr, *Input Devices.* Academic Press, Orlando, FL, USA, 1990.
482. J. Shi and C. Tomasi, "Good features to track," in *Proc. IEEE Int'l Conf. on Computer Vision and Pattern Recognition*, 21-23 June 1994, pp. 593–600.
483. B. Shneiderman, *Designing the User Interface: Strategies for Effective Human-Computer Interaction.* Addison-Wesley Longman Publishing Co., Boston, MA, USA, 1997.
484. ——, *Leonardo's Laptop: Human Needs and the New Computing Technologies.* Cambridge, MA, USA: MIT Press, 2002.
485. E. H. Shortliffe, *Computer-based medical consultation: MYCIN.* New York, NY: Elsevier, 1976.
486. C. L. Sidner, "Building spoken-language collaborative interface agents," in *Practical Spoken Dialog Systems*, D. A. Dahl, Ed. Kluwer Academic Publishers, 2004, pp. 197–226.
487. J. Sietsma and R. Dow, "Creating artificial neural networks that generalize," *Neural Networks*, vol. 4, pp. 67–79, 1991.
488. T. Sikora, "The MPEG-7 visual standard for content description – an overview," *IEEE Trans. Circuits Syst. Video Technol.*, vol. 11, no. 6, pp. 696–702, 2001.
489. M. Silfverberg, I. S. MacKenzie, and T. Kauppinen, "An isometric joystick as a pointing device for handheld information terminals," in *Proc. of Graphics Interface*, B. Watson and J. W. Buchanan, Eds., 2001, pp. 119–126.
490. S. Siltanen, M. Hakkarainen, O. Korkalo, T. Salonen, J. Sääski, C. Woodward, T. Kannetis, M. Perakakis, and A. Potamianos, "Multimodal user interface for augmented assembly," in *Proc. of IEEE Int'l Workshop on Multimedia Signal Processing*, 2007.
491. S. Siltanen and J. Hyväkkä, "Implementing a natural user interface for camera phones using visual tags," in *Proceedings of the 7th Australasian User Interface Conference (AUIC2006)*, 2006, pp. 113 – 116.
492. J. Siroux, M. Guyomard, F. Multon, and C. Remondeau, "Oral and gestural activities of the users in the Georal system," in *International Conference on Cooperative Multimodal Communication*, vol. 2, Eindhoven, The Netherlands, 1995, pp. 287–298.
493. J. Sivic and A. Zisserman, "Video Google: A text retrieval approach to object matching in videos," in *Proc. IEEE Int'l Conf. on Computer Vision*, vol. 2, Oct. 2003, pp. 1470–1477.
494. M. Slaney and M. Covell, "FaceSync: A linear operator for measuring synchronization of video facial images and audio tracks," in *Proc. Advances in Neural Information Processing Systems*, 2001.
495. A. W. M. Smeulders, M. Worring, S. Santini, A. Gupta, and R. Jain, "Content-based image retrieval at the end of the early years," *IEEE Trans. Pattern Anal. Mach. Intell.*, vol. 22, no. 12, pp. 1349–1380, 2000.
496. J. R. Smith and S. F. Chang, "Visualseek: a fully automated content-based image query system," in *Proc. ACM Int'l Conference on Multimedia.* ACM Press New York, NY, USA, 1997, pp. 87–98.

497. J. R. Smith, S. Basu, C.-Y. Lin, M. R. Naphade, and B. Tseng, "Integrating features, models and semantics for content-based retrieval," in *Proc. Int'l Workshop on Multimedia Content-Based Indexing and Retrieval*, September 2001, pp. 95–98.
498. M. Smith and T. Kanade, "Video skimming and characterization through the combination of image and language understanding techniques," in *Proc. IEEE Int'l Conf. on Computer Vision and Pattern Recognition*, 1997, p. 775.
499. R. Snelick, U. Uludag, A. Mink, M. Indovina, and A. Jain, "Large scale evaluation of multimodal biometric authentication using state-of-the-art systems," *IEEE Trans. Pattern Anal. Mach. Intell.*, vol. 27, no. 3, pp. 450–455, March 2005.
500. C. G. M. Snoek, M. Worring, J.-M. Geusebroek, D. C. Koelma, F. J. Seinstra, and A. W. M. Smeulders, "The semantic pathfinder: Using an authoring metaphor for generic multimedia indexing," *IEEE Trans. Pattern Anal. Mach. Intell.*, vol. 28, no. 10, pp. 1678–1689, October 2006.
501. C. G. Snoek and M. Worring, "Multimodal video indexing: A review of the state-of-the-art," *Multimedia Tools and Applications*, vol. 25, no. 1, pp. 5–35, January 2005.
502. M. Sonka, V. Hlavec, and R. Boyle, *Image Processing Analysis, and Machine Vision.* PWS Publishing, 1999, ch. 6 & 14.
503. K. Spärck Jones, S. Walker, and S. E. Robertson, "A Probabilistic Model of Information Retrieval: Development and Comparative Experiments - Part 1 and 2," *Information Processing and Management*, vol. 36, no. 6, pp. 779–840, 2000.
504. K. Stanney, S. Samman, L. Reeves, K. Hale, W. Buff, C. Bowers, B. Goldiez, D. Nicholson, and S. Lackey, "A paradigm shift in interactive computing: Deriving multimodal design principles from behavioral and neurological foundations," *International Journal of Human-Computer Interaction*, vol. 17, no. 2, pp. 229–257, 2004.
505. C. Stauffer and W. Grimson, "Learning patterns of activity using real-time tracking," *IEEE Trans. Pattern Anal. Mach. Intell.*, vol. 22, no. 8, pp. 747–757, Aug. 2000.
506. B. E. Stein and M. A. Meredith, *The Merging of the Senses.* MIT Press Cambridge, MA, 1993.
507. F. W. M. Stentiford, "Attention based similarity," *Pattern Recognition*, vol. 40, no. 3, pp. 771–783, 2006.
508. R. J. Sternberg, *Cognitive Psychology*, 4th ed. Thomson Wadsworth, 2006.
509. A. Stolcke, Y. König, and M. Weintraub, "Explicit word error minimization in N-best list rescoring," in *Proc. European Conf. on Speech Communication and Technology*, 1997.
510. D. Stork and M. Hennecke, Eds., *Speechreading by Humans and Machines.* Berlin, Germany: Springer, 1996.
511. J. Sturm, B. Cranen, F. Wang, J. Terken, and I. Bakx, "Effects of prolonged use on the usability of a multimodal form-filling interface," in *Spoken Multimodal Human-Computer Dialogue in Mobile Environments.* Springer, The Netherlands, 2004, pp. 329–348.
512. B. Suhm and A. Waibel, "Towards better language models for spontaneous speech," in *Proc. Int'l Conf. on Spoken Language Processing*, 1994.
513. X. Sun and M. Kankanhalli, "Video summarization using R-sequences," *Real-time imaging*, vol. 6, no. 6, pp. 449–459, Dec 2000.

514. H. Sundaram and S. F. Chang, "Computable scenes and structures in films," *IEEE Trans. Multimedia*, vol. 4, no. 4, pp. 482–491, 2002.
515. M. Suzuki, Y. Kajiura, A. Ito, and S. Makino, "Unsupervised language model adaptation based on automatic text collection from WWW," in *Proc. Int'l Conf. on Speech Communication and Technology*, 2006.
516. D. M. J. Tax and R. P. W. Duin, "Support vector domain description," *Pattern Recognition Letters*, vol. 20, no. 11-13, pp. 1191–1199, 1999.
517. L. Taycher, L. Cascia, and S. Sclaroff, "Image digestion and relevance feedback in the imagerover www search engine," in *Int'l Conf. on Visual Information Systems*, San Diego, Dec. 1997, pp. 85–94.
518. H. Teager and S. Teager, "Evidence of nonlinear sound production mechanisms in the vocal tract," in *Speech Production and Speech Modelling*. Kluwer Academic, 1990, pp. 241–261.
519. S. Theodoridis and K. Koutroumbas, *Pattern Recognition*, 3rd ed. Acad. Press, 2006.
520. A. N. Tikhonov and V. Y. Arsenin, *Solutions of Ill-posed Problems*. Washington DC: Winston & Sons, 1977.
521. C. Tillmann and H. Ney, "Word triggers and the EM algorithm," in *Proc. of the Workshop Computational Natural Language Learning (CoNLL)*, 1997, pp. 117–124.
522. A. Tomkins, "Social and semantic structures in web search," in *Proc. IEEE/WIC/ACM International Conference on Web Intelligence*, Silicon Valey, CA, 2007.
523. S. Tong and E. Chang, "Support vector machine active learning for image retrieval," in *Proc. ACM Int'l Conference on Multimedia*. Ottawa, Canada: ACM Press, 2001, pp. 107–118.
524. S. Tong and D. Koller, "Support vector machine active learning with applications to text classification," in *Proc. Int'l Conf. on Machine Learning*. Morgan Kaufmann, 2000, pp. 999–1006.
525. B. U. Töreyin, Y. Dedeoglu, and A. E. Çetin, "Hmm based falling person detection using both audio and video." in *ICCV Workshop on HCI*, 2005, pp. 211–220.
526. B. U. Toreyin, E. B. Soyer, I. Onaran, and A. E. Cetin, "Falling person detection using multi-sensor signal processing," *EURASIP Journal on Advances in Signal Processing*, 2007.
527. A. Treisman and G. Gelade, "A feature integration theory of attention," *Cognit. Psychology*, vol. 12, no. 1, pp. 97–136, 1980.
528. B. Truong, C. Dorai, and S. Venkatesh, "New enhancements to cut, fade, and dissolve detection processes in video segmentation," in *Proc. ACM Int'l Conference on Multimedia*, 2000, pp. 219–227.
529. N. Tsingos, E. Gallo, and G. Drettakis, "Perceptual audio rendering of complex virtual environments," in *Proc. ACM Int'l conference on Computer Graphics and Interactive Techniques*, 2004.
530. G. Tür, D. Hakkani-Tür, A. Stolcke, and E. Shriberg, "Integrating prosodic and lexical cues for automatic topic segmentation," *Computational Linguistics*, vol. 21, no. 1, pp. 31–57, 2001.
531. M. Turk and A. Pentland, "Face recognition using eigenfaces," in *Proc. IEEE Int'l Conf. on Computer Vision and Pattern Recognition*, 1991, pp. 586–591.

532. M. Turunen, "Jaspis - a spoken dialogue architecture and its applications," Ph.D. dissertation, University of Tampere, Department of Information Studies, 2004.
533. M. Turunen and J. Hakulinen, "Jaspis 2 - an architecture for supporting distributed spoken dialogues," in *Proc. European Conf. on Speech Communication and Technology*, Geneva, Switzerland, 2003, pp. 1913–1916.
534. G. Tzanetakis and P. Cook, "MARSYAS: A framework for audio analysis," *Organized Sound*, vol. 4, no. 30, pp. 169–175, 2000.
535. ——, "Musical genre classification of audio signals," *IEEE Trans. Speech Audio Process.*, vol. 10, no. 5, pp. 293–302, July 2002.
536. S. Uchihashi, J. Foote, A. Girgensohn, and J. Boreczky, "Video manga: generating semantically meaningful video summaries," in *Proc. ACM Int'l Conference on Multimedia*, 1999, pp. 383–392.
537. M. Utiyama and H. Isahara, "A statistical model for domain-independent text segmentation," in *Proc. Annual Meeting of the Association for Computational Linguistics*, 2001, pp. 499–506.
538. A. Valli and J. Véronis, "Étiquetage grammatical de corpus oraux : problèmes et perspectives," *Revue française de linguistique appliquée*, vol. 4, no. 2, pp. 113–133, 1999.
539. J. R. Vallino, "Interactive Augmented Reality," Ph.D. dissertation, Department of Computer Science, University of Rochester, 1998.
540. V. Vapnik, *Statistical Learning Theory*. New York: Wiley-Interscience, 1998.
541. G. B. Varile and A. Zampolli, *Survey of the State of the Art in Human Language Technology*. Cambridge University Press, 1997.
542. A. Vassiliou, A. Salway, and D. Pitt, "Formalizing stories: sequences of events and state changes," in *Proc. of IEEE Int'l Conference on Multimedia and Expo*, vol. 1, 2004, pp. 587–590.
543. D. Vaufreydaz, M. Akbar, and J. Rouillard, "Internet documents: A rich source for spoken language modeling," in *Proc. IEEE Workshop Automatic Speech Recognition and Understanding*, 1999.
544. D. Vergyri, K. Kirchhoff, K. Duh, and A. Stolcke, "Morphology-based language modeling for arabic speech recognition," in *Proc. Int'l Conf. on Spoken Language Processing*, 2004.
545. C. Vertan and N. Boujemaa, "Upgrading color distributions for image retrieval: can we do better?" in *International Conference on Visual Information Systems (Visual2000)*, November 2000.
546. F. Vignoli and S. Pauws, "A music retrieval system based on user-driven similarity and its evaluation," in *Proc. Int'l Conf. on Music Information Retrieval*, London, UK, September 11-15 2005, pp. 272–279.
547. P. Viola and M. Jones, "Robust real-time face detection," *Int'l J. of Comp. Vis.*, vol. 57, no. 2, pp. 137–154, 2004.
548. M. Vlachos, P. Yu, and V. Castelli, "On periodicity detection and structural periodic similarity," in *SIAM International Conference on Data Mining*, 2005.
549. E. Voorhees, "Using WORDNET for Text Retrieval," in WORDNET*: An Electronic Lexical Database*, C. Fellbaum, Ed. The MIT Press, 1998.
550. E. Voutsakis, E. G. Petrakis, and E. Milios, "Intellisearch: Intelligent search for images and text on the web," in *Image Analysis and Recognition (ICIAR 2006)*, Povoa de Varzim, Portugal, Sept. 18-20 2006, pp. 697–708.

551. E. Voutsakis, E. Petrakis, and E. Milios, "Weighted link analysis for logo and trademark image retrieval on the web," in *Proc. of IEEE/WIC/ACM Int'l Conference on Web Intelligence*, Compiegne, France, Sept. 2005, pp. 581–585.
552. VTT, "Phonemouse demo software," http://www.vtt.fi/multimedia/.
553. W. Wahlster, "Towards symmetric multimodality: Fusion and fission of speech, gesture, and facial expression," in *KI : Advances in Artificial Intelligence: 26th Annual German Conference on AI.* Springer, 2003, pp. 1–18.
554. ——, *SmartKom: Foundations of Multimodal Dialogue Systems.* Springer-Verlag, New York, Secaucus, NJ, USA, 2006.
555. M. T. Wallace, G. E. Roberson, W. D. Hairston, B. E. Stein, J. W. Vaughan, and J. A. Schirillo, "Unifying multisensory signals across time and space," *Exp. Brain Research*, vol. 158, pp. 252–258, 2004.
556. F. Wang, Y.-F. Ma, H.-J. Zhang, and J.-T. Li, "A generic framework for semantic sports video analysis using dynamic Bayesian networks," in *International Multimedia Modelling Conference*, 2005.
557. J. Z. Wang, J. Li, G. Wiederhold, and O. Firschein, "System for screening objectionable images using Daubechies' wavelets and color histograms," in *International Workshop on Interactive Distributed Multimedia Systems and Telecommunication Services*, 1997, pp. 20–30.
558. J. Wang, S. Zhai, and J. Canny, "Camera phone based motion sensing: interaction techniques, applications and performance study," in *Proc. ACM Symposium on User Interface Software and Technology*, 2006.
559. Y. Wang, Z. Liu, and J.-C. Huang, "Multimedia content analysis-using both audio and visual clues," *IEEE Signal Process. Mag.*, vol. 17, no. 6, pp. 12–36, Nov. 2000.
560. D. J. Ward and D. J. C. MacKay, "Fast hands-free writing by gaze direction," *Nature*, vol. 418, p. 838, 2002.
561. D. J. Ward, "Adaptive computer interfaces," Ph.D. dissertation, University of Cambridge, 2001.
562. C. Ware and H. Mikaelian, "An evaluation of an eye tracker as a device for computer input," in *Proc. ACM-SIGCHI conference on Human factors in computing systems*, 1987.
563. M. Weintraub, Y. Aksu, S. Dharanipragada, S. Khudanpur, H. Ney, J. Prange, A. Stolcke, F. Jelinek, and E. Shriberg, "LM95 project report: Fast training and portability," Center for Language and Speech Processing, Johns Hopkins University, Tech. Rep., 1996.
564. D. A. White and R. Jain, "Similarity indexing with the SS-tree," in *12th International Conference on Data Engineering*, 26 Feb. - 1 Mar. 1996, pp. 516–523.
565. C. D. Wickens and H. J. G., *Engineering Psychology and Human Performance.* Prentice Hall, NJ, 2000.
566. J. Wilkinson and B. Devlin, "The material exchange format (mxf) and its application," *SMPTE journal*, vol. 111, no. 9, pp. 378–384, 2002.
567. I. H. Witten and E. Frank, *Data Mining: Practical Machine Learning Tools and Techniques with Java Implementations.* Morgan Kaufmann, Academic Press, 2000, ch. 4.
568. W. Wolf, "Hidden markov model parsing of video programs," in *Proc. IEEE Int'l Conf. Acous., Speech, and Signal Processing*, 1997, pp. 2609–2611.
569. L. Wu, K. Sycara, T. Payne, and C. Faloutsos, "FALCON: Feedback adaptive loop for content-based retrieval," in *Proc. Int'l Conf. on Very Large Data Bases*, Cairo, Egypt, Sept. 2000, pp. 297–306.

570. Z. Wu and M. Palmer, "Verb semantics and lexical selection," in *Proc. Annual Meeting of the Association for Computational Linguistics*, New Mexico State University, Las Cruces, New Mexico, 1994, pp. 133–138.
571. L. Xie, P. Xu, S.-F. Chang, A. Divakaran, and H. Sun, "Structure analysis of soccer video with domain knowledge and hidden Markov models," *Pattern Recognition Letters*, vol. 25, no. 7, pp. 767–775, 2004.
572. Y. Yaşaroğlu and A. A. Alatan, "Summarizing video: content, features & hmm topologies," in *Proc. Int. Workshop Very Low Bitrate Video Coding*, 2003, pp. 101–110.
573. M. M. Yeung and B.-L. Yeo, "Video visualization for compact presentation and fast browsing of picturial content," *IEEE Trans. Circuits Syst. Video Technol.*, vol. 7, pp. 771–785, 1997.
574. L. Ying, S.-H. Lee, C.-H. Yeh, and C.-C. Kuo, "Techniques for movie content analysis and skimming," in *IEEE Signal Process. Mag.*, vol. 23, no. 2, Mar 2006, pp. 79–89.
575. L. Ying, S. Narayanan, and C. Kuo, "Content-based movie analysis and indexing based on audiovisual cues," *IEEE Trans. Circuits Syst. Video Technol.*, vol. 14, no. 8, pp. 1073–1085, Aug. 2004.
576. M. Ylikerälä and H. Kuukkanen, "Pluggable 3D stereographics," in *Articles on Experiences 4 - Digital Media & Game. Kylänen, Mika (Ed.). Lapland Centre of Expertise for the Experience Industry (LCEEI).*, 2006, pp. 168 – 176.
577. N. B. Yoma, F. McInnes, and M. Jack, "Weighted matching algorithms and reliability in noise canceling by spectral subtraction," in *Proc. IEEE Int'l Conf. Acous., Speech, and Signal Processing*, vol. 2, 1997, pp. 1171–1174.
578. N. Yoma and M. Villar, "Speaker verification in noise using a stochastic version of the weighted viterbi algorithm," *IEEE Trans. Speech Audio Process.*, vol. 10, no. 3, pp. 158–166, 2002.
579. S. Young, "A review of large-vocabulary continuous-speech," *IEEE Signal Process. Mag.*, vol. 13, no. 5, pp. 45–57, 1996.
580. S. Young, G. Evermann, D. Kershaw, G. Moore, J. Odell, D. Ollason, D. Povey, V. Valtchev, and P. Woodland, "The HTK book (for HTK version 3.2)," Cambridge University Engineering Department, Tech. Rep., 2002.
581. S. Young, N. Russell, and J. Thornton, "Token passing: A simple conceptual model for connected speech recognition systems," Cambridge University Engineering Dept, Tech. Rep. CUED/F-INFENG/TR38, 1989.
582. A. L. Yuille, "Energy functions for early vision and analog networks," *Biological Cybernetics*, vol. 61, pp. 115–123, 1989.
583. A. L. Yuille and H. H. Bülthoff, *Perception as Bayesian Inference.* Cambridge University Press, 1996, ch. Bayesian Decision Theory and Psychophysics, pp. 123–161.
584. J. Zacks and B. Tversky, "Event structure in perception and conception," *Psychological Bulletin*, no. 127, pp. 3–21, 2001.
585. J. M. Zacks, T. S. Braver, M. A. Sheridan, D. I. Donaldson, A. Z. Snyder, J. M. Ollinger, R. L. Buckner, and M. E. Raichle, "Human brain activity time-locked to perceptual event boundaries," *Nature Neuroscience*, vol. 4, no. 6, pp. 651–655, June 2001.
586. S. Zhai and P. Milgram, *Quantifying Coordination in Multiple DOF Movement and its Application to Evaluating 6 DOF Input Devices.* ACM Press/Addison-Wesley Publishing Co., New York, NY, USA, 1998.

587. Y. Zhai, Z. Rasheed, and M. Shah, "Semantic classification of movie scenes using finite state machines," *IEE Proc. - Vision, Image, and Signal Processing*, vol. 152, no. 6, pp. 896–901, 2005.
588. D. Zhang, D. Gatica-Perez, S. Bengio, I. McCowan, and G. Lathoud, "Modeling individual and group actions in meetings: A two-layer HMM framework," in *Proc. IEEE Int'l Conf. on Computer Vision and Pattern Recognition Workshop*, vol. 7, 2004, pp. 117–124.
589. H.-J. Zhang, Z. Chen, W.-Y. Liu, and M. Li, "Relevance feedback in content-based image search," in *Proc. 12th Int'l Conf. on New Information Technology (NIT)*, Beijing, China, Aug. 2003, pp. 29–31, (invited keynote).
590. H.-J. Zhang and Z. Su, "Improving CBIR by semantic propagation and cross-mode query expansion," in *Proc. Int'l Workshop on Multimedia Content-Based Indexing and Retrieval*, September 2001, pp. 83–86.
591. T. Zhang and C. C. J. Kuo, "Audio content analysis for online audiovisual data segmentation and classification," *IEEE Trans. Speech Audio Process.*, vol. 9, no. 4, pp. 441–457, 2001.
592. R. Zhao and W. Grosky, "Narrowing the semantic gapimproved text-based web document retrieval using visual features," *IEEE Trans. Multimedia*, vol. 4, no. 2, pp. 189–200, June 2002.
593. X. S. Zhou and T. S. Huang, "Unifying keywords and visual contents in image retrieval," *IEEE Multimedia*, vol. 9, no. 2, pp. 23–33, 2002.
594. ——, "Relevance feedback for image retrieval: a comprehensive review," *Multimedia Systems*, vol. 8, no. 6, pp. 536–544, 2003.
595. Z. Zhu and T. S. Huang, *Multimodal Surveillance: Sensors, Algorithms, and Systems.* Artech House Publishers, Jul. 2007.
596. Y. Zhuang, Y. Rui, T. Huang, and S. Mehrotra, "Adaptive key frame extraction using unsupervised clustering," in *Proc. IEEE Int'l Conf. on Image Processing*, 1998, pp. 866–870.
597. X. Zou and B. Bhanu, "Tracking humans using multi-modal fusion," in *Proc. IEEE Int'l Conf. on Computer Vision and Pattern Recognition Workshop.* Washington, DC, USA: IEEE Computer Society, 2005, p. 4.
598. E. Zwicker and H. Fastl, *Psychoacoustics, Facts and Models*, 2nd ed., ser. Series of Information Sciences. Berlin: Springer, 1999, vol. 22.

Index

1D projection 137
3D interfaces 56

augmented reality 61

acoustic model 57
  adaptation 71
acoustic models 59
action classification 135, 136
action recognition 127, 128, 142
action spotting 142
Active Appearance Models 120
active learning 229
adaptable interfaces 53, 69, 70
adaptation 68, 295
adaptive interfaces 68
adaptive multimedia 80
ambient intelligence 68
angular kernel 231
annotated image 261
Applications 43
  Audio-Visual ASR 43
  Biometrics 46
  Broadcast News 45
  images 46
  meetings 47
  sports 44
  TV Structuring 45
AROnSite 324
asycnrhonous HMM 92
Audio 132
audio descriptors *see* audio feature extraction
audio feature extraction 245
  critical bands 245
  Rhythm Patterns 245
  Statistical Spectrum Descriptors 245
audio features 23, 179
  generic/specific 23
  MFCC 24
  pitch 24
  short-term energy 24
  short/long-term 23
  speaking rate 25
  ZCR 24
audio processing 179
audio similarity perception 242
audio test collections 246
audiovisual 3, 18
audiovisual automatic speech recognition 111
audiovisual fusion 179
audiovisual integration 91, 97
audiovisual saliency 179
augmented reality 311, 314, 320, 322
authorities 265
autocorrelation 132
automatic speech recognition 201
Automatic Speech Recognition (ASR) *see* speech recognition

background subtraction 145
Baum-Welch 136
Baum-Welsh 139
Bayesian 3, 137
Bayesian Belief Networks (BBN) 70
Bayesian decision theory 8

Bayesian estimation 8
Bayesian inference 10
biometric identification 68

CBIR 222
Christmas Carols 242
classification feature 148
click to talk 288
clustering 325
co-citation analysis 265
cognition 7
cognitive psychology 8
collaborative
  authoring 80
  filtering 72, 78
collection analysis module 273
color histogram 130
common meaning representation 65
compositionality 288
computational attention 179
conceptual content 221
conceptual feature vector 223
conceptual similarity 224
confidence measures 202, 211
consensus decoding 209
consistency 286, 295
content based
  image retrieval 78
Content Based Image Retrieval 222
content-based image retrieval 261
content-case analysis 128
context aware 318
context awareness 74
context-free grammar 142
crawler module 272
cricket 130
cross-modal integration 3
curl 138

desktop metaphor 55
Dialogue density 163
dialogue manager 282
Dialogue Manager (DM) 57
Dialogue scene 159
Dialogue velocity 163
direct manipulation 55
direct parsing 128
discourse markers 213
discrete cosine transform 148

dynamic bayesian networks 107
dysvideo 136

electronic tag 319
energy spectrum 263
Euclidean distance 244
event detection 179
Expectation-Maximization 118
eye tracking 60

fast fourier transform 148
feature extraction 148
feature structures 64
features 5
fight detection 149
Film Syntax 158
Finite State Machine (FSM) 57
form-filling 288
fusion 3, 19, 111, 153

gestalt psychology 8
gesture based application 322
gesture based interaction 316, 317, 322
gesture interfaces 60
global motion estimation 130
GOMS model 52
Graphical User Interfaces *see* GUI
GUI 50, 55, 58, 62, 81, 83
  toolkits 83

handwriting recognition 135
haptic 316
haptic interfaces 61
head mounted display 314
Head Mounted Displays (HMD) 61
hidden markov model 127
Hidden Markov Model (HMM) 57
hierarchical HMM 103
HITS 260
HMD *see* head mounted display
HMM 127, 134–136, 139
  continuous 135, 137
  discrete 135
  topology 140
Hough transform 129
hubs 265
Human Computer Interaction (HCI) 50
Human Model Processor (HMP) 51

hybrid descriptor 221
hybrid image search 223
hybrid retrieval systems 260
hypernym graph 225
hypernymy 224

illicit content 133
illicit content analysis 128
image analysis 261
image content 260, 261
image retrieval 259
image retrieval on the Web 260
information retrieval 212, 259
intensity histogram 262
interactive image retrieval 221
Interactive Voice Response (IVR) 59
interface guidelines 83
intermodal 5, 16
intramodal 5, 16

key concepts 223
key-frame selection 179

language model 57, 202
  adaptation 71
language model adaptation 212, 214, 215
language model interpolation 214
Laplace kernel 231
layered HMM 92
lexical cohesion 213
link analysis 260
Logical story unit 159
logo 261
logo-trademark detection 263
logo-trademark similarity 263

map based user interfaces 244
Markov Decision Process (MDP) 73
Maximum Likelihood 12
Maximum-A-Posteriori 12
McGurk effect 14
measurement noise compensation 111
mixed-initiative 284
mobile augmented reality *see* augmented reality
mobile interfaces 74
modality efficiency 291
modality synergy 280, 293
modality-selection 288
model based parsing 128, 134
Model-View-Controller *see* MVC
moment invariants 263
monomodal 3
morpho-syntactic knowledge 206
morpho-syntactic rescoring 208
morphology 205
most ambiguous and orthogonal examples 232
most ambiguous examples 232
motion estimation 315, 317
Motion Field 131
motion trajectories 131
MPEG 131
MPEG-7 23
MPEG-7 Standard 157
mulitstream models 92
multi-agent architectures 81
multi-touch 56
multi-touch screen 313, 316
multicue 5
multimedia 3
multimedia fission 62
multimedia maps 79
multimedia retrieval 70
multimedia skimming 79
multimedia summarization 79
multimedia systems
  adaptive 70
multimodal 3, 5
  architectures 81
  frameworks 82
  integration pattern 67
  mutual disambiguation 67
  synergistic error correction 67
multimodal dialogue systems 279
multimodal fusion 62, 63, 92
multimodal interfaces 62, 279
multimodal processing 179
multimodal synergy 62
multistream HMM 92
music information retrieval 243
  content-based 243
  cultural data 243
  song lyrics 242, 243
    lyrics fetching 246
music map 325
music maps 326

MVC 52, 72
  paradigm 53, 54, 66, 80
MVC paradigm 281

n-class model 202
n-gram model 202
Natural Language Generation (NLG) 57
natural language processing 201
Natural Language Understanding (NLU) 57
NFC 319

object actions 131
object classification 148
ontology 224
open-mike 288

PageRank 260
parsing 135
pca 130
perception 3, 7
periodicity 132
philosophy 8
PhoneMouse 322
physical browsing 319
PicASHOW 261
PlaySOM 325
PocketSOM 325
pornographic 127, 132
pragmatics 205
Principal Component Analysis 130

queries by example 260
queries by example image 260
query expansion 269
query focused graph 266
query point movement 269
query uncertainty 260

RBF kernel 231
relevance feedback 71, 73, 229, 260, 268
retrieval by image annotations 260
retrieval by image content 260
retrieval module 273
RFID 319
rotation 138

Scenes 158
score-oriented Viterbi search 104
segment models 91, 98
segmentation 145
Self-Organizing Map 243
  adaptation function 244
  BMU selection 244
  multimodal 249
  quantitative evaluation 249
  visualization 244
semantic
  annotation 78
  fusion 63, 64
  gap 78
  multimedia understanding 78
  parsing
    robust 57
  unification 65
  web 82
semantic gap 222, 242
semantic persistence 286
semantic projection 228
semantic similarity 224, 261
Semantic Similarity Retrieval Model 264
semantics 205
sensation 7
Shot accuracy 161
Shots 158
shout detection 150
silhouette 148
similarity adaptation 269
similarity measure 225
skin 131, 137
smart mobile terminal 313
snooker 129, 130, 135, 141
SOM based user interfaces *see* map based user interfaces
speech dictation 59
speech interfaces 58
speech recognition 56, 57
speech synthesis 57
Spoken Dialogue Systems (SDS) 57, 59
sport action tracking 130
sport analysis 128
sport media analysis 127
SSRM 264
state machine 135
stereo display 314

Stereogames 323
storage module 273
Story unit 159
stream weights 112, 115
strong fusion 22
SVM scale invariance 231
SymBall 322
symmetric multimodality 287
synergistic error correction 288
syntactics 205

tactile 316
tagging, ASR transcripts 207
tagging, part-of-speech 206
talking heads 68
tennis 129, 141
TEOCEP 150
term re-weighting 269
text features 246
  tf × *idf* model 246
  bag-of-words models 246
  term weighing 246
text segmentation 213, 214
text-to-speech synthesis (TTS) 58
topic adaptation 212
topic segmentation 107
touchscreen 326
trademark 261
trajectory 135
turn-taking 285

unification integration 64
usability 51, 52
usability principles 52
  consistency 53
  familiarity 53
  predictability 53
  transparency 53
user model 69
  adaptation 69
  application 69
user-initiative 284

Vector Space Model 264
video annotation 179
video processing 179
Video shot string 165
video structuring 91
video summarization 179
view classification 129
virtual reality 61
visemes 68
visual dominance effect 51
visual marker 321
visual tag 319
Viterbi 130, 137–139
voice browser 84
VoiceXML 83

wavelet 148
weak fusion 20
Weighted PicASHOW 267
WIMP interface 55
word error minimization 209
WordNet 264
Wordnet 224
World Wide Web 259
WPicASHOW 267
WWW 259
WYSIWYG 55

Zooming User Interfaces (ZUI) 56

Printed in the United States of America